THE
PUSHCART PRIZE, VIII:
BEST OF THE
SMALL PRESSES
1983-1984 Edition

THE PUSHCART PRIZE, VIII:

BeST OF THE SMALL PRESSES

...WITH AN INDEX TO THE FIRST EIGHT VOLUMES

EDITED BY BILL HENDERSON
with the Pushcart Prize editors

Introduction by Gail Godwin

AVON
PUBLISHERS OF BARD, CAMELOT, DISCUS AND FLARE BOOKS

Note: nominations for this series are invited from any small, independent, literary book press or magazine in the world. Up to six nominations—tear sheets or copies selected from work published in that calendar year—are accepted by our October 15 deadline each year. Write to Pushcart Press, P.O. Box 380, Wainscott, N.Y. 11975 if you need more information.

Pushcart Press sends special thanks to The Helen Foundation of Salt Lake City for its generous awards to the authors of our lead short story, poem, and essay.

AVON BOOKS
A division of
The Hearst Corporation
1790 Broadway
New York, New York 10019

First Avon Printing, April, 1984

AVON TRADEMARK REG. U.S. PAT. OFF. AND IN
OTHER COUNTRIES, MARCA REGISTRADA, HECHO EN
U.S.A.

Printed in the U.S.A.

DON 10 9 8 7 6 5 4 3 2 1

Acknowledgements

The following works are reprinted by permission of the publishers and authors.

"Summer, An Elegy" © 1982 The Iowa Review
"A Small Good Thing" © 1982 Ploughshares © 1983 Alfred Knopf Co.
"Judgment" © 1982 Antaeus and Kate Wheeler
"The Time, The Place, The Loved One" © 1982 Paris Review
"Uncle Balt and the Nature of Being" © 1982 Conjunctions
"How To Write A Poem" © 1982 Paris Review
"Prayer For the Dying" © 1982 TriQuarterly
"Robo-Wash" © 1982 Mississippi Review
"Age" © 1982 Ploughshares
"The Stench" © 1982 Micah Publications © 1980 Jillian Becker
"Samba De Los Agentes" © 1982 Paris Review
"The Dishwasher" © 1982 Mississippi Review
"The Company We Keep: Self-Making In Imaginative Art, Old and New" © 1982 Daedalus, reprinted by permission of Daedalus, Journal of the American Academy of Arts and Sciences, Vol. III, 4, Cambridge, MA
"Avant-Garde Mastery" © 1982 TriQuarterly
"Being and Judaism" © 1982 Georgia Review
"Crane and Carlsen: A Memoir" © 1982 Raritan: A Quarterly Review
"The Eight Stages of Translation" © 1982 Kenyon Review and © 1983 Rowan Tree Press
"What Literature Means" © 1982 Partisan Review
"Memories of Unhousement, A Memoir" © 1982 Salmagundi
"Notes On Failure" © 1982 Hudson Review and Joyce Carol Oates
"The Decimation Before Phraata" © 1982 Antaeus and Alan Dugan
"Remembering Titian's Martyrdom of St. Lawrence" © 1982 Ironwood
"Persimmons" © 1982 American Poetry Review
"Sitting Between Two Mirrors" © 1982 Poetry
"Zoe" © 1982 Kenyon Review
"Quarrel" © 1982 Poetry
"The House That Fear Built: Warsaw, 1943" © 1982 Chelsea
"Moles" © 1982 Ohio Review
"The Weaver" © 1982 Northwest Review
"The Longing" © 1982 Cutbank
"The Reedbeds of The Hackensack" © 1982 Kenyon Review
"Hidden Justice" © 1982 Georgia Review
"Lining Up" © 1982 Grand Street
"Great-Aunt Francesca" © 1982 Ploughshares
from "A Sequence on Sidney Lanier" © 1982 MSS
"Carolyn At Twenty" © 1982 The Signpost Press
"A Valediction" © 1982 Ploughshares
"Those Destroyed By Success" © 1982 Poetry
"Each Bird Walking" © 1982 The Iowa Review
"Sonnet" © 1982 Missouri Review
"The Pond At Dusk" © 1982 The Iowa Review
"Dream Vision" © 1982 Threepenny Review
"I Knew I'd Sing" © 1982 Kayak
"Procession" © 1982 Hudson Review and Philip Booth
"Marcus Garvey Arrested at 125th Street Station" © 1982 Agni Review
"Hamlen Brook" © 1982 Poetry
"Confederate Graves in Little Rock" © 1982 Crazyhorse
"The Man of Many L's" © 1982 Seattle Review
"The End of the World" © 1982 Copper Canyon Press
"The Woman Who Lives In The Botanical Gardens" © 1982 Alexis De Veaux. First published in Open Places.
"The Desire And Pursuit of The Part" © 1982 The Iowa Review
"That Bright Grey Eye" © 1982 Ironwood
"Indian Boarding School: The Runaways" © 1982 Frontiers: A Journal of Women Studies
"Sapphics Against Anger" © 1982 Threepenny Review
"Tutka Bay, Alaska" © 1982 Blackwells Press
"Graveyard Day" from Shiloh and Other Stories by Bobbie Ann Mason. Copyright © 1982 by Bobbie Ann Mason. Originally appeared in Ascent. Reprinted by permission of Harper and Row Inc.

O<small>N THE OCCASION</small> of Pushcart Press' Tenth Anniversary, this book is dedicated to the hundreds of writers and editors who have helped us over the years; it is also dedicated to George A. Plimpton and friends and their Project Pushcart—an author's independent bookselling march down New York's Fifth Avenue (complete with pushcarts) that inspired the naming of our press a decade ago.

EDITOR'S NOTE

Since the founding of *The Pushcart Prize* series, it has been my honor to introduce each edition. This year I am pleased to pass this honor on to Gail Godwin.

Gail Godwin has published fiction and essays in many little magazines, including *North American Review, TriQuarterly, Iowa Review, The Lamp In The Spine, Paris Review, Story Quarterly, The James Joyce Quarterly, The Harvard Advocate* and *Antaeus*. She is the author of a short story collection and five novels, most recently *A Mother and Two Daughters*.

Gail Godwin is the first in a list of distinguished authors who will write the introductions to future editions of *The Pushcart Prize*.

BILL HENDERSON

INTRODUCTION:

About Pushcart Prize VIII

by GAIL GODWIN

"If anything is obvious about each if us, it is that we are very different persons depending on the art we are living with or in."

> WAYNE C BOOTH
> "The Company We Keep: Self-Making in
> Imaginative Art, Old and New."

> "Tell me," I said,
> "something I can't forget."

> TESS GALLAGHER
> "Each Bird Walking."

THIS IS to me the most invigorating, thought-provoking collection of writing that the Pushcart Press has yet published. And that is saying a lot, because its standards have been high ever since its first *Pushcart Prize* volume was published in 1976, "to rescue some of the wonderful writing appearing in small presses from oblivion," as Editor Bill Henderson expressed its purpose.

It does not surprise me that the material in this volume is of such extraordinarily high quality, because more and more of the really original and unforgettable writing in this country is finding its way into the multitudinous small presses that have sprung up all over the land. There are reasons for this, reasons that are both ominous

11

and energizing. What is happening reminds me very much of a natural phenomenon that took place in my own front yard last spring. One morning I went out and found the lawn massed with tiny maple seedlings. A local tree expert explained that the big maples, traumatized into action by a fierce two-year onslaught of gypsy moths, had mobilized deep down in their genes and produced this amazing spate of seedlings in order to ensure that there would always be maples.

One hopes there will always be maples, just as one hopes there will always be fine, vigorous writing, the healthy kind that grows honestly and stubbornly out of its own roots and sources, and attains its unique form by branching towards the light according to its individual needs and attributes.

However, (if you will indulge me in my metaphor a bit longer), healthy writing is vulnerable to predators, too. Its spirit and originality can be sapped, its actual content influenced, altered— or ignored—by the corporate policies that increasingly shape the mass market magazines. I speak from personal experience here. Recently, one mass market magazine that had bought a story of mine asked permission to cut one third of the story shortly before press time *because the magazine was running short of space for all the ads it had booked!* I refused in an indignant huff, and the magazine ran the story uncut. But what if I had been a writer just starting out, eager to see myself in print at last: would I have had the courage to say no?

In another recent confrontation with the gypsy moths of corporate publishing, I was beseeched by a magazine to send them anything new I had written. So I sent a new story of which I was very proud, although I had qualms about the magazine's somewhat gaudy and confused new format, which made it difficult to separate editorial content from advertising. Did I really want to see this story, which was an important one to me, broken up into little chunks to make way for the almighty cigarette and perfume ads? I needn't have worried, however, because the editor who had requisitioned the story returned it with abject apologies. What to say? She had been "wild" about it, but there had just been a shakeup at the magazine: it was now "targeting" to a "more contemporary" readership, and, as my story was set in the nineteen-fifties, she was afraid that disqualified it from being contemporary.

Which, translated into corporate language, means that these mythical "targeted" readers out there, poor stunted souls, are not capable of being interested in anything not taking place in the immediate present. Surely a contemptuous image of the reader you want for your magazine and an image based on invalid premises as well. (Wayne Booth has some salient things to say about the many reductive forms of taste-shaping going on in our culture today in his penetrating essay, "The Company We Keep: Self-Making in Imaginative Art, Old and New," which appears in this volume). Because every reader knows that it's not when or where a story takes place that engages the imaginative attention; it's the texture and quality of human life going on in the story that makes it memorable or forgettable. I think particularly of a story in this volume, Ellen Gilchrist's "Summer, An Elegy"; it is set in a bygone time and place, but it sticks with you, it haunts you, because of its acute rendering of certain human propensities (for sorrow, for guilt, for celebration and propitiation of the past through memory) that remain as timeless—and therefore as contemporary—as ever.

But, just as in nature, the news is never all bad. While many of the old showcases for good writing are dying or withering away under the pressure for sameness that will lead to mass profits, an exciting and pluralistic array of alternative publishing sources is attracting both new and established writers. (Witness the contents of last year's *Pushcart Prize VII* which sparkles with old and new names alike.)

Fifteen years ago, when I began sending out my stories with their accompanying stamped and self-addressed envelopes, it was understood among aspiring writers that the "underground" way of getting your work read eventually by larger audiences was to publish first in a little magazine. Then the more perspicacious of the New York magazine and book editors, ever on the lookout for fresh talent, would write and ask you if you had any more stories like the one he/she had just read in the latest issue of *TriQuarterly* or *The Iowa Review*. Or maybe you had a novel in progress?

Now things have turned around some. Writers who have long since found their way into mass circulation are seeking out small presses for their work; certain of those New York editors themselves have gone "underground" and are publishing *their* fiction in little magazines (for instance Gordon Lish, Knopf editor and former fiction editor of *Esquire* in its last vintage years, has a story, "How to Write a Poem," in this volume.) The small presses continue, of course, to attract the beginning, aspiring writer, as they always did, but why have so many seasoned writers gone back to licking stamps?

Perhaps because they value small, dedicated readerships—the kinds of readers who really look forward to reading their *Southern Review* or their *Kenyon Review*—more than they value some mass-produced "targeted" readership that might be the figment of Madison Avenue's imagination. Perhaps, like myself, they would rather see their work presented in a lucid, unbroken form, so that the perfect reader we dream of, that involved, reflective reader who has both the time and the long attention span, may turn the thick white pages and live completely in the presence of our art, undistracted by the yelps and bids for attention from dozens of different commercial products.

In the case of prolific writers, writers like Joyce Carol Oates, whose provocative essay, "Notes on Failure," appears in this collection, a considerable and varied number of magazines is needed just to hold the work; and if the scope of a writer's work is broad, magazines representing a wide spectrum of styles and interests will be required. *All* writers—seedlings and solidly-rooted alike—require sufficient space and freedom to *play* with their art, to pursue their visions unstinted by arbitrary word allotments and suitable story situations dictated by conglomerates and corporations with something else on their minds besides good writing. Raymond Carver felt required by the demands of his art to revise and expand an already published and well-known story. Thanks to *Ploughshares*, the new story, a remarkable outgrowth of the first, appears in *Pushcart VIII*, "A Small, Good Thing."

In the course of my own publishing history, certain literary magazines have been like special friends, the kind of friends who are willing to tolerate—and even to encourage—my idiosyncrasies, obsessions, and explorations. What they seem to want from me is what I require most from myself at the time. And because I am expanded, made more daring, by their latitude, I have often attempted things I might not have done had I been inhibited by the exclusiveness of magazines that identify themselves with particular reader tastes, or had I been trying to squeeze my vision into the latest oligarchic prescription for what is "contemporary."

The first story I ever had accepted for publication was taken by the *North American Review*, and it would have been my first published story, as well, had I not been so naive about what one did with author's proofs. So overwhelmed was I to see myself in print, after years of waiting, that I proudly sent these proofs to my mother. A year went by, I had another story accepted by another magazine, and flushed with the triumph of this, I wrote rather haughtily to Robley Wilson, Jr., at *North American Review*, inquiring whether he ever planned to run my story. He wrote back a charming letter saying that he had assumed I was still making changes in the proofs and hadn't wanted to rush me. We subsequently became friends, and while I still lived in Iowa, we would meet occasionally for lunch at a place half-way between Iowa City and Cedar Rapids and have long and intimate dialogues about writing and everything else.

I also have a fond respect for the *Paris Review*, because twice in my life when I had written stories that I was afraid nobody but myself would find the story in, George Plimpton immediately found the stories and published them with relish.

In recent years I have written a lot for *Antaeus*. This is because Daniel Halpern keeps asking me for just the kind of thing I am never sure I will be able to write until I write it, and which always surprises me after I have written it. What writer can resist such a temptation?

🔥 🔥 🔥

THE
PEOPLE WHO HELPED

FOUNDING EDITORS—*Anaïs Nin (1903-1977), Buckminster Fuller (1895-1983), Charles Newman, Daniel Halpern, Gordon Lish, Harry Smith, Hugh Fox, Ishmael Reed, Joyce Carol Oates, Len Fulton, Leonard Randolph, Leslie Fiedler, Nona Balakian, Paul Bowles, Paul Engle, Ralph Ellison, Reynolds Price, Rhoda Schwartz, Richard Morris, Ted Wilentz, Tom Montag, William Phillips. Poetry editor: H. L. Van Brunt.*

EDITORS—*Walter Abish, Ai, Elliott Anderson, John Ashbery, Robert Boyers, Joseph Brodsky, Wesley Brown, Hayden Carruth, Raymond Carver, Malcolm Cowley, Paula Deitz, Steve Dixon, M. D. Elevitch, Loris Essary, Ellen Ferber, Carolyn Forché, Stuart Friebert, Jon Galassi, Tess Gallagher, Louis Gallo, George Garrett, Louise Glück, David Godine, William Goyen, Jorie Graham, Linda Gregg, Barbara Grossman, Michael Harper, DeWitt Henry, J. R. Humphreys, John Irving, June Jordan, Karen Kennerly, Galway Kinnell, Mary Kinzie, Carolyn Kizer, Jerzy Kosinski, Richard Kostelanetz, Seymour Krim, Maxine Kumin, Stanley Kunitz, James Laughlin, Seymour Lawrence, Naomi Lazard, Herb Leibowitz, Denise Levertov, Stanley Lindberg, Thomas Lux, Mary MacArthur, Daniel Menaker, Frederick Morgan, Howard Moss, Cynthia Ozick, Jayne Anne Phillips, Robert Phillips, George Plimpton, Stanley Plumly, Eugene Redmond, Ed Sanders, Teo Savory, Grace Schulman, Harvey Shapiro, Leslie Silko, Charles Simic, Dave Smith, William Stafford, Gerald Stern, David St. John, Bill and Pat Strachan, Ron Sukenick, Barry Targan, Anne Tyler, John Updike, Samuel Vaughan, David Wagoner, Derek Walcott, Ellen Wilbur, David Wilk, Yvonne, Bill Zavatsky.*

17

CONTRIBUTING EDITORS FOR THIS EDITION—Bo Ball, Jim Barnes, Charles Baxter, Michael Blumenthal, Michael Dennis Browne, Richard Burgin, Fred Busch, Kathy Callaway, Steve Cannon, Siv Cedering, Kelly Cherry, Naomi Clark, Christopher Clausen, Marilyn Coffey, Philip Dacey, Guy Davenport, Susan Strayer Deal, Terrence Des Pres, Rita Dove, Jane Flanders, H. E. Francis, Jack Gilbert, Ellen Gilchrist, William Gilson, Matthew Graham, Thom Gunn, Lyn Hejinian, Don Hendrie Jr., Michael Hogan, John Hollander, David Ignatow, Elizabeth Inness-Brown, Janet Kauffman, Shirley Kaufman, Cinda Kornblum, Marilyn Krysl, Josephine Jacobsen, Miriam Levine, Philip Levine, Romulus Linney, Steven Liu, Garry Locklin, Frank MacShane, David Madden, Clarence Major, Adrianne Marcus, Dan Masterson, Cleopatra Mathis, Colleen McElroy, Heather McHugh, Michael McFee, Sandra McPherson, Judy Moffett, Charles Molesworth, Jennifer Moyer, Lisel Mueller, Carol Muske, Naomi Shihab Nye, David Ohle, Sharon Olds, Mary Oliver, Simon Ortiz, Linda Pastan, Joyce Peseroff, Mary Peterson, Robert Pinsky, Jarold Ramsey, David Ray, Leo Romero, William Pitt Root, Michael Ryan, Sherod Santos, Philip Schultz, Lynne Sharon Schwartz, Richard Smith, Gary Soto, Marcia Southwick, Elizabeth Spires, Maura Stanton, Pamela Stewart, David St. John, Elizabeth Tallent, Mary TallMountain, Julia Thacker, Elizabeth Thomas, Barbara Thompson, Sara Vogan, Barbara Watkins, C.K. Williams, Harold Witt, David Wojahn, Christine Zawadiwsky, Patricia Zelver, Paul Zimmer.

ROVING EDITOR—*Gene D. Chipps*

EDITORS AT LARGE—*Kirby and Liz Williams*

DESIGN AND PRODUCTION—*Ray Freiman*

JACKET DESIGN—*Barbara Lish*

EUROPEAN EDITOR—*Andrew Motion*

MANAGING EDITOR—*Helen Handley*

EDITOR AND PUBLISHER—*Bill Henderson*

PRESSES FEATURED IN THE FIRST EIGHT PUSHCART PRIZE EDITIONS

Agni Review
Ahsahta Press
Ailanthus Press
Alcheringa/Ethnopoetics
Alice James Books
American Literature
American PEN
American Poetry Review
Amnesty International
Anaesthesia Review
Antaeus
Antioch Review
Apalachee Quarterly
Aphra
The Ark
Ascent
Assembling
Aspen Leaves
Aspen Poetry Anthology
Barlenmir House
Barnwood Press
Beloit Poetry Journal
The Bellingham Review
Bilingual Review

Bits Press
Black American Literature Forum
Black Rooster
Black Scholar
Black Sparrow
Black Warrior Review
Blackwells Press
Blue Cloud Quarterly
Blue Wind Press
BOA Editions
Bookslinger Editions
Boxspring
Burning Deck Press
Caliban
California Quarterly
Canto
Capra Press
Cedar Rock
Center
Chariton Review
Chelsea
Chicago Review
Chouteau Review
Chowder Review
Cimarron Review
Cincinnati Poetry Review
City Lights Books
Clown War
CoEvolution Quarterly
Cold Mountain Press
Columbia: A Magazine of Poetry and Prose
Confluence Press
Confrontation
Conjunctions
Copper Canyon Press
Cosmic Information Agency
Crawl Out Your Window
Crazy Horse
Cross Cultural Communication
Cross Currents
Curbstone Press

Cutbank
Dacotah Territory
Daedalus
Decatur House
December
Dreamworks
Dryad Press
Duck Down Press
Durak
East River Anthology
Fiction
Fiction Collective
Fiction International
Field
Firelands Art Review
Five Trees Press
Frontiers: A Journal of Women Studies
Gallimaufry
Genre
The Georgia Review
Ghost Dance
Goddard Journal
The Godine Press
Graham House Press
Grand Street
Graywolf Press
Greensboro Review
Greenfield Review
Hard Pressed
Hills
Holmgangers Press
Holy Cow!
Hudson Review
Icarus
Iguana Press
Indiana Writes
Inwood Press
Intermedia
Intro
Invisible City
Iowa Review

Ironwood
The Kanchenjunga Press
Kansas Quarterly
Kayak
Kenyon Review
Latitudes Press
L'Epervier Press
Liberation
Linquis
The Little Magazine
Living Hand Press
Living Poets Press
Logbridge-Rhodes
Lowlands Review
Lucille
Lynx House Press
Manroot
Magic Circle Press
Malahat Review
Massachusetts Review
Michigan Quarterly
Milk Quarterly
Montana Gothic
Montana Review
Micah Publications
Missouri Review
Mississippi Review
Montemora
Mr. Cogito Press
MSS
Mulch Press
Nada Press
New America
New England Review
New Letters
North American Review
North Atlantic Books
North Point Press
Northwest Review
Obsidian

Oconee Review
October
Ohio Review
Ontario Review
Open Places
Oyez Press
Painted Bride Quarterly
Paris Review
Parnassus: Poetry In Review
Partisan Review
Penca Books
Penumbra Press
Pentagram
Persea: An International Review
Pequod
Pitcairn Press
Ploughshares
Poet and Critic
Poetry
Poetry Northwest
Poetry Now
Prairie Schooner
Prescott Street Press
Promise of Learnings
Quarry West
Quarterly West
Rainbow Press
Raritan: A Quarterly Review
Red Cedar Review
Red Clay Books
Red Earth Press
Release Press
Revista Chicano-Riquena
River Styx
Rowan Tree Press
Russian *Samizdat*
Salmagundi
San Marcos Press
Seamark Press
Seattle Review

Second Coming Press
The Seventies Press
Shankpainter
Shantih
Shenandoah
A Shout In The Street
Sibyl-Child Press
Small Moon
The Smith
The Spirit That Moves Us
Southern Poetry Review
Some
The Sonora Review
Southern Review
Southwestern Review
Spectrum
St. Andrews Press
Story Quarterly
Sun & Moon
Sun Press
Sunstone
Tar River Poetry
Tendril
Telephone Books
Texas Slough
THIS
Threepenny Review
13th Moon
Transatlantic Review
Three Rivers Press
Thorp Springs Press
Thunder's Mouth Press
Toothpaste Press
TriQuarterly
Truck Press
Tuumba Press
Undine
Unicorn Press
Unmuzzled Ox
Unspeakable Visions of the Individual

Vagabond
Virginia Quarterly
Water Table
Washington Writers Workshop
Western Humanities Review
Westigan Review
Wickwire Press
Willmore City
Word-Smith
Xanadu
Yale Review
Yardbird Reader
Y'Bird

CONTENTS

THE
PUSHCART PRIZE, VIII:
BEST OF THE
SMALL PRESSES
1983-1984 Edition

♨ ♨ ♨

A SMALL, GOOD THING

fiction by RAYMOND CARVER

from PLOUGHSHARES

nominated by PLOUGHSHARES, *Elizabeth Inness-Brown, Joyce Carol
Oates, Robert Phillips, George Plimpton, Ellen Wilbur and Patricia
Zelver*

SATURDAY AFTERNOON she drove to the bakery in the shopping
center. After looking through a loose-leaf binder with photographs
of cakes taped onto the pages, she ordered chocolate, the child's
favorite. The cake she chose was decorated with a space ship and
launching pad under a sprinkling of white stars at one end of the
cake, and a planet made of red frosting at the other end. His name,
SCOTTY, would be in raised green letters beneath the planet. The
baker, who was an older man with a thick neck, listened without
saying anything when she told him the child would be eight years
old next Monday. The baker wore a white apron that looked like a
smock. Straps cut under his arms, went around in back and then to
the front again where they were secured under his heavy waist. He
wiped his hands on his apron as he listened to her. He kept his
eyes down on the photographs and let her talk. He let her take her
time. He'd just come to work and he'd be there all night, baking,
and he was in no real hurry.

She gave the baker her name, Ann Weiss, and her telephone
number. The cake would be ready on Monday morning, just out of
the oven, in plenty of time for the child's party that afternoon. The
baker was not jolly. There were no pleasantries between them, just
the minimum exchange of words, the necessary information. He
made her feel uncomfortable, and she didn't like that. While he
was bent over the counter with the pencil in his hand, she studied
his coarse features and wondered if he'd ever done anything else
with his life besides be a baker. She was a mother and thirty-three

years old, and it seemed to her that everyone, especially someone the baker's age—a man old enough to be her father—must have children who'd gone through this special time of cakes and birthday parties. There must be that between them, she thought. But he was abrupt with her, not rude, just abrupt. She gave up trying to make friends with him. She looked into the back of the bakery and coud see a long, heavy wooden table with aluminum pie pans stacked at one end, and beside the table a metal container filled with empty racks. There was an enormous oven. A radio was playing country-western music.

The baker finished printing the information on the special order card and closed up the binder. He looked at her and said, "Monday morning." She thanked him and drove home.

On Monday morning, the birthday boy was walking to school with another boy. They were passing a bag of potato chips back and forth and the birthday boy was trying to find out what his friend intended to give him for his birthday that afternoon. Without looking, he stepped off the curb at an intersection and was immediately knocked down by a car. He fell on his side with his head in the gutter and his legs out in the road. His eyes were closed, but his legs began to move back and forth as if he were trying to climb over something. His friend dropped the potato chips and started to cry. The car had gone a hundred feet or so and stopped in the middle of the road. A man in the driver's seat looked back over his shoulder. He waited until the boy got unsteadily to his feet. The boy wobbled a little. He looked dazed, but okay. The driver put the car into gear and drove away.

The birthday boy didn't cry, but he didn't have anything to say about anything either. He wouldn't answer when his friend asked him what it felt like to be hit by a car. He walked home, and his friend went on to school. But after the birthday boy was inside his house and was telling his mother about it, she sitting beside him on the sofa, holding his hands in her lap, saying, "Scotty, honey, are you sure you feel all right, baby?" thinking she would call the doctor anyway, he suddenly lay back on the sofa, closed his eyes, and went limp. When she couldn't wake him up, she hurried to the telephone and called her husband at work. Howard told her to remain calm, remain calm, and then he called an ambulance for the child and left for the hospital himself.

Of course, the birthday party was cancelled. The child was in the hospital with a mild concussion and suffering from shock. There'd been vomiting, and his lungs had taken in fluid which needed pumping out that afternoon. Now he simply seemed to be in a very deep sleep—but no coma, Doctor Francis had emphasized; no coma, when he saw the alarm in the parents' eyes. At eleven o'clock that Monday night when the boy seemed to be resting comfortably enough after the many X-rays and the lab work, and it was just a matter of his waking up and coming around, Howard left the hospital. He and Ann had been at the hospital with the child since that morning, and he was going home for a short while to bathe and to change clothes. "I'll be back in an hour," he said. She nodded. "It's fine," she said. "I'll be right here." He kissed her on the forehead, and they touched hands. She sat in a chair beside the bed and looked at the child. She was waiting for him to wake up and be all right. Then she could begin to relax.

Howard drove home from the hospital. He took the wet, dark streets very fast, then caught himself and slowed down. Until now, his life had gone smoothly and to his satisfaction—college, marriage, another year of college for the advanced degree in business, a junior partnership in an investment firm. Fatherhood. He was happy and, so far, lucky—he knew that. His parents were still living, his brothers and his sister were established, his friends from college had gone out to take their places in the world. So far he had kept away from any real harm, from those forces he knew existed and that could cripple or bring down a man, if the luck went bad, if things suddenly turned. He pulled into the driveway and parked. His left leg began to tremble. He sat in the car for a minute and tried to deal with the present situation in a rational manner. Scotty had been hit by a car and was in the hospital, but he was going to be all right. He closed his eyes and ran his hand over his face. In a minute, he got out of the car and went up to the front door. The dog was barking inside the house. The telephone rang and rang while he unlocked the door and fumbled for the light switch. He shouldn't have left the hospital, he shouldn't have. "God dammit!" he said. He picked up the receiver and said, "I just walked in the door!"

"There's a cake here that wasn't picked up," the voice on the other end of the line said.

"What are you saying?" Howard asked.

"A cake," the voice said. "A sixteen dollar cake."

Howard held the receiver against his ear, trying to understand. "I don't know anything about a cake," he said. "Jesus, what are you talking about?"

"Don't hand me that," the voice said.

Howard hung up the telephone. He went into the kitchen and poured himself some whiskey. He called the hospital. But the child's condition remained the same; he was still sleeping and nothing had changed there. While water poured into the tub, Howard lathered his face and shaved. He'd just stretched out in the tub and closed his eyes when the telephone began to ring. He hauled himself out, grabbed a towel, and hurried through the house, saying "Stupid, stupid," for having left the hospital. But when he picked up the receiver and shouted, "Hello!" there was no sound at the other end of the line. Then the caller hung up.

He arrived back at the hospital a little after midnight. Ann still sat in the chair beside the bed. She looked at Howard, and then she looked back at the child. The child's eyes stayed closed, the head was still wrapped in bandages. His breathing was quiet and regular. From an apparatus over the bed hung a bottle of glucose with a tube running from the bottle to the boy's arm.

"How is he?" Howard said. "What's all this?" waving at the glucose and the tube.

"Doctor Francis's orders," she said. "He needs nourishment. He needs to keep up his strength. Why doesn't he wake up, Howard? I don't understand, if he's all right."

Howard put his hand against the back of her head. He ran his fingers through her hair. "He's going to be all right. He'll wake up in a little while. Doctor Francis knows what's what."

After a time he said, "Maybe you should go home and get some rest. I'll stay here. Just don't put up with this creep who keeps calling. Hang up right away."

"Who's calling?" she asked.

"I don't know who, just somebody with nothing better to do than call up people. You go on now."

She shook her head. "No," she said, "I'm fine."

"Really," he said. "Go home for a while, and then come back and spell me in the morning. It'll be all right. What did Doctor Francis say? He said Scotty's going to be all right. We don't have to worry. He's just sleeping now, that's all."

A nurse pushed the door open. She nodded at them as she went to the bedside. She took the left arm out from under the covers and put her fingers on the wrist, found the pulse, and then consulted her watch. In a little while she put the arm back under the covers and moved to the foot of the bed where she wrote something on a clipboard attached to the bed.

"How is he?" Ann said. Howard's hand was a weight on her shoulder. She was aware of the pressure from his fingers.

"He's stable," the nurse said. Then she said, "Doctor will be in again shortly. Doctor's back in the hospital. He's making rounds right now."

"I was saying maybe she'd want to go home and get a little rest," Howard said. "After the doctor comes," he said.

"She could do that," the nurse said. "I think you should both feel free to do that, if you wish." The nurse was a big Scandinavian woman with blond hair. There was the trace of an accent in her speech.

"We'll see what the doctor says," Ann said. "I want to talk to the doctor. I don't think he should keep sleeping like this. I don't think that's a good sign." She brought her hand up to her eyes and let her head come forward a little. Howard's grip tightened on her shoulder, and then his hand moved to her neck where his fingers began to knead the muscles there.

"Doctor Francis will be here in a few minutes," the nurse said. Then she left the room.

Howard gazed at his son for a time, the small chest quietly rising and falling under the covers. For the first time since the terrible minutes after Ann's telephone call to him at his office, he felt a genuine fear starting in his limbs. He began shaking his head, trying to keep it away. Scotty was fine, but instead of sleeping at home in his own bed he was in a hospital bed with bandages around his head and a tube in his arm. But this help was what he needed right now.

Doctor Francis came in and shook hands with Howard, though they'd just seen each other a few hours before. Ann got up from the chair. "Doctor?"

"Ann," he said and nodded. "Let's just first see how he's doing," the doctor said. He moved to the side of the bed and took the boy's pulse. He peeled back one eyelid and then the other. Howard and Ann stood beside the doctor and watched. Then the doctor turned back the covers and listened to the boy's heart and lungs with his stethoscope. He pressed his fingers here and there on the abdomen. When he was finished he went to the end of the bed and studied the chart. He noted the time, scribbled something on the chart, and then looked at Howard and Ann.

"Doctor, how is he?" Howard said. "What's the matter with him exactly?"

"Why doesn't he wake up?" Ann said.

The doctor was a handsome, big-shouldered man with a tanned face. He wore a three-piece suit, a striped tie, and ivory cuff-links. His grey hair was combed along the sides of his head, and he looked as if he had just come from a concert. "He's all right," the doctor said. "Nothing to shout about, he could be better, I think. But he's all right. Still, I wish he'd wake up. He should wake up pretty soon." The doctor looked at the boy again. "We'll know some more in a couple of hours, after the results of a few more tests are in. But he's all right, believe me, except for that hair-line fracture of the skull. He does have that."

"Oh, no," Ann said.

"And a bit of a concussion, as I said before. Of course, you know he's in shock," the doctor said. "Sometimes you see this in shock cases."

"But he's out of any real danger?" Howard said. "You said before he's not in a coma. You wouldn't call this a coma then, would you, doctor?" Howard waited. He looked at the doctor.

"No, I don't want to call it a coma," the doctor said and glanced over at the boy once more. "He's just in a very deep sleep. It's a restorative, a measure the body is taking on its own. He's out of any real danger, I'd say that for certain, yes. But we'll know more when he wakes up and the other tests are in. Don't worry," the doctor said.

"It's a coma," Ann said. "Of sorts."

"It's not a coma yet, not exactly," the doctor said. "I wouldn't want to call it coma. Not yet anyway. He's suffered shock. In shock cases this kind of reaction is common enough; it's a temporary reaction to bodily trauma. Coma. Well, coma is a deep, prolonged unconsciousness that could go on for days, or weeks even. Scotty's not in that area, not as far as we can tell anyway. I'm certain his condition will show improvement by morning. I'm betting that it will anyway. We'll know more when he wakes up, which shouldn't be long now. Of course, you may do as you like, stay here or go home for a time. But by all means feel free to leave the hospital for a while if you want. This is not easy, I know." The doctor gazed at the boy again, watching him, and then he turned to Ann and said, "You try not to worry, little mother. Believe me, we're doing all that can be done. It's just a question of a little more time now." He nodded at her, shook hands with Howard again, and then he left the room.

Ann put her hand over her child's forehead. "At least he doesn't have a fever," she said. Then she said, "My God, he feels so cold though. Howard? Is he supposed to feel like this. Feel his head."

Howard touched the child's temples. His own breathing had slowed. "I think he's supposed to feel this way right now," he said. "He's in shock, remember? That's what the doctor said. The doctor was just in here. He would have said something if Scotty wasn't okay."

Ann stood there a while longer, working her lip with her teeth. Then she moved over to her chair and sat down.

Howard sat in the chair next to her chair. They looked at each other. He wanted to say something else and reassure her, but he was afraid too. He took her hand and put it in his lap, and this made him feel better, her hand being there. He picked up her hand and squeezed it. Then he just held her hand. They sat like that for a while, watching the boy and not talking. From time to time he squeezed her hand. Finally, she took her hand away.

"I've been praying," she said.

He nodded.

She said, "I almost thought I'd forgotten how, but it came back to me. All I had to do was close my eyes and say, 'Please, God, help us, —help Scotty'; and then the rest was easy. The words were right there. Maybe if you prayed too," she said to him.

"I've already prayed," he said. "I prayed this afternoon, yesterday afternoon, I mean, after you called, while I was driving to the hospital. I've been praying," he said.

"That's good," she said. For the first time now, she felt they were together in it, this trouble. She realized with a start it had only been happening to her and to Scotty. She hadn't let Howard into it, though he was there and needed all along. She felt glad to be his wife.

The same nurse came in and took the boy's pulse again and checked the flow from the bottle hanging above the bed.

In an hour another doctor came in. He said his name was Parsons, from Radiology. He had a bushy moustache. He was wearing loafers, a western shirt, and a pair of jeans.

"We're going to take him downstairs for more pictures," he told them. "We need to do some more pictures, and we want to do a scan."

"What's that?" Ann said. "A scan?" She stood between this new doctor and the bed. "I thought you'd already taken all your X-rays."

"I'm afraid we need some more," he said. "Nothing to be alarmed about. We just need some more pictures, and we want to do a brain scan on him."

"My God," Ann said.

"It's perfectly normal procedure in cases like this," this new doctor said. "We just need to find out for sure why he isn't back awake yet. It's normal medical procedure, and nothing to be alarmed about. We'll be taking him down in a few minutes," this doctor said.

In a little while two orderlies came into the room with a gurney. They were black-haired, dark-complexioned men in white uniforms, and they said a few words to each other in a foreign tongue as they unhooked the boy from the tube and moved him from his bed to the gurney. Then they wheeled him from the room. Howard and Ann got on the same elevator. Ann stood beside the gurney and gazed at the child. She closed her eyes as the elevator began its descent. The orderlies stood at either end of the gurney without saying anything, though once one of the men made a comment to the other in their own language, and the other man nodded slowly in response.

Later that morning, just as the sun was beginning to lighten the windows in the waiting room outside the X-Ray department, they brought the boy out and moved him back up to his room. Howard and Ann rode up on the elevator with him once more, and once more they took up their places beside the bed.

They waited all day, but still the boy did not wake up. Occasionally one of them would leave the room to go downstairs to the cafeteria to drink coffee and then, as if suddenly remembering and feeling guilty, get up from the table and hurry back to the room. Doctor Francis came again that afternoon and examined the boy once more and then left after telling them he was coming along and could wake up any minute now. Nurses, different nurses than the night before, came in from time to time. Then a young woman from the lab knocked and entered the room. She wore white slacks and a white blouse and carried a little tray of things which she put on the stand beside the bed. Without a word to them, she took blood from the boy's arm. Howard closed his eyes as the woman found the right place on the boy's arm and pushed the needle in.

"I don't understand this," Ann said to the woman.

"Doctor's orders," the young woman said. "I do what I'm told to do. They say draw that one, I draw. What's wrong with him, anyway?" she said. "He's a sweetie."

"He was hit by a car," Howard said. "A hit and run."

The young woman shook her head and looked again at the boy. Then she took her tray and left the room.

"Why won't he wake up?" Ann said. "Howard? I want some answers from these people."

Howard didn't say anything. He sat down again in the chair and crossed one leg over the other. He rubbed his face. He looked at his son and then he settled back in the chair, closed his eyes, and went to sleep.

Ann walked to the window and looked out at the parking lot. It was night and cars were driving into and out of the parking lot with their lights on. She stood at the window with her hands gripping the sill and knew in her heart that they were into something now, something hard. She was afraid, and her teeth began to chatter until she tightened her jaws. She saw a big car stop in front of the hospital and someone, a woman in a long coat, got into the car. For a minute she wished she were that woman and somebody, anybody, was driving her away from here to somewhere else, a place where she would find Scotty waiting for her when she stepped out of the car, ready to say *Mom* and let her gather him in her arms.

In a little while Howard woke up. He looked at the boy again, and then he got up from the chair, stretched, and went over to stand beside her at the window. They both stared out at the parking lot. They didn't say anything. But they seemed to feel each other's insides now, as though the worry had made them transparent in a perfectly natural way.

The door opened and Doctor Francis came in. He was wearing a different suit and tie this time. His gray hair was combed along the sides of his head, and he looked as if he had just shaved. He went straight to the bed and examined the boy. "He ought to have come around by now. There's just no good reason for this," he said. "But I can tell you we're all convinced he's out of any danger. We'll just feel better when he wakes up. There's no reason, absolutely none, why he shouldn't come around. Very soon. Oh, he'll have himself a dilly of a headache when he does, you can count on that. But all of his signs are fine. They're as normal as can be."

"Is it a coma then?" Ann asked.

The doctor rubbed his smooth cheek. "We'll call it that for the time being, until he wakes up. But you must be worn out. This is hard. Feel free to go out for a bite," he said. "It would do you good. I'll put a nurse in here while you're gone, if you'll feel better about going. Go and have yourselves something to eat."

"I couldn't eat," Ann said. "I'm not hungry."

"Do what you need to do, of course," the doctor said. "Anyway, I wanted to tell you that all the signs are good, the tests are positive, nothing at all negative, and just as soon as he wakes up he'll be over the hill."

"Thank you, doctor," Howard said. He shook hands with the doctor again. The doctor patted Howard's shoulder and went out.

"I suppose one of us should go home and check things," Howard said. "Slug needs to be fed, for one thing."

"Call one of the neighbors," Ann said. "Call the Morgans. Anyone will feed a dog if you ask them to."

"All right," Howard said. After a while he said, "Honey why don't you do it? Why don't you go home and check on things, and then come back? It'll do you good. I'll be right here with him. Seriously," he said. "We need to keep up our strength on this. We'll want to be here for a while even after he wakes up."

"Why don't you go?" she said. "Feed Slug. Feed yourself."

"I already went," he said. "I was gone for exactly an hour and fifteen minutes. You go home for an hour and freshen up. Then come back. I'll stay here."

She tried to think about it, but she was too tired. She closed her eyes and tried to think about it again. After a time she said, "Maybe I will go home for a few minutes. Maybe if I'm not just sitting right here watching him every second he'll wake up and be all right. You know? Maybe he'll wake up if I'm not here. I'll go home and take a bath and put on clean clothes. I'll feed Slug. Then I'll come back."

"I'll be right here," he said. "You go on home, honey, and then come back. I'll be right here keeping an eye on things." His eyes were bloodshot and small, as if he'd been drinking for a long time. His clothes were rumpled. His beard had come out again. She touched his face, and then she took her hand back. She understood he wanted to be by himself for a while, to not have to talk or share his worry for a time. She picked up her purse from the nightstand, and he helped her into her coat.

"I won't be gone long," she said.

"Just sit and rest for a little while when you get home," he said. "Eat something. Take a bath. After you get out of the bath, just sit for a while and rest. It'll do you a world of good, you'll see. Then come back down here," he said. "Let's try not to worry. You heard what Doctor Francis said."

She stood in her coat for a minute trying to recall the doctor's exact words, looking for any nuances, any hint of something behind his words other than what he had said. She tried to remember if his expression had changed any when he bent over to examine the child. She remembered the way his features had composed themselves as he rolled back the child's eyelids and then listened to his breathing.

She went to the door where she turned and looked back. She looked at the child, and then she looked at the father. Howard nodded. She stepped out of the room and pulled the door closed behind her.

She went past the nurses' station and down to the end of the corridor, looking for the elevator. At the end of the corridor she turned to her right where she found a little waiting room where a Negro family sat in wicker chairs. There was a middle-aged man in a khaki shirt and pants, a baseball cap pushed back on his head. A large woman wearing a house dress and slippers was slumped in one of the chairs. A teenaged girl in jeans, hair done in dozens of little braids, lay stretched out in one of the chairs smoking a

cigarette, her legs crossed at the ankles. The family swung their
eyes to her as she entered the room. The little table was littered
with hamburger wrappers and styrofoam cups.

"Franklin," the large woman said as she roused herself. "Is about
Franklin?" Her eyes widened. "Tell me now, lady," the woman
said. "Is about Franklin?" She was trying to rise from her chair, but
the man had closed his hand over her arm.

"Here, here," he said. "Evelyn."

"I'm sorry," Ann said. "I'm looking for the elevator. My son is in
the hospital, and now I can't find the elevator."

"Elevator is down that way, turn left," the man said as he aimed
a finger.

The girl drew on her cigarette and stared at Ann. Her eyes were
narrowed to slits, and her broad lips parted slowly as she let the
smoke escape. The Negro woman let her head fall on her shoulder
and looked away from Ann, no longer interested.

"My son was hit by a car," Ann said to the man. She seemed to
need to explain herself. "He has a concussion and a little skull
fracture, but he's going to be all right. He's in shock now, but it
might be some kind of coma too. That's what really worries us, the
coma part. I'm going out for a little while, but my husband is with
him. Maybe he'll wake up while I'm gone."

"That's too bad," the man said and shifted in the chair. He shook
his head. He looked down at the table, and then he looked back at
Ann. She was still standing there. He said, "Our Franklin, he's on
the operating table. Somebody cut him. Tried to kill him. There
was a fight where he was at. At this party. They say he was just
standing and watching. Not bothering nobody. But that don't mean
nothing these days. Now he's on the operating table. We're just
hoping and praying, that's all we can do now." He gazed at her
steadily.

Ann looked at the girl again, who was still watching her, and at
the older woman who kept her head down, but whose eyes were
now closed. Ann saw the lips moving silently, making words. She
had an urge to ask what those words were. She wanted to talk more
with these people who were in the same kind of waiting she was in.
She was afraid, and they were afraid. They had that in common.
She would have liked to have said something else about the
accident, told them more about Scotty, that it had happened on the
day of his birthday, Monday, and that he was still unconscious. Yet

she didn't know how to begin. She stood there looking at them without saying anything more.

She went down the corridor the man had indicated and found the elevator. She stood for a minute in front of the closed doors, still wondering if she was doing the right thing. Then she put out her finger and touched the button.

She pulled into the driveway and cut the engine. She closed her eyes and leaned her head against the wheel for a minute. She listened to the ticking sounds the engine made as it began to cool. Then she got out of the car. She could hear the dog barking inside the house. She went to the front door, which was unlocked. She went inside and turned on lights and put on a kettle of water for tea. She opened some dog food and fed Slug on the back porch. The dog ate in hungry little smacks. It kept running into the kitchen to see that she was going to stay. As she sat down on the sofa with her tea, the telephone rang.

"Yes!" she said as she answered. "Hello!"

"Mrs. Weiss," a man's voice said. It was five o'clock in the morning, and she thought she could hear machinery or equipment of some kind in the background.

"Yes, yes! What is it?" she said. "This is Mrs. Weiss. This is she. What is it, please?" She listened to whatever it was in the background. "Is it Scotty, for Christ's sake?"

"Scotty," the man's voice said. "It's about Scotty, yes. It has to do with Scotty, that problem. Have you forgotten about Scotty?" the man said. Then he hung up.

She dialed the hospital's number and asked for the third floor. She demanded information about her son from the nurse who answered the telephone. Then she asked to speak to her husband. It was, she said, an emergency.

She waited, turning the telephone cord in her fingers. She closed her eyes and felt sick to her stomach. She would have to make herself eat. Slug came in from the back porch and lay down near her feet. He wagged his tail. She pulled at his ear while he licked her fingers. Howard was on the line.

"Somebody just called here," she said. She twisted the telephone cord. "He said, he said it was about Scotty." She cried.

"Scotty's fine," Howard told her. "I mean he's still sleeping. There's been no change. The nurse has been in twice since you've been gone. They're in here every thirty minutes or so. A nurse or else a doctor. He's all right."

"Somebody called, he said it was about Scotty," she said.

"Honey, you rest for a little while, you need the rest. Then come back here. It must be that same caller I had. Just forget it. Come back down here after you've rested. Then we'll have breakfast or something."

"Breakfast," she said. "I don't want any breakfast."

"You know what I mean," he said. "Juice, something, I don't know. I don't know anything, Ann. Jesus, I'm not hungry either. Ann, it's hard to talk now. I'm standing here at the desk. Doctor Francis is coming again at eight o'clock this morning. He's going to have something to tell us then, something more definite. That's what one of the nurses said. She didn't know any more than that. Ann? Honey, maybe we'll know something more then. At eight o'clock. Come back here before eight. Meanwhile, I'm right here and Scotty's all right. He's still the same," he added.

"I was drinking a cup of tea," she said, "when the telephone rang. They said it was about Scotty. There was a noise in the background. Was there a noise in the background on that call you had, Howard?"

"I don't remember," he said. "Maybe the driver of the car, maybe he's a psychopath and found out about Scotty somehow. But I'm here with him. Just rest like you were going to do. Take a bath and come back by seven or so, and we'll talk to the doctor together when he gets here. It's going to be all right, honey. I'm here, and there are doctors and nurses around. They say his condition is stable."

"I'm scared to death," she said.

She ran water, undressed, and got into the tub. She washed and dried quickly, not taking the time to wash her hair. She put on clean underwear, wool slacks, and a sweater. She went into the living room where the dog looked up at her and let its tail thump once against the floor. It was just starting to get light outside when she went out to the car.

She drove into the parking lot of the hospital and found a space close to the front door. She felt she was in some obscure way responsible for what had happened to the child. She let her thoughts move to the Negro family. She remembered the name "Franklin" and the table that was covered with hamburger papers, and the teenaged girl staring at her as she drew on her cigarette. "Don't have children," she told the girl's image as she entered the front door of the hospital. "For God's sake, don't."

She took the elevator up to the third floor with two nurses who were just going on duty. It was Wednesday morning, a few minutes before seven. There was a page for a Doctor Madison as the elevator doors slid open on the third floor. She got off behind the nurses, who turned in the other direction and continued the conversation she had interrupted when she'd gotten into the elevator. She walked down the corridor to the little alcove where the Negro family had been waiting. They were gone now, but the chairs were scattered in such a way that it looked as if people had just jumped from them the minute before. The table top cluttered with the same cups and papers, the ashtray was filled with cigarette butts.

She stopped at the nurses' station just down the corridor from the waiting room. A nurse was standing behind the counter, brushing her hair and yawning.

"There was a Negro man in surgery last night," Ann said. "Franklin was his name. His family was in the waiting room. I'd like to inquire about his condition."

A nurse who was sitting at a desk behind the counter looked up from a chart in front of her. The telephone buzzed and she picked up the receiver, but she kept her eyes on Ann.

"He passed away," said the nurse at the counter. The nurse held the hairbrush and kept on looking at her. "Are you a friend of the family or what?"

"I met the family last night," Ann said. "My own son is in the hospital. I guess he's in shock. We don't know for sure what's wrong. I just wondered about Mr. Franklin, that's all. Thank you." She moved down the corridor. Elevator doors the same color as the walls slid open and a gaunt, bald man in white pants and white canvas shoes pulled a heavy cart off the elevator. She hadn't noticed these doors last night. The man wheeled the cart out into the corridor and stopped in front of the room nearest the elevator and consulted a clipboard. Then he reached down and slid a tray out of the cart. He rapped lightly on the door and entered the room. She could smell the unpleasant odors of warm food as she passed the cart. She hurried past the other station without looking at any of the nurses and pushed open the door to the child's room.

Howard was standing at the window with his hands behind his back. He turned around as she came in.

"How is he?" she said. She went over to the bed. She dropped her purse on the floor beside the nightstand. She seemed to have been gone a long time. She touched the child's face. "Howard?"

"Doctor Francis was here a little while ago," Howard said. She looked at him closely and thought his shoulders were bunched a little.

"I thought he wasn't coming until eight o'clock this morning," she said quickly.

"There was another doctor with him. A neurologist."

"A neurologist," she said.

Howard nodded. His shoulders were bunching, she could see that. "What'd they say, Howard? For Christ's sake, what'd they say? What is it?"

"They said they're going to take him down and run more tests on him, Ann. They think they're going to operate, honey. Honey, they are going to operate. They can't figure out why he won't wake up. It's more than just shock or concussion, they know that much now. It's in his skull, the fracture, it has something, something to do with that, they think. So they're going to operate. I tried to call you, but I guess you'd already left the house."

"Oh, God," she said. "Oh, please, Howard, please," she said, taking his arms.

"Look!" Howard said then. "Scotty! Look, Ann!" He turned her toward the bed.

The boy had opened his eyes, then closed them. He opened them again now. The eyes stared straight ahead for a minute, then moved slowly in his head until they rested on Howard and Ann, then traveled away again.

"Scotty," his mother said, moving to the bed.

"Hey, Scott," his father said. "Hey, son."

They leaned over the bed. Howard took the child's hand in his hands and began to pat and squeeze the hand. Ann bent over the boy and kissed his forehead again and again. She put her hands on either side of his face. "Scotty, honey, it's mommy and daddy," she said. "Scotty?"

The boy looked at them, but without any sign of recognition. Then his eyes scrunched closed, his mouth opened, and he howled until he had no more air in his lungs. His face seemed to relax and soften then. His lips parted as his last breath was puffed through his throat and exhaled gently through the clenched teeth.

The doctors called it a hidden occlusion and said it was a one-in-a-million circumstance. Maybe if it could have been detected somehow and surgery undertaken immediately, it could have saved him. But more than likely not. In any case, what would they have been looking for? Nothing had shown up in the tests or in the X-rays. Doctor Francis was shaken. "I can't tell you how badly I feel. I'm so very sorry, I can't tell you," he said as he led them into the doctors' lounge. There was a doctor sitting in a chair with his legs hooked over the back of another chair, watching an early morning TV show. He was wearing a green delivery room outfit, loose green pants and green blouse, and a green cap that covered his hair. He looked at Howard and Ann and then looked at Doctor Francis. He got to his feet and turned off the set and went out of the room. Doctor Francis guided Ann to the sofa, sat down beside her and began to talk in a low, consoling voice. At one point he leaned over and embraced her. She could feel his chest rising and falling evenly against her shoulder. She kept her eyes open and let him hold her. Howard went into the bathroom, but he left the door open. After a violent fit of weeping, he ran water and washed his face. Then he came out and sat down at the little table that held a telephone. He looked at the telephone as though deciding what to do first. He made some calls. After a time, Doctor Francis used the telephone.

"Is there anything else I can do for the moment?" he asked them.

Howard shook his head. Ann stared at Doctor Francis as if unable to comprehend his words.

The doctor walked them to the hospital's front door. People were entering and leaving the hospital. It was eleven o'clock in the morning. Ann was aware of how slowly, almost reluctantly she moved her feet. It seemed to her that Doctor Francis was making them leave, when she felt they should stay, when it would be more the right thing to do, to stay. She gazed out into the parking lot and then turned around and looked back at the front of the hospital. She began shaking her head. "No, no," she said. "I can't leave him here, no." She heard herself say that and thought how unfair it was

that the only words that came out were the sort of words used on
TV shows where people were stunned by violent or sudden deaths.
She wanted her words to be her own. "No," she said, and for some
reason the memory of the Negro woman's head lolling on the
woman's shoulder came to her. "No," she said again.

"I'll be talking to you later in the day," the doctor was saying to
Howard. "There are still some things that have to be done, things
that have to be cleared up to our satisfaction. Some things that
need explaining."

"An autopsy," Howard said.

Doctor Francis nodded.

"I understand," Howard said. Then he said, "Oh, Jesus. No, I
don't understand, Doctor. I can't, I can't. I just can't."

Doctor Francis put his arm around Howard's shoulders. "I'm
sorry. God, how I'm sorry." He let go of Howard's shoulders and
held out his hand. Howard looked at the hand, and then he took it.
Doctor Francis put his arms around Ann once more. He seemed
full of some goodness she didn't understand. She let her head rest
on his shoulder, but her eyes stayed open. She kept looking at the
hospital. As they drove out of the parking lot, she looked back at
the hospital once more.

At home, she sat on the sofa with her hands in her coat pockets.
Howard closed the door to the child's room. He got the coffee
maker going and then he found an empty box. He had thought to
pick up some of the child's things. But instead he sat down beside
her on the sofa, pushed the box to one side, and leaned forward,
arms between his knees. He began to weep. She pulled his head
over into her lap and patted his shoulder. "He's gone," she said.
She kept patting his shoulder. Over his sobs she could hear the
coffee maker hissing in the kitchen. "There, there," she said
tenderly. "Howard, he's gone. He's gone and now we'll have to get
used to that. To being alone."

In a little while Howard got up and began moving aimlessly
around the room with the box, not putting anything into it, but
collecting some things together on the floor at one end of the sofa.
She continued to sit with her hands in her coat pockets. Howard
put the box down and brought coffee into the living room. Later,
Ann made calls to relatives. After each call had been placed and
the party had answered, Ann would blurt out a few words and cry

for a minute. Then she would quietly explain, in a measured voice, what had happened and tell them about arrangements. Howard took the box out to the garage where he saw the child's bicycle. He dropped the box and sat down on the pavement beside the bicycle. He took hold of the bicycle awkwardly so that it leaned against his chest. He held it, the rubber pedal sticking into his chest. He gave the wheel a turn.

Ann hung up the telephone after talking to her sister. She was looking up another number, when the telephone rang. She picked it up on the first ring.

"Hello," she said, and she heard something in the background, a humming noise. "Hello!" she said. "For God's sake," she said. "Who is this? What is it you want?"

"Your Scotty, I got him ready for you," the man's voice said. "Did you forget him?"

"You evil bastard!" she shouted into the receiver. "How can you do this, you evil son of a bitch?"

"Scotty," the man said. "Have you forgotten about Scotty?" Then the man hung up on her.

Howard heard the shouting and came in to find her with her head on her arms over the table, weeping. He picked up the receiver and listened to the dial tone.

Much later, just before midnight, after they had dealt with many things, the telphone rang again.

"You answer it," she said. "Howard, it's him, I know." They were sitting at the kitchen table with coffee in front of them. Howard had a small glass of whisky beside his cup. He answered on the third ring.

"Hello," he said. "Who is this? Hello! Hello!" The line went dead. "He hung up," Howard said. "Whoever it was."

"It was him," she said. "That bastard. I'd like to kill him," she said. "I'd like to shoot him and watch him kick," she said.

"Ann, my God," he said.

"Could you hear anything?" she said. "In the background? A noise, machinery, something humming?"

"Nothing, really. Nothing like that," he said. "There wasn't much time. I think there was some radio music. Yes, there was a radio going, that's all I could tell. I don't know what in God's name is going on," he said.

She shook her head. "If I could, could get, my hands, on him." It came to her then. She knew who it was. Scotty, the cake, the telephone number. She pushed the chair away from the table and got up. "Drive me down to the shopping center," she said. "Howard."

"What are you saying?"

"The shopping center. I know who it is who's calling. I know who it is. It's the baker, the son-of-a-bitching baker, Howard. I had him bake a cake for Scotty's birthday. That's who's calling. That's who has the number and keeps calling us. To harass us about the cake. The baker, that bastard."

They drove out to the shopping center. The sky was clear and stars were out. It was cold, and they ran the heater in the car. They parked in front of the bakery. All of the shops and stores were closed, but there were cars at the far end of the lot in front of the cinema. The bakery windows were dark, but when they looked through the glass they could see a light in the back room and, now and then, a big man in an apron moving in and out of the white, even light. Through the glass she could see the display cases and some little tables with chairs. She tried the door. She rapped on the glass. But if the baker heard them he gave no sign. He didn't look in their direction.

They drove around behind the bakery and parked. They got out of the car. There was a lighted window too high up for them to see inside. A sign near the back door said, "The Pantry Bakery, Special Orders." She could hear faintly a radio playing inside and something—an oven door?—creak as it was pulled down. She knocked on the door and waited. Then she knocked again, louder. The radio was turned down and there was a scraping sound now, the distinct sound of something, a drawer, being pulled open and then closed.

Someone unlocked the door and opened it. The baker stood in the light and peered out at them. "I'm closed for business," he said. "What do you want at this hour? It's midnight. Are you drunk or something?"

She stepped into the light that fell through the open door. He blinked his heavy eyelids as he recognized her.

"It's you," he said.

"It's me," she said. "Scotty's mother. This is Scotty's father. We'd like to come in."

The baker said, "I'm busy now. I have work to do."

She had stepped inside the doorway anyway. Howard came in behind her. The baker moved back. "It smells like a bakery in here. Doesn't it smell like a bakery in here, Howard?"

"What do you want?" the baker said. "Maybe you want your cake? That's it, you decided you want your cake. You ordered a cake, didn't you?"

"You're pretty smart for a baker," she said. "Howard, this is the man who's been calling us. This is the baker man." She clenched her fists. She stared at him fiercely. There was a deep burning inside her, an anger that made her feel larger than herself, larger than either of these men.

"Just a minute here," the baker said. "You want to pick up your three day old cake? That it? I don't want to argue with you, lady. There it sits over there, getting stale. I'll give it to you for half of what I quoted you. No. You want it? You can have it. It's no good to me, no good to anyone now. It cost me time and money to make that cake. If you want it, okay, if you don't, that's okay too. I have to get back to work." He looked at them and rolled his tongue behind his teeth.

"More cakes," she said. She knew she was in control of it, of what was increasing her. She was calm.

"Lady, I work sixteen hours a day in this place to earn a living," the baker said. He wiped his hands on his apron. "I work night and day in here, trying to make ends meet." A look crossed Ann's face that made the baker move back and say, "No trouble now." He reached to the counter and picked up a rolling pin with his right hand and began to tap it against the palm of his other hand. "You want the cake or not? I have to get back to work. Bakers work at night," he said again. His eyes were small, mean-looking, she thought, nearly lost in the bristly flesh around his cheeks. His neck was thick with fat.

"We know bakers work at night," Ann said. "They make phone calls at night too. You bastard," she said.

The baker continued to tap the rolling pin against his hand. He glanced at Howard. "Careful, careful," he said to Howard.

"My son's dead," she said with a cold, even finality. "He was hit by a car Monday morning. We've been waiting with him until he died. But of course, you couldn't be expected to know that, could you? Bakers can't known everything. Can they, Mr. Baker? But he's dead. He's dead, you bastard!" Just as suddenly as it had welled in her the anger dwindled, gave way to something else, a dizzy feeling of nausea. She leaned against the wooden table that was sprinkled with flour, put her hands over her face and began to cry, her shoulders rocking back and forth. "It isn't fair," she said. "It isn't, isn't fair."

Howard put his hand at the small of her back and looked at the baker. "Shame on you," Howard said to him. "Shame."

The baker put the rolling pin back on the counter. He undid his apron and threw it on the counter. He looked at them, and then he shook his head slowly. He pulled a chair out from under a card table that held papers and receipts, an adding machine and a telephone directory. "Please sit down," he said. "Let me get you a chair," he said to Howard. "Sit down now, please." The baker went into the front of the shop and returned with two little wrought-iron chairs. "Please sit down you people."

Ann wiped her eyes and looked at the baker. "I wanted to kill you," she said. "I wanted you dead."

The baker had cleared a space for them at the table. He shoved the adding machine to one side, along with the stacks of note paper and receipts. He pushed the telephone directory onto the floor, where it landed with a thud. Howard and Ann sat down and pulled their chairs up to the table. The baker sat down too.

"I don't blame you," the baker said, putting his elbows on the table. "First. Let me say how sorry I am. God alone knows how sorry. Listen to me. I'm just a baker. I don't claim to be anything else. Maybe once, maybe years ago I was a different kind of human being, I've forgotten, I don't known for sure. But I'm not any longer, if I ever was. Now I'm just a baker. That don't excuse my offense, I know. But I'm deeply sorry. I'm sorry for your son, and I'm sorry for my part in this. Sweet, sweet Jesus," the baker said. He spread his hands out on the table and turned them over to reveal his palms. "I don't have any children myself, so I can only imagine what you must be feeling. All I can say to you now is that I'm sorry. Forgive me, if you can," the baker said. "I'm not an evil man, I don't think. Not evil, like you said on the phone. You got to understand that what it comes down to is I don't know how to act anymore, it would seem. Please," the man said, "let me ask you if you can find it in your hearts to forgive me?"

It was warm inside the bakery. In a minute, Howard stood up from the table and took off his coat. He helped Ann from her coat.

The baker looked at them for a minute and then nodded and got up from the table. He went to the oven and turned off some switches. He found cups and poured coffee from an electric coffee maker. He put a carton of cream on the table, and a bowl of sugar.

"You probably need to eat something," the baker said. "I hope you'll eat some of my hot rolls. You have to eat and keep going. Eating is a small, good thing in a time like this," he said.

He served them warm cinnamon rolls just out of the oven, the icing still runny. He put butter on the table and knives to spread the butter. Then the baker sat down at the table with them. He waited. He waited until they each took a roll from the platter and began to eat. "It's good to eat something," he said, watching them. "There's more. Eat up. Eat all you want. There's all the rolls in the world in here."

They ate rolls and drank coffee. Ann was suddenly hungry, and the rolls were warm and sweet. She ate three of them, which pleased the baker. Then he began to talk. They listened carefully. Although they were tired and in anguish, they listened to what the baker had to say. They nodded when the baker began to speak of loneliness, and the sense of doubt and limitation that had come to him in his middle years. He told them what it was like to be childless all these years. To repeat the days with the ovens endlessly full and endlessly empty. The party food, the celebrations he'd worked over. Icing knuckle-deep. The tiny wedding couples stuck into cakes. Hundreds of them, no, thousands by now. Birthdays. Just imagine all those candles burning. He had a necessary trade. He was a baker. He was glad he wasn't a florist. It was better to be feeding people. This was a better smell anytime than flowers.

"Smell this," the baker said, breaking open a dark loaf. "It's a heavy bread, but rich." They smelled it, then he had them taste it. It had the taste of molasses and coarse grains. They listened to him. They ate what they could. They swallowed the dark bread. It was like daylight under the fluorescent trays of light. They talked on into the early morning, the high pale cast of light in the windows, and they did not think of leaving.

THE END OF THE WORLD

by THOMAS MCGRATH

from PASSAGES TOWARD THE DARK (Copper Canyon Press)

nominated by David Wilk

The end of the world: it was given to me to see it.
Came in the black dark, a bulge in the starless sky,
A trembling at the heart of the night, a twitching of the webby
flesh of the earth.
And out of the bowels of the street one beastly, ungovernable
cry.

Came and I recognized it: the end of the world.
And waited for the lightless plunge, the fury splitting the rock.
And waited: a kissing of leaves: a whisper of man-killing ancestral
night—
Then: a tinkle of music, laughter from the next block.

Yet waited still: for the awful traditional fire,
Hearing mute thunder, the long collapse of sky.
It falls forever. But no one noticed. The end of the world
provoked
Out of the dark a single and melancholy sigh

From my neighbor who sat on his porch drinking beer in the
dark.
No: I was not God's prophet. Armageddon was never
And always: this night in a poor street where a careless irreverent
laughter
Postpones the end of the world: in which we live forever.

%% %% %%

THE COMPANY WE KEEP: SELF-MAKING IN IMAGINATIVE ART, OLD AND NEW

by WAYNE C. BOOTH

from DAEDALUS

nominated by David Madden

> A voice comes to one in the dark. Imagine.
> —Samuel Beckett, *Company*

> How will literature survive the development of other media of communication? . . . The day when the Book ceases to be the principal vehicle of knowledge, will not literature have changed its meaning once again? Perhaps we are quite simply living through the last days of the Book.
> —Gérard Genette, "Structuralism and Literary Criticism"

> It really is of importance, not only what men do, but also what manner of men they are that do it.
> —John Stuart Mill, *On Liberty*

The Many Imaginative Worlds We Live In

WHEN I WAS FOUR OR FIVE YEARS OLD, a salesman came to our door and somehow managed to talk my father into buying a set of books he could not afford: *My Book House*. Memory says that we shelved many volumes, perhaps ten or twelve—certainly it seemed to me that there were more than any human being could ever exhaust. All these wonderfully gilded books (I have recently discovered that there were only six), and all for creatures like me! The ones on the right were for little children; the ones on the left were for "when you get older and learn to read."

They were all profusely illustrated, in a style that I now suppose was vaguely Pre-Raphaelite. Splendid knights, on marvelous steeds with flaring nostrils, battled with ugly, but obviously vulnerable, dragons, to rescue sinewy princesses. The princesses quickly became confused in my mind with various "girls of my dreams," creatures of an imagination set on fire by various popular songs then current. We did not hear those songs on any radio; there was no radio in our home in the twenties. The same mother who read to me from the books bought the sheet music and sang them to us, to her own accompaniment on the piano.

"Art," you see, was already doing its work, creating a kind of culture of the imagination. But it was a highly commercial kind, obviously, most of its work done by salesmen moving door-to-door in the pursuit of profit, culture be damned. And here I am, more than half a century later, able to remember more about the set of illustrated books and those popular songs than I can about anything my parents said or did at the time—except, of course, for negative moments when punishment was vigorous. I can remember making up songs of my own, no doubt borrowed from favorites like "Hello, Central, Give Me Heaven," "You Can't Holler Down My Rain Barrel," and one about the ancient story of a sweet little "babe in the woods" who lay down and died, with her brother.

I asked my mother, in a burst of creative egotism, why nobody ever learned to sing *my* songs, since after all I was more than willing to learn *theirs*. I can't remember her answer, and I can barely remember snatches of two of "my" songs. But I can remember dozens of theirs, and when I sing them, even now, I sometimes feel again the emotions, and see the images, that they aroused then. Thus who I am now—the very shape of my soul—was to a surprising degree molded by the works of "art" that came my way.

I set "art" in quotation marks, because much that I experienced in those early books and songs would not be classed as art according to most definitions. But for the purposes of appraising the effects of "art" on "life" or "culture," and especially for the purposes of thinking about the effects of the "media," we surely must include every kind of artificial experience that we provide for one another. What better word have we than "art" to cover every piece of imitation-life, every experience invented for the sake of supplementing or counteracting or criticizing or evading or enhancing "life"?

In this sense of the word, all of us are from the earliest years fed a steady diet of art, and the quality of our lives at any given moment will, to a surprising degree—some these days would say to an appalling degree—depend on the quality of what we ingest. But the metaphor of nourishment is misleading; it suggests that we are talking about health as some future value, judging food (or poison) only as it might be tested empirically by some medical team ten minutes or ten years later. When we talk in that way about the future effects of art, and especially about what print and video culture are likely to do to us, we disregard the qualities met in the moment of eating, the quality of the meal itself, and of what might be called the aftertaste, the quality of the mind that is full of *this* kind of melody or verse rather than *that* kind.

Was I enjoying a good childhood, *as* I listened or read, sang "real" songs or imagined others? I would sit and dream of those Pre-Raphaelite lords and ladies, sit quietly for hours, singing my songs, dreaming of "my" adventures. I would charge up glass mountains, tiptoe into the chambers of sleeping maidens, their seductive forms—oh, yes!—chastely concealed under "counterpanes" with flowery patterns, like those that illustrated *A Child's Garden of Verses*. Soon I was making my own variations, transforming in imagination characters from my daily round. I found to my delight that, by a simple decision to daydream, I could rescue my current love, Virginia Shelley, from a cloudburst; reaching down from my seat upon my charger, I would touch her hand and we would at once float up a kind of dry funnel in what was otherwise a terrifying thunderstorm. Out over the threatened streets we flew, just like the magical people in the books, together at last, untouched by the rain, unafraid of the thunder, marveled at by the soggy crowds of weaklings who looked up at us from below.

By then I was able to read some of the stories in *My Book House* on my own. I read them again and again—though some were already almost memorized. I thumbed them forwards and backwards; I chanted them aloud, sitting and dreaming over one page for as long as my dreams required. And sometimes, with lots of

time on my hands, I would just ramble from the middle of one
story to the next, wondering what would happen if Cinderella got
lost in "Puss in Boots."

All Americans of my generation will be able to summon their
own memories to dramatize how different our childhood experience was from that of children reared in later years on radio, on
movies, on TV. During my hours of dreaming, in the 1920s,
nobody from outside my own head ever imposed a flashing series
of scene changes on my "screen." Until I had my first radiant
"video" experience (not what people now generally call video, but
the movie *Ramona*, when I was perhaps eight or nine), I experienced no work of "art" one tenth as exciting, visually, as "Sesame
Street" or even the next commercial you will see on the screen.
Compared with almost every child in America today, I had a mind
that was sluggish and impoverished, awkward in its inferences
from visual signs, uninformed about the possibilities for excitement in the world.

Sluggish, uninformed, impoverished. Or was it reflective, independent, uncluttered, tranquil? We are quickly tempted into
heavy judgments in these matters, even when we attempt pure
description. I must move, before I am done here, to some overt
evaluating, but the truth is that we have no established ways of
talking about the relative value, as nourishment for a growing child
or fading adult, of the various foods offered us in the 1920s or
1980s. Before we explore any such language, it will be better to
step tentatively into some more raw description.

On a recent vacation, my wife and I and two friends talked a
good deal about two movies of 1981, *Reds* and *My Dinner with
André*. We also followed a daily schedule of reading a given short
story, each of us privately, and then discussing it later in the day.
Our third activity, during those aggressively cultural ten days, was
reading aloud for an hour or so from *Ulysses*, and discussing as we
read.

Our only plan had been to "do some reading aloud together, and
maybe discuss a story or two." But by the time we were done, we
had accumulated a complicated variety of experiences with art,
none of them quite like those of my childhood.

There were, most obviously, three experiences that might be
called direct or primary: the moments spent in direct contact with

the work. With the movies, that had of course been a one-time affair, already for some weeks fading in memory. With the short stories, it was time spent alone, transforming words into images and events; but that primary experience was extended by the secondary experience of discussion, checking memory and refining first impressions. With *Ulysses*, a work that all of us had previously read, or read at, the primary experience was communal and complex. For the most part, it was inextricably combined with secondary artistic experience: analysis, debate, and reflection were intertwined with the reading. But there were also moments that were almost as unmediated by reflection as the most direct and engrossed moments had been when Beatty/Reed faced down the commissars.

About all of the works, then, we engaged in a kind of reflection and debate that had never disturbed my childhood reading. But discussion of the movies was seriously hampered by our fading memories. Reading and rereading the printed stories, alive there before us, we could let them grow under our hands. Thus there was a fundamental contrast between works that were still somehow in process as we discussed and works that offered us only a closed memory of direct experience. The two movies led to discussions that were generally the most animated. Nobody actually struck anyone in anger, as people are said to do about some TV characters, but it was clear that, despite our lifetime commitments to literature, we were more passionately committed to our opinions about those two average movies, weeks after viewing them, than to our contrasting views about *Ulysses* or the short stories we had before us. Two of us "liked" *Reds* much more than did the other two; two of us disliked *My Dinner with André* intensely, while the other two thought it a valuable experiment. "Wonderful that Malle should attempt such a *daring* violation of what makes a 'good movie.' " Because we were free, like my younger self, to "waste" whatever time we pleased, we could talk indefinitely about our reasons for liking or disliking. We agreed that Beatty didn't know how to combine the political and romantic lines of *Reds;* we disagreed about whether André was a pretentious bore or a fascinating, though troubled, pioneer of the spirit. We disagreed about whether anyone responsible had recognized just how superficial and cliché-ridden was the conversation between André and Wally.

But with all our leisure, we soon began to run out of topics derived from memory of the movies themselves, and we might have ground to a halt if we had depended on *their* motive power. The primary experience, after all, was further and further in the past. Even if we had been able to locate another showing some-where, we could never really "consult the text," though we were aware that certain fortunate students of film have the equipment needed to do so. Again and again some one of us would mention details that the others had overlooked, but there was no way to verify any memory. "Well, I guess I'll just have to see it again," or "I don't *want* to see it again. All I want to see is whether, as you claim, the camera was making that ironic point against André."

With all our variety, there was one experience we did *not* have, sixty miles from the nearest TV or movie theatre, and with no radio, newspaper, or magazines available: a one-time encounter, with no chance to look again at details, and with little chance for discussion or private reflection—that is to say, the most frequent artistic experience in America today. TV programming, the art that is shared more widely than any other, assumes that whatever critical thought occurs will be itself broadcast: an occasional critic on the "Today Show" telling us what to think, in language cleverer than we ourselves could manage; an occasional talk show about "issues" reduced for quick consumption. Any such intrusion of a reflective voice is followed quickly by a fresh visual sensation: primary experience of a kind so immediate as almost to be called un*media*ted. Whatever one may think about that kind of uncompli-cated primacy, we knew none of it as we read and talked.

What Difference Does It Make?

The usual way of taking the media seriously is to talk about their consequences—most often, for the growth of children. We are flooded both with indictments of sex and violence on TV, and with replies that either deny the adequacy of the evidence of bad consequences or that see TV as only a symptom, not a cause. Such debate is not necessarily pointless. If we can finally prove that children who watch a great deal of TV have indeed been maimed, then it is possible—remotely possible—that we may find ways of controlling the medium without sacrificing essential freedoms for all concerned. But studies of consequences suffer from the defects that plague all empirical studies of cause and effect in human behavior: they seem never to be decisive, nor can investigators agree on how to conduct them or on how to evaluate even the most decisive results once they are in. If a given number of children are more violent after watching a given number of programs, how are we to prove that getting their natural violence out of their systems is not a good thing, a kind of vaccination while they are so young that they can't do a lot of harm? If we then turn, in a kind of desperation, to longitudinal studies, we must wait for ten or twenty years to decide whether to act—and meanwhile, the harm, if any, continues to be perpetrated.[1]

But the most serious limitation of consequence talk is that it tells us nothing about the quality of the lives lived *during* a given artistic experience. It is one thing to show that an experience changes people's behavior; it is quite another thing, obviously more important even though more difficult, to show that an experience is desirable or undesirable in itself *as* experience.

Though the distinction tends to get lost in our future-oriented society,[2] we all recognize it when we are thinking, not about other people's development, but about what is for *us* worth doing. Nobody can believe that all ways of "spending time" have equal value. Indeed, it is a constant assumption of our society—of our advertising, of our book reviews and criticism of the arts, of our easy talk about the difference between good spectator sports and bad, good and lousy baseball games, good and bad days—that some hours justify or enhance life, others poison it. And today, as in the past, people talk about our various forms of "art" as more or less adequate ways of providing a "good time." Only when we set out to prove something about good or bad effects do we forget our assumption that, *regardless* of consequences, some moments spent with books and plays and TV and movies are worth living, while others leave us wondering whether the best for man is never to be born.

What kind of "good time" was I leading during my days with fairy stories and folk tales? What is the quality of my life during my three hours and forty minutes attending the movie *Reds*, or my occasional half-hour with Johnny Carson, or my three hours with Agatha Christie's *Curtains*, or the weeks of life spent reading and rereading Jane Austen's *Emma?* If anything is obvious about each of us, it is that we are very different persons depending on the art we are living with or in. The lives we live *in the moment* of the living are more or less defensible according to whether the worlds we live in prove to be habitable. Difficult as talk about such matters is, surely nothing could be more important than keeping alive the great critical traditions of describing and appraising the quality of experience made possible by different works and different kinds of work. Let others measure consequences, then, as we consider for a while here the quality of induced life that is enjoyed as we surrender to the different media. We can return, in the last two sections of this essay, to talk about consequences in a way that will be somewhat different from asking whether, in a world in which everybody is already violent in one degree or another, more children bop each other after watching a given kind of television.

We have already begun on our task, merely by trying to describe a variety of experiences with different media. Suppose we push farther into this immensely threatening terrain (acknowledging from the beginning that we will overgeneralize), and ask four neglected questions—neglected in talk about *these* matters, though of course we refer to them a good deal in other contexts: *Where* are we—that is, what kind of world or space do we inhabit, as we experience a given medium? *Who* are we, as we read or listen or look? *Who* dwells there *with* us? And—moving slightly in the direction of future consequences again—*what* do we desire, what do we hope for, in the imagined world we have entered?

Where Do We Live Our Imaginative Lives?[3]

To describe where we are might seem an easy task: we are placed into this or that locale—the Bronx, a space station on Aldebaran, a battlefield outside the walls of Troy, an eighteenth century drawing room, the riot-filled streets of the Left Bank in 1968, the ruins of Beirut in 1982, a TV newsroom with weather maps on the walls. But difficulties arise as soon as we distinguish the incidental results of a particular program schedule or library shelf from what is essential to the medium. Our questions then become, Where are we *always* when watching TV or a movie? Where are we *always* when reading a story? If we can answer such general questions, we shall be on our way to locating who we are made to be, since where we live is part of the definition of who we are.

Like all of our questions, this one is ambiguous and difficult. Suppose we take it as asking *where the action takes place*. With all of our immense critical outpouring about the various media, I can find hardly anything about this question put in the form that makes it interesting. And of course we find no experimental data to aid us: "mental experiments" of the kind this piece is built on are for now all we have.[4]

Perhaps it is different for those whose first imaginative experience was with video and not with Grimm, but for me, the action of all TV drama takes place somehow in a physical location behind, or in some sense *in*, the set. At the movies, the action takes place "back there" or "out there," sometimes even out there in Hollywood if I become slightly disengaged: I "see" a set, not a scene. In every case, even when most fully lost in the action, I am somehow outside of it, not responsible for it. It is true that I more easily and uncritically lose all awareness of the "real" world when watching a movie than when reading a book or watching a play on the stage. (I have heard it said that people brought up on legitimate theater "lose" themselves at a play more than at the movies, but it's hard for me to believe it.) And yet I am by no means as close to any screened action as I am to those actions that occur in my head as I read. The set and the screen are themselves always *located*, with the action taking place on the other side of it. In this sense, all of the screened actions occur *in the same place*, and they occur in total independence of anything I do.

This fixity of location, and the pace of events within a location, are especially striking when, watching TV, I discover that the family and I can circle the set, leave it, tune it out, come back to it, talk to each other over it—and the action carries on, indifferent to us. When we come back, the events in that fixed scene (regardless of whether the imagined "country" is a spaceship or the servants' quarters in an English mansion) have continued inexorably in our absence (unless of course, it was commercial-time, and then it is the commercials that have ignored our absence). Nothing that might have happened to me in the interval could make the slightest difference. The weekly newspaper columns summarizing "What Happened on the Soaps"[5] testify to the radical independence of the box from our own activity; "they" carry on their restless lives, such as they are, hastening toward their predictable doom (death for the minor characters, and for the others, not death, but lowered ratings and final withdrawal), whether I attend or not.

Printed stories are not like that. Though it may sometimes seem that the general outlines of their plots are fixed for all time, in fact they depend on me. Most obviously, the book I read is not itself the physical location of anything that occurs "in" it. The action takes place in a country somehow in my head, yet freed to occur in a space *not* in my head, let alone confined to some box or screen. *I* make the streets, the buildings, the people, the clothing, in a space that is in my head yet is larger than any "set" could ever be. If I get up from my chair and move to the kitchen for a sandwich, that "country" goes with me. In one sense, the action stops until I continue my creative work, yet in another sense, the world "in there" goes on shifting and changing as I munch. The action is, in other words, internal, mine in a way that is not true of the action on, or in, a screen.

No controlled study will ever show whether the effects of this difference are good or bad, but there can be no question about their being immense and complicated. No doubt the very fixities that from my present viewpoint seem troublesome will prove to have values of a kind that now escape me. Anticipating the questions, Who dwells there with us, who addresses us? we might even speculate about the valuable comfort we all find—a comfort not to be found from the fluid narratives of print culture—from knowing that all those TV people, obviously in some sense alive and kicking, are out there going about their incredibly eventful lives, regardless of whether I attend. *Those* lives carry on, no matter what happens to me today; *I am not responsible there,* and the holiday from life they give me is what keeps me going. In their fixities is my peace. Perhaps we have here a new form of religious solace—not an eternal world to look forward to, but at least a world that will prove to be indestructible for my own time, and thus in a way timeless. It may even be that a steady diet of such reassurance will, for people living *fully* in our time, provide a necessary base for enduring the daily flux, while a steady diet of printed narra-tives, consumed in private and with a strong sense of personal responsibility, will produce either self-pitying introverts, suffering in elitist isolation from the crowd, or nervous ineffectual worrywarts, miserable about not solving the shifting, ambiguous problems that printed narratives often evoke.

But I am getting ahead of my story. Hard as it is to evaluate the differences, there can be no doubt that they are great. Regardless of what dwelling in the two locations leads me to *become,* I am obviously living a totally different kind of life as I take in or re-create these narratives *now.* And one can hardly make that kind of statement without at the same time worrying about consequences—again to leap ahead a bit—consequences of a kind far more profound than will result from this or that content of any narrative. Our society is in fact conducting, with the new media as with many other technological developments, an *un*controlled experiment of vast proportions, the results of which we will never fully know. After all, we experimenters who might evaluate the results are shifting our natures daily, as our imaginations are schooled to work *this* way rather than *that.* Our way of appraising the results will be itself determined by those results: another reason for speculating about qualities now, without waiting for social scientists to get their act together.

Who Are We?

TOURISTS/SOJOURNERS/NATURALIZED CITIZENS

I have already suggested that we have less opportunity to dwell for long with the movies and TV dramas we enjoy than with narratives in print. It is true that, by taking special effort, the studiously inclined can now turn video tapes into a kind of book, "thumbing the pages," reflecting on forms, discovering ever more profound themes. But by and large, a video drama, like traditional stage drama, expects us to pass this way only once, or at most to visit by chance once again at some future time.

As tourists, viewing everything from a distance as it happens "out there," we are of course not expected to participate in the affairs of state. We have no right and no opportunity to change anything, and no responsibility whatever for what goes on. We are expected to be, not participant observers, but rather sympathetic bystanders. Reading a story, in contrast, I must be engaged with it at every moment, or it simply stops. If I stop moving, I may gain or lose by my shift of attention, depending on what I attend to, but I do not lose any sequence that will have gone on past me, when I return. This country needs me.

PASSIVE RECEIVERS OF FROZEN INPUT/ACTIVE CREATORS

This radical difference in the degree of active control is most evident in the absolute control video exercises over our visual imagery. As the four of us talked on vacation, our images of a given character in the movies were much more precise and—so far as we could tell—much more alike than anything we had derived from our reading. John Reed was vividly and forever fixed as our image of Beatty; Zinoviev was forever Jerzy Kosinski; André was forever Malle's André. We tourists had been shown the people of that land once and for all, and with no exercise of our capacity to imagine figures of our own. We could no more substitute a different appearance for Reed than we could imagine a different New York City or Polish-Russian border. Though we were all, as it turned out, quite puzzled about the moral and political intentions of *Reds*, its visual intentions were so powerful that none of us is ever likely to break entirely free of them, no matter how many books we may read about the historical characters. Yet we all knew that the historical Reed and Louise Bryant and Zinoviev must have been vastly different from what we were shown, that the movie made up whatever images it needed to ensure its effect of seeming like history, and that everyone and everything was thus permanently Beattyfied for us.

The experience with all of the printed narratives was in this respect entirely different. Our talk was not only less excited; it included many more moments of silence, and of course it allowed for something entirely excluded by the movies, an unimpassioned reference back to the text, which was, after all, right there in front of us. But in another sense, the story—the events experienced by characters "imagined in our heads"—was not there in front of us, not in the sense or to the degree that the movie had been when we first viewed it. Searching the text could never be a return to see directly what the image in fact *was;* it had to be a search for evidence about what it was still to *become*. Since we as readers had been required to make whatever images constituted our story— images of character, of scene, of sequence—as disputatious but

reflective *re*readers we had to continue remaking those images as
we discussed. Thus the stories were still in process of being
"written," and still are in process now, in my head, as I write this
essay; from beginning to end I am schooled in imagining.

This continuing process can affect every part of our "reading":
tone of voice, facial expression, the lighting of scenes, the presumed inner feeling of all characters, the significance of what
anyone does. On vacation, we were often shocked to discover that
our fellow readers had made quite "indefensible" inferences about
all of these matters, not only about how a character appeared
physically, but about whether a character's experience was tragic
or comic, pathetic or contemptible. A given gesture might be seen
as angry and defiant by one reader and as pathetically resigned by
another, the physical accompaniment entirely different for each.
Again and again one of us would say something like, "Oh, the dress
is not *that* shade of blue—the point in this story is surely that
everything is faded out to pastels," or "But you've overlooked the
repeated reference to the shadows. Don't you see that the room
must be of a kind that will represent . . ."

In these and other ways, the stories and their characters shifted
under our scrutiny. We were, in short, prolonging the primary
experience *as* we discussed. Most of the stories grew in stature as
we talked; a couple of them shrank before our eyes; but none
remained what they had been. The important point is that the
change was not only in their "meanings" (shifts of meaning occurred in discussing the movies, too), but that we were steadily
engaged in imaginative recreation. The primary experience shifted
as we engaged in the secondary experience. The engagement was
thus inherently more sustained and imaginatively active—not
because we spent more time (in fact, we spent on no story as much
time as we spent originally just reviewing *Reds*), but because the
different media offered different invitations.

I have heard it said that this striking fixity of image given by the
visual media (and the resulting passivity in the receiver) is curable
by some sort of "technological fix"—that there can be no theoretical limit to what the new media can do. Perhaps. No doubt
technology will continue to improve our access to movies and TV,
so that energetic students will increasingly find it possible to do
term papers on structure and themes. But even as they do so, the
precision of image will be reinforced: whatever happens to other

meanings, visual meanings will have been created, once and for all, by the originators. In short, it is hard to see how anyone can eliminate the fundamental difference between media in which some kind of physical reality has established a visual scene *before* the viewer starts to work on it, and those like radio and print that can use only language for description—language that is always no more than an invitation to thought and imagination, never a solid presentation of finished reality.

This point perhaps should be illustrated with a closer look at a printed description. Show me any man or woman on the screen, any screen, and that will *be* forever that man or woman. But what do I do if you tell me, as does E. M. Forster in *Howards End,* that a young man "seemed a gentleman. . . . To a feminine eye there was nothing amiss in the sharp depressions at the corners of his mouth, nor in the rather box-like construction of his forehead. He was dark, clean-shaven, and seemed accustomed to command"?[6] What I must do is to begin some hard work of the imagination. Again: if you show me, on any screen, a given London residential square, it will be forever *that* square. But what must I do if you tell me the following?

> Their house was in Wickham Place, and fairly quiet, for a lofty promontory of buildings separated it from the main thoroughfare. One had the sense of a backwater, or rather of an estuary, whose waters flowed in from the invisible sea. . . . Though the promontory consisted of flats—expensive, with cavernous entrance halls . . . —it fulfilled its purpose, and gained for the older houses opposite a certain measure of peace. These, too, would be swept away in time, and another promontory would rise upon their site, as humanity piled itself higher and higher on the precious soil of London.[7]

What I am required to do by such a passage underlines a further difference in the qualities of mind and heart expected of us when we visit these contrasting kingdoms. The video arts tell us precisely what we should see, but their resources are thin and cumbersome for stimulating our moral and philosophical range. Those who enter Forster's world are expected to be interested in questions that would be almost impossible to raise with any precision in video. How could any screen portray as much moral and intellectual meaning as is packed into the sentence: "These, too, would be swept away in time, and another promontory would rise upon their site, as humanity piled itself higher and higher on the precious soil of London." As sheer thought, this is by no means uncharacteristically deep or rich for fiction, but the concentration of proferred ideas is intense indeed, as compared with any "information" that could be conveyed by mere visual sequences. Perhaps each of the four major overt ideas of the sentence could be suggested by sufficiently elaborate sequences. Even the notion that the soil is precious could perhaps be given by a series of frames, accompanied with commentary spoken by some character who has been established as speaking reliably for the values of the work. If we became really desperate, we could always fall back on "voice over." But even at best, the result would be relatively indefinite. And meanwhile, the other three claims made by the sentence would remain unspoken. By the time a film maker had worked to convey the meaning of this sentence, any movie would be half over, and most TV dramas would already have been replaced on the screen by three others.[8]

UNLIMITED SENSATION/FOCUSED REFLECTION

We visitors to the realms of gold discover a further curious presupposition about what we will be able and willing to attend to. A full photographic frame presents an unlimited range of points on which one *might* focus attention and from which one could derive "the meaning" of the frame. It is true that skillful directors and cameramen know how to limit that potential infinity. But do what they will, they leave us always with the question, "Of the possible centers of attention here, which one shall I take as significant, and which shall I simply ignore? Does it *mean* something that the hero has a wart beneath his left eye?" In any printed story, a wart under the left eye carries some sort of weight: it has been chosen from thousands of other possible details. Even in detective stories, which depend on planting irrelevancies, the wart means something as a deliberate deflection of attention. But in video, innumerable warts are simply *there*, accidents that even the most skillful director cannot eliminate completely. The result is that we visitors are habituated to a kind of looseness of attention; no detail can mean very much, when some details can mean nothing. And there is always an open invitation for the eye to wander to some further sensation.

Thus reflective study and imaginative inventiveness are to some degree against the grain of the medium. The producers may hope to make the new media as "arty" in this respect as are serious literature and the traditional graphic arts, but they can never go all the way: we continue—even in the most gloomily metaphysical of scenes by Bergman or Antonioni—to revel in the precise and almost infinitely various and rapidly flowing imaginative worlds they have cooked up for us. We do not sit before the object and use it as a stimulus for our own invention of new worlds of our own or reflections about events as they occur[9]—not at least to the degree encountered in reading.

In reading, even of the shoddiest stuff, I am given one word, one phrase, one sentence, one relatively unfixed image at a time, just as the author wrote them—or rather, as the author decided to place them after trying out various orders. Every mentioned detail thus comes labeled: "Attend to *this*." Even the most dramatic label is still visually vague, requiring imaginative work to bring it to life. "Her dress, a bright red silk, was so dazzling that he at first hardly noticed her face." Well, yes, I've seen ladies like that in that kind of dress, so my imagination works one or another of their characteristics into the scene. The result may be quite inappropriate—a stereotyped bitch, when the author means an angel or a woman who resists such stereotyping? But my mistake may not ultimately matter, not to the essential quality of my activity, because I have time, sitting alone in the light, turning my own pages, to revise my imaginings, to readjust my types, to reclothe the lady, as it were, to study her face, the face that I have myself made. And what I study, when the fiction is any good, is not her face, finally, but her character.

COMFORTABLE STEREOTYPING/RESISTANCE TO SIMPLICITIES

A further expectation about *my* character as visitor to video seems to follow from all of these. I am expected to engage willingly in stereotyping. I am not given time, after all, to engage in anything else.

I stereotype morally: this world consists almost entirely of heroes and villains. It is true that all narrative requires some moral simplifying. But printed fiction has found ways of resisting it, and even stage and film can prod us a bit. But TV, by all the evidence so far, subsists on moral stereotypes.

I stereotype intellectually; there simply is no time to do anything else. The highly particular images presented by particularized actors will be much too confusing to make a story line, unless the issues can be taken in at a glance or word. The screen thus reinforces a general trend in *all* media toward simplification and polarization of the unlimited complexities of our lives. As citizen of the country presented to me by TV, whether that country is literally the United States or some imagined world, I learn quickly that all problems could be solved simply, if only other people would think about them the way I am being taught to do *now*. It is no news to say that anybody who has read a book—any book, even the most distorted—on any subject will be appalled by the simplifications of that subject in any movie or TV program. There are simply no movies or TV programs, regardless of the depth of the chosen subjects, that make intellectual demands of the kind expected of even the most watered-down philosophical or scholarly text, or of the printed fiction that critics take seriously.

It is hard to decide how much of this constriction of mind is inherent in the medium and how much simply in market conditions (the pitch, after all, must be made to the average viewer). We should learn soon, as home-chosen TV becomes more widespread. But what is important here is that, even if the medium were someday to overcome this limitation and become as sustained in its thought as Aristotle, the limitations I am concerned with would remain: the passivity of imaginative engagement, with a resulting simplified emotional engagement.

No doubt there will be great consequences for our future selves from all of these controls over our characters as we enter and leave the video worlds. But we do not know, we cannot prove, what those consequences will be. What we do know, what we need no experimental proof for, is that our lives are lived in *these* ways, sitting now before the screen, and not in other possible ways. The selves, souls, persons, characters that we are likely to become as a result of living in a print or a video culture for decades will matter greatly, but they are unavailable as evidence in our debates. The selves that we *are* now as we live in these worlds are to some degree known—at first hand. We have met the victims, here in our living rooms.

With Whom Do We Dwell? Who Addresses Us?

Who I *am*, in a given imaginative encounter, is inseparable from the question of the kind of people I'm living *with*. Voices come to me from these screens and from these printed stories. Who converses with me here? What kind of companionship is being offered? What company do I keep?

The voice of movies and TV come to us as we sit in the dark or half-light, sometimes alone, but more often in company. In all emotional drama, whether comic or sad, the company becomes crucial. When those we are with laugh or weep, we are more inclined to laugh or weep. When they remain silent, groan, walk out of the theater or leave for a snack, we are forced, by the company we keep, to modify our listening. We watch differently. The members of the company *in* the screen-world know about all that, play to it, make the comedy or pathos work by "playing" on the audience. In comedy, they provide evidences of amused company in *that* world too: studio audiences or canned laughter. In tragedy and pathos, that won't work so well, and we are given instead shots of minor characters weeping.

The voices of literature come to us, usually, as we sit alone, in the light. (On vacation, the four of us did read aloud some to each other. But how many people do that these days?) Even if someone else is present in the room, we read alone, except for the company of the author.

The new media thus support me, reassure me, provide me with a more visible and lively company. Print puts me on the spot, whispers to me of something only the author and I will understand, threatens me, finally, with loneliness, unless the author is very good company indeed. In the literature I most admire, especially the modern literature, I sense that the author writes specifically to me—there may, at most, be one or two others in this world of mine qualified to catch all the nuances.

It is by no means self-evident that the essentially lone, private experience of reading is a better way to live than to join those new, lively companies provided by video. For me, the most magical transport comes in fact not when reading alone, but when I share art in company—as in classical theater, great music festivals, reading aloud together, playing chamber music. But of course movie audiences—and even more obviously TV companies—do not work quite like that. And when we look at the company we keep *behind* the screen, most particularly the company of producers, the differences become really striking.

As viewer, I am part of a vast company exercising remote control through the ratings, a company that demands an unlimited supply of entertainment. The tube, representing those mostly anonymous producers, will provide—must provide—what I demand of it. The tube will not die: the company I keep as I watch it will go on eternally. Reading any beloved author, in contrast, I know that I dwell with someone whose powers are finite; the "supply" of this precise kind of company will someday come to an end. Though I can return to the author after he or she dies, we share, in our private companionship, a deep knowledge of our precious and poignant limitations.

The tube implies, insofar as it can, that there are no limits. Though producers may give us a few bad programs this season, they cannot afford to let us down, because our company is their bread and butter. If we are to dwell together in a global village, sitting before the screen, it will be a village in which none of the elders ever dies. When death in fact occurs—President Kennedy dies almost before our eyes, Johnny Carson is aging and will someday surely die—it will not finally matter very much, because the tube has promised us that some other show will easily take over the top ratings.

But who are these immortal producers? The company offered to me by the screens is unlimited, immensely varied, and largely anonymous. It is more varied, potentially, than even my library shelves. In the first place, it can draw on the riches of those shelves. What is more, no book can offer me the sheer, joyful gift that a fine juggler, dancer, singer, or gymnast can: TV and movie producers can purchase these gifts for me. No book can possibly duplicate the gift of energy and concentrated courage and abandon of the "performance" of a football or soccer game. The tube offers me, not in its dramatic efforts, but in its images of real people doing what they do best, an endless supply of that supreme gift— the drama of the best that is in one.

The best authors try to do that too, implying: "Here I give you

my notion of what living can be—it can be what it is during these
moments we spend together." It may seem, then, that we have
only to compare the quantity and quality of gifts offered by two
equally good companions. And once we say that, must we not
recognize that the world is enriched more broadly and variously by
the new media than could ever be done by print? Must we not add
that print will never provide as much good company from as many
cultures—all periods and climes and genres—as TV can?

Something seems wrong in this judgment. The gifts do not really
come to us unmediated, on TV or on the movie screen. They have
been chosen by a team of directors and associates. The juggler I
see on the "Tonight Show" has been *chosen* to entertain me; if I
saw him on the street, collection hat in front of him, I would accept
or reject this offer of his gift, unmediated. It must be better, for
him, to be paid by Carson than to be on the street with only my
interest or my charity to depend on. Yet I wonder. Is it only a
cheap nostalgia that leads me to see more dignity in a street
performer, living in poverty, offering a gift that too many passersby
don't even notice, than in the same performance offered (as
mediated by teams of organizers) on the screen? The juggler
himself has not changed, essentially, but the gift now comes from
someone else—the producers. I recently saw a young trapeze
artist perform, for the first time ever, four somersaults in a midair
pass. It was a marvelous thing to see, but it was packaged in the
dulcet tones of one of those "60 Minutes" people, watered down to
seem really quite ordinary, the drama of the first three unsuccess-
ful tries reduced to something staged. The total "act" was easy,
muffling the immense achievement of the artist himself.

Like all of the questions I have raised, this one about the quality
of a proferred gift cannot be answered simply. But a simple
distinction operates here that one finds implacably controlling our
responses to gifts from friends in everyday affairs. If you offer me a
gift of something that you would yourself like to receive, if it is
something that you respect as a gift, I accept it with love. If you
offer me something that expresses your contempt for my taste, if
you would yourself feel contempt or loathing for what you offer me,
I have a right to feel—indeed I cannot help feeling—that the gift is
no gift at all. All the evidence shows that most producers of TV
shows, unlike that trapeze artist, offer gifts of the second kind.
Indeed, they fall all over themselves claiming that they do not

themselves watch the kind of stuff they produce, and they claim that they would much prefer a world in which better shows were demanded by the public. Nobody who pays any attention to the public statements of executives can believe that anyone except perhaps the frontline performer is giving his or her best.

One might argue that this blight is not in the least inherent to the medium, but only to our present methods of financing it. After all, our culture seems to produce as much hack work in print as on TV. The producers of a great proportion of our printed matter must surely view it with as much contempt as any TV producer feels for the day's offering. But all evidence so far suggests that the medium of TV itself for some reason *builds in* a contempt for us and our life. When anything we care for passes through its hands, what comes out is a single statement: None of this matters very much.

What Is My Heart's Desire?

DOES ANYTHING MATTER?

There is a sense in which a steady diet of TV, like the printed narratives that most resemble it in brevity and stereotyping, seems to say that nothing matters, really. Whether I like a show greatly or detest it, there are no great consequences for me or for the makers. Just as the news (on both TV and radio, as in their predecessors on the movie screen, e.g., "Time Marches On") reduces every event to the same reductive "spot," so the dramatic fictions are reduced to a few moments in which nothing matters except whether I have not turned the dial.

Defenders of TV can point to fronts of resistance—the various efforts at "in-depth" news, the solemn moments when great classics like *The Scarlet Letter* are given an hour or so of uninterrupted time. No doubt the producers of "60 Minutes" or "Brideshead Revisited" think of themselves as offering matters that matter. Presumably they can sometimes even pass the "hack test": Would I watch this show if someone else had produced it? And they manage to persuade many viewers that serious issues are being addressed seriously, and significant theatre being produced artistically. But somehow they can never escape the effect of the medium, its short attention span, its sheer quantity of appeals, its easy fixations of vivid imagery. One emerges from any extended viewing period, whether of the "best" or the worst, in a state of floating indifference.

The most obvious exceptions are those momentous public events when we all have the wrenching illusion that we are there, as during the week following President Kennedy's assassination. That whole event mattered a great deal to every viewer. As Robert Stein says, "In my own memory, John Kennedy's funeral is as *real* as anything that happened to me in combat during World War II." Given the existence of such moments and our convictions about them, we can hardly say that "nothing matters" to us as we watch TV. Indeed, the more deeply we consider the question, the more obvious it becomes that to the steady viewer, whether in times of crisis or during the innumerable crises in the dramas, a great deal matters. The interesting question is what and how it matters, considering the trivialization of subjects and the casual indifference of viewers about what they watch—provided they can watch *something*.

WHAT DO WE DESIRE IN THE NEWS ABOUT "REAL LIFE"

Print culture allows for, though by no means ensures, sustained attention to issues. Books, articles in *Daedalus*, presuppose readers willing to spend not just the time necessary to read a discussion but the impulse to compare contrasting and sustained views. Video culture is, by contrast, a culture of the superficially informed, the hasty, the indifferent.

Consider one of the more "serious" shows about issues, "60 Minutes." It will each week present four or five melodramatic vignettes, of perhaps ten or twelve minutes each, all in a form requiring me to make up my mind on issues of world-shaking importance. Indeed, I find that I *do* make up my mind, all too easily. They have given me the stereotypes that I need in making up my mind: the villainous insurance executive, obviously cheating the sensitive victim in the wheelchair, suffering while holding the cute child in his lap; the snarling prime minister of the contemptuously treated little country down under; the helpless old woman facing the impersonal forces of the bureaucracy—all followed by a cheery little vignette, in the final few moments, about the surprisingly widespread use of horses still in our modern age. The result: since everything matters equally, nothing matters really. Or rather: what matters is narrowed to a range chosen from among the available favorable outcomes; what matters is to move fast to the reward waiting at the end.

And what is the reward? A sense that somebody out there, *in* there, is taking care of these issues in quick order. Though for some viewers the effect may be despair, as the melodramas pile up, supported as they are by the nightly picture of mayhem throughout the world, the general effect is to reassure me about quick fixes in the world, and to make me sick with desire for similar quick fixes in my own troubles. What I am taught to desire is *relief*, as instantaneous as that promised in the analgesic ads; I have been taught to expect it, as the images of trouble shift refreshingly and painlessly from moment to moment.

LESSONS OF DESIRE IN NARRATIVE

Like traditional ethical criticism of literature, conventional criticism of drama in the new media, from the earliest movies on, has usually focused on the overt content as decent or indecent, virtuous or vicious. Virtue presented and properly rewarded thus earns a favorable judgment, vice triumphant is anathema. (Note that even the most avant-garde critic is likely to work in the same scheme, simply substituting up-to-date terms for virtue and vice: a "mind-shattering, no-holds-barred, devastatingly mischievous exposé of bourgeois pieties" is of course virtuous.) Since the creation of mass culture, some critics have worked on a simple scheme of highbrow versus lowbrow. A production of *The Scarlet Letter* financed by the National Endowment for the Humanities is of course good, even if deadly boring and shorn of all the complexities that Hawthorne cared for; while anything pop is by definition to be rejected. Though most actual examples of such well-meant judgments are absurd, the reaction of some political liberals who, for fear of encouraging censorship, have rejected all ethical, moral, or political judgments, is equally absurd. Surely the trick is to find some way of talking about the ethical and political effects of art that will get beneath a given surface image; even the most "objectionable" image may or may not be hurtful even to a child, depending on what is done with it *in the whole formed experience of the work*. Though there may be some specific images that are good or bad in themselves, I can think of none. It is our experience of the form into which each image fits that determines the quality of our deepest habits of desire.

Such "aesthetic habits" (call them that, though to do so obscures their being simultaneously aesthetic and practical) are built out of two kinds of formal experience. The first is the experience of a pattern of desire played upon, inevitably, by any temporal story. You simply cannot make an interesting story without playing upon patterns of hope, fear, and anticipation. The typical fairy tale leads us to desire (and to expect) a happy outcome through a combination of the protagonist's efforts and some kind of fantastic intervention, the happiness consisting in the possession of some conventional good: gold, a prince or princess, revenge, security. The typical nineteenth century popular novel teaches us in much the same way to desire, through many hours of trials and tribulations, a happy ending that is again defined in conventional terms: for the women in the story (and hence for us readers, male or female), it is marriage to the ideal male; for the men, it is such a marriage combined with some sort of public honor, defined as wealth or fame or power. The typical highbrow novel of the modern period teaches us that it is wickedness and folly to seek such conventional goods, and that what we should desire is some deeper quality like maturity, self-knowledge, artistic integrity, or moral courage. Though there is obviously a great range in the quality of the experience offered by different exemplars of all of these "plottings of desire"—ranging from the cheapest form of a Horatio Alger-like grab for success to the subtleties of Stephen Dedalus's struggle for artistic independence and power—the basic pattern of *reliance on future payoff* is reinforced by all.

The same values are of course reinforced by most dramas on TV or movie screen. To build a successful plot, the most obvious requirement is that the designer create a strong desire for some payoff that is just barely conceivable as within reach, given the probable length of the work in hand. When I begin a 300-page book called a novel, I can expect a long series of variegated instabilities to be faced and overcome before the final chapter. When I go to a movie, I can expect two hours, more or less, of frustration of desire before reward comes. When I turn on a TV drama, my usual expectations are for at most an hour of seeming-pain before joy reigns. And finally, when I experience the little thirty-second dramas offered me in the commercials, my hopes and fears, scratched into almost instant irritation, must be assuaged (though only partially, or I will not go out and buy) with an almost instant image of happy reward. These patterns, I must repeat, are entirely independent of the content; the differences would remain even if the characters in the novel found their bliss in final possession of a Mercedes-Benz, while the stick-characters on the thirty-second sales pitch found *theirs* in learning how to live right by reading the complete works of Plato. What we are talking about is habits of desire, expectations about how desires and their fulfillment work.

One modern definition of "the aesthetic" consists of a simple—if not simple-minded—repudiation of the entire domain of desire. Whenever we seek some good in the future, we violate the domains of art, where pure aesthetic contemplation reigns supreme. The definition has done great harm in the critical world, by leading to a denigration of *all* appetites and satisfactions; the rapid impoverishment of the palette that has resulted, in all the arts— though not, praise God, for all artists in *any* of the arts—makes one of the weirdest instances in history of the triumph of abstract theory over the plain teachings of everyday experience. (Yes, I am thinking of the "interesting" and impoverished experiences offered by John Cage and his successors, and of most other minimalists I know.)

But we need not repudiate all habits of desire to recognize a great qualitative difference between those arts that work to make the journey as valuable as the destination and those that "have no time" for anything but increasing hope for final success. Though the typical nineteenth century novel may have been excessively goal-oriented, helping to build generations of success-mongers, the form of the novel allowed, even encouraged, an entirely different message: it is not where you go that matters but how you get there. You have time, we are told by those mammoth novels that Henry James called "great fluid puddings," time to pause now, to savor, to elaborate, to look at your surroundings. Though you care, as I the novelist care, about achieving a final happiness for our Pip, our Dorothea Brooke, our Emma Woodhouse, our Richard Feverell, you and I both care even more about the quality of their souls, the quality of what they say and do as we travel with them. We are thus encouraged, as we read, to linger, to reread, to extract parts and reflect on them, just as we all were led to reflection by the stories of our childhood.

I have just finished reading Paul Theroux's *The Mosquito Coast*. A few months ago I read Russell Hoban's *Ridley Walker*, and a few weeks before that, Wright Morris's autobiographical account, *Will's Boy*. In each work, a pre-adolescent narrator-hero grapples with a decayed or decaying adult world, trying to understand people and impersonal forces that adults themselves do not understand. In all three accounts, everything en route matters as much or more than the outcome. Not only does every detail count in one's picture of the "worlds" presented; not only does each moment of the work build toward another moment that makes the first one matter more. In all three, we quickly learn that what happens to *this* boy should matter very much to everyone. After thirty pages I care more about the quality *now* of Ridley Walker and Charlie Fox and the young Wright Morris than I have ever cared about any imagined man, woman, or child on TV.

I am not making the sentimental point that they all made me weep; they did not. For the most part they made me laugh, often in ways close to my laughter in *Huckleberry Finn*. No, the point is that they made me care, made me care about what they cared for: about making sense out of a baffling world, surviving the incomprehensions and cruelties of adults, moving through troubled youth to mature decision—and above all, discovering how to act well in the world. Even the "two-hour forms"—traditional drama, modern movies, an occasional drama on PBS—are to some degree able to resist, in a similar way, the mindless pursuit of quickly fulfilled desire. There is, after all, time enough, time for soliloquy, for experiment with camera angle, for exploring a secondary character, for moving into a beautiful setting with a deliberate savoring of detail.

But we are now in general repudiating all that. Our culture seems to have "decided" to specialize in short spans, dividing experience into breathless desire-fulfillment patterns lasting from less than fifteen minutes to under an hour. What the decision means, we all know at first hand. Most of us fight it as best we can, either by refusing to watch or by obtaining the new network-free devices that take us back to the time span of traditional drama. But meanwhile the dominant culture of most Americans, the art we live by (many of us for scores of hours each week), teaches not simply the short attention span that educators have long noticed in children who have been "boxed in" from birth, but an attention to quick (though of course future) gratification. Here is the image, "real," fixed, lacking in only one simple thing to complete its happiness: a mate, a promotion, a killing of the bad guys, *anything* that can stand for a happy outcome. The dramatic resources of video seem permanently suited to imaginations of desire that are relatively scrappy, relatively passive, relatively frozen by the pre-imaginings of the makers, relatively resistant to reflection and reconsideration. Such patterns can be used, obviously, in the service of any uncomplicated surface value whatever. Any Christian preacher can use them to tout a desire for a particular brand of salvation, as some sects have long since discovered (though their cheap vignettes-of-easy-salvation do not get onto prime time: try early Sunday morning). Any political system, program, or candidate can use them to push a given sloganized ideology. Any moral majority or well-heeled minority can use them to combat any given wicked thought or action. What they cannot be used for is to celebrate the possibilities of life lived *now* or of leisurely reflection about life in all its complexities.

Commerce, Consequences, Remedies

Though my main subject here has been those features of the media that are largely or entirely independent of differences in content, the subject of the quick fix requires a brief look at the effect of commercials and of commercial pressures on a content that might, in an ideal world, be radically different.

When I began this exercise in speculation, I was determined not to load the dice against TV. Too many indictments seem to me to be conducted on a level that would condemn the sex and violence in the Bible or Shakespeare as much as anything found in the most blatant rip-off. But I have now arrived at what looks like a highly pessimistic judgment indeed—pessimistic because I see no way that we can effectively "go back"; no hope that we are going to decide, now that we know something about the effects of the grand experiment, to cancel it; no real chance that we can reverse the disastrous effects, on print culture itself, of the patterns of desire taught us by video culture. Even knowing how chancy all predictions about the future of various media have been in the past, I feel fairly confident that the dominance of video will increase, not diminish, and that its shattering effects on who we are will become more evident as the new forms of computer-video triumph. *They* are obviously even shallower than the older forms, which at least made gestures toward portraying people, while the new multibillion dollar art form, Pac-Man and its siblings, reduces our imaginative world to the precharted ravages of gaping mechanical maws and exploding metal.

In short, I suspect that the sheer visual excitement made available by video is too much for the race to resist. But there is one by-product of the discovery of this art-domain that we could modify if we decided that it was important to do so. Clearly, there is no absolute bond linking video and commercial corruptions. And it is equally clear that some of the worst ravages of scrappiness, frenzy, and greed result, not from anything inherent in video, but from how we have chosen to use it. As we witness a growing separation of home viewing from the imposed choices of network programming and the studios' quest for blockbuster movies, it is important to recognize just how much is at stake. Though nothing we can do will enable either video or print to match each other's effects, it seems probable that if video artists could be freed from their present bonds the worst losses might still be reversed. Our best hope for that, obviously, and our chief defensive weapon, in a culture that promises, at least in the short run, to become increasingly "videotic," is a developed practice of ethical criticism—by which I mean, of course, not a criticism that pushes a given moral creed, but one in which critics, in a sense dwelling together "in company," reflect on how the media shape the "ethos" of selves and societies.

What direction might such criticism take, when turned upon those brilliant flashing commercials that fill our nights and days?

Most traditional narrative has relied on imitating the seemingly natural form: "roused appetite—fulfilled appetite." But one prominent subgroup of narratives has always rivaled this pattern, the kind that rouses appetites and refuses to gratify them *within the form*. Pornography is the most obvious example, but every sensual pleasure and every passion can be exploited in what could be called the "pornographic structure": maximizing the desire and then cutting short the form, leaving the reader or viewer to complete the cycle in the real world. Satiric works are always in this form: People or institutions taken from the real world are made as contemptible as possible, leading us to desire their punishment, comic or serious, and to express our scorn actively in the real world. Literary works in themselves can only properly punish types and images, not real persons, but they can lead us to desire or detest real persons of a similar type. Some verbal descriptions (and many video portrayals) of food express the same pattern, leading us toward the refrigerator rather than toward any formal resolution in the art work. These pornographic patterns all depend on the fact that words can never satisfy actual hungers, whether for sex, revenge, or food. They are thus all essentially in conflict with the central enterprise of this essay—the search for experiences so valuable *now* that consequent actions seem, let us say, inconsequential.

If we think about advertising in general as depending on this same pattern—an inherently half-completed form leading to extra-formal modes of completion—then we can see more clearly the staggering scope of the revolution that we have all undergone in this century, first in print, then in radio, and now in video.[10] Except for underground works of sexual pornography and satire, pre-video narrative culture provided all who shared it (whether literate or not) with completed forms (printed advertisement, the obvious exception, lacked the resources of narrative). It is no doubt true that those forms were in one sense still not shut off from effects in the practical world. Their consumers could be left with a strong desire for "more of the same," or with fantasies about finding a real "girl of my dreams" to match the figures of romance. Still, nothing in pre-advertising times, and nothing in printed advertising, came even close to the specialization in frustration that TV culture has achieved. It could be said, of course, that not just TV ads, but the whole of modern culture leads to the "I want, I want . . ." that Saul Bellow attributed to Henderson. But TV culture makes previous "want-makers" seem puny. Even those who in effect make their living by proving, with their criticism, that they are too smart to be taken in by such stuff, are in fact strongly influenced by it, both its content (though that is not our main concern) and its repetitive form.

It would be tedious, unnecessary, and in itself unpersuasive, to describe any chance sampling from the day's fare. Every viewer knows from experience that the essential form of these tidbits is what I am calling pornographic: unlike even the shoddiest TV drama or talk show, the commercial is obviously and blatantly organized to leave itself uncompleted, to make us desire something that by definition the present moment cannot supply. The activity that its imaginings would stimulate is not an activity of the imagination at all, but an activity of possession. If I imagine anything, it is only the steps I must take to go downtown and get my hands on that new possession.[11]

It would be flatly against the purposes of such an art to provide any sense that this experience in itself, or repetitions of it, or reflection about it, will be enough. Many commercials do indeed these days come perilously close to violating their own purpose; it may turn out to be more fun to sit and watch these clever little dramas than to go shopping. While waiting for the glorious day when TV thus gives us everything we might conceivably want, suppose we look closely at the qualities of the primary experience of watching one of the most successful of these, the AT&T spot that Michael Arlen follows, brilliantly and relentlessly, in *Thirty Seconds*.[12] Arlen's interest is different from ours. With great patience and quiet irony, he traces an immensely painstaking and expensive path from conception through months of labor to thirty seconds of TV time, every second designed to make us want to "reach out and touch someone far away. Give 'em a call."

There is nothing subtle or disguised about the message, and its overt ethical content is quite unobjectionable. Each episode is designed to carry the same moral: telephone calls can bring joy to your life by enabling you to "reach out" to someone far away. (The company, Arlen tells us, originally stressed a theme of giving pleasure to others by calling them, but it soon caught onto the need to stress the pleasure taken by the caller.) "From the beginning, AT&T wanted us to overcome the negative emotions associated with long-distance," one of the advertisers tells Arlen. "For years, there has been a definitely *negative, uncasual* quality to a lot of long-distance calling. AT&T wanted us to emphasize the *casual, positive* aspect: long-distance is fun, it's easy, it's cheap." The ad is designed to move "the twenty-five-to-forty-nine age bracket, and the tilt is definitely toward the female, seeing that women initiate sixty percent of all residence long-distance phone calls."[13] Nothing wrong here, so far: surely the more long-distance calling among friends and relatives, the better. Here is how they design vicarious experience to increase our loving calls:

1. Open an older man in a "show-biz" setting. He's standing while listening, perhaps with his eyes closed, on phone. [Note association with fun, vitality.]
2. Cut to living-room scene with the corner of the rug thrown back. Little girl is tap-dancing with shiny new tap shoes. Proud father holds phone down near tapping as mother beams proudly. [Continuity of generations; parental pride.]
3. Cut back to elderly man as he smiles more widely and begins to impulsively dance to the same step himself. [The phone makes you want to dance; it expresses your love for family.]
4. Cut to brand-new Army recruit with brand-new short haircut. He's rubbing his head [and phoning home about it: when lonely you can keep in touch].
5. Cut to barber friend or dad sitting in his own barber chair; laughing. [Troubles shared by phone give joy.]
6. Cut to gal standing on head in yoga position. She's on the phone. [Phone is useful in all positions, situations, ages. And it's fun because funny.]
7. Cut to another gal doing the same. [Share, share, share.]
8. Cut to young man in cowboy getup—hats, jeans, etc. He has just competed in a rodeo, still has number on back and chest and is a little the worse for wear. . . . He's on the phone and happy [because he's sharing news of his victory; the phone brings good news, not bad].
9. Cut to young woman in jockey outfit just fresh from the race. She's full of mud. She's talking very happily on the phone. [More victory, more joy.]
10. Cut to locker room with hockey player waiting on phone. Lots of bustling around him. [Victory? Slight suspense.]
11. Cut to toothless little boy on phone in same uni-

form, whooping it up [about his father's victory;
more victory, more joy].

12. Cut back to locker room as champagne is poured
over his head and he breaks into a big toothless
smile. Freeze on smile [identical to his son's: the
phone thus identified with father-son love, with
triumph in life].[14]

The final version adds some features; it gets a baby and a black
girl into the act. (Why did it take them so long to think of a baby?)
But it is essentially still a cluster of sentimental moments associat-
ing the telephone with the viewer's desire for love and victory and
laughter. The makers rightly assume that we all desire these
things, and if we can be made to desire them even more, and then
to associate the desire with the next telephone call as fulfillment,
we will make more long-distance calls.

All this is perhaps obvious, and we might be tempted to say that
such superficial dramas are not worth our attention; nobody takes
them seriously, except perhaps some of the hundreds of "artists"
who make each one, and the advertisers themselves. But it takes
no very deep analysis to show that they are among the primary
forces shaping modern American character, as we have defined
character.

What are the qualities of the imaginative experience provided
by such an intensely crafted piece as the AT&T ad?

1. Like all video, the ad is of course visually intense, requiring
considerable quickness and sophistication of inference, not from
verbal but from visual signs. It tends to deflect our attention from
the words. Yet it is accessible to every experienced viewer,
however "illiterate" in other media. Mastery of this language
apparently comes as naturally as learning to talk. In this, such
mastery is unlike learning to read, which is a highly artificial
process that in one sense is never fully mastered.

2. It assumes a passive level of *mental* attention (if we can
contrast the mental to what the mind does in processing visual
imagery); redundancy is thus essential, redundancy about every
point. Each episode must mean exactly the same thing.

3. It allows for no ambiguities, either of image or of meaning.
Moral values are either suppressed entirely or taken for granted
(i.e., it is a good thing to "reach out and touch someone").

4. It forbids reflection. Both within the ad and in the movement from ad to ad we see one immediate sensation replaced quickly by another immediate sensation. To study the sequence, to think about anything at all, may increase one's admiration for the maker's skill, but it will always be subversive of the "artist's" true intent.

5. It identifies our deepest human emotions—love of family, desire for success, enjoyment of laughter, joy in dancing—with a material acquisition. In doing so, it denies every possible context for such emotions except instant gratification.

6. It requires me to view all people as stereotypes. In the invention of quickly recognized types, it is more resourceful than any previous art form except perhaps the comic strip. Raw types can be the only sort of "persons" taken in at such speed.

7. It portrays the goal of life as victory at the end of the day, not as conducting an effective or proper life en route. There can *be* no route, only *want*, followed at once by gratification. In this world, the winners are the ones who use those phones. There are no losers. Nobody calls mother for comfort after loss; nobody calls to tell of unexpected death or the loss of a job. The phone company would, of course, refuse to sponsor an ad that appealed to losers; losers will not have the money to make long-distance calls. All pain and all sense of struggle must be eliminated from this world.

Of course, there is nothing inherent in the nature of brief spots that requires mindless good cheer; they could just as well convey a mindless repetition of despair and emptiness, like some modern fiction, or a mindless repetition of political slogans, as happens both at home and abroad. In a sense, these short forms are as ideologically neutral as a computer—except for the fundamental ideology of repeated desire. The primary experience will always be of the same general kind, whether the product advertised is a new edition of Shakespeare's works, to make your family cultured, a new form of meditation or exercise, to make you serene or healthy, or a new deodorant or pantyliner to keep you fresh all day.

8. The company I keep (not of course the stick figures in the stories but their creators) do not respect me; they are not companions, but manipulators. Insofar as I am inclined to admire them, I do not admire their human depth or warmth or wisdom but their raw skill. If I infer an "author" or team of authors responsible for the presentation, I cannot think of them as friends who are themselves captured by any message conveyed. Unlike the im-

plied authors of great fiction, they are admirable at most as instructors in technique: I can learn from them how to do this clever stuff. Or I may envy them their pay. As everyone knows, the actors in the ads get paid more than the actors in the programs; it is evident to anyone who watches for a few hours at almost any time of day that more attention and money have gone into the ads than into the shows they *seem* to interrupt. Yet we also know, from the statements of those executives who write about their experience, that they do not themselves respect their art as art. No one of the creators has ever claimed that he (I've seen none by women) so admired a given ad that he could not resist going out at once to buy the product. At most, they will say that they admire what they know to be mastery of a set of tricks.

In commercials, then, we encounter primary experience that seems the antithesis, in every conceivable respect, of the kind of imaginative experience that children encounter in fairy stories, or that we adults find in reading what we call literature. "Thirty Seconds" is a relatively benign version of the creature: "Reach out and touch someone" is no doubt a more humanly defensible message than "Why do *you* use Preparation H?" or Steve Allen pretending that he can play a piano in a Ford. But the specific content, I must repeat, doesn't matter much as compared with the patterns of desire conveyed by the form: happiness is identified with something more or less costly, to be obtained in the immediate future; the makers are paid to portray this something, not to give us good company in an otherwise troubled world. The whole enterprise could not be better designed to produce a restlessness of spirit antithetical to reflection or thoughtful analysis. Whatever analysis we perform will be, like Arlen's book about this one advertising program, entirely divorced from, and ultimately hostile to, the ends sought by the work itself. The best printed narratives have always stimulated criticism that *appreciates* their value, in several senses of the word. The best TV criticism, and certainly the best criticism of the commercials, seems always to engage in *de*preciation.

To say all this is not quite the same thing as simply reviving McLuhan's slogan, "The medium is the message." It is to say that the effects of the medium in shaping the primary experience of the viewer, and thus the quality of the self during the viewing, are radically resistant to any elevation of quality in the program content: as viewer, I become *how* I view, more than *what* I view. And the gloomy conclusion must be that, unless we can change their present characteristic forms, the new media will surely corrupt whatever global village they create; you cannot build a world community out of misshapen souls.

A Hint at Conclusion: The Problem of Evaluation

Such speculation, much of it going far beyond any conceivable testing with hard evidence, "raises more questions than it answers"—a bit of socialscientese that I detest when others resort to it. About the only point that is beyond question is the immense power of the new voices to shape us anew. Difficult as it is to evaluate the differences, we are differently shaped by "Rumpelstiltskin," by *Ulysses,* by Johnny Carson, by "Dallas," by "Sesame Street," and by those thirty seconds.

Unfortunately for my case, the question of whether a given change in our habits of self-making is to be judged for better or worse cannot be answered quite as simply as I may have suggested. It is not at all hard to think of complicating objections. There are, for example, surely as many threatening corruptions of the printed word these days as of video. Certainly the print culture that I see disappearing nevertheless spawns today about as much hackwork, contemptuous of me as company, as does video culture. Indeed, the characters in the average soap or commercial are treated with relative respect, as compared with the monstrous abuses that now fill the pages of magazines like *Penthouse* or of many a best-selling book. Second, it is by no means as easy as I have implied to decide whether a given quality in current offerings—in any medium, new or old—is inherent to the medium or an accident of our times and economies. Nothing I have said can settle old controversy about whether the awfulness of TV, and of the kinds of printed fiction that are now produced and distributed like toothpaste, are causes or effects of this or that social reality. What's more, print itself was never—as Plato pointed out—an unequivocal good for souls or cultures. And finally, it is not obvious that we ever had a print culture of the kind my comments tend to idealize; indeed it may well be that ours is really no less a print culture than was mine as a child. And even in that culture, was not

my imagination being fixed, not only by the illustrations of those
lovely books, but by romantic patterns as potentially harmful as
those that poor Emma Bovary imbibes from what Flaubert considers the dreadfully destructive romantic novels read in her
childhood?

Wherever we may come out when we face such complexities, we
cannot doubt that each of us grapples daily with a barrage of "art"
unmatched in quantity and (potentially) unequaled in range by
anything known to previous generations. Whether our lives make
sense, then, whether we can in any way offer a defense of our
works and days within this culture, depends more than ever before
on our developing two great traditional arts: the art of rigorous
selection from offerings of all comers, friends, hacks, and con men;
and the art of engaging together in the kind of critical talk that
alone can protect us from selections that are arbitrary and dog-
matic. By sharing our grounds for selection, we can create moments that turn even the trashiest offering into a genuinely *good*
time. In short, whether the time spent with any medium is
redeemed or wasted is not entirely in the control of the masters;
we still have some choice about who we are to be, exercised
whenever we choose how to talk about our would-be pushers and
shapers.

It is by no means fashionable to talk as if a person's choice of
artistic company could make the difference between a good life and
a bad one, *now*. Obviously I am saying something as offensive as
that. But must we not recognize that to keep company with all the
suitors our society sends to our door will be to ensure, as times are,
a life of frenzy if not of despair?

REFERENCES

1. In May 1982 a study by the National Institute of Mental Health concluded
that there is now "overwhelming evidence of a causal relationship between
violence on television and later aggressive behavior." Letty Cottin Pogrebin, in
Growing Up Free: Raising Your Child in the 80's (New York: McGraw Hill, 1980),
gives a disturbing summary of the quantitative role of TV in our children's lives. I
quote here her scary extracts from various studies, but not the documentation she
provides for each claim: "More American homes have television than have heat or
indoor plumbing. The average TV set is turned on for 6½ hours per day. Most
children begin watching television at 2.8 *months* of age. Three- to five-year-olds
watch TV 54 hours a week. By the time a child enters kindergarten, she or he has

spent more time in the TV room than a four-year college student spends in the classroom. By the time a child graduates from high school, he or she will have spent less than 12,000 hours in front of a teacher and more than 22,000 hours in front of a television set. By age seventeen, each child has seen 350,000 commercials." She reports one survey that found 20 percent of children aged four to six preferring television to their mothers and 44 percent preferring it to their fathers. Junior high-school students, another study claims, "believe television" more than they believe their parents, teachers, friends, or books, radios, or newspapers (p. 393).

2. I find it curious that in our time one has to labor to explain this distinction. In the nineteenth century, even hardheaded utilitarians like John Stuart Mill took it for granted as fundamental in all deliberation about how a society should be run. In *On Liberty*, for example, Mill again and again distinguishes between the consequences that a policy might have for society and the quality of life that it might encourage or discourage in individuals. In arguing for the importance of allowing citizens to exercise free choice, he says, "It is possible that he [the citizen] might be guided in some good path, and kept out of harm's way," without cultivating his personal qualities. "But what will be his comparative worth as a human being? It really is of importance, not only what men do, but also what manner of men they are that do it" (Chapter 3, "Of Individuality," par. 4).

3. Having defined "art" in the broadest possible way, I am here narrowing the definition of "imagination" somewhat, bringing it closer to its roots. In what follows, I am thinking for the most part of what is quite literally "imagined" in our minds, "imitations"—though not of a separately existing reality. The term necessarily expands outward from specific colored shapes to include those shapes *in action,* and finally, it spills over to the moral qualities of those shapes: *that* woman, dressed *that* way, is a sympathetic image, while that other one is hateful, or puzzling, or doomed.

4. Our best performers of such mental experiments have been Marshall McLuhan and Father Walter Ong. It is unfortunate that McLuhan's love of highjinks and his frequently absurd praise for TV obscured the immensely imaginative way in which he opened up new domains for criticism of the media. Though I hope to say something more than that "the medium is the message," it is unlikely that I would be talking in this way if McLuhan had not written, again and again, sentences like this: "We still cannot free ourselves of the delusion that it is how a medium is used that counts, rather than what it does to us and with us. This is the zombie stance of the technological idiot." The other sharpest influence I am aware of is Lessing, though I only scratch the surface of what would follow from taking him seriously in matters like these.

5. Perhaps readers of *Daedalus* do not follow these weekly summaries with the assiduity they deserve, so I shall quote one of the fourteen that appeared in the *Chicago Tribune* on May 29, 1982: " 'All My Children'—7—noon—Erica returned to Brandon's arms, then was miffed that he had accepted a Hong Kong job offer. Cliff exploded when Nina hired Mrs. Gurney as a live-in nursemaid and when Nina also accepted the presidency of Courtland Computers. Palmer's fake medic, Dr. Bentley, warned Donna she would die if she continued her pregnancy. Jesse played up to Angie after she caught him smooching Vera, who he

later dumped. Angie's ma was dismayed by Jesse's appearance and manner. Phoebe flaunted the fact that she prefers Melanie over Carrie for Chuck. Harry enticed Benny to continue gambling even though Benny did not have enough money to keep searching for Estelle." If you have doubts about some of the locutions here, do not blame me; the quotation is accurate.

6. 1921, chapter 3.

7. Ibid., chapter 2.

8. I resist talking here about the many thematic connections—"only connect"—that this passage suggests with other parts of the novel; such patterns are equally accessible to any dramatized version, except, of course, for the implacable restrictions provided by the uninterrupted pace of the stage or screen.

9. At first sight, it might seem that traditional drama is precisely like the new scenic media in these respects. After all, plays are designed to be viewed once, with no conventional opportunity for any "reader" to slow the pace, return to reconsider earlier parts, or to sit and muse on what is meant. And the visual effect of theater seems as fixed by the director and actors as it is in a movie or TV drama.

But there is, as many critics have pointed out, a great difference between our experience of the visual reality in the theater and on the screen. In the theater, not even the most naive spectator ever loses a sense of living in a double world: the world of the stage and the world that the stage portrays. Olivier is both Olivier and Othello, and the pleasure of watching "them" interact, as it were, is an essential part of our primary experience. In contrast, photographic media, though obviously less "personal" or "human" in that the screen is imposed between spectators and flesh-and-blood human beings, just as obviously "mediate" less; directors have always known that we tend to identify screen roles with real life. When naive viewers send gifts and telegrams and long personal letters to the "good" characters portrayed on TV, and threaten real violence to the villains, they are really responding precisely as the medium asks them to. The fullest success, for any TV series, is to have one or another character become so real to the viewers that their minds are as fully occupied by his or her troubles as they would be by troubles in real life. But the fullest success for a "legitimate" actor is to be known as capable of an impressive range of characters—and thus identifiable with none.

10. It is not generally remembered on what a high pitch of public service radio broadcasting was launched. Robert Stein summarizes the story in *Media Power: Who is Shaping Your Picture of The World* (1972): "The channels were owned by the people and licensed by the government. In return for using the public airwaves, broadcasters were pledged to 'serve the public interest, convenience or necessity.' At the start, serving and selling were not considered compatible. Addressing the first conference of broadcasters in 1922, Herbert Hoover, then Secretary of Commerce, declared: 'It is inconceivable that we should allow so great a possibility for service, for news, for entertainment, for education and for vital commercial purposes to be drowned in advertising chatter.' In 1930 William Paley of CBS told a Senate Committee that during a recent week on his network 'the actual time taken for advertising mention was seven-tenths of one per cent of all our time.'"

11. Many shows are plainly pornographic in another sense: the thing to be

possessed is a stick-woman reduced to the mindless essentials of male gratification—the nicest toy in the display case. But to dwell on that kind of corruption
would lead us back to the subject that I have been trying—with only limited
success—to rule to one side for a while: the appalling *content* of too many current
artistic experiences, whether in video or print.

12. New York, 1980.
13. Ibid., pp.12-13, 47.
14. Ibid. pp. 69-70.

% % %

EACH BIRD WALKING

by TESS GALLAGHER

from THE IOWA REVIEW

nominated by THE IOWA REVIEW, *Elizabeth Inness-Brown, David Wojahn and Patricia Zelver*

Not while, but long after he had told me,
I thought of him, washing his mother, his
bending over the bed and taking back
the covers. There was a basin of water
and he dipped a washrag in and
out of the basin, the rag
dripping a little onto the sheet as he
turned from the bedside to the nightstand
and back, there being no place

on her body he shouldn't touch because
he had to and she helped him, moving
the little she could, lifting so he could
wipe under her arms, a dipping motion
in the hollow. Then working up from
the feet, around the ankles, over the
knees. And this last, opening
her thighs and running the rag firmly
and with the cleaning thought
up through her crotch, between the lips,
over the V of thin hairs—

as though he were a mother
who had the excuse of cleaning to touch
with love and indifference,
the secret parts of her child, to graze
the sleepy sexlessness in its waiting
to find out what to do for the sake
of the body, for the sake of what only
the body can do for itself.

So his hand, softly at the place
of his birth-light. And she, eyes deepened
and closed in the dim room.
And because he told me her death as
important to his being with her,
I could love him another way. Not
of the body alone, or of its making,
but carried in the white spires of trembling
until what spirit, what breath we were
was shaken from us. Small then,
the word *holy*.

He turned her on her stomach
and washed the blades of her shoulders, the
small of the back. "That's good," she said,
"That's enough."

On our lips that morning, the tart juice
of the mothers, so strong in remembrance, no
asking, no giving, and what you said, this
being the end of our loving, so as not to hurt
the closer one to you, made me look to see
what was left of us with our sex
taken away. "Tell me," I said,
"something I can't forget." Then the story
of your mother, and when you finished
I said, "That's good, that's enough."

THE DECIMATION BEFORE PHRAATA

(A VARIATION AFTER THE GREEK)

by ALAN DUGAN

from ANTAEUS

nominated by Carolyn Kizer, Lisel Mueller and Sherod Santos

The army marched by for days and was admired by all
of us for its silence, discipline, and carrion eagles.
Rank after rank marched by in right order and step,
each man heavily packed and armed and looking like the next.
Every night they built a town with towers and walls.
Every morning they tore it down and marched away.
We withdrew when they attacked, attacked when they withdrew
and lived high off their baggage train, killing a few,
losing a few—it was our same old free-style army game—
but they, those killers, had been broken into slaves
and feared their officers more than they feared the enemy.
This they were right to do: once when they broke some "rule"
before our Phraata, we heard them beg for punishment,
so they fell in and counted off and each tenth man
was pulled out of line and killed with his own sword.
They called this "decimation" and did it to strengthen their
    "wills."
What a people! They killed more of them than we did, but
they beat us anyhow. Then they marched away!
They didn't take what they came for, our defenseless Phraata.

That empire is incomprehensible, but we are in it.
They came back for Phraata and now we are the light horse
auxiliary of the XIth Legion (Augustan) of the Empire
and have no home. The Legionnaires still shout
to their officers, "Please decimate us!" The officers
always do, as we watch, and they always win,
and we and our horses are with them on the flanks
because there's nowhere else to go and nothing else
for us barbarians to do or be: it's a world empire.

🔥 🔥 🔥

PRAYER FOR THE DYING

fiction by WILLIS JOHNSON

from TRIQUARTERLY

nominated by TRIQUARTERLY

THE DAY YAKOV KAPUTIN died he managed to make the nurse understand that he wanted to see Father Alexey. Yakov had lived in America for thirty years but he did not speak English. He scribbled a faint, wiggly number on the paper napkin on his lunch tray and pointed a long knobby finger back and forth between the napkin and his bony chest. "You want me to call, do you, dear?" the nurse asked in a loud voice that made Yakov's ears ring. Yakov could not understand what she said but he nodded, *"Da."*

When the telephone rang Father Alexey was just dozing off. It was July. Crickets were chirring in the long dry grass outside his window. The priest was lying in his underwear listening to a record of Broadway show tunes on the new stereo his mother had bought him. His long beard was spread out like a little blanket on his chest. The window shade was down and a fan was softly whirring.

He thought it was the alarm clock that rang and tried to turn it off.

"Mr. Kaputin wants you to come to the hospital," the nurse said with finality, as if announcing some binding decision from above.

He did not know how long he had slept. He felt shaky and unfocused.

"I can't," he said.

"Is this the Russian priest?"

"This is Father Alexey." His voice seemed to echo far away from him. "I'm busy just now."

"Well, we're all busy, dear," the nurse said. She paused as if waiting for him to see the truth in that and do the right thing.

"What is it this time?" Father Alexey said with a sigh.

"I just came from him," the nurse began to converse chattily.

("That's better now," her tone seemed to say.) "He's a real sweet-heart. He wrote your number down. He didn't touch his lunch, or his breakfast. I don't think he feels well. Of course we can't understand a word he says, and he can't understand us . . ."

"He never feels well," Father Alexey said irritably. "You usually do not feel well when you have cancer."

"Well," the nurse said indignantly. "I've called. I've done *my* duty. If you don't want to come . . ."

Father Alexey sighed another large sigh into the receiver. He hated the hospital. He hated the way it smelled, the way grown men looked in little johnny coats, the way Yakov's bones were all pointed. Besides that, it was very hot out. During the entire morning service not even the hint of a breeze had come in the door of his little church. In the middle of a prayer he thought he might faint. He had had to go into the Holy of Holies and sit down.

"It's not a matter of 'not wanting,'" he said pointedly. "I'll have to adjust my schedule, and that's not always easy. I don't know when I can be there. I have to try to find a ride."

He lay for a while longer with the fan blowing on him, his hands clasped on his soft white stomach. The sheet under him was clean and cool. He looked tragically at the window shade. It was lit up like a paper lantern.

Father Alexey lived next to the church in an old house with a cupola, fancy molding and derelict little balconies. A rusty iron fence tottered around the unmowed yard. Once every seven or eight years one or two sides of the house got a coat of paint. The different shades of paint and the balusters missing from the little balconies gave the house a patched, toothless look. On rainy days water dripped down the wall next to Father Alexey's bed. He complained to Mr. Palchinsky, the president of the Union of True Russians, which owned the house. Mr. Palchinsky got the Union to provide each room with a plastic bucket. Father Alexey would have tried to fix the roof himself but he did not know how to do it. Yakov said he knew how to do it but he was too old to climb a ladder and besides they did not have a ladder.

Yakov's room was next to Father Alexey's. Each night after the old man said his prayers he would say good night to the priest through the wall.

Father Alexey did not always answer. Yakov was a nice man but he could be a pain. He was always talking, telling stories about himself. Yakov in the forest, Yakov in the Civil War, Yakov in the labor camp, Yakov tending flower beds for some big shot in White Plains. Father Alexey knew them all. And whenever he made an observation with which Yakov did not agree, Yakov would say, "You're young yet. Wait a while. When you're older, you'll see things more clearly."

The priest knew it was one of the things people in town said about him: he was young. He tried to look older by wearing wire-rimmed glasses. He was balding, and that helped. Not that it was a bad thing to say, that he was young. If people really wanted to be disparaging—as when the Anikanov family got mad at him because he forgot to offer them the cross to kiss at their mother's memorial service—they went around reminding their neighbors that he was not Russian at all but an American from Teaneck; if they knew about his mother being Polish they called him a Pole; they brought up the fact that he once had been a Catholic. If they wanted to truly drag his name through the mud, they called him a liberal, even though he almost always voted Republican.

Yakov had been to the hospital before, once when he had his hernia and once for hemorrhoids. This time, even before they knew it was cancer, he sensed he wouldn't be coming home. He was, after all, almost ninety years old. He carefully packed his worn suit, the photographs of his wife, his Army medal, some old books that looked as if they had been rained on, into cardboard boxes which he labeled and stacked in his room. He left an envelope with some money with Father Alexey and also his watering pail for his geraniums. When the car came he didn't want to go. Suddenly he was afraid. Father Alexey had to sit with him in his room, assuring him it was all right, he was going to get well. He carried Yakov's suitcase out to the car. Yakov was shaking. When Father Alexey waved good-bye the old man started to cry.

The hospital was in the city, fifteen miles away. Once a week the senior citizens' bus took people from the town to the shopping center, which was only a mile from the hospital, and you could get a ride if there was room. But if you did not have a car and it was not Thursday, you had to call Mikhail Krenko, the dissident. He had a little business on the side driving people to the city for their errands.

Krenko worked nights on the trucks that collected flocks from the chicken barns. He had arrived in town one day after jumping off a Soviet trawler. It was said that he offered a traffic policeman two fresh codfish in exchange for political asylum. People suspected he was a spy. They were almost certain he had Jewish blood. Why else, they asked each other, would the Soviets have given him up so easily? Why had he come to live in a godforsaken town that did not even have a shopping center?

Krenko was a short man with limp yellow hair and a round face like a girl. He chewed gum to cover the smell of his liquor, sauntered with his hands in his pockets and did not remove his hat upon entering a house, even with an ikon staring him in the face. In the churchyard one Sunday people overheard him call Mr. Palchinsky *Papashka*—"Pops." Anna Kirillovna Nikulin told of the time she rode to the city with him and he addressed her as Nikulina—not even *Mrs.* "Here you are, Nikulina," he said, "the drugstore."

Some female—an American; young, by the sound of her—answered when Father Alexey dialed his number.

"He's in the can," she said.

"Well, would you call him, please?" he said impatiently.

"Okay, okay, don't have a kitten."

She yelled to Krenko. "I don't know—some guy having a kitten," she said.

When Krenko came on the telephone, the priest said as sarcastically as he could, "This is Father Alexey—the 'guy' from your church."

"Hey, you catch me hell of time, with pants down."

"I called you," Father Alexey replied stiffly, "because one of my parishioners happens to be very ill."

He hung his communion kit around his neck and went to wait for Krenko in the sparse shade of the elm tree in front of the house. Only a few branches on the old tree still had leaves. In some places big pieces of bark had come off. The wood underneath was as dry and white as bone.

Across the street was the town's funeral home. Sprays of water from a sprinkler and a couple of hoses fell over the trim green grass and on the flowers along the walk. Father Alexey held his valise with his holy vestments in one hand and in the other his prayer book, a black ribbon at the prayers for the sick. He could feel the sweat already running down his sides.

He thought how it would be to strip off his long hot clothes and run under the spray, back and forth. He saw himself jumping over the valise, he took off his hat and wiped his face and bald head with his handkerchief. He fluttered the handkerchief in the air. In a minute it was dry.

Then from behind him a window opened and he heard Mrs. Florenskaya call. He pretended not to hear. He did not turn around until the third time.

"Oh, hello, Lidiya Andreyevna," he said, holding the bright sun behind his hand.

"Somewhere going *batiushka?*" the old woman asked in her crackly voice.

"Yes," the priest said reluctantly.

"Good," Mrs. Florenskaya said. "*Ich komme.*"

The Union of True Russians had bought the house as a retirement home (it had been a fine, sturdy house, the home of a sea captain; the church next door had been the stable for his carriage horses) and at one time all the rooms and flats had been occupied. Everyone was gone now, dead or moved away—mostly dead. The whole parish had grown older all at once, it seemed. Now with Yakov in the hospital, Father Alexey was alone in the old house with Mrs. Florenskaya. Every day she shuffled up and down the empty, echoing hallway in her worn slippers and Father Alexey would hear her crying. In nice weather she cried out on the porch. The first time he heard her—it was shortly after he had arrived to take over the parish a year ago (his predecessor, Father Dmitri, had started to drink and was transferred back to New York)— Father Alexey had run upstairs to see what was wrong. Mrs. Florenskaya listened to his beginner's Russian with a happy expression on her face, as if he were trying to entertain her. Then she had replied in a mixture of English and German, although he didn't know any German, that a bandit was stealing spoons from her drawer.

He no longer asked.

After a minute the front door opened and the little woman came spryly down the stairs carrying a cane which she did not seem to need. A paper shopping bag and an old brown purse hung from one arm. She was wearing a kerchief and a winter coat.

"Where going *Sie*, little father?" She came into the shade and smiled up at him.

When he told her about Yakov, she sighed heavily. "Old people just closing eyes," she said. Her chin started to wobble.

"Aren't you hot in that coat, Lidiya Andreyevna?" he asked.

She pulled a wadded tissue out of her pocket. "*Sie* young man, *Sie* can *arbeiten*. I am old." She wiped her nose, then lifted her chin in the air. "I *arbeiten* in Chicago," she said proudly. "In fine hotel."

Father Alexey looked down the empty street.

"He's late," he said.

"*Ja*," the old woman said emphatically, as if he had confirmed all she had said. "Many *zimmer* taken care of; wash, clean, making beds."

A short distance from where they stood the road dropped steeply to the river. Father Alexey could see the far bank and the dark pines of the forest beyond. The sky was blue and still. The leaves were motionless on the trees, as if they were resting in the heat. Above the brow of the hill, Father Alexey saw two heads appear then slowly rise like two plants pushing up into the sun. The heads were followed by two bodies, one long, one square. They came up over the hill and came slowly in the heat toward the priest and Mrs. Florenskaya. They were dressed for the city, the woman in a dress with flowers, the man in a suit and tie. The woman was the long one. The man was sheer and square like a block of stone. As they drew near, the man took the woman's arm in his thick hand and stopped her short of the shade. They looked back down the road. The man checked his watch.

Bending around the priest, Mrs. Florenskaya peered at them with curiosity.

"Good heavens," she said at last in Russian, "why are you standing in the sun? Come here, dearies, with us."

The man gave them half a smile. "It's all right," he said as if embarrassed. But the woman came right over.

"Thank you," she said as if the shade belonged to them. "That hill! We had to stop four times. Stepanka, come join these nice people." She took him by the arm. "Now that's much better—no?"

Father Alexey introduced himself and said in Russian that the weather was very hot.

"Fedorenko," the man said but he did not offer his hand. He added in English: "My wife."

"*Ach, Sie sprechen Englisch!*" Mrs. Florenskaya said delightedly. "I, too!"

From time to time Father Alexey ran into them in the market or on the street. The man was Ukrainian, the woman Byelorussian.

The woman would always smile. Once in a while the man nodded stiffly. On Sundays Father Alexey would see them pass by on their way to the Ukrainian church.

"Are you waiting for someone?" the man's wife asked, continuing the English. "We're supposed to meet Mr. Krenko here."

"He was supposed to be here ten minutes ago," the priest said.

"We're going to do a little shopping," the woman informed them. "Stepan's not allowed to drive. It's his eyes. They wouldn't renew his license. We're going to get some glasses for him. He doesn't want them. He thinks they'll make him look old."

"Not old," her husband said sharply. "Don't need it. What for spend money when don't need it?"

"You see?" she said hopelessly.

As they waited the sun grew hotter. They inched closer together under the tree. They could see the heat coming up from the road and from the black shingles of the roofs that showed above the hill. Mrs. Fedorenko fanned her face. Mrs. Florenskaya unbuttoned her coat. They stared longingly at the glistening spray of water across the way. There was a rainbow in the spray and the water glistened on the green grass and on the flowers and on the lawn sign on which the undertakers had painted in gold an Orthodox cross beside the regular Christian one.

Finally they heard an engine straining. Up over the hill through the waves of heat came Krenko's car. It was a big car, several years old, all fenders and chrome. Upon reaching level ground it seemed to sigh. It came up to them panting.

Krenko pushed open the front door.

"You're late," Father Alexey told him. With a look of distaste, he set his valise with his holy vestments on Krenko's zebra-skin seat. Mr. and Mrs. Fedorenko climbed into the back, followed by Mrs. Florenskaya who nudged Mr. Fedorenko into the middle with her bony hip.

"Where is she going?" Krenko said.

"Ask her," the priest shrugged.

"Where you going, lady?"

"Never mind," Mrs. Florenskaya said.

"Not free, you know. Cost you money."

"*Ja*. Everything all time is money."

"Ten dollars," Krenko said.

"*Ja, ja.*"

"You have?"

Mrs. Florenskaya took a rag of a bill out of her pocketbook and waved it angrily under Krenko's nose. She put it back and snapped her purse. "Everything is money," she said. Tears suddenly rolled out from under her eyeglasses.

"Crazy old woman," Krenko muttered.

"May we go?" Father Alexey said.

They drove around the block onto the main street of the town. On the street was the market, the bank, the hardware store, the laundromat, the boarding house where old people who did not belong to the Union of True Russians lived, and a variety store where they sold pizzas. Part way down the hill Krenko stopped and blew the horn.

"Another passenger, I presume?" Father Alexey said.

"Make it when sun is shining," Krenko winked.

From a door marked "Private" stepped Marietta Valentinova, the famous ballerina who lived over the hardware store. A white cap with green plastic visor kept the sun from her small severe face. Krenko got out and opened the front door, giving her a mock bow, which she ignored.

She had been at the St. Vladimir's Day service that morning at Father Alexey's church. Several members of the parish were named Vladimir, so there had been a good attendance in spite of the heat, more than a dozen. St. Olga's Day a few days earlier had not been nearly so succesful, but then there was only one Olga in town, and she was sick and couldn't come. Marietta Valentinova had stood in her usual place in the center, where she was in range of any idle chatter, which she would silence at once with a scalding look. She also kept an eye on the ikon candles. She did not like to let them burn down more than halfway, and all during the service she was blowing them out and removing them from their holders. People who had lit the candles complained about it to each other but none dared say anything to her. On Sundays or saints' days, it didn't matter, she put a dollar in the basket. No one had ever seen her take back change. But she was very severe.

"Good afternoon, Marietta Valentinova," Father Alexey said. "*Ya yedu v gospital.*"

The ballerina glanced at his valise. One corner of her small red mouth lifted slightly. "I thought you have been looking thin," she teased him in English. "That's the trouble with being monk: no wife to feed you."

"It's Yakov Osipovich," he said, reddening.

"Well," she said, "shall you move over or must I stand in sun all day?"

"Maybe you get in first, lady," Krenko said. "With such little legs you fit better in middle."

"I will thank you to pay attention to your own legs. And also your manner. Who do you think you are, blowing that horn?"

"Like joking with her," Krenko winked when the priest got out to let the ballerina in.

"How about the air conditioning?" Father Alexey said when Krenko got back behind the wheel.

"Okay. First got to put up all windows," Krenko said. Then he turned a switch. Air blew out from under the dashboard.

"I think that's the heat," said Father Alexey.

"Is okay," Krenko said. "Got to cool up."

They drove to the bottom of the hill and turned up along the river. The water lay flat and colorless between banks of colorless clay. Soon they were in the woods. The road ran over the tops of hills and down to stream beds filled with rocks. The undergrowth was dense and tangled and they could not see the river. They passed a farmhouse with a barn propped up by poles. In a clearing slashed in the woods a mobile home squatted like a gypsy, its children and its trash strewn round the yard.

The air was blowing out, but the car was stifling. They were squeezed together, Father Alexey with his valise on his lap. Marietta Valentinova smelled Krenko sweating. She moved a fraction closer to the priest, who had pulled out his handkerchief and was wiping his face.

"If I don't get some air, I am going to faint," Marietta Valentinova said.

Krenko moved the switch another notch. The hot air blew out harder.

"Sometimes takes couple minutes," he said.

"In a couple of minutes we will be cooked," the ballerina said. "Can't you see I'm dying?"

"Hold it!" Krenko said. He felt under the dashboard. "Now is coming."

Father Alexey wiggled his small white fingers in the air blowing on his knees. It was still hot.

"*Now* is coming," Krenko said confidently.

"Open a window," the ballerina commanded.

"You going to let air condition out . . ."

"Did you hear me?" she said in a voice so severe that everyone at once rolled down his window.

"Thank God," said the priest as the hot wind blew in on them. They put their hands out into it, groping for a current of coolness.

After a while Mrs. Fedorenko said, "It was very hot in New Jersey, too. That's where we lived."

"Hot like hell," Krenko agreed, although he had never been to New Jersey. "Here is not hot."

"I am very glad to hear that this is not hot," the ballerina said. She held a hanky over her mouth as they passed a chicken barn.

"More hot in California," Mr. Fedorenko said. "I been all over United States. Many Ukrainian people live in California. Many Russian, too," he added for the benefit of the ballerina who had cocked her ear toward him, showing him her profile, the raised eyebrow. "And many Ukrainian. Not same thing."

"Do tell us about it," the ballerina said haughtily. To Marietta Valentinova there was no such thing as a Ukrainian. That was modern nationalist nonsense. What was the Ukraine?—*Malorossiya*, Little Russia. They were all Russians.

"You are from New Jersey, *batiushka*?" Mrs. Fedorenko asked to change the subject.

"Yes. It is very hot in New Jersey. I haven't been to California."

"*I* in Chicago *arbeiten*," Mrs. Florenskaya said.

"You were saying something about the *malorossy*, I believe?" the ballerina said.

"Not Little Russians, lady. Ukrainian."

"All right, Stepanka. Did you hear? *Batiushka* also lived in New Jersey."

Mr. Fedorenko folded his heavy arms. "Don't call us *malorossy*."

"I don't call you anything," the ballerina smiled coldly.

"No?" Mr. Fedorenko pushed forward his big chin. "What are you calling ten million Ukrainians? The ones Russia starved?"

"If you are speaking of the Soviet Union, I'll thank you not to call it Russia," the ballerina said. "I even hate to say that word— *soviet*."

"Okay," Krenko said, "long time ago—okay?"

"I have a question," Father Alexey said.

"You, too," said Mr. Fedorenko accusingly. His face was very red.

"Me too, what?"

"Stepanka," Mrs. Fedorenko implored.

"I see you Four July parade. See you turn away when Ukrainian club marching. You don't remember, huh?"

"I didn't turn away."

"I wouldn't blame you if you did," the ballerina said. "I certainly would."

"I didn't."

"That's enough, Stepanka."

"Maybe I just looked somewhere else," the priest said. "There is a big difference between looking somewhere else at a given moment and turning away."

"Of course there is," Mrs. Fedorenko assured him.

"I know how is seeing," her husband said.

"All right, Stepanka. What were you going to ask before, *batiushka*? You had a question."

"I don't know," the priest said dejectedly. After a moment he said, "I guess I was going to ask why everyone is speaking English."

"You're absolutely right," Mrs. Fedorenko said. "You need to learn." And then she said something in Russian, or Ukrainian, or Byelorussian, which Father Alexey did not quite catch. In the conversation that followed, he heard many words he knew but there were many words in between—they spoke so quickly— which he could not understand.

Then there was silence.

He looked around and saw the others looking at him.

"*Nu?*" the ballerina said.

"*Shto?*" he asked.

"*Shto ti dumayesh?*"

"*Shto?*"

"Heavens, my dear Father Alexey," the ballerina changed to English. "We are talking about poor Mr. Kaputin. Haven't you been listening?"

"Of course I've been listening."

"Well, then?"

"Well, what?"

"Is he getting better? You did say you were going to see him?"

"Yes, of course, Marietta Valentinova. I know. I understand." He had picked out Yakov's name in the wash of words but assumed they were talking about the old man's geraniums. Yakov grew them in his window box. They were big and healthy flowers, all from pinchings from other people's flower pots, and it was the thing people saw when they walked past the house. Father Alexey shifted the valise on his lap. His clothes were stuck to him.

"The nurse said he wasn't feeling well," he said. "Who knows what that means? Last time they said the same thing and I went all the way there and there was nothing wrong with him. He was fine. He just wanted someone to talk to. I walk in and he says, 'I'm glad you came, *batiushka*. Have you paid my electric bill? I think I paid it before I came here, but I can't remember.' I told him everything was taken care of. 'That's good,' he says. 'I was worried. So how are you, *batiushka*? It's hot out, isn't it?' "

"How sweet," the ballerina said.

"Sweet? It cost me—the church—ten dollars."

"Don't blame me," Krenko said. "They don't give the gas away yet."

There were more farms, more rocky fields and unpainted houses that tilted one way and another. Then more woods broken by raw-cut clearings full of stumps and weeds and plastic toys and house trailers on cement blocks.

Of the farms and houses, Father Alexey could almost pick which was Russian, which American. None of the people in them had money, you could see that easily enough, but the American ones almost seemed to be the way they were out of stubbornness. There was something in a savage, defiant way willful about the broken porches, the rusty machinery outside the barns. The Russian yards were unkempt only with weeds and overgrown grass and the woods coming closer and closer. They had little gardens, just tiny patches, with flowers and a few vegetables. Father Alexey started to get depressed.

"Did you ever think," he said, looking out the window, "that you would be here?"

No one said anything.

"Are you speaking to me?" Marietta Valentinova said.

"Yes. To anyone."

"Think I would be here? Of course not. Who would?"

"Then why did you come?"

"We're getting personal, I see." But she wasn't angry.

"I'm sorry. I was just thinking . . ."

"You want to know? All right, I came for my health."

Mr. Fedorenko gave a guffaw. His wife pulled at his sleeve.

"It's true. Why would I leave New Jersey? I had a nice apartment. When I danced I got good write-ups. You should see the people who came to my ballets. You could barely find a seat. And it wasn't a small auditorium in that school, either. Only thing, the air was no good for my health. All that pollution. So where does a Russian go? You've got to have a church. So you go where there are Russians. At least there there were people with intelligence," she added over her shoulder. "Not like this godforsaken place."

"How many people lived in New Jersey!" Mrs. Fedorenko said before her husband could say anything. "We like it here, though," she said, patting Mr. Fedorenko's thick square hand. "We've had enough big things—the war, DP camp. After the camp we went to Venezuela. On Monday morning you turned on the radio and if there was a revolution you didn't have to go to work. Too many things. Here it's small and quiet. And Stepan always wanted to live near a river. He says that way you will never starve."

"I live in this place eighteen year," declared Mrs. Florenskaya. "*Achtzehn jahr,*" she added for Father Alexey's benefit. "All in this old house."

"Eighteen years," said the ballerina sadly. "I couldn't stand this place so long." But she already had been in the town more than half that.

Father Alexey calculated. Eighteen years ago he was nine years old. It was a whole year in his life, but all he could remember of being nine was being in the fourth grade and Sister Rita St. Agnes being his teacher, a stern little woman with thick black eyebrows who had seemed to take to him after his father died. "The boy with the laughing eyes," she called him affectionately. Sometimes he looked into the mirror to see why she called him that. The eyes belonged to a bald, not very old person who was expected to be full of answers for people far older than he, people who were afraid of getting sick and of nursing homes and hospitals and what was going to happen to them. He dispensed answers like the holy water he flung on heads and shoulders at a feast-day procession. Answers for death and fear and sadness and stolen spoons. And in all his life he had only lived in New Jersey with his mother and in the monastery in New York and now in a little town no one had ever heard of. How could he know?

In another eighteen years he would be forty-five. How much

would he know then? Would he see things more clearly, as Yakov said? Krenko, the ballerina might still be around. Krenko probably would be in jail, he thought with some satisfaction, or in the real estate business or some scheme, making money one way or another. The ballerina would be an old woman if she were still alive. The others would surely be dead. Most of the people in the parish would be dead.

He was becoming more and more alone in the world.

The shopping center was on a long broad avenue that ran between the interstate and the city. It once had been a road of fine old houses with wide porches and broad lawns and beds of marigolds and tulips. A few remained. Dentists and lawyers had their offices in them. The rest had been torn down for the fast-food restaurants, gas stations and bargain stores that lined the road like a crowd at a parade. Krenko drove into the shopping center parking lot from the back road that came up from the river and discharged his passengers in front of the K-Mart. He'd be back in two hours, he said.

Father Alexey let the ballerina out and got back in the front seat. His cassock was wet and wrinkled where the valise had been.

"Look like you piss yourself," Krenko said and laughed.

In the hospital Father Alexey carried his valise in front of him to hide the wet place. Two teenaged girls snickered behind him on the elevator. A small boy who got on with his mother gawked up at him all the way to the seventh floor. "Hey, mister—you look like something," the boy said when the elevator stopped.

Father Alexey marched to the nurses' station and set his valise down hard. Then he remembered the wet place and covered it with his prayer book.

"You're here for Mr. Kaputin?" asked the nurse who was there.

"Yes," Father Alexey said curtly. "Are you the one who called?"

"No, Mrs. Dinsmore has gone." She came into the corridor. She was a tall woman with narrow shoulders and a tired face. Even before she said anything, Father Alexey knew that Yakov was going to die.

"The doctor has been in," she said.

He followed her to the room. Yakov was asleep, long and gaunt under the sheet. There was a thick sweet smell in the room. Yakov's bones looked as if they might pop through his face. With each breath his mouth puffed out like a frog's. On the stand beside his bed was an ikon of the Holy Mother of Kazan and a vase with daisies whose petals were falling off.

Father Alexey touched the old man's arm. His eyes blinked open. For a while he stared up at the priest. "It's you," he said.

"How are you feeling, Yakov Osipovich?" the priest asked in Russian.

"I saw my mother." Yakov's voice was hoarse and old. He took a long time between his words.

"Where did you see her?"

"She went away. There are fewer Russians, *batiushka* . . ."

He began to talk incoherently, something about apples in his father's orchard. The words came out in pieces that did not fit, as if something had broken inside of him.

The nurse brought a glass of tea. Father Alexey cooled it with his breath.

"Here, Yakov Osipovich," he said, raising the old man's head. The tea rose halfway up the glass straw, then sank back into the glass.

"Try again, Yakov Osipovich. Pull harder."

"Shall I try?" the nurse asked.

Father Alexey took his communion kit from around his neck. "I don't think it matters," he said.

The nurse went out quietly, leaving the door ajar.

Father Alexey arranged articles from his kit and others from his valise on the stand beside Yakov's bed and put on his holy vestments. He took the ribbon from the place he had marked in his book, then turned through the pages to the prayers for the dying.

He read quietly, occasionally making a cross over the old man's head. Yakov gazed up at him in silence and a kind of wonder, his mouth agape.

The priest softened a piece of bread in a little wine.

"Yakov Osipovich," he said, "are you sorry for your sins?"

The old man looked from the priest's face to the hand with the bread. Then his eyes closed. The priest shook him. "Yakov Osipovich," he said. "Say yes."

He tried to put the bread into Yakov's mouth but the old man's teeth were clenched. He slipped the bread between Yakov's lips, tucking it back into his cheek. Eventually Yakov's mouth began to move. He chewed fast, as if he were hungry.

Yakov opened his eyes just once more. Father Alexey was

putting his things away. He heard Yakov's voice behind him. The old man was looking at him calmly.

"How did you come?" he said.

The priest came and sat beside him. "I found a ride. Are you feeling better?"

"Then you have to pay."

"Don't worry about it, Yakov Osipovich."

"Well, I'll straighten it out with you later, *batiushka*."

Krenko was parked outside the emergency door in a place marked "Doctors Only."

"You make me wait long time," Krenko said. Father Alexey could smell liquor on him.

"I'm sorry."

"Not me, I don't care. But little dancing lady going to be mad like hell."

Marietta Valentinova sputtered at them half the way home. Tiny drops of saliva landed on the dashboard. Father Alexey watched them evaporate, leaving little dots. At last she stopped. They became aware of his silence.

"*Batiushka?*" Mrs. Fedorenko said.

After a while Krenko said, "Well, you got to go everybody sometimes."

"Where going?" Mrs. Florenskaya said.

"Mr. Kaputin," Mrs. Fedorenko told her gently.

"*Ja, alles,*" the old woman said, "*alles kaput. Mein man, meine kinder. Alles* but me."

The sun was gone from the window shade when Father Alexey got back to his room and lay down on his bed. It was still light, it would be light for a while yet. He turned on his fan to move the air and looked at the wall through which Yakov had said good night. He heard Mrs. Florenskaya upstairs in the hallway. She was starting in again.

The priest switched on the stereo with the record from the afternoon. But he could still hear her.

"Christ," he said, and turned up the volume.

THOSE DESTROYED BY SUCCESS

by WILLIAM DICKEY

from POETRY

nominated by Adrianne Marcus and Stanley Lindberg

The very large pasteboard replica of the general,
his medals pasted from his chest
down over his washboard belly,
is propped up at the podium and squeaks.
Skillful technicians amplify and dilute
what he appears to be saying, until the audience,
which is comatose anyway from the brandy
and the smuggled cigars, grunts
approvingly into its paunches.
It will be all right.

Even the general, even the president,
who is weeping in the Oval Office
at the thought of having to give up
the least hangnail of power, even
the great poet whose voice has become
so identifiable that we genuflect
hearing it, shutting off our minds
to the recognition that it is only a voice now,
even these, before their success, were men.
Inside them, as they are towed, great
helium balloons in the Macy's Christmas parade,
there may still be men rattling,
but how are we to know?

I watch you richochet
from banquet to banquet, from
radio to talk show, and I think
"That is my friend. She is in
real danger." And you watch me
in a suit with a vest, and wearing a
Countess Mara tie, accepting
with judicious well-phrased thanks.

Both of us need to remember that
we are no good, no good, really.
Neither of us can speak fluent Greek.
Both of us can cook, but last night
I ruined a perfectly possible chicken soup,
and I still remember when your stove caught fire
and you had to redecorate the kitchen.

To be destroyed by success, I think
you do need to begin to believe
you can do anything and everything
and as the belief grows
little bits of the brain fall off
and turn into recalcitrant diamonds.
And eventually you are only a scatter of diamond
and a hollow where the ability to fail once was.

Keep reminding me, and I will keep
reminding you. Remember that
you cannot tell east from west, remember
that in separate cars, you leading
and then I leading, it once
took us two hours to find the freeway.
Remember the Christmas Day in Bucks County
when I was trying to call Seattle, and
the long-distance operator began to try
to put long-distance calls through me
in the upstairs bedroom,
and when I explained I was only trying
to call Seattle, said: "You poor thing."

Even if the money comes, let us be poor
and spend it rapidly on British Leyland
motor cars that collapse when scolded
and on fish poachers for which we have
no fish. And after the banquet
at which multiples of ourselves have toasted
multiples of ourselves many times over
and turned red in the face, let us go back
to a shabby hotel room and talk
about what went wrong, and remember
how dangerous it is to be right, and how
dangerous to be powerful, even in small things.

MOLES

by MARY OLIVER

from THE OHIO REVIEW

nominated by THE OHIO REVIEW, *Jane Flanders and William Stafford*

Under the leaves, under
the first loose
levels of earth
they're there—quick
as beetles, blind
as bats, shy
as hares but seen
less than these—
traveling
among the pale girders
of appleroot,
rockshelf, nests
of insects and black
pastures of bulbs
peppery and packed full
of the sweetest food:
spring flowers.
Field after field
you can see the traceries
of their long
lonely walks, then
the rains blur
even this frail
hint of them—
so excitable,

so plush,
so willing to continue
generation after generation
accomplishing nothing
but their brief physical lives,
pushing and shoving
with their stubborn muzzles against
the whole earth,
finding it
delicious.

MEMORIES OF UNHOUSEMENT, A MEMOIR

by CLARK BLAISE

from SALMAGUNDI

nominated by SALMAGUNDI

I.

Before the Interstate system obliterated the old America, you used to come upon them at country cross-roads: clusters of white arrows tipped in black, pointing in every direction. Somewhere on the Plains you would see it, slow down, and be thrilled: *Denver 885*, it would say, or *New Orleans 1045*, or better yet, *Los Angeles 2000*. How they got there, who decided on the city and the mileage, I'll never know. Perhaps they had taken over from the whitewashed rocks, the dabs of tar, left by earlier waves of lost, impatient travelers, when twenty or thirty miles a day was more than fair measure. Nowadays, the green mirror-studded billboards conspire to keep our minds on the effortlessly attainable, the inevitable. No more than two destinations, they seem to say, don't tease us with prospects greater than our immediate ambition. *Glens Falls,* the one nearest to me now says *Saratoga Springs 18*.

We are deprived of that special thrill when our destination, our crazy, private destination, made its first appearance in one of those black-tipped clusters. No reason at all that on a road between Chicago and Madison, just outside Beloit, Wisconsin, WINNIPEG should miraculously appear. Yet in 1949 when I was nine and guiding my father on our longest trip home, it did. Nine hundred

121

miles in a '47 Chevy, with its split windshield, high fenders and curved chrome bars over the dashboard radio, for my salesman-father was a typical, fifteen-hour long haul. But for old-times' sake he'd break journey in Detroit Lakes, he said. Detroit Lakes, in northern Minnesota, was where they'd honeymooned in 1939. Up there in the headwaters of the Mississippi is where I was conceived, I suppose.

I was born in Fargo, North Dakota, in 1940. Along with Roger Maris and William Gass and Larry Woiwode. In that *Ragtime* spirit that haunts us all, I sometimes think of my mother pushing the pram, of Mrs. Woiwode pushing hers, of little Roger Maris, then six, dashing past us, bat on shoulder. Billy Gass, a bifocular teen-ager, squints a moment at these figures of life, then returns to the ice castle of his imagination. "The Pedersen Kid" crystallizing even then. *Beyond the Bedroom Wall* gurgles in his stroller. Babe Ruth's assassin takes a few mean cuts. I am the only Canadian writer born in Fargo, North Dakota.

There is nothing obscure, really, about Fargo. In 1977, at a cocktail party in New Delhi, India, I found myself talking to an agreeable, white-haired American with a professional manner, the U.S. Agricultural attache. My India-born wife was serving that year as the director of a Canadian academic-exchange program. She was a quasi-diplomat.

"I consider myself half a Canadian, really," he said.

"I'm more than half American myself," I replied.

We shared a smile, wondering who would explain himself first. "I was born in North Dakota," I said. Then, covering my tracks, I added, "My parents had just emigrated."

"I was about to say almost the same thing. Where in North Dakota?"

"Fargo."

"Amazing."

He was the first North Dakotan I had ever met. "What year would that have been,' he asked. "Forty, forty-one?"

"April, 1940."

"I was just finishing my M.A. at North Dakota State that spring. My wife was an O.B. nurse."

Parallel lives were beginning to converge, as though a collision course, plotted by children on separate planets, had suddenly become inevitable. We said together, "St. John's Hospital."

I added, "Dr. Hanna."

He called his wife over. As she put her drink down and turned to join us, he said, "How would you like to meet the first person you ever saw?"

We always returned to Winnipeg whenever my father ran out of work. Or when unmentionable things occurred. We had left Pittsburgh in 1945, Cincinnati in 1943, Fargo in 1942, and—a week before—Leesburg, Florida. Everytime we left, we headed back to Winnipeg, my mother's city.

My father was from the village of Lac Megantic, a few mountain ridges north of Maine, directly south of Quebec City. Winnipeg must have been a torture to him. I remember him, slicing luncheon meats in an upstairs bedrom in my grandmother's house, sipping beer and smoking Canadian cigarettes whose cork-tips inflamed his lips, next to a leaking window; he never spoke of his dislikes. He never warned us. He merely acted without apology. He was probably not entirely sane.

Once in Pittsburgh, in an outburst that still lies blottered somewhere, he'd discovered a fellow-salesman sneaking back to the floor just minutes after ducking out for lunch. While my father supposedly ate—he had a weakness for restaurants, for sitting at a table and being served, a leisurely lunch bespoke respectability—the other salesman let himself out of the men's room cubicle, where he'd downed a sandwich, and let himself back on the floor. He'd intended a clear hour to himself, writing up every sale and crediting himself with every commission. The rules dictate full credit to the lone name on the final bill. It discourages lunch-hours, among other things.

My father was hiding in the other cubicle. He came back and found the scab writing up one of his juicier sales. My father, even at his most sociopathic, could be a charming man. I came to fear those eruptions of charm. Frenchmen, as Quebeckers of his generation were usually called ("Hey, Frenchie!") are often very charming. Especially to Americans. My father looked more Jewish than French, more gypsy than Jew. He spoke furniture-yiddish and ring-Italian. I am his genetic miscue. Though always impeccably dressed—his code was as inflexible as an autodidact's stiff vocabulary—he appears to me now, two years dead, in a bandana and earrings, a billowing black shirt and dark, baggy pants, tucked into his greasy boots. There should be a tribe, somewhere, that combines all his somber talents.

My father possessed—or, rather, it possessed him—a murderous temper. He had pounded out twenty victories in three weight-divisions, in two countries, under various names that served him like flags of convenience, until finally being hammered himself by an eventual champion. Thereafter he'd confined his skills to Canada's most successful export industry, helping assure the delivery of Montreal's finest whiskey to parched, Prohibition-dry New York. I learned all this later from his last wife, a cautious woman with police connections in Pittsfield, Massachusetts. She'd had his record routinely checked, after marrying him and growing suspicious. Fifty years ago, or longer now, he'd "been known" to every policeforce between Troy and Burlington. No gesture in the universe is ever lost. They never pinned murder on him, but there had been assault and manslaughter and even an accessory charge, later dropped. He was in the hospital by then, bounced between surgery and intensive care; legs gone, lungs clotted, a face reduced to that sloping nose and fleshy, slightly-folded ears.

The charm and the sledge-hammer. It is 1945, a year I cannot believe I've lived through. We are on the fifth floor of the Pittsburgh Sears, during the putative lunch-break of two very hungry salesmen. My father called his colleague over. He asked him to bring the order book. He smiled so graciously at the customers, his customers from a missed supper the night before, that they were reassured. *No, no*, he grinned, *quite all right*.

The order book was long and narrow and thick. Gripped at its bound end and then snapped against a flat object, it emitted a sharp, satisfying crack, like a solid jab or a clean base hit. The flat, astonished cheek of the salesman was such a surface and my father tatooed each cheek as though they'd been the alternate sides of a small punching bag, until, even with slaps, a cheek like a leather bag can gradually unravel.

That finished him with Sears and for awhile, banished him from the States. We crossed into Canada at Niagara Falls that midnight and were in Winnipeg three days later. That was the earlier time, 1945. Canada was still at War, the same war that (I was told) had sent us to North Dakota in 1939. Canada, part of Britain's war effort, would be on the front lines as soon as the Luftwaffe finished mopping up. German U-Boats already controlled the Gulf of St.

Lawrence. The French islands of St. Pierre and Miguelon, off the coast of Newfoundland, were rebelling against the Vichy regime; no one knew how long that would last, a fog-bound Casablanca. Newfoundland and Labrador, British crown colonies and still ten years away from joining Canada, would of course be ceded to the Nazis, just like the Channel Islands. The Frenchies in Quebec refused to fight an English War; Adrien Arcand and his brown-shirts were poised for a *putsch*, whenever Hitler ordered it. Which left Ontario, in 1939 and '40, feeling itself in the probable front-line of combat, with Lindbergh-style collaborationists controlling the States, the *Bunds* of Buffalo stirring up border-hate. I'd never been in a War. In Pittsburgh of 1945, I didn't feel part of a War, not like Winnipeg.

My father, a French-Canadian, never even considered fighting an English war. By his lights, justly so. He was barely over-age for the American draft. Brawny, steel-making Pittsburgh had been a good place for a salesman to sit out the hostilities. But for that unprincipled salesman and my father's temper, we might have stayed; no gesture in the universe escapes consequence.

This is my first memory: the soldiers at Canadian customs, their jaunty berets. The smell of a different tobacco in the air. My uncle in his Colonel's khaki, the Passchendaele medals on his chest, smoking thick pieces of glass for me and my cousins. The scientists of the free world had gathered in Winnipeg in 1945 for a spectacu-lar view of a solar eclipse. I remember my twin cousins, limber girls of eight, doing backward flips all around my grandmother's house.

II.

For most Canadians the differences between their country and the United States are minimal. The majority of English-speaking Canadians cross the border without papers, taking their places in the United States (we like to think) as nobler sorts of Americans. More respectful, less bumptious, better educated. Lofty types, a touch disdainful; Galbreaths all. We queue up, we don't litter. Compare any large Canadian city with an American counterpart: the difference is obvious and public pride is deeply layered. If we saw anything drop from a car window, or onto the sidewalk, my mother would mutter, "Americans!" There is something to it. Most public facilities in the United States resemble relics from a combat zone. It's hard for Canadians to avoid a little smugness, even those who emigrate.

But there is another kind of Canadian; smaller in number but infinitely richer in influence, who pounces upon every distinction, magnifies it and cherishes the disparity. It might be said that he keeps alive a certain Confederation Flame, for without his voice, Canada would certainly yield to profit and convenience and become, officially, a clean and prosperous corner of the United States. It might be said they are the reason Canada was created and the reason it still exists: to draw fine distinctions, to show that individual liberty and the pursuit of happiness is not the only reason for existing as a nation. To many Canadians, the American is a person who doesn't hesitate shooting a stranger for running over his lawn, for honking at a red light. These Canadians prefer their quiet, more authoritarian country, the sovereignty of parliament and not the litigious individual. They read Canadian magazines and sometimes British, they go only to movies listed as "Canadian or Foreign"; thus acknowledging the peculiar status of things American, they watch (and listen) exclusively to the CBC. Mention "the States" to them and you might pull a blank. "I was in Fargo once," a cousin might say. "Small town. Ugly."

"New York? God, no thanks. You can get killed there."

The only Canadians I know who genuinely *like* the United States are of course the French-speakers. And for good reason. The French-Canadian, when he leaves home on this continent, is tolerated only in the United States. In Toronto, I have heard the familiar retort, "Speak White!" I've seen my (one-time) fellow Torontonians demand of young Quebec tourists, chatting away on the immaculate Toronto subway, to *please* remember where they are; that so much jabbering in French is giving everyone a headache and no matter what Trudeau is trying to do to the country it won't work because it was settled when Wolfe defeated Montcalm and affirmed when they hanged Louis Riel and they ought to hang Rene Levesque too. On Prince Edward Island, in a tourist home modelled on Anne of Green Gables, the landlady, in showing us our rooms and remarking on my Quebec license plates (but not on my French name) confided in me, "the white man built this country! What are the French trying to do?"

At Old Orchard Beach, *l'etat Maine*, or in many parts of south

Florida, America has capitulated to the French fact. Commercial greed, a tradition of tolerance, or simple confidence conspire to make French a conquering language. And all winter long, the tanned Quebecois flock back to Dorval Airport in the most outrageous motley of straw hats and Palm Beach T-shirts, straw bags stuffed with grapefruit. The last Americans. Levesque said as much, appealing to Americans for support: I am the George Washington of my people. I hear more *joual* on the streets of New York than in Toronto.

When my father quit the liquor-escorting business, after deserting his first two wives, he found himself in depression-cold Montreal, thirty-seven, unskilled though not untalented. He'd always sold things, apart from special services, and now he offered his salesmanship to the T. Eaton Company, then considered the world's largest department store. Montreal was Canada's most important city. If wealth had been preserved in those desperate years, it was to be found in the English community of Montreal, a minority of the population with a corner on nearly all its commercial holdings.

My father spoke good English. After all, he'd been up and down the Hudson Valley both as a fighter and as a smuggler and most of his family, by this time, had settled in Manchester, New Hampshire and Fall River, Massachusetts. It was fluent English, the way Trudeau's and Levesque's is fluent, but it was different from his French. A little coarser, with damns and hells when he didn't need them, and other words inappropriate to their context. In English he could be emphatic but not always convincing. At the same time, his childhood and adolescent French had deserted him. He had underworld French, but in truth he had no language, no voice; only expletives. It came as a shock to me, towards the very end of his life, when in a wheelchair he visited us in Paris and confided, "If I went back to Montreal I could speak French again. A couple of months and I could speak it as good as you."

The point is this. First, by unstated rules, and then by directive, he was not permitted to serve English-speaking customers. For him, it would be the priests and nuns, the spinsters with anglicized taste, the maids and charladies of Cote-des-Neiges and Westmount wealth. Whenever the blustery, regimental sorts with their Great War medals still on their blazer pockets came in, my father was instructed to call Mr. Fraser to come over and help, and eventually, write up the sale. I enter the story only because the interior decorator, to whom he once complained, spoke to the manager. She seemed to be a fair-minded woman, educated, European-trained, and from the West. In 1939 she became his third wife, and they headed off to Winnipeg, and from Winnipeg my father wrote letters and Sears of Fargo gave him a chance. They went to Detroit Lakes to celebrate.

My first long exposure to Canada took place ten years later, following one of my father's failures in the southern part of the United States. Oh, I know what drives a Canadian, especially a French-speaking one, farther and farther south, until he can go no further! Warmth. Heat. *Look, son, how it shimmers!* Light as thick as syrup bouncing off our car. Seat leather that sizzles. *Ouch!* my mother cried. Oh, give me a home where the highway ahead looks wet twelve months a year! He was made for swimming trunks; a dark man with an hourglass build who could sleep all day in the sun and glow like walnut at night. Mosquitoes found him unappealing. Women did not. There were so many I lost count, once I learned how to measure them. The only truth I have to go on is that *any* woman he talked to outside of the strictest necessity: any waitress, any bank-teller, any secretary, any neighbor—any woman whose first name he knew (or denied knowing)—was also his part-time companion. Otherwise, he avoided women all together. What could he possibly talk about?

We'd driven up from Florida. Those clustered signposts served us well: *Atlanta 605. New Orleans 590.* We were tearing around America, rolling double-sixes around the old Monopoly board. One day for Florida, another for Georgia. Then they came fast: Tennessee, Kentucky, Indiana, Illinois, and before the half-week was out, that sign in Beloit: *Winnipeg 945.* We were in the green and watery states now, in the lee of Canada: Wisconsin and Minnesota. We were in Fargo for an afternoon and I wandered down the main street of my, and Roger's hometown. He was fifteen now; prime for scouting. We drove past the house we'd lived in, that spring of 1940: Fifth Street, S. E.

They identified the next door neighbor's house for me; we knocked but no one was home. Their name was Hinckle. Mr. Hinckle, back in the summer and fall of 1940, had loved to hold me (my father did not); the only infant-pictures I have were taken by

Mr. Hinckle, or by his wife while I was in his arms. A great many years later, in 1973, I published a book of short stories in Canada which, by luck, was reviewed in the Minneapolis *Tribune*. A line in the review moved me, and I repeat it here: "by opening himself to us, he makes it possible for us to better know ourselves." And a few weeks later I received, forwarded by my publisher, a letter from a nursing home in St. Paul, from Mrs. Hinckle, writing in a firm hand, asking if I had possibly been born in Fargo in 1940. She'd never had children, but she'd always thought herself a mother to me. Mr. Hinckle would have been so happy to read this marvelous review. It was in one of those stories that I had written, *no gesture in the universe is ever lost*, in a context that I had tried to make absurd. Now I know that it is the core of all my beliefs.

III

That afternoon in Fargo as I walked on Fifth Street, S.E., feeling attached to the concrete that had possibly supported my pram and to the trees that had, years earlier, bloomed in Mrs. Hinckle's lens, a car slowed down and a window unrolled. Those were Manitoba windows, with their inside sheets of frost-free plastic, and I responded to them as emblems of an even earlier, purer hometown than Fargo. Winnipeg was where all my mother's memories came to rest, where my grandparents and all my relatives lived, and it being only five hours away, it was the city where I would be spending that night and, for all I knew, the rest of my life.

"Sonny?" the driver asked. A resonant, kindly, crinkly, northern voice. He had sandy hair and a reddish moustache. No Americans wore moustaches in those days, except cads and lovers in Hollywood movies. Thirty years ago, Canadians really looked and sounded different, surrogates of Britain, even in border-state situations. (I realize now that *of course*, especially in border confrontations with the United States, Canadians enjoy their only dominance: the might of Vancouver, Calgary, Winnipeg, Toronto and Montreal, exerted against the puny, unpeopled northern fringes of Washington, Montana, North Dakota, and upstate New England. The only exceptions were Detroit and Buffalo, and even there Canadians felt a moral smugness.) I knew which side of this particular border I belonged on.

"Sonny?"

"Yessir?" I answered, still the obedient, drawling Southern boy. "You from around here?"

Judging from the way my cousins were about to receive me, pretending (I thought) not to understand a word I said, I must have answered, "*Ah wuz boned raht cheach.*"

"Then pardon my French but where the Hell is the Moorhead Bridge?"

Moorhead, Minnesota, faces Fargo from across the Red River. My mother had had her first labor pains on that bridge, where she walked every day. She'd made it sound (as she always did, in all her stories) an exciting chase, which side got an agent to her first. I'd felt myself competed for: the underpopulated hunger of North Dakota against the progressive Sky Blue Waters of Minnesota. A North Dakota birth was just right for me: manageably modest, yet special. Minnesota was too important, too American, it mattered too much in the American scheme of things. If I had to be born an American, let it be North Dakota.

And then it just spilled out. "Y'all lookin for St. Boniface, aincha?"

The driver's head sort of rested, rolling slightly, on the edge of the window, unable to compute, precisely, what had just been heard. St. Boniface was the French-speaking twin city of Winnipeg, just across this same Red River. The river only divided states in America; in Canada it symbolized infinitely more. My cousins in Winnipeg had never crossed the river except to skim far eastward, into the fishing waters of the Whiteshell, near Kenora. Whenever my father visited Winnipeg, he found many reasons to go over to St. Boniface and he often took me with him. Winnipeg was that kind of city to me; a macrocosm of my family, a microcosm of the country, achingly close yet out of reach from the town of my birth.

"Did you *hear* that?" the man was asking, turning to his wife and elderly passengers in the back seat. *St. Boniface* and snorts of laughter. "Yes, son. How do I get to your St. Boniface?"

Of course I didn't have the slightest notion. If we were on Fifth, I reasoned, the numbers probably got smaller as they approached the water. My own street ran slightly downhill; I pointed the car straight ahead.

My parents came along shortly. We drove down the main street, visited Sears—the agent of our Americanization—and then we were gone again, following the river north to Grand Forks, and eventually, Pembina, the border, and Emerson, where Canada started. Like many children, I suppose, I held my breath till we crossed the border and inhaled deeply of Canadian air, convinced it was something purer than the stuff I'd just expelled.

Of all the distinctions I have invented in my life, (and come to believe in, with the force of myth), the differences between Canada and the United States—so frail in reality, so inconsequential in the consciousness of America or the world or even most Canadians—is still my last, my most important illusion. It matters, or it mattered until very recently, that a border exists. That people so similar should be formed in different ways. That because I inherited those differences, I should have something special to say on both sides of the border. Through my childhood and adolescence and well into my adulthood, to the ragged fringe of middle age, the faith in a Canada being of a different order of history, experience and humanity, granted me an identity. It was never easy to claim it, but I never doubted it was there, and that I belonged to it. And because of having an identity there, it seemed that I had a prior understanding of Canadian temperament. My humor was Canadian humor. Even with an absurd, rural Florida accent, things I said in Canada, to Canadians, were invariably appreciated, understood on several levels, inflated beyond my own understanding. Canada cultivated an unused part of me that America had never touched. The significant blob of otherness in my life has always been Canada; it sits like a helmet over the United States, but I was the only person who felt its weight.

North, North, North: that glorious direction. The provincial bison-shield of Manitoba, the narrow highway that cut through the wheatfields on the left and the French-speaking hamlets along the river on our right, their lone church-steeples gleaming (to my mother's disgust) higher than the bluffs that hid the rest of the town, and seeming even taller than the wheat elevators that stretched westward, each of them announcing a calloused, sun-reddened Protestant town. And then, the highway divided, trolley tracks appeared, and we were in Winnipeg.

I think often of the compass points. Like the arrow-clusters at cramped country crossroads, the cardinal directions all move me; I dream restless dreams of that *setting out* feeling, of entering a highway for what you know to be a long drive, and reading that

first, firm, challenge to the continent. *East*. And I would see
fishing boats and a pounding rocky surf and the great cities and I
would think (in my southern, and mid-western days) *yes*, that's the
best direction. East for me. Culture, history, people, excitement,
sophistication. But then, on my only trip to California, undertaken
with a group of high school seniors from Pittsburgh, I thrilled to
those days of unbroken signposts: *West, West, West*, and even
when the land was flat or Appalachian-rolling, I'd be thinking of
buttes and mesas and sawtooth mountains and I'd think of getting
properly lost in all that space, and feeling free. Well, this was
North: this was just about as far North as anyone could imagine;
watery and glistening and cold, as though the sign itself should be
read under a stream of icy water; I think of North and I think of
Hamm's Beer and Land o'Lakes butter and of the lakes and pure
forests of the Canadian shield, that area that stops just a few hours
east of Winnipeg, where town names again turn French and
people along the highway are unmistakably Indian.

Most of my life has been spent on the southern fringes of the
shield and though my opinion of its charms has changed—it is time
again for heat—it is still the direction that defines me. North.
Northern. I like the northern winter not because of sportiness in
me or delight in the bracing qualities of a stern climate, but merely
for its obliging me to stay indoors. North gives justification for the
torpid side of my personality (that I'm on best terms with) to take
over.

I think that is why SOUTH has no charm for me at all; it is the
only cardinal point that fails to conjure an unreal, dreamlike
essence of itself. When I think of the north Florida and south
Georgia I knew, I remember only walls of leggy pine with slash
marks on their trunks, hung with resin buckets, and I remember
the Coke machines in country gas stations where for a nickel I
could lift a heavy metal lid (I can remember the first whiff of that
cold, moist air, I remember the pleasure of trailing my fingers in
that iced water), spot a bottle cap in one of the metal tracks and
glide it along to the spring-catch my nickel had released. And I can
remember draining those stubby little Coke bottles with their
raised, roughened letters on the side, always checking the bottom
to see where it had been bottled, how far it had come, though
nearly all were good ol' bottles from Plant City and Orlando. Well,

all I remember of *South* is sand and heat and thirst and skies and the color of sweaty undershirts, spotted with buzzards.

IV.

On Wolseley Drive in Winnipeg, on the banks of the Assiniboine, my grandparents had their house. Three hours away, my aunt and uncle had an even larger home, with a basement full of hunting rifles, decoys, canoes and kayaks, and a special room for a billiards table. Since my uncle was in those days a writer and commercial artist as well as president of the Wheat Pool—and was soon to become Winnipeg's best-known television personality—and my aunt was a broadcaster, they had studios and libraries on their second floor. The third floor held guest rooms and an attic full of bundled magazines going back to the beginning of *National Geographic* and *Readers' Digest*, as well as the splashy American weeklies like *Life* and *Saturday Evening Post*. They kept the hunting and fishing magazines, and everything Canadian, particularly everything relating to the Prairies and especially Manitoba. Nothing important had ever been thrown out. The house was virtually a computer, although means of retrieval were still a little primitive.

That house, and their lives, represented something to me called Canada, that was more than merely attractive; it was compelling. In the various towns and cities of my first ten years, we had always lived in small apartments carved out of old servants' quarters, on the fringe of other people's families, and we always seemed to be sharing some vital function of other people's lives. Kitchens, bathrooms, entrances, hall-ways, washing facilities. Maybe that's why, in years to come when we finally rented our own duplexes, my father celebrated by roaming around in his boxer shorts all day Sunday and from the moment he returned home. I used to wonder about that. In my favorite TV show, "Father Knows Best", Robert Young ("Jim Anderson") always came home in a suit and changed to an elbow-patched tweed or corduroy jacket. Whatever it was, Canada, by virtue of its cool, English houses and its politeness and its streetcars and its formalities and its formidable understanding of everything going on in the world, as well as in the city, was a more interesting place to live than America. It was certainly more complicated, with French instructions running down the sides and backs of every food package. My parents had moved back to Canada at a time when its differences from the United States were unforced but extreme; whatever seemed foreign to me on a perceptual level was nevertheless perfectly comprehensible on a level of precognition. Or, to put it in the terms I would later live by, Canada was a novel that others found dull and difficult, but that I found interesting and accessible from the beginning. You could say that my life was a dissertation on the subject of Canada and the United States, and what it is like, being a part of both.

I visited my aunt and uncle every day and shot pool in the basement by myself or with my cousin. My parents and I stayed at my grandmother's and between the houses and the school, I became a Canadian.

My grandmother was a classic of the grandmother type; too old to have a life of her own, but young enough to manage the lives of several others. She was small but sturdy, she had wit and a deadpan delivery that was the first to ever "get me going" as she put it—the first person subtler than my comprehension. She had taken up driving and a wee bit of smoking and drinking (the sign of an amateur in these matters: she kept her cigarettes loose in an old sugarbowl in the kitchen cupboard, and she would smoke a cigarette only at predictable times of morning and evening and when the dough was rising after a first good punch-down).

My grandfather, when awake, was the focus of our awareness, though not of our attention. While he was up, we all kept an eye on him. He was classically senile: a bald, tall, stooped old patriarch, a one-time doctor, a breeder of flowers and fruit trees and an importer of draft horses, the consolidator of an insurance group—a man of great substance in Western Canada. Up on the second floor, in the room occupied by my parents and me, I would read the volumes of Who's Who in Western Canada that told my grandfather's tale ("The Luther Burbank of Canada"), and I never tired of reading the biographies of him in the Canadian Readers' Digest, the Who's Who and all the profiles in the various medical and insurance journals. Canada's best-known novelist of that time and place, Frederick Philip Grove, had even based a novel on him. From those biographies I learned the name of the various prize-winning peaches and apples he'd introduced, the prize-winning horses he'd bred and I learned to feel a touch of family pride whenever we passed an office of the Wawanesa Mutual, the insurance company he had headed. *Everyone* in Winnipeg seemed to be famous, all of my relatives had wealth and power and visibility; casual visitors to my uncle's house turned out to be cabinet ministers, American governors, authors. When I walked down the street with my aunt or uncle, people stopped and often turned around to watch as they walked by. After the bruised, violent anonymous lives we'd lived in those mildewed Southern towns, Winnipeg was like a jolt of pure, cold oxygen, the only place left in the world that conformed to the notions of reality I'd gotten from reading and from my own intense imagining.

At the age of seventy-five, my grandfather was merely a disturbing presence. He was strong and stern and he kept himself busy through a ten-hour workday in his old study and sometimes in the living room, underlining every sentence in every book and magazine in the house. He did not know his name, or that of his wife and daughters (he'd had nine daughters and one son, and all five of the survivors visited regularly except the son in Toronto, and my mother). His memory had deserted him while he was in his early fifties, and as a doctor he'd recognized—it had been his father's fate as well—and had gotten out of medicine, and cut back on the insurance. He'd retired, physically exhausted, with a heart condition. The insurance company had treated him generously. His faculties continued to fail. He was apparently alert enough, in 1940, when my mother brought me up from Fargo for my first visit, to feel the bumps on my head and declare, "Don't worry, Annie, this boy will never be a fighter." So far as I can determine, he never spoke to me, or of me, again. His heart repaired itself, as it often does in bodies suddenly relieved of stress, and he had his work, the underlining of every word in the *Free Press* and *Tribune*, and all those stacks of magazines. That was my Canada and that was my grandfather's house: a place where everything was intact and even madness could be quietly accommodated. There was, in fact, only one thing that could not be housed, because he was not organically a part of it, and that was my father.

"See what *he* wants," my grandmother would ask, not unkindly. She was as afraid of giving offense as my father was; therefore they worked out elaborate systems of mutual avoidance. He rarely came downstairs. Whenever he did, an aroma of tobacco preceded him by at least a minute, and my grandfather would lay his pencil down, carefully marking his place in the work still before him, stand, and—high, quivering voice fierce with rage—order him out. "How dare you, sir, walk across my carpet with your dirty workman's boots? Out, Out, I say!" My father, in Winnipeg, never went outside in the winter, and was always in slippers. My grandfather was furious, muttering , "the cheek, the gall! I will report this insolence to Stewart, don't think I won't!" That would be the sign for my mother, first, to interpose herself. "It's all right, daddy, he's Leo, your son-in-law." Stewart had been a stable-hand, imported from Scotland like all the Clydesdales. Now my grandfather was in a proper Victorian rage, throwing my mother aside, "I don't know why you're shielding him, Lillie, but I'm getting to the bottom of this. I won't rest—" by which time my father had sneaked back up the stairs, cursing to himself and my grandfather would be left standing, hands clenched, undecided over the next challenge. All the women in his life were "Lillie," my grandmother's name, except my grandmother, who was usually just "mother." After he died, at the age of eighty-two, my grandmother had her own few bad years, heaping invectives on her husband, not for those last twenty inglorious years, but for the years of his magnificent achievement, the *Who's Who* years. Who, or what, to believe? Even as I write this, my own mother is close to enacting the dramas of her parents, and as I reach back into these events of thirty years ago, I'm aware that truth is simply a matter of framing and reframing. I've chosen to believe certain versions, I've rejected others. I too was blessed with a gifted memory and I've worn it down by now to something dull and ordinary and I fear that the family disease awaits me.

When my grandfather's fists unclenched he'd go back to the chair and begin the assault on a new column of print.

The winter of 1950 was one of the snowiest in Winnipeg history. It would lead to a flood that is still remembered, to sandbags in my aunt's and grandmother's backyards, to those canoes and kayaks pushing off directly from the driveway and bringing relief a few blocks downstream. And, as the head of the Red Cross, it would be my aunt's finest hour: in the pictures we were sent (by that time we too had pushed off; they caught up with us in Cleveland, in a rooming house on Euclid Avenue), my aunt and uncle would be bundled in their parkas, under helmets with the Red Cross painted on the sides, and it would remind me of British Air Raid wardens.

The pictures were grainy, black and white, some of them smeared from rainwater on the lenses (a beautiful, accidental effect; what would be its equivalent in language?). I should like that talent—to capture activity, strain, sleeplessness, peril, the direction of a thousand lives and millions of dollars, and the muddy, ice-choked river racing by the fixed point of my grandmother's backyard, tossing boulders of ice, houses, trucks, with the fury of a horizontal Niagara.

That would be the spring. Right now, it is still a hard, Siberian winter day. Winnipeg exists, paradoxically, by virtue of its relative mildness, its southern latitude. Southern only for Canada; America had abandoned any attempt to colonize the lands north of the Twin Cities. Winnipeg should not exist, except as an urban planner's act of defiance, an experiment on the heartless Russian model. But it does exist, as Edmonton exists, as Montreal exists, and the effects of that anomaly—the intense self-consciousness, the isolation , the pride, the shame and absurdity of carrying on normal life at forty below zero—creates a population that fills the studios and board-rooms and lecture halls of Canada with so much talent that old Winnipeggers form a kind of talent-Mafia in Toronto. Some drained south, the Monty Halls and David Steinbergs and Erving Goffmans, but most defied the dominant pulls of the continent and headed East. Winnipeg, meaning "muddy water," is built on one of the very few north-flowing rivers in North America. Maybe there's more of a social component to geology than we had ever suspected.

The people of the city are proud of their winters, proud of their simple survival. They were afraid of softness, at least in my mother's family, and they were constantly headed deeper North, as though to test themselves, as though Winnipeg represented some degenerate, sub-tropical fringe of sybaritic abandonment. My cousins began their kayaking at ten or so, portaging to rivers and lakes right to the shores of Hudson's Bay. They had a farm in the Sand Hills in the western part of the province, where they grew flax and ran trap lines, and in the fall I went with them— Florida child that I was then, accent and all—and learned to shoot at an early enough age to avoid the normal hesitancies and sentimentalities of the urban academic. I learned to hunt like a farmer, like a competitor and protector; I concentrated on gophers and red-winged blackbirds.

V.

One Saturday deep in the winter of 1949-50, my grandmother asked me to go up to Portage Avenue to see Mr. McArdle and to bring back the meat-order, which she was phoning in. I was given directions to find the shop, but no money. From what I could see, no money ever entered or left my grandmother's house. Accounts were rendered, usually in person, by well-dressed men who waited in the parlor. Tea and biscuits would be served. My grandfather would be on good behavior, looking from face to face, following conversations, or so it seemed, laughing when others laughed. Sundays would bring visits of an elderly threesome of spinster sisters, "The Bonnycastle Girls," who dressed in sybillant black satins, who exuded the kinds of perfume associated with toilet waters and colognes, something closer to a "scent" than a "fragrance," like a liquified powder. They had visited my grand-mother every Sunday for the past forty years, although no one (on our side, at least) was quite prepared to explain to me if they were friends from a different time and place, or relatives, or perhaps, inherited obligations, the weekly visit a form of interest on an unpayable capital. I joined the group enthusiastically smiling and following faces much like my grandfather, until one day when I got too close and detected odors under the cologne and realized something disagreeable was being hidden; there was, in fact, no attempt being made to attract.

I walked up Stiles to McArdle's. The street was packed with white-frame houses behind their deeply snowy yards. I am re-minded now, in their winter settings, of a street like an occluded lower jaw, all the way up to Portage Avenue. One long block under the winter sun, in the winds of thirty-five below. "It's nippy outside. Bundle up. Don't tarry," said my grandmother.

I have seen most of the world's major cities by now, but Portage Avenue in the early Fifties remains for me something special, like a Russian movie, molded on a scale of epic tedium that nevertheless achieves a certain indifferent weight. If we could rid our minds of notions of charm and beauty and still be receptive to urban grandeur, then Portage Avenue, the east-west axis of Winnipeg and half the province of Manitoba, would stand as a model. It was conceived on a scale of spaciousness in keeping with the open fields and possibly in revenge for the two thousand miles of crabbed forest at its back. It was wide, straight, and flat, and down its middle in its own private *maidan,* rolled the endless herd of rumbling streetcars. Standing at Stiles, I could look a couple of miles to the west, the buildings showing not a single variation in height and not a single uniformity of design, and spot, *in embryo* as it were, the line of streetcars that would be passing me in the next half hour. Since no one could stand outside more than ten minutes anyway, it was most compassionate of the transport commission to flood the rails with more cars than any city had a right to expect. That was my Winnipeg; a city of prompt and endless convenience.

I presented my request to the aproned, blood-stained, gray-haired man with the scholarly glasses. "What would it be, now?" he asked, the voice foreign yet attractive to me, able to squeeze out twice as many words per second as my slow, hateful speech. I was working on reducing my accent, for I knew from overhearing my parents in their bed that we were finished in the South anyway. I hoped we'd never leave Winnipeg. I was getting more "ays" and fewer "uhs" into every line, though I still couldn't force myself into Canadian pronunciations of *zed* and *shedule*. Canadian spellings all looked right to me; "honour" seemed a graver concept with its extra vowel intact.

"I've come for the meat order," I said.

"I can see that."

"My grandmother called you."

He squinted. Obviously he was expected to know every child in his square mile. "And who might she be, now?"

I gave the name.

His face broke into a *Saturday Evening Post* cover of recognition. The bushy white eyebrows shot up, the rimless glasses slipped, the lips formed an "Oh!" and fell, arms outstretched, against his countertop, as though doing a cheating, standing push-up.

"Why, it's the wee bairn! Why dinja say, lad? You're the wee American bairn she's been talking about. What's your name again?"

"Clark."

"Clar-r-r-k." he rolled the name like a large, succulent, choco-late-covered cherry. "Now isn't that fine! Clarrrk is music to my ears, it is."

It was a name I despised, and had paid for repeatedly in Southern schools. Clark Bars and Clark Kent and Clark Gable were the extent of my visibility in the American world, and to be named after any of them, as they all assumed I had, was an assault on the rituals of Southern dignity. I realize now that a name like Clark, in those years, was a tribal name—there were two Clarks (first names) and innumerable Clarkes (last name) in the school I now attended, including a teacher, and some of them conformed to my notion of what Clarks inevitably were like. Clarks in America had all been wounded, and they bore their wounds with minimal grace. In Canada they competed with Icelandics for places on the hockey team.

I was, however, even in Winnipeg, a little uneasy with my last name, which was clearly unique—Blais—and which added unpronouncibility to the earlier charge of exploitativeness. I couldn't understand why we didn't spell it "Blaze" since that was the way it usually came out, though I'd heard through my father that it was really an unpleasant little burp of a name, a little like "Bligh" and sometimes "Blay", so that there was no consistency to it, not even a spelling that conformed in any way to its sound. It didn't help matters that I couldn't pronounce my own name; it seemed a minimal expectation in one who took some pride in his academic achievements. My first name outweighed my second name, with its crispness and neat, hard bracketing of a single vowel with two of the most forceful consonant-clusters in the English language. That first name of mine was like an ice-cube; the last name was a head-cold. It had seemed to me, at eight and nine and ten, that the greatest mystery in the world, and the greatest potential for terror, were locked in the letters of my two names. I spent hours in my grandfather's old study, now a laundry room, using his old doctor's fountain pen-set and his old stacks of prescription pads, practicing signatures that would eliminate that last sound from my name.

"How is the old gentleman?" asked Mr. McArdle.

"Just fine."

"A bit of a handful now and then, I reckon. He likes to go for his strolls, y'know. In the summer, of course."

"He's fine."

"But a great man, in his time."

I deposited the "wee gift" that my grandmother had bundled for me: two thick slices of her fresh cracked-wheat bread, separated by waxed paper from a savory, crusty meat. These were unknown foods to me.

"Steak and kidney pie, ay, laddie?" In my previous life as a Southerner, carrying gifts to tradesmen was unthinkable (so was the idea of a special butchershop in those small Florida towns we'd inhabited; my mother had gone to the town's lone chain-store outlet, around back where the black people had their service-window opening onto the alley by the garbage cans, to ask for items that were our meat-staples but which were cat-food or "nigger food" down there—liver, kidneys, sweetbreads, and above all, tongue, her favorite, and my lunch-time sandwich, which could make my classmates retch as I bit into it).

"I have the order," he told me. "I was going to drop it off myself later on, when Cam comes in. My son, Campbell."

I nodded.

"How are your cousins? Fine lads. Clar-r-r-k's my name, too. Clarrrk McArrrdle. Clark's historically a MacArthur, you know. Like that Yankee general. The MacArthur tartan is one we can wear. What's your last name? I don't believe they ever told me."

I told him.

He frowned, screwed up his jolly old elf's face, as though preparing for some ultimate test of strength. But his voice came out muted, almost choked.

"You're an American lad, you say."

"Yes, sir."

"I've never in all my born days heard a name like that. You don't look a Chink. Are you sure you got it right?"

I told him it was my name as best I could pronounce it. He took it, as I half-intended, as approximating "Bligh."

"That's a very sorry name, if you ask me," he said. He stabbed at a piece of my grandmother's pie. "English to boot."

"No sir," I charged. "It's Canadian. French-Canadian, actually."

And here, in a butcher shop on Portage Avenue, I stepped ever so briefly behind the veil, out of the tribal tent, into the special solitude of Canadian life. The butcher's face was simply blank. It registered nothing; as though I'd not even come in or had not been seen. I had meant to say, *naw, it's not one of those foreign British things* . . . it's Canadian. My relatives maintained a discreet silence on things American, but for British institutions they manifested a keen dislike. Whenever the BBC news came on, every day at noon, beginning as it always did with an upper-class twit intoning news of the Royal Family, such as "The King today . . ."

my cousin would pipe up, ". . . cut a long, wet one in the Royal Crapper," or some such; it was still an era when Canadian national- ists looked to America for a counter-weight to the British presence. And definitely I was not an American, if you could overlook my accent. I am grandma's boy, and the Old Gentleman's grandson, and I've come to take my place here, trading steak and kidney pie for a few hand-picked lobes of glistening calves' liver. And I can prove I belong; I've got a Canadian name. The only words I knew with "Canadian" in them had "French-" in front of them. It went with "Canadian" the way "early" and "All-" went with "American," as a completion, an intensification of an otherwise ungraspable concept.

"No one ever said that," said the butcher. He moved behind the counter as though the floor were spread with coals; he jabbed out liver from a porcelain tray with a normal dinner fork, and then let it slide off the fork onto waxed paper, with a look that hovered on disgust.

"Understand me, Master Clarrrk," he said. "I have nothing in the world against you parrsonally. But I canna abide the French, as a race. They should stay in St. Bonny and not go mucking with the white races. That's my final warrd on the subject." He wrapped the liver in a purplish, brown paper and tied it neatly with cords. "Good day, lad," he said. "My best to the old folks."

VI.

Up on the second floor, in the bedroom we had converted to an apartment, with a hotplate for my father's coffee and a small skillet for my mother's eggs—the smoke-filled haven of my father—a small drama was being enacted that would alter all our lives. My mother had reactivated her old teacher's permit and was, by now, substituting on a near-daily basis in various parts of the city. I was in school, struggling to overcome the deficiencies of a rural South- ern background; thanks to family connections, I was not routinely demoted two grades (as was the case with American transfers), and was managing, with after school tutoring, to make a successful transition to the world of ink and nibs, formulas, and long composi- tions. I was singing British folk songs instead of Military Service Hymns: no one sang "O, Canada!" louder than I, every morning in the hall. And for the first time, I was enjoying my classmates. In

Florida, students were to be tolerated or avoided while pursuing the fugitive pleasures of the text. Here, there was no schoolyard fighting, despite the tempting target I must have offered. The captains of the various team-sports—most of them imposing Icelandic boys with names like Thordarson and Thorlakson—would choose me first, simply because I was obviously the worst. Selections were made in ascending order of competence. They took time to teach me the unfamiliar games, British Bulldog and broom hockey, and would even stop the action if they saw I was too hopelessly out of place.

No one could have been more displaced than my father. He'd ask me when it was safe to go downstairs and to slip outside (this necessitated checking on my grandfather and enduring his scolding for having snuck into the house from "the stables"). Whenever I'm sitting on a bus these days and see a passenger still outside, devouring the stub of a cigarette and then filling his lungs with a final drag before stepping aboard—to let it out all over the bus—I think back to my father and the way he transformed that house into a Saturday night tavern simply by coming downstairs. My grandmother smoked her cigarettes with barely any smoke, let alone after-smell.

He had been going to St. Boniface, and to the furniture stores in the Jewish North End of Winnipeg, the parts of town rich in contacts for the life he knew. Like my mother, he had a transferable skill. He worked a few days, and decided things were too slow, too old-fashioned. He didn't know the Canadian furniture scene anymore, and the American brands, when carried, were far too expensive. Of course he didn't mention anything to us about working or about looking for other work. That wouldn't be his style.

One day after school I went upstairs to read old magazines and the *Who's Who*. My father was there (he rarely was), at his place by the window, looking out on the snowy roof, up Stiles Street to Portage, in the distance. On his knees was a letter. On the window ledge were some notebook pages he must have stolen from me. When he saw me, he folded the letter back in the envelope. I tried to show I wasn't interested, but a small suitcase on the bed was packed.

I went over to my cousin's to shoot pool. My grandfather was sleeping; my father would have no trouble. I couldn't imagine where we'd be going next, but *West*, I remember excited me. I felt ready for it now.

I played pool till the phone rang. My aunt called me from the head of the stairs, "Clark, your mother."

No, I said, I hadn't seen him. I didn't know anything about it. She was crying. What can I *tell* them? she cried. I was looking for an apartment for us, she said. *We agreed; we'd try to settle down.*

He was gone, all right. Shirts, suits, shoes, and car: the salesman's clearing-out. My mother was already reframing it for her mother's and sister's sake: "Leo decided he could do better in the States. He's following a lead in . . . (I made it up: Denver) . . . Denver. He'll send for us when he locates an apartment." I even believed in Denver; I looked up a city-map and tried to memorize the grid. Years later, pursuing my own studies of another Franco-American whose life—given a different dominance in our family—I might have crossed, I again encountered those heroic late-forties and 1950 Denver streets of Neal Cassady and Jack Kerouac; madness to push this further, though a message to me seems to linger. Kerouac and Cassady were my father's world, the one he never escaped, and he died back inside it, in New Hampshire, as desolately as Kerouac did in his mother's transplanted Lowell kitchen in Florida. His father's name was Leo.

On the sheet of notebook paper, I found drafts of a letter to us that was never, finally, left. It said more or less what we expected; he'd gotten a lead, it looked good, and he trusted himself to make a better personal impression than he could in a letter mailed from Winnipeg. If he got it, we'd live better than we ever had. My mother, too, gazed out over the roof, down Stiles, at that one; no need to say the obvious.

She didn't notice the rest of the page, which wasn't a proper letter at all. It was a page of signature. His signature. *Lee Blaise*, it said, up and down several rows. Then, Lee R. Blaise, up and down many more.

"Lee Blaise," I said to myself. Yes, Yes. Clark Blaise. It looked right. It balanced. It was anchored.

🔥 🔥 🔥

HOW TO WRITE A POEM

fiction by GORDON LISH

from THE PARIS REVIEW

nominated by Gene Chipps

I TELL YOU, I am no more a sucker for this thing of poetry than the next fellow is. I mean, I can take it or leave it—a certain stewarded pressure, some modulated pissing and moaning, the practiced claims of a seasonal heart. But once in a blue moon I have in hand a poem whose small unfolding holds me to its period. It needn't be any great shakes, such a poem. I don't care two pins for what its quality is. Christ, no—literature's not what I look to poetry for.

Fear is.

You know. Fear—like *terror*.

You keep your head on straight, there'll be this breeze you'll start to feel, a sort of dainty sussuration of the words. That's when you can bet the poor sap's seen it coming at him—an ordinary universe, the itemless clutter of an unraveling world. First chance he gets, it's a whole new ball game, touching bases while he races home free, that little telltale wind on the page you're looking at as the gutless poet starts to work up speed.

Maybe I don't like poets—or people. But I just love to catch a poet at it, and then test myself against the thinglessness that made him cut and run. What I do is I pick it up where the poet's nerve dumped him, where he just couldn't stand to see there's still nothing in a place where something never was.

It's no big deal. You just face down what he, in his chickenheart, couldn't. Then you type your version up and sign your name. Next thing you do is get it printed as your own, sit back and listen to them call you brave.

It's the safest theft, a stolen poem—and who, tell me, doesn't steal something? Besides, show me what a poet dares demand his

145

right to. A public reading? Public subsidy? But certainly not a grand banality. Least of all the very one his cowardice dishonored! Forget it—this is a person who's afraid.

What brings me to these brusque disclosures is an experience of recent vintage, a poem I took over from a certain someone who is a woman, and have since passed off—not without applause—as my own.

Nothing to it.

Just you watch.

The text—I mean the one that came before me—tells us of a thing as follows: two women, the poet and a widow, the bereaved missus of the lover of the poet.

For how long had the lovers been lovers?

Long enough.

And the deceased deceased?

A less long time than that.

Whatever the precise numbers, we are talking about an adulterous liaison of the usual order.

Routine. The loved and the loveless.

Of course, the poet is herself married. But since her spouse never enters the poem by more than intimation, we are led, I think, to conclude that his relation to all this is of no concern and of less importance. I mean, insofar as people going and fucking whom they weren't supposed to, the poet's spouse doesn't figure into any of this at all. He does not *press,* that is—at least not on the mounting prospect of what we're sure must be coming.

Not so the dead man's wife. What I am suggesting is—what is suggested by the poet in the poem (oh yes, the poet, as I said, is *in* the poem, in the poem and speaking)—is that an air of discovery thickens over things very greatly: the unsuspecting widow, her husband's sneaky copulations. But, naturally, that's where we're headed, where the original text is taking us—toward exposure, toward widow-know-all.

(As for the one party the poem pays no mind to, now that the poet's version has been published—in not nearly so distinguished a setting as mine was—doesn't *he* know all too, even as I write this?

But perhaps the spouses of poets don't read poetry.

Perhaps that's why the poet was in this fix in the first place.

Fair enough—we'll stand agreed the poet had her reasons.)

What does it matter one way or the other, the poet's hubby, what he knows or doesn't? It's plain we're not required to render him more than passing notice. The poet urges as much.

One dismissive reference.

What happens is this.

In the poem, remember?

We see the poet and the widow at the widow's. Newly back from the cemetery? We're not informed. Just this—a blustery day, late autumn, late morning, the women in pullovers and cardigans, greys, tans, tweeds, second sweaters draped over shoulders, legs scissored back under buttocks.

A living room, a fire. Comfy. Cozy.

Are the principals seated on the floor?

I think so. I like to think so.

What we're told is the poet's here to lend a hand—help sort the dead man's papers, be good company, a goodly solace, a presence in a very empty house. So we see the women being women together, being friends together, fingering what the dead man said.

(Was he a poet, too? More than likely. Nowadays, there are many, many poets.)

We see them grieving lightly, smoothing skirts, reminiscing, sipping tea, making tidy. Well, we hear this, see that—I don't recollect if the poet really kept her senses keyed to this or that event. So we see or hear their speeches when they reach into a carton to read aloud a bit of this or that.

You know. Order, memory, fellowship. A little weeping. Women's shoulders, women's sweaters.

Nice.

When—you guessed it—there's the wife with her hand at the bottom of a carton, and then her hand up and out, a neat packet in it, envelopes, a certain shape and paper, a certain fragrance, the dead man's record of the poet's indiscretion—letters that give account of passion.

My God!

Etc., etc., etc.

But let's be adults here. It's not as bad as all that. After all, the man's dead and buried. Quite beyond scolding. The widow's seen plenty. The poet is a poet. Life is . . . life.

Oh, well.

So there we are (at the poet's placing), watching women being wiser—hearing them cry a little, hearing them laugh a little, and then, at last, seeing them, as veterans will, embracing.

I'm not so sure who speaks first, nor what the poet said was said—the poet's poem being somewhere in my household, but I being too caught up in this to get up to go and check. Let's just say the widow says, "All these years, all these years. And who *was* he? He was who you talked to in these letters."

And the poet?

Who remembers?

But I expect she says whatever's said to someone being spacious just for your benefit. Perhaps this: "No, no, no—it was you who had the best of him, the substance, the husband, the man." Etc., etc.

The deceased, in pursuit of this assertion, is then celebrated, in four deft lines, for his performance in the four arduous capacities of husband, citizen, father, provider.

Is there guile in this? Does the poet mean for us to take a tiny signal?

Consider—four roles, four lines? Why such a sweet symmetry? Is this art or artfulness? And consider even further: Is there or is there not a difference?

What's crucial is who's kidding—the poet in the poem or the poet that's outside it?

Balance, I really hate balance. A proper disproportion, that's the nervy thing.

So there they are, poet and widow, usurper and usurped. Unclothed as it were—even pretty close to naked—each of them jumpy to reach out and grab the nearest covering.

Which is the other.

So they hurry up and bury their embarrassment in the terry-cloth offered up by bodies.

Another embrace. Sort of sisterly. Good hugging. But it goes from there to a thing you'd call carnal. At which point, the poem has furnished us with the bulk of its text, the day (get this!) having, in its pliant time, accomplished (the poet tells us) a like progress.

So it's dusk when the two women make their way to bed, to do what the poet then gives us to imagine. But before we know it, the poet reappears, having projected (she explains) her astral body back to the room where she left us. We see, via her sight, the letters lying strewn among the papers. We see teacups, saucers, purses, shoes, two outer sweaters. We see these things as things at first, items on the widow's Chinese carpet.

The rest of the poem? Now there you have it! For it now labors to extract from the figure of these particulars a facsimile of the human spectacle, something serviceable in the way of meaning, the event quantified, the lesson learned.

This was the poem the poet published and that I—the genius that I am for spotting where a work has turned from the fearful vision in it—have since rewritten and passed along for eight dollars and the fun.

Now let me tell you what I did.

In my poem, nothing's different. Word for word, it's all the same—up until the astral body comes back for a summary. Just like the phony poet, I take a look around. I see the same artifacts, all the stuff that produced this emptiest of rooms.

I mean, I see the letters and the teacups and the sweaters and the shoes. These things and all the poet saw. But in my poem, where they are is on a span of decent-grade, wall-to-wall broadloom, bought when the price was reduced.

Now you know what art is.

And notice, was I ever even once a person in that house?

Skip it. It's all the same to me—the goddamn fancy carpet, what's on it, and its whereabouts.

PERSIMMONS

by LI-YOUNG LEE

from AMERICAN POETRY REVIEW

nominated by Mary Kinzie and Maura Stanton

In sixth grade Mrs. Walker
slapped the back of my head
and made me stand in the corner
for not knowing the difference
between persimmon and precision.
How to choose

persimmons. This is precision.
Ripe ones are soft and brown spotted.
Sniff the bottoms. The sweet one will be fragrant.
How to eat: put the knife away, lay down newspaper.
Peel the skin tenderly, not to tear the meat.
Chew the skin, suck it, and swallow.
Now, eat the meat of the fruit, so sweet,
all of it to the heart.
Donna undresses, her stomach is white.
In the yard, dewy and shivering with crickets,
we lay naked,
face-up, face-down.
I teach her Chinese.
Crickets: chu chu. Dew: I've forgotten.
Naked: I've forgotten.
Ni, wa: you and me.
I part her legs,
remember to tell her
she is beautiful as the moon.

Other words that got me in trouble were
fight and fright, wren and yarn.
Fight was what I did when I was frightened,
fright was what I felt when I was fighting.
Wrens are small, plain birds,
yarn is what one knits with.
Wrens are soft as yarn.
My mother made birds out of yarn.
I loved to watch her tie the stuff;
a bird, a rabbit, a wee man.

Mrs. Walker brought a persimmon to class
and cut it up so everyone could taste
a *Chinese apple*.
Knowing it wasn't ripe or sweet,
I didn't eat, but watched the other faces.

My mother said every persimmon had a sun
inside, something golden, glowing,
warm as my face.

Once, in the cellar, I found two wrapped in newspaper,
forgotten and not yet ripe.
I took both and set them on my bedroom windowsill,
where every morning a cardinal sang, *The sun, the sun*.

Finally understanding
he was going blind,
my father sat up all one night
waiting for a song,
a ghost, or something.
I gave him the persimmons,
swelled, heavy as sadness,
and sweet as love.

This year, in the muddy lighting of my parents' cellar,
I rummage, looking for something I lost.
My father sits on the tired, wooden stairs,
black cane between his knees, hand over hand,
gripping the handle.

He is so happy that I'm home.
I ask him how his eyes are, a stupid question.
All gone, he answers.

Under some blankets, I find a box of three scrolls.
I sit by him and untie them.
Three paintings by my father:
Hibiscus leaf, a white flower.
Two cats preening.
Two persimmons, so full they want to drop off the cloth.

He raises both hands to touch the cloth,
asks, *Which is this?*

This is persimmons, Father.

Oh, the feel of the wolftail on the silk,
the strength, the perfect tension
in the wrist.
I painted them hundreds of times eyes closed.
These I painted blind.
Some things never leave a person;
scent of the hair of one you love,
the texture of persimmons,
in your palm, the ripe weight.

CONFEDERATE GRAVES
IN LITTLE ROCK

by RICHARD HUGO

from CRAZYHORSE

nominated by CRAZYHORSE, *Jim Barnes and Steve Cannon*

Far from these stones, in my country wind shouts
but shouts no name. It hustles north
locked on one heading forever, and salmon enter
rivers on the dead run starting that remorseless
drive home to funereal pools. Children
seem forever preserved in youth by a fresh rain
out of the south, and birds ride thermals
with the easy wisdom of wings.

If I can, I'll die in that weather of home.
This air's not mine. The hum of various insects
compounds the heat. Not one cloud, not
one faint touch of wind. I arbitrarily pick
one name, a 16-year-old boy, John Brock
who fell holding the banner of battle in hands
calloused on his father's farm. He was home
in this heat. He could say: I'm dying at home.

I row among the dead stumps in a lake.
My bass plug settles and I reel at the speed
I believe fish swim. Nothing. I'd carve names
on stumps to resurrect the souls of dead trees
and make sure someone remembers the forest
that cracked off one terrible tornado ago.
That air howled "rebel" and the name of a family
destroyed by a blue rain of artillery.

In North Little Rock, poverty's shacks
fill with song. They're singing the last rites of one
more victim of murder—the mean word uttered—
the kind gun fired—the usual forms
filled out and filed—the usual suspect jailed.
They're singing from graves created by wrongs
that go back before wars were recorded
or graves marked by stones.

Maybe the best graves stay unmarked, the right words
never find themselves cut into stone.
Whatever the weather it could be home for one
blood or another. For certain the best wars
wear down for personal reasons. It's hard
to do battle in breezy country where sun
lights the highway and one cloud shades
your car, whatever speed you drive.

QUARREL

by ELLEN BRYANT VOIGT

from POETRY

nominated by Michael Blumenthal, Stanley Lindberg, and David Wojahn

Since morning they have been quarreling—
the sun pouring its implacable white bath
over the birches that are undressing
slyly, from the top down—and they hammer
at each other with their knives, nailfiles,
graters of complaint as the day unwinds,
the plush clouds lowering a gray matte
for the red barn. Lunch, the soup like
batting in their mouths, last week,
last year, they're moving on to always
and never, their shrill pitiful children
crowd around but they see the top of this
particular mountain, its glacial headwall,
the pitch is terrific all through dinner
and they are committed, the sun long gone,
the two of them back to back in the blank
constricting bed, like marbles on aluminum—
O this fierce love
that needs to reproduce in one another
wounds inflicted by the world.

𝅛 𝅛 𝅛

GRAVEYARD DAY

fiction by BOBBIE ANN MASON

from ASCENT

nominated by ASCENT

Holly, swinging her legs from the kitchen stool, lectures her mother on natural foods. Holly is ten.

Waldeen says, "I'll have to give your teacher a talking-to. She's put notions in your head. You've got to have meat to grow."

Waldeen is tenderizing liver, beating it with the edge of a saucer. Her daughter insists that she is a vegetarian. If Holly had said Rosicrucian, it would have sounded just as strange to Waldeen. Holly wants to eat peanuts, soyburgers, and yogurt. Waldeen is sure this new fixation has something to do with Holly's father, Joe Murdock, although Holly rarely mentions him. After Waldeen and Joe were divorced last September, Joe moved to Arizona and got a construction job. Joe sends Holly letters occasionally, but Holly won't let Waldeen see them. At Christmas he sent Holly a copper Indian bracelet with unusual marks on it. It is Indian language, Holly tells her. Waldeen sees Holly polishing the bracelet while she is watching TV.

Walden shudders when she thinks of Joe Murdock. If he weren't Holly's father, she might be able to forget him. Waldeen was too young when she married him, and he had a reputation for being wild, which he did not outgrow. Now she could marry Joe McClain, who comes over for supper almost every night, always bringing something special, such as roast or dessert. He seems to be oblivious to what things cost, and he frequently brings Holly presents. If Waldeen married Joe, then Holly would have a stepfather—something like a sugar substitute, Waldeen imagines. Shifting relationships confuse her. She doesn't know what marriage means anymore. She tells Joe they must wait. Her ex-husband is still on her mind, like the lingering after-effects of an illness.

Joe McClain is punctual, considerate. Tonight he brings fudge ripple ice cream and a half-gallon of Coke in a plastic jug. He kisses Waldeen and hugs Holly.

Waldeen says, "We're having liver and onions, but Holly's mad 'cause I won't make Soybean Supreme."

"Soybean *Delight*," says Holly.

"Oh, excuse me!"

"Liver is full of poison. The poisons in the feed settle in the liver."

"Do you want to stunt your growth?" Joe asks, patting Holly on the head. He winks at Waldeen and waves his walking stick at her playfully, like a conductor. Joe collects walking sticks, and he has an antique one that belonged to Jefferson Davis. On a gold band, in italics, it says Jefferson Davis. Joe doesn't go anywhere without a walking stick, although he is only thirty. It embarrasses Waldeen to be seen with him.

"Sometimes a cow's liver just explodes from the poison," says Holly. "Poisons are *oozing* out."

"Oh, Holly, hush, that's disgusting." Waldeen plops the pieces of liver onto a plate of flour.

"There's this restaurant at the lake that has Liver Lovers' Night," Joe says to Holly. "Every Tuesday is Liver Lovers' Night."

"Really?" Holly is wide-eyed, as if Joe is about to tell a long story, but Waldeen suspects Joe is bringing up the restaurant—Sea's Breeze at Kentucky Lake—to remind her that it was the scene of his proposal. Waldeen, not accustomed to eating out, studied the menu carefully, wavering between pork chops and T-bone steak and then suddenly, without thinking, ordering catfish. She was disappointed to learn that the catfish was not even local, but frozen ocean cat. "Why would they do that," she kept saying, interrupting Joe, "when they've got all the fresh channel cat in the world right here at Kentucky Lake?"

During supper, Waldeen snaps at Holly for sneaking liver to the cat, but with Joe gently persuading her, Holly manages to eat three bites of liver without gagging. Holly is trying to please him, as though he were some TV game show host who happened to live in the neighborhood. In Waldeen's opinion, families shouldn't shift memberships, like clubs. But here they are, trying to be a family. Holly, Waldeen, Joe McClain. Sometimes Joe spends the weekend, but Holly prefers weekends at Joe's house because of his shiny wood floors and his parrot that tries to sing "Inka Dinka Doo." Holly likes the idea of packing an overnight bag.

Waldeen dishes out the ice cream. Suddenly inspired, she suggests a picnic Saturday. "The weather's fairing up," she says.

"I can't," says Joe. "Saturday's graveyard day."

"Graveyard day?" Holly and Waldeen say together.

"It's my turn to clean off the graveyard. Every spring and fall somebody has to rake it off." Joe explains that he is responsible for taking geraniums to his grandparents' graves. His grandmother always kept the pot in her basement during the winter, and in the spring she took it to her husband's grave, but she had died in November.

"Couldn't we have a picnic at the graveyard?" asks Waldeen.

"That's gruesome."

"We never get to go on picnics," says Holly. "Or anywhere." She gives Waldeen a look.

"Well, okay," Joe says. "But remember, it's serious. No fooling around."

"We'll be real quiet," says Holly.

"Far be it from me to disturb the dead," Waldeen says, wondering why she is speaking in a mocking tone.

After supper, Joe plays rummy with Holly while Waldeen cracks pecans for a cake. Pecan shells fly across the floor, and the cat pounces on them. Holly and Joe are laughing together, whooping loudly over the cards. They sound like contestants on "Let's Make a Deal." Joe Murdock wanted desperately to be on a game show and strike it rich. He wanted to go to California so he would have a chance to be on TV and so he could travel the freeways. He drove in the stock car races, and he had been drag racing since he learned to drive. Evel Knievel was his hero. Waldeen couldn't look when the TV showed Evel Knievel leaping over canyons. She told Joe many times, "He's nothing but a show-off. But if you want to break your fool neck, then go right ahead. Nobody's stopping you." She is better off without Joe Murdock. If he were still in town, he would do something to make her look foolish, such as paint her name on his car door. He once had WALDEEN painted in large red letters on the door of his LTD. It was like a tattoo. It is probably a good thing he is in Arizona. Still, she cannot really understand why he had to move so far away from home.

After Holly goes upstairs, carrying the cat, whose name is Mr. Spock, Waldeen says to Joe, "In China they have a law that the men have to help keep house." She is washing dishes.

Joe grins. "That's in China. This is *here*."

Waldeen slaps at him with the dish towel, and Joe jumps up and grabs her. "I'll do all the housework if you marry me," he says. "You can get the Chinese to arrest me if I don't."

"You sound just like my ex-husband. Full of promises."

"Guys named Joe are good at making promises." Joe laughs and hugs her.

"All the important men in my life were named Joe," says Waldeen, with pretended seriousness. "My first real boyfriend was named Joe. I was fourteen."

"You always bring that up," says Joe. "I wish you'd forget about them. You love *me*, don't you?"

"Of course, you idiot."

"Then why don't you marry me?"

"I just said I was going to think twice is all."

"But if you love me, what are you waiting for?"

"That's the easy part. Love is easy."

In the middle of "The Waltons," C. W. Redmon and Betty Mathis drop by. Betty, Waldeen's best friend, lives with C.W., who works with Joe on a construction crew. Waldeen turns off the TV and clears magazines from the couch. C. W. and Betty have just returned from Florida and they are full of news about Sea World. Betty shows Waldeen her new tote bag with a killer whale pictured on it.

"Guess who we saw at the Louisville airport," Betty says.

"I give up," says Waldeen.

"Colonel Sanders!"

"He's eighty-four if he's a day," C. W. adds.

"You couldn't miss him in that white suit," Betty says. "I'm sure it was him. Oh, Joe! He had a walking stick. He went strutting along—"

"No kidding!"

He probably beats chickens to death with it," says Holly, who is standing around.

"That would be something to have," says Joe. "Wow, one of the Colonel's walking sticks."

"Do you know what I read in a magazine?" says Betty. "That the Colonel Sanders outfit is trying to grow a three-legged chicken."

"No, a four-legged chicken," says C.W.

"Well, whatever."

Waldeen is startled by the conversation. She is rattling ice cubes, looking for glasses. She finds an opened Coke in the refrigerator, but it may have lost its fizz. Before she can decide whether to open the new one Joe brought, C. W. and Betty grab glasses of ice from her and hold them out. Waldeen pours the Coke. There is a little fizz.

"We went first class the whole way," says C.W. "I always say, what's vacation for if you don't splurge?"

"I thought we were going to buy *out* Florida," says Betty. "We spent a fortune. Plus, I gained a ton."

"Man, those jumbo jets are really nice," says C.W.

C.W. and Betty seem changed, exactly like all people who come back from Florida with tales of adventure and glowing tans, except that they did not get tans. It rained. Waldeen cannot imagine flying, or spending that much money. Her ex-husband tried to get her to go up in an airplane with him once—a $7.50 ride in a Cessna—but she refused. If Holly goes to Arizona to visit him, she will have to fly. Arizona is probably as far away as Florida.

When C.W. says he is going fishing on Saturday, Holly demands to go along. Waldeen reminds her about the picnic. "You're full of wants," she says.

"I just wanted to go somewhere."

"I'll take you fishing one of these days soon," says Joe.

"Joe's got to clean off his graveyard," says Waldeen. Before she realizes what she is saying, she has invited C.W. and Betty to come along on the picnic. She turns to Joe. "Is that okay?"

"I'll bring some beer," says C.W. "To hell with fishing."

"I never heard of a picnic at a graveyard," says Betty. "But it sounds neat."

Joe seems embarrassed. "I'll put you to work," he warns.

Later, in the kitchen, Waldeen pours more Coke for Betty. Holly is playing solitaire on the kitchen table. As Betty takes the

Coke, she says, "Let C.W. take Holly fishing if he wants a kid so bad." She has told Waldeen that she wants to marry C.W., but she does not want to ruin her figure by getting pregnant. Betty pets the cat. "Is this cat going to have kittens?"

Mr. Spock, sitting with his legs tucked under his stomach, is shaped somewhat like a turtle.

"Heavens, no," says Waldeen. "He's just fat because I had him nurtured."

"The word is *neutered!*" cries Holly, jumping up. She grabs Mr. Spock and marches up the stairs.

"That youngun," Waldeen says with a sigh. She feels suddenly afraid. Once, Holly's father, unemployed and drunk on whiskey and Seven-Up, snatched Holly from the school playground and took her on a wild ride around town, buying her ice cream at the Tastee-Freez, and stopping at Newberry's to buy her an "All in the Family" Joey doll, with correct private parts. Holly was eight. When Joe brought her home, both were tearful and quiet. The excitement had worn off, but Waldeen had vividly imagined how it was. She wouldn't be surprised if Joe tried the same trick again, this time carrying Holly off to Arizona. She has heard of divorced parents who kidnap their own children.

The next day Joe McClain brings a pizza at noon. He is working nearby and has a chance to eat lunch with Waldeen. The pizza is large enough for four people. Waldeen is not hungry.

"I'm afraid we'll end up horsing around and won't get the graveyard cleaned off," Joe says. "It's really a lot of work."

"Why's it so important, anyway?"

"It's a family thing."

"Family. Ha!"

"Why are you looking at me in that tone of voice?"

"I don't know what's what anymore," Waldeen wails. "I've got this kid that wants to live on peanuts and sleeps with a cat—and didn't even see her daddy at Christmas. And here *you* are, talking about family. What do you know about family? You don't know the half of it."

"What's got into you lately?"

Waldeen tries to explain. "Take Colonel Sanders, for instance. He was on 'I've Got A Secret' once, years ago, when nobody knew who he was. His secret was that he had a million-dollar check in his pocket for selling Kentucky Fried Chicken to John Y. Brown. *Now* look what's happened. Colonel Sanders sold it but didn't get rid of it. He's still Colonel Sanders. John Y. sold it too and he can't get rid of it either. Everybody calls him the Chicken King, even though he's governor. That's not very dignified, if you ask me."

"What in Sam Hill are you talking about? What's that got to do with families?"

"Oh, Colonel Sanders just came to mind because C.W. and Betty saw him. What I mean is, you can't just do something by itself. Everything else drags along. It's all *involved*. I can't get rid of my ex-husband just by signing a paper. Even if he *is* in Arizona and I never lay eyes on him again."

Joe stands up, takes Waldeen by the hand, and leads her to the couch. They sit down and he holds her tightly for a moment. Waldeen has the strange impression that Joe is an old friend who moved away and returned, years later, radically changed. She doesn't understand the walking sticks, or why he would buy such an enormous pizza.

"One of these days you'll see," says Joe, kissing her.

"See what?" Waldeen mumbles.

"One of these days you'll see. I'm not such a bad catch."

Waldeen stares at a split in the wallpaper.

"Who would cut your hair if it wasn't for me?" he asks, rumpling her curls. "I should have gone to beauty school."

"I don't know."

"Nobody else can do Jimmy Durante imitations like I can."

"I wouldn't brag about it."

On Saturday Waldeen is still in bed when Joe arrives. He appears in the doorway of her bedroom, brandishing a shiny black walking stick. It looks like a stiffened black racer snake.

"I overslept," Waldeen says, rubbing her eyes. "First I had insomnia. Then I had bad dreams. Then—"

"You said you'd make a picnic."

"Just a minute. I'll go make it."

"There's not time now. We've got to pick up C.W. and Betty."

Waldeen pulls on her jeans and a shirt, then runs a brush through her hair. In the mirror she sees blue pouches under her eyes. She catches sight of Joe in the mirror. He looks like an actor in a vaudeville show.

They go into the kitchen, where Holly is eating granola. "She promised me she'd make carrot cake," Holly tells Joe.

"I get blamed for everything," says Waldeen. She is rushing around, not sure why. She is hardly awake.

"How could you forget?" asks Joe. "It was your idea in the first place."

"I didn't forget. I just overslept." Waldeen opens the refrigerator. She is looking for something. She stares at a ham.

When Holly leaves the kitchen, Waldeen asks Joe, "Are you mad at me?" Joe is thumping his stick on the floor.

"No. I just want to get this show on the road."

"My ex-husband always said I was never dependable, and he was right. But *he* was one to talk. He had his head in the clouds."

"Forget your ex-husband."

"His name is Joe. Do you want some juice?" Waldeen is looking for orange juice, but she cannot find it.

"No." Joe leans on his stick. "He's over and done with. Why don't you just cross him off your list?"

"Why do you think I had bad dreams? Answer me that. I must be afraid of *something.*"

There is no juice. Waldeen closes the refrigerator door. Joe is smiling at her enigmatically. What she is really afraid of, she realizes, is that he will turn out to be just like Joe Murdock. But it must be only the names, she reminds herself. She hates the thought of a string of husbands, and the idea of a step-father is like a substitute host on a talk show. It makes her think of Johnny Carson's many substitute hosts.

"You're just afraid to do anything new, Waldeen," Joe says. "You're afraid to cross the street. Why don't you get your ears pierced? Why don't you adopt a refugee? Why don't you get a dog?"

"You're crazy. You say the weirdest things." Waldeen searches the refrigerator again. She pours a glass of Coke and watches it foam.

It is afternoon before they reach the graveyard. They had to wait for C.W. to finish painting his garage door, and Betty was in the shower. On the way, they bought a bucket of fried chicken. Joe said little on the drive into the country. When he gets quiet,

Waldeen can never figure out if he is angry or calm. When he put the beer cooler in the trunk, she caught a glimpse of the geraniums in an ornate concrete pot with a handle. It looked like a petrified Easter basket. On the drive, she closed her eyes and imagined that they were in a funeral procession.

The graveyard is next to the woods on a small rise fenced in with barbed wire. A herd of Holsteins grazes in the pasture nearby, and in the distance the smokestacks of the new industrial park send up lazy swirls of smoke. Waldeen spreads out a blanket, and Betty opens beers and hands them around. Holly sits down under a tree, her back to the gravestones, and opens a Vicki Barr flight stewardess book.

Joe won't sit down to eat until he has unloaded the geraniums. He fusses over the heavy basket, trying to find a level spot. The flowers are not yet blooming.

"Wouldn't plastic flowers keep better?" asks Waldeen. "Then you wouldn't have to lug that thing back and forth." There are several bunches of plastic flowers on the graves. Most of them have fallen out of their containers.

"Plastic, yuck!" cries Holly.

"I should have known I'd say the wrong thing," says Waldeen.

"My grandmother liked geraniums," Joe says.

At the picnic, Holly eats only slaw and the crust from a drumstick. Waldeen remarks, "Mr. Spock is going to have a feast."

"You've got a treasure, Waldeen," says C.W. "Most kids just want to load up on junk."

"Wonder how long a person can survive without meat," says Waldeen, somewhat breezily. Suddenly, she feels miserable about the way she treats Holly. Everything Waldeen does is so roundabout, so devious, a habit she is sure she acquired from Joe Murdock. Disgusted, Waldeen flings a chicken bone out among the graves. Once, her ex-husband wouldn't bury the dog that was hit by a car. It lay in a ditch for over a week. She remembers Joe saying several times, "Wonder if the dog is still there?" He wouldn't admit that he didn't want to bury it. Waldeen wouldn't do it because he had said he would do it. It was a war of nerves. She finally called the Highway Department to pick it up. Joe McClain, at least, would never be that barbaric.

Joe pats Holly on the head and says, "My girl's stubborn, but she knows what she likes." He makes a Jimmy Durante face which causes Holly to smile. Then he brings out a surprise for her, a bag of trail mix, which includes pecans and raisins. When Holly pounces on it, Waldeen notices that Holly is not wearing the Indian bracelet her father gave her. Waldeen wonders if there are vegetarians in Arizona.

Blue sky burns through the intricate spring leaves of the maples on the fence line. The light glances off the gravestones—a few thin slabs that date back to the last century and eleven sturdy blocks of marble and granite. Joe's grandmother's grave is a brown heap.

Waldeen opens another beer. She and Betty are stretched out under a maple tree and Holly is reading. Betty is talking idly about the diet she intends to go on. Waldeen feels too lazy to move. She watches the men work. While C.W. rakes leaves, Joe washes off the gravestones with water he brought in a camp carrier. He scrubs out the carvings with a brush. He seems as devoted as a man washing and polishing his car on a Saturday afternoon. Betty plays he-loves-me-he-loves-me-not with the fingers of a maple leaf. The fragments fly away in a soft breeze.

From her Sea World tote bag, Betty pulls out playing cards with Holly Hobbie pictures on them. The old-fashioned child with the bonnet hiding her face is just the opposite of Waldeen's own strange daughter. Waldeen sees Holly secretly watching the men. They pick up their beer cans from a pink, shiny tombstone and drink a toast to Joe's great-great-grandfather Joseph McClain, who was killed in the Civil War. His stone, almost hidden in dead grasses, says 1841-1862.

"When I die, they can burn me and dump the ashes in the lake," says C.W.

"Not me," says Joe. "I want to be buried right here."

"*Want* to be? You planning to die soon?"

Joe laughs. "No, but if it's my time, then it's my time. I wouldn't be afraid to go."

"I guess that's the right way to look at it."

Betty says to Waldeen, "He'd marry me if I'd have his kid."

"What made you decide you don't want a kid, anyhow?" Waldeen is shuffling the cards, fifty-two identical children in bonnets.

"Who says I decided? You just do whatever comes natural. Whatever's right for you." Betty has already had three beers and she looks sleepy.

"Most people do just the opposite. They have kids without thinking. Or get married."

"Talk about decisions," Betty goes on. "Did you see 'Sixty Minutes' when they were telling about Palm Springs? And how all those rich people live? One woman had hundreds of dresses and Morley Safer was asking her how she ever decided what on earth to wear. He was *strolling* through her closet. He could have played *golf* in her closet."

"Rich people don't know beans," says Waldeen. She drinks some beer, then deals out the cards for a game of hearts. Betty snatches each card eagerly. Waldeen does not look at her own cards right away. In the pasture, the cows are beginning to move. The sky is losing its blue. Holly seems lost in her book, and the men are laughing. C.W. stumbles over a footstone hidden in the grass and falls onto a grave. He rolls over, curled up with laughter.

"Y'all are going to kill yourselves," Waldeen says, calling to him across the graveyard.

Joe tells C.W. to shape up. "We've got work to do," he says.

Joe looks over at Waldeen and mouths something. "I love you"? Her ex-husband used to stand in front of the TV and pantomime singers. She suddenly remembers a Ku Klux Klansman she saw on TV. He was being arrested at a demonstration, and as he was led away in handcuffs, he spoke to someone off-camera, ending with a solemn message, "I *love* you." He was acting for the camera, as if to say, "Look what a nice guy I am." He gave Waldeen the creeps. That could have been Joe Murdock, Waldeen thinks. Not Joe McClain. Maybe she is beginning to get them straight in her mind. They have different ways of trying to get through to her. The differences are very subtle. Soon she will figure them out.

Waldeen and Betty play several hands of hearts and drink more beer. Betty is clumsy with the cards and loses three hands in a row. Waldeen cannot keep her mind on the cards either. She wins accidentally. She can't concentrate because of the graves, and Joe standing there saying "I love you." If she marries Joe, and doesn't get divorced again, they will be buried here together. She picks out a likely spot and imagines the headstone and the green carpet and the brown leaves that will someday cover the twin mounds. Joe and C.W. are bringing leaves to the center of the graveyard and piling them on the place she has chosen. Waldeen feels peculiar, as if the burial plot, not a diamond ring, symbolizes the promise of marriage. But there is something comforting about the thought, which she tries to explain to Betty.

"Ooh, that's gross," says Betty. She slaps down a heart and takes the trick.

Waldeen shuffles the cards for a long time. The pile of leaves is growing dramatically. Joe and C.W. have each claimed a side of the graveyard, and they are racing. It occurs to Waldeen that she has spent half her life watching guys named Joe show off for her. Once, when Waldeen was fourteen, she went out onto the lake with Joe Suiter in a rented pedal-boat. When Waldeen sees him at the bank, where he works, she always remembers the pedal-boat and how they stayed out in the silver-blue lake all afternoon, ignoring the people waving them in from the shore. When they finally returned, Joe owed ten dollars in overtime on the boat, so he worked Saturdays, mowing yards, to pay for their spree. Only recently in the bank, when they laughed over the memory, he told her that it was worth it, for it was one of the great adventures of his life, going out in a pedal-boat with Waldeen, with nothing but the lake and time.

Betty is saying, "We could have a nice bon-fire and a wienie roast—what *are* you doing?"

Waldeen has pulled her shoes off. And she is taking a long, running start, like a pole vaulter, and then with a flying leap she lands in the immense pile of leaves, up to her elbows. Leaves are flying and everyone is standing around her, forming a stern circle, and Holly, with her book closed on her fist, is saying, "Don't you know *any*thing?"

𝄞 𝄞 𝄞

THE DISHWASHER

fiction by ROBERT MCBREARTY

from MISSISSIPPI REVIEW

nominated by MISSISSIPPI REVIEW, *Patricia Goedicke and Elizabeth Inness-Brown*

I'M A DISHWASHER IN A RESTAURANT. I'm not trying to impress anybody. I'm not bragging. It's just what I do. It's not the glamorous job people make it out to be. Sure, you make a lot of dough and everybody looks up to you and respects you, but then again there's a lot of responsibility. It weighs on you. It wears on you. Everybody wants to be a dishwasher these days, I guess, but they've got an idealistic view of it.

"C'mon kid, c'mon kid, hustle, hustle, move 'em," the manager's calling in that friendly, staccato voice of his, pushing me on. "Move 'em kid, rinse that crap off, kid, first into the side sink, we don't want all that grease and stuff in the main sink, c'mon, *hustle*. WE'RE GETTING BEHIND!"

(The waiters, waitresses, cook are there now too, right behind him, cheering me on.)

"C'mon, we need some silverware, we need some plates, we got people waiting, they're getting fierce out there. Give me a god-damn plate for Christ's sake."

"Okay, kid," the manager says, "after you rinse off all that ketchup and chicken bones into the side sink, throw the plates and stuff into the soapy water in the main sink. Let 'em soak. Now as they're soaking, dig in there, that's right dig in there and—"

"Into all that grime and gray-black sudsy water, sir?" I ask.

"That's right. Scoop for the ones that have been soaking. Scoop!" (He makes a scooping motion with his hand.)

"I think this one's ready, sir."

168

"Whats' that? . . . Egg yolk . . . I see egg yolk on that, Christ, get that off."

The cook shouts in that cheerful, chiding voice of his, "You *turkey!* I got eggs ready, I got hamburgers, I got fries, I got onion rings, I got grease popping up in my eyes, but I don't have a lousy plate to put anything on. *Turkey!*" (The cook respects me a lot, and knows I take it in stride. He mumbles and swears some more, but I know that's just his style when he's tense.)

"All right, kid." (The manager's bent over with me now. We're both bent right over that steaming, bubbling, smelly sink together. He's got his top button loose. I can see the sweat pouring off of his face. He's breathing heavy, but his face is set dead and calm now, though I know what's going on under the surface. I respect him for his self control since he has a generally florid personality.)

"Okay, kid, how ya feeling?"

"I'm okay," I say.

"You got your mind on something today, don't you?"

I shake my head. "I'm just getting warm."

"You don't seem like you're really with it."

A plate squirts out of my soapy, slippery hands. I grab for it, knock it back up in the air, it twirls, the manager grabs for it, and sends it twisting back up in the other direction. I grab for it again, but it slides through my hands like trying to grab a fish in the water, and lands with a sick sounding clang and breaks into pieces on the floor.

The manager looks at me and coughs. He sort of stares up at the ceiling for awhile, as if wondering if it's ready for a new paint job. I watch the colors in his face change to red. I know he feels as badly about this as I do.

"Thank God it wasn't a glass," I say, "those really bust into bits."

"Are you happy here?" he asks me.

"Sure."

"I mean, are you really happy?"

(The manager takes a personal as well as a professional interest in me. I respect him for that.) "Of course," I say, "who wouldn't be?"

"Okay, we're going to forget about that one," he says. "It was just a plate." He gives a funny sort of laugh, short violent bursts of air, as if someone is standing behind him and giving him bear hugs.

"I don't mean to be *rude*," Sally, the waitress, comes back to say, "but people are really getting downright hostile. Some fellow out there is claiming he's having a low blood sugar attack. Can't we at least get them some coffee?"

The manager breathes. "Okay, let's start from scratch again. A whole new ballgame. You give the cups just a quick rinse. Okay, just a quick rinse, and then you put them on that tray, and then you run them through the machine, one cycle, takes five minutes, you take them out of the machine, you carry the tray out to the front where the waitress can get to them. Okay?"

"What tray?"

"That one."

"Oh. The blue one?"

He makes a funny little sound again, sort of a cross between laughing and gagging. "Yeah," he says, taking me suddenly by the arm in an affectionate gesture and leading me to the tray in question. He takes my hand in his in a fatherly way and places it on the tray. He rubs my hand across the tray so that I will get a good feel of it.

"Hard rubber?" I say.

"That's right. Hard rubber," he says.

"It doesn't melt in the machine?"

"No. Never. This is the tray that you will use. This is the tray that you will run through the machine with the coffee cups on it."

"Oh, okay," I say.

We bend back over the sink. The steam rises into my nostrils and I give a little laugh.

"What's funny?" the manager asks.

"I think of Macbeth. You know, the witch's cauldron."

"Oh, you think of Macbeth."

"I saw the movie," the cook calls. "Pretty weird." He gives a high pitched laugh. I know he's stoned.

Sally comes back. "I'm *not* going back out there," she says. "*I'm* the one who has to take all the guff when something isn't ready. I'm *not* going back out there until I can give them something."

"Tell them some jokes," the cook calls. "Do a little dance for them, Sally baby."

"I just wish *somebody* would tell me what's going on back here."

"Look, we got some paper cups," the manager says. "Stall them, give them some water in paper cups."

"Water in paper cups, beautiful," she says.

"One time in Atlanta," the cook starts.

"Oh, shut up," the manager says. "Just cook and shut up."

The cook slams down his spatula. "You riding me, man? You want me to walk off? You want me to walk off right now?"

"Lay off, Charlie. I didn't mean anything."

"You riding me?"

"Forget it. Okay? I'm sorry."

"You can do the cooking, you like it so much," he mumbles. But he goes back to flipping the hamburger patties. (The manager and the cook always have a friendly, lively, give-and-take. I respect their relationship a lot.)

"Okay kid, how we doing?" the manager says, rolling up his shirt sleeves. He edges in next to me at the sink, and stares at me, intent, and asks, looking down now at the gray stinking water, "You want me to go in there with you? You want me to go down in there with you?"

I put a tentative hand into the water. I go down a few inches. Something heavy, with a harsh, leathery feel butts up against my hand, and I jerk back. You never know what's floating around down there. I take a deep breath though, and say, "I'll handle it. I'll do it. Let me just try it my way."

He sighs heavily. He looks suddenly tired and old. "Okay, give it a go."

And I do. The plates come back with ketchup smeared across them, chicken bones, crumpled napkins, bits of bread dripping gravy, cigarettes stuffed out in egg yolks, mutilated french fries. I knock the the paper and bones and ashes off into the trash can under the sink. Then I give a quick rinse in the sink to get the main crap off, then I drop them into the sudsy water of the main sink to soak off any crusty stuff. I scoop back into the sink, pull something out, give a quick wipe, and then put everything on a tray and run it through the machine on a five minute cycle. The machine finishes. (Meanwhile, waiting for the machine, I keep up with the other stuff, knock the crap off, rinse, soak, scoop, wipe.) The machine gives a buzz. I throw it open. Great clouds of steam boil my facial flesh. Sort the plates, silverware, glasses, cups. Run the plates over to the cook. Run the cups and glasses out front where the waitress can get to them. The waitress runs back, grabs the plates from the cook that he's just filled with food, meanwhile crying out, "Two fries, three deluxe burgers, one without onions, two chicken dinners, substitute peas for corn on one of them."

"Substitute peas for corn," the cook repeats scornfully. He doesn't respect people who want substitutions.

But I'm really moving now. Trash off. Crap off. Rinse. Soak. Scoop. Wipe. Machine. Remove. Sort. Run over to the cook. I'm moving and the manager's calling out in his staccato voice, "Okay, kid, now we're going, now we're going, keep 'em moving, way to go kid, keep it up, we're catching up now," and out of the corner of my eye I catch the cook giving me a quick glance and nodding his head approvingly. The kid's okay, he's thinking, the kid's going to be okay. Sally, hustling by, gives me a little pat on the shoulder. "*Okay*," she says, "*Okay*." (I respect her and may be falling in love with her.)

The manager's grinning now. "Okay, doing a good job tonight, boys, yes sir. We're starting to do a good job. How we coming on the chicken, Charlie?"

"Chicken's okay," he says, "let's move the potatoes."

"I could move the potatoes," I say, "where do you want them?"

"No, kid, that's okay." The manager calls to Sally, "Move the potatoes. How's the cole slaw?"

"They ain't going for the cole slaw," Charlie says. "Day cook put too much mayonnaise, I think. You got to watch the mayonnaise on the cole slaw."

We're *going*, yes, sir. I'm hot. I'm really hot. I'm sweating and shaking, but I'm moving fast, and the manager even says, "Hey, slow it down, don't kill yourself."

"No sir, I won't. I'm okay."

You can feel it when a restaurant's moving. Everybody's working in synchronization. You hear dishes and forks rattling, grease hissing. You feel like you're beating *them*. And them's the customers. The customer's out to get you and you're out to get them, and if you make them happy, you've *beaten* them.

"Slow it down, kid, slow it down," the manager says, "don't burn yourself out."

And then Sally comes back into the grill area, and we all know, before she's said anything, that something's gone wrong.

"What is it, Sally?" the manager asks.

Slowly, she raises up a silver spoon for all of us to see. "Greasy," she says. "Somebody sent it back. Said it was greasy."

She looks down. None of us say anything. The cook whistles and turns back to his burgers, flipping them slowly and methodically. The manager takes the spoon from her, and tosses it back into the gray-black sudsy water. "Wash it again for the clown out there," he says.

I go back to my dishes, but I feel sick and disappointed inside. Later though the manager takes me aside and says gruffly, "It wasn't your fault. Dont' get down. It was a tough break. The wrong spoon, the wrong guy . . ."

Later, down in the basement, I talk to the famous old janitor, who is mopping with slow, steady strokes.

"You like it here?" I ask. "You like the work?"

"Ah, I used to," he says. "I liked the reputation, you know. I liked the girls that came with it."

"But you don't like it anymore?"

"Ah, now it's just money. Everybody's in it for the money. And I go along with them. I take what I can get. But I always loved it too. I was pretty good in my day." He sweeps his hand around at the clean looking rows of canned goods. "It all starts down here with me, you know. I make a mistake one day and it's all up. Yeah, I'm tired of the responsibility. I think I'm going to hang it up pretty soon."

"What will you do then?"

"I'm thinking about getting me a condominium in Vail. I've got a hell of a lot put away over the years." He chuckles and runs a hand through his thin white hair. "I guess I did all right after all."

I watch him go on mopping, mopping with even, steady, sliding strokes, that shows me that while he has probably never been truly gifted, not gifted in the way I sense I am in my field, he has made up for it with dedication, reliability, and respect.

🔥 🔥 🔥

THE POND AT DUSK

by JANE KENYON

from THE IOWA REVIEW

nominated by THE IOWA REVIEW *and Joyce Peseroff*

When a fly wounds the water the wound
soon heals. Swallows tilt and twitter
overhead, dropping now and then toward
the outward-radiating signs of food.

The green haze on the trees changes
into leaves, and what looks like smoke
floating over the neighbor's barn
is nothing but apple blossoms.

But sometimes what looks like disaster
is disaster. Then the men struggle
with the casket, just clearing the pews;
then long past dark a woman sits,
distracted, over the ledger and the till.

SITTING BETWEEN TWO MIRRORS

by JAMES BAKER HALL

from POETRY

nominated by Sherod Santos

What I like best
is making lists of what I like
best. The good days

are inventories, near & far. I seldom leave
without a book. Where would I go without a book?
You would say my life is a lottery—
that I am the only one

without a ticket. You would say
your life is better—you say it over & over,
you do. What do I do? I put things in boxes.

I move boxes around. I have many things,
some of them mine. I care for them.
That is what I do. I do simple things.
I move them around clearing places
to move them around. I tell you
I do things, over & over.
Now you tell me

something. Talk is what you do. It comforts
me to hear you talk. You would say that you are
mine too, my not-simple thing. Say it
again, today, I want to hear you say
something, today. I wash your clothes.
I buy you fresh bread.
I get the paper

to see what day it is. I laugh. I act
as though I know what day it is. I laugh
again—it comforts me to hear you
laugh. I talk

on the phone. I water the plants while I talk
on the phone. I make coffee while I talk
on the phone. I am a person
like anyone else. I act
like a person. A person

calls & says whatever it is
a person says. Says
today. A person says today.
I say today

over & over, getting it straight. Getting it
straight is what I do, I want to get it
straight. I say

What did you say?
Tell me something again,
comfort me.
Today? Yes, today.
Is that it?
And when is that?

္ ္ ္

from A SEQUENCE ON SIDNEY LANIER

by ANDREW HUDGINS

from MSS

nominated by MSS

Postcards of the Hanging: 1869

1. Clifford, we've grown too far apart.
   So yesterday I bought some postal cards
   and have resolved to send them all to you.
   But what to say? I'm doing well
   and Mary says to say she's doing fine.

2. Remember the large oak beside Hall's barn?
   This afternoon I saw a nigger hanged from it
   For spitting on a white girl's shoes.
   Or so he said. She said he grabbed her breast.
   I suspect the truth is somewhere in between.
   When he said *shoes*, they went berserk.

3. Last night, disturbed, I woke at four o'clock.
   I'd dreamed but couldn't recollect the dream.
   So I got up and studied law
   until I smelled the bacon, eggs, and tea,
   and ate myself into the solid world.

4. In church it hit me like a cannonball:
   I'd dreamed of feet—such gorgeous feet,
   so soft and smooth and dainty pink,
   they looked as if they'd never walked on the earth,
   as if they were intended just to walk on air.

5. As far as hangings go, this one was quiet.
   By the time they got him to the tree, they'd calmed.
   They sat him on a mule and slipped the noose
   around his neck. He sang—or started to—
   "Swing Low, Sweet Chariot," but lost his place,
   and when he paused somebody slapped the mule
   across the rump. It wouldn't move,
   and finally they had to push the mule
   from underneath the colored man.

6. The bottoms of his boots were not worn through.
   Those boots! They kicked and lashed above the mule
   and tried to get a purchase on the air
   before they stilled and seemed to stand on tip-toe
   lke another acorn hanging from the oak.

7. A colored peddlar who had stopped to watch
   asked them if he could have the dead man's boots.
   "He can't use dem gennelmens," he said.
   "And dese ol' boots of mine is shot."
   "Why sure, old timer, Take the boots
   and anything else you want off this dead fool."
   "I thank ya kindly, gennelmens. Jus' the boots."

8. I blacked my boots after supper tonight—
   walking boots, working boots, Sunday shoes,
   and even the calvary boots I wore
   when we were living on horseback in the war.
   That Charlie was a handsome horse!
   When I was through, my hands were black
   as the dead man's hands. Even my face was smudged.
   Now clean, the boots give off an eerie glow
   like a family of cats lined up beside the fire.

9. Does this make sense to you? This afternoon
    I walked five miles into the woods,
    sat down in a clearing in the pines,
    and sobbed and sobbed until my stomach hurt.
    When I stopped, I tied the laces together,
    slung the freshly dirty boots around my neck,
    and walked, barefooted, home. When I got there
    my feet were sticking to the ground with blood
    and lots of dirt was clinging to the skin.
    It helped a bit. I'm doing better now
    and Mary says to say she's doing fine.

SUMMER, AN ELEGY

fiction by ELLEN GILCHRIST

from THE IOWA REVIEW

nominated by THE IOWA REVIEW, *Gordon Lish and David Wojahn*

HIS NAME WAS SHELBY after the town where his mother was born, and he was eight years old and all that summer he had to wear a little black sling around the index finger of his right hand. He had to wear the sling because his great-granddaddy had been a famous portrait painter and had paintings hanging in the White House.

Shelby was so high-strung his mother was certain he was destined to be an artist like his famous ancestor. So, when he broke his finger and it grew back crooked, of course they took him to a specialist. They weren't taking any chances on a deformity standing in his way.

All summer long he was supposed to wear the sling to limber up the finger, and in the fall the doctor was going to operate and straighten it. While he waited for his operation Shelby was brought to Bear Garden Plantation to spend the summer with his grandmother and as soon as he got up every morning he rode over to Esperanza to look for Matille.

He would come riding up in the yard and tie his saddle pony to the fence and start talking before he even got on the porch. He was a beautiful boy, five months younger than Matille and a head shorter, and he was the biggest liar she had ever met in her life.

Matille was a lonely little girl, the only child in a house full of widows. She was glad of this noisy companion fate had delivered to Issaquena County right in the middle of a World War.

Shelby would wait for her while she ate breakfast, helping himself to pinch-cake, or toast, or cold cornbread, or muffins, walking around the kitchen touching everything and talking a mile a minute to anyone who would listen, talking and eating at the same time.

"My daddy's a personal friend of General MacArthur's," he would be saying. "They were buddies at Auburn. General MacArthur wants him to come work in Washington but he can't go because what he does is too important." Shelby was standing in the pantry door making a pyramid out of the Campbell's Soup cans. "Every time my daddy talks about going to Washington my momma starts crying her head off and goes to bed with a backache." He topped off the pyramid with a can of tomato paste and returned to the present. "I don't know how anyone can sleep this late," he said. "I'm the first one up at Bear Garden every single morning."

Matille would eat breakfast as fast as she could and they would start out for the bayou that ran in front of the house at the end of a wide lawn.

"Did I tell you I'm engaged to be married," Shelby would begin, sitting next to Matille in the swing that went out over the water, pumping as hard as he could with his thin legs, staring off into the sky.

"Her daddy's a colonel in the Air Corps. They're real rich." A dark secret look crossed his face. "I already gave her a diamond ring. That's why I've got to find the pearl. So I can get enough money to get married. But don't tell anyone because my momma and daddy don't know about it yet."

"There aren't any pearls in mussels," Matille said. "Guy said so. He said we were wasting our time chopping open all those mussels."

"They do too have pearls," Shelby said coldly. "Better ones than oysters. My father told me all about it. Everyone in New Orleans knows about it."

"Well," Matille said, "I'm not looking for any pearls today. I'm going to the store and play the slot machine."

"You haven't got any nickels."

"I can get one. Guy'll give me one." Guy was Matille's uncle. He was 4-F. He had lost an eye in a crop-dusting accident and was having to miss the whole war because of it. He couldn't get into the Army, Navy, Marines or Air Corps. Even the Coast Guard had turned him down. He tried to keep up a cheerful face, running around Esperanza doing the work of three men, being extra nice to everyone, even the German war prisoners who were brought over from the Greenville Air Force Base to work in the fields.

He was always good for a nickel, sometimes two or three if Matille waited until after he had his evening toddies.

"If you help me with the mussels I'll give you two nickels," Shelby said.

"Let me see," Matille said, dragging her feet to slow the swing. It was nice in the swing with the sun beating down on the water below and the pecan trees casting a cool shade.

Shelby pulled a handkerchief from his pocket and untied a corner. Sure enough, there they were, three nickels and a quarter and a dime. Shelby always had money. He was the richest boy Matille had ever known. She stared down at the nickels, imagining the cold thrill of the slot machine handle throbbing beneath her touch.

"How long?" she said.

"Until I have to go home," Shelby said.

"All right," Matille said. "Let's get started."

They went out to the shed and found two rakes and a small hoe and picked their way through the weeds to the bayou bank. The mud along the bank was black and hard-packed and broken all along the water line by thick tree roots, cypress and willow and catalpa and water oak. They walked past the cleared-off place with its pier and rope swings and on down to where the banks of mussels began.

The mussels lay in the shallow water as far as the rake could reach, an endless supply, as plentiful as oak leaves, as plentiful as the fireflies that covered the lawn at evening, as plentiful as the minnows casting their tiny shadows all along the water's edge, or the gnats that buzzed around Matille's face as she worked, raking and digging and chopping, earning her nickels.

She would throw the rake down into the water and pull it back full of the dark-shelled, inedible, mud-covered creatures. Moments later, reaching into the same place, dozens more would have appeared to take their place.

They would rake in a pile of mussels, then set to work breaking them open with the hoe and screwdriver. When they had opened twenty or thirty, they would sit on the bank searching the soft flesh for the pearl. Behind them and all around them were piles of rotting shells left behind in the past weeks.

"I had my fortune told by a voodoo queen last Mardi Gras," Shelby said. "Did I ever tell you about that? She gave me a charm made out of a dead baby's bone. You want to see it?"

"I been to Ditty's house and had my fortune told," Matille said. "Ditty's real old. She's the oldest person in Issaquena County. She's older than Nannie-Mother. She's probably the oldest person in the whole state of Mississippi." Matille picked up a mussel and examined it, running her finger inside, then tossed it into the water. Where it landed a dragonfly hovered for a moment, then rose in the humid air, its electric-blue tail flashing.

"You want to see the charm or not?" Shelby said, pulling it out of his pocket.

"Sure," she said. "Give it here."

He opened his hand and held it out to her. It looked like the wishbone from a tiny chicken. "It's voodoo," Shelby said. He held it up in the air, turning to catch the sunlight. "You can touch it but you can't hold it. No one can hold it but the master of it. Here, go on and touch it if you want to."

Matille reached and stroked the little bone. "What's it good for?" she said.

"To make whatever you want to happen. It's white magic. Momma Ulaline is real famous. She's got a place on Royal Street right next to an antique store. My Aunt Katherine took me there when she was babysitting me last Mardi Gras."

Matille touched it again. She gave a little shudder.

"Well, let's get back to work," Shelby said, putting the charm into his pocket, wiping his hands on his playsuit. His little black sling was covered with mud. "I think we're getting someplace today. I think we're getting warm."

They went back to work. Shelby was quiet, dreaming of treasure, of the pearl that lay in wait for him, of riches beyond his wildest dreams, of mansions and fine automobiles and chauffeurs and butlers and maids and money, stacks and stacks of crisp five-dollar bills and ten-dollar bills and twenty-dollar bills. Somewhere in Steele's Bayou the pearl waited. It loomed in his dreams. It lay in wait for him beneath the roots of a cypress or water oak or willow.

Every morning when he woke he could see it, all morning as he dug and raked and chopped and Matille complained and the hot sun beat down on the sweating mud and the stagnant pools of minnows and the fast-moving, evil-looking gars swimming by like gunboats, all day the pearl shone in his mind, smooth and mysterious, cold to the touch.

They worked in silence for awhile, moving downstream until they were almost to the bridge.

"Looks like we could get something for all these shells," Matille said, examining the inside of one. It was all swirls of pink and white, like polished marble. "Looks like they ought to be worth something!"

"We could make dogfood out of the insides," Shelby said. "Mr. Green Bagett had a dog that ate mussels. My grandmother told me all about it. He would carry them up to the road in his mouth and when the sun made them open he would suck out the insides." Shelby leaned on his hoe, making a loud sucking noise. "He was a dog named Harry after Mr. Bagett's dentist and he would eat mussels all day long if nobody stopped him."

"Why don't we carry these mussels up to the road and let the sun open them?" Matille said.

"Because it takes too long that way," Shelby said. "This is quicker."

"We could make ashtrays out of the shells," Matille said.

"Yeah," Shelby said. "We could sell them in New Orleans. You can sell anything in the French Quarter."

"We could paint them and decorate them with flowers," Matille said, falling into a dream of her own, picturing herself wearing a long flowered dress, pushing a cart through the crowded streets of a city, selling ashtrays to satisfied customers.

Now they were almost underneath the bridge. Here the trees were thicker and festooned with vines that dropped into the water like swings. It was darker here, and secret.

The bridge was a fine one for such a small bayou. It was a drawbridge with high steel girders that gleamed like silver in the flat Delta countryside. The bridge had been built to connect the two parts of the county and anyone going from Grace to Baleshed or Esperanza or Panther Brake or Greenfields had to pass that way. Some mornings as many as seven cars and trucks passed over it. All day small black children played on the bridge and fished from it and leaned over its railings looking down into the brown water, chunking rocks at the mud turtles or trying to hit the mean-looking gars and catfish that swam by in twos or threes with their teeth showing.

This morning there were half a dozen little black boys on the bridge and one little black girl wearing a clean apron. Her hair was in neat cornrows with yellow yarn plaited into the braids. Her head looked like the wing of a butterfly, all yellow and black and brown and round as it could be.

"What y'all doing?" the girl called down when they got close enough to hear. "What y'all doing to them mussels?"

"We're doing an experiment," Shelby called back.

"Let's get Teentsy and Kale to help us," Matille said. "Hey, Teentsy," she called out, but Shelby grabbed her arm.

"Don't get them down here," he said. "I don't want everyone in the Delta in on this."

"They all know about it anyway," Matille said. "Guy told Grand-daddy everyone at the store was laughing about us the other day. He said Baby Doll was busting a gut laughing at us for chopping all these mussels."

"I don't care," Shelby said, putting his hands on his hips and looking out across the water with the grim resignation of the born artist. "They don't know what we're doing it for."

"Well, I'm about worn out," Matille said. "Let's go up to the store and get Mavis to give us a drink."

"Let's open a few more first. Then we'll get a drink and go over to the other side. I think it's better over there anyway. There's sand over there. You got to have sand to make pearls."

"We can't go over there," Matille said. "That's not our property. That's Mr. Donleavy's place."

"He don't care if we dig some mussels on his bayou bank, does he?"

"I don't know. We got to ask him first. He's got a real bad temper."

"Let's try under this tree," Shelby said. "This looks like a good place. There's sand in this mud." He was bending down trying the mud between his fingers, rubbing it back and forth to test the consistency. "Yeah, let's try here. This feels good."

"What y'all tearing up all those mussels for," Kale called down from his perch on the bridge. "They ain't good for nothing. You can't even use them for bait."

"We're gonna make ashtrays out of them," Shelby said. "We're starting us an ashtray factory."

"Where about?" Kale said, getting interested, looking like he would come down and take a look for himself.

"Next to the store," Shelby said. "We're gonna decorate them and sell them in New Orleans. Rich folks will pay a lot for real mussel ashtrays."

"That ought to hold them for awhile," he said to Matille. "Let them talk about that at the store. Come on, let's open a few more. Then we'll get us a drink."

"All right," Matille said. "Let's try under this tree." She waded out into the water until it was up to her ankles, feeling the cold mud ooze up between her toes. She reached out with the rake. It caught, and she began pulling it up the shore, backing as she pulled, tearing the bark off the edges of the tree roots. The rake caught in the roots and she reached down to free it.

"Matille!" Shelby yelled. "Matille! Look out!" She heard his voice and saw the snake at the same moment, saw the snake and Shelby lifting the hoe and her hand outlined against the water, frozen and dappled with sunlight and the snake struggling to free itself and the hoe falling toward her hand, and she dropped the rake and turned and was running up the bank, stumbling and running, with Shelby yelling his head off behind her, and Teentsy and Kale and the other children rose up from the bridge like a flock of little blackbirds and came running down the hill to see what the excitement was.

"I got him," Shelby yelled. "I cut him in two. I cut him in two with the hoe. I got him."

Matille sank down on the edge of the road and put her head on her knees.

"She's fainting," Kale called out, running up to her. "Matille's fainting."

"No, she ain't." Teentsy said. "She's all right." Teentsy sat down by Matille and put a hand on her arm, patting her.

"It was a moccasin," Shelby yelled. "He was big around as my arm. After I killed him the top half was still alive. He struck at me four times. I don't know if I'm bit or not."

"Where's he gone to now?" Kale said.

"I don't know," Shelby said, pulling off his shirt. "Come look and see if he bit me." The children gathered around searching Shelby's skin for bite marks. His little chest was heaving with excitement and his face was shining. With his shirt off he looked about as big around as a blue jay. His little black sling was flopping around his wrist and his rib cage rose and fell beneath the straps of his seersucker playsuit.

"Here's one!" Teentsy screamed, touching a spot on Shelby's back, but it turned out to be an old mosquito bite.

"Lay down on the ground," Kale yelled, "where we can look at you better."

"Where do you *think* he bit you?" Teentsy said.

But Shelby was too excited to lay down on the ground. All he wanted to do was jump up and down and tell his story over and over.

Then the grown people heard the commotion and came out from the store. Mavis Findley and Mr. Beaumont and Baby Doll and R.C. and Overflow came hurrying down the road and grabbed hold of Shelby so they could see where the snake bit him.

"Didn't nothing bite him, Mr. Mavis," Kale said. "He kilt it. He kilt it with the hoe."

"He almost chopped my hand off," Matille said, but no one was listening.

Then Mavis and Baby Doll and Overflow escorted Matille and Shelby back to the big house with the black children skipping along beside and in front of them like a disorderly marching band.

By the time the procession reached the house the porch was full of ladies. Matille's mother and grandmother and great-grandmother and several widowed aunts had materialized from their rooms and were standing in a circle. From a distance they looked like a great flowering shrub. The screen door was open and a wasp buzzed around their heads threatening to be caught in their hairnets.

The ladies all began talking at once, their voices rising above and riding over and falling into each other in a long chorus of mothering.

"Thank goodness you're all in one piece," Miss Babbie said, swooping up Matille and enfolding her in a cool fragrance of dotted

Swiss and soft yielding bosom and the smell of sandalwood and the smell of coffee and the smell of powder.

Miss Nannie-Mother, who was 96, kissed her on the forehead and called her Eloise, after a long-dead cousin. Miss Nannie-Mother had lived so long and grown so wise that everyone in the world had started to look alike to her.

The rest of the ladies swirled around Shelby. Matille struggled from her grandmother's embrace and watched disgustedly from the doorframe as Shelby told his story for the tenth time.

"I didn't care what happened to me," Shelby was saying. "No rattlesnake was biting a lady while I was in the neighborhood. After I chopped it in two the mouth part came at me like a chicken with its head cut off."

"He almost chopped my hand off," Matille said again, but the only ones listening to her were Teentsy and Kale, who stood by the steps picking petals off Miss Teddy's prize pansies and covering their mouths with their hands when they giggled to show what nice manners they had.

"This is what comes of letting children run loose like wild Indians," Miss Teddy was saying, brandishing a bottle of Windsor nail polish.

"Whatever will Rhode Hotchkiss think when she hears of this?" Miss Nell Grace said.

"She'll be terrified," Miss Babbie answered. "Then go straight to her knees to thank the Lord for the narrow escape."

"I knew something was going to happen," Miss Hannie Clay said, her hands still full of rickrack for the smock she was making for her daughter in Shreveport. "I knew something was coming. It was too quiet around here all morning if you ask my opinion."

Matille leaned into the door frame with her hands on her hips watching her chances of ever going near the bayou again as long as she lived growing slimmer and slimmer.

Sure enough, when Matille's grandfather came in from the fields for the noon meal he made his pronouncement before he even washed his hands or hung up his hat.

"Well, then," he said, looking down from his six feet four inches and furrowing his brow. "I want everyone in this house to stay away from the bayou until I can spare some men to clear the brush. Shelby, I'm counting on you to keep Matille away from there, you hear me?"

"Yes sir," Shelby said. He stood up very straight, stuck out his hand and shook on it.

Now he's done it, Matille thought. Now our luck's all gone. Now nothing will be the same.

Now the summer wore on into August, and Shelby and Matille made a laboratory in an old chicken house, and collected a lot of butterflies and chloroformed them with fingernail polish remover, and they taught a fox terrier puppy how to dance on his hind legs, and spent some time spying on the German prisoners, and read all the old love letters in the trunks under the house, and built a broad jump pit in the pasture, but it was not the same. Somehow the heart had gone out of the summer.

Then one morning the grown people decided it was time for typhoid shots, and no matter how Matille cried and beat her head against the floor she was bathed and dressed and sent off in the back seat of Miss Rhoda's Buick to Doctor Findley's little brick office overlooking Lake Washington.

As a reward Matille was to be allowed to stay over at Bear Garden until the pain and fever subsided.

In those days vaccinations were much stronger than they are now, and well cared-for children were kept in bed for twenty-four hours nursing their sore arms, taking aspirin dissolved in sugar water and being treated as though they were victims of the disease itself.

Miss Rhoda made up the twin beds in Shelby's mother's old room, made them up with her finest Belgian linens and decorated the headboards with Hero medals cut from cardboard and hand-painted with watercolors.

The bedroom was painted ivory and the chairs were covered with blue and white chintz imported from Paris. It was the finest room Matille had ever slept in. She snuggled down in the pillows admiring the tall bookcases filled with old dolls and mementos of Carrie Hotchkiss's brilliant career as a Rolling Fork cheerleader.

Miss Rhoda bathed their faces with lemon water, drew the Austrian blinds and went off for her nap.

"Does yours hurt yet?" Shelby said, rubbing his shot as hard as he could to get the pain going. "Mine's killing me already."

"It hurts some," Matille said, touching the swollen area. "Not too much." She was looking at Shelby's legs, remembering something Guy had shown her, something that had happened a long time ago, something hot and exciting, something that felt like fever, and like fever, made everything seem present, always present, so that she could not remember where or how it had happened or how long a time had passed since she had forgotten it.

"Just wait till tonight," Shelby rattled on. "You'll think your arm's fixing to fall off. I almost died from mine last year. One year a boy in New Orleans did die. They cut off his arm and did everything they could to save him but he died anyway. Think about that, being in a grave with only one arm." Shelby was talking faster than ever, to hide his embarrassment at the way Matille was looking at him.

"I can't stand to think about being buried, can you?" he continued, "all shut up in the ground with the worms eating you. I'm getting buried in a mausoleum if I die. They're these little houses up off the ground made out of concrete. Everyone in New Orleans that can afford it gets buried in mausoleums. That's one good thing about living here."

"You want to get in bed with me?" Matille said, surprised at the sound of her own voice, so clear and orderly in the still room.

"Sure," Shelby said, "if you're scared. It scares me to death to think about being buried and stuff like that. Are you scared?"

"I don't know," Matille said. "I just feel funny. I feel like doing something bad."

"Well, scoot over then," Shelby said, crawling in beside her.

"You're burning up," she said, putting a hand on his forehead to see if he had a fever. Then she put her hand on his chest as if to feel his heartbeat, and then, as if she had been doing it every day of her life, she reached down inside his pajamas for the strange hard secret of boys.

"I want to see it, Shelby," she said, and he lay back with his hands stiff by his sides while she touched and looked to her heart's content.

"Now you do it to me," she said, and she guided his fingers up and down, up and down, up and down the thick tight opening between her legs.

The afternoon was going on for a long time and the small bed was surrounded by yellow light and the room filled with the smell of mussels.

Long afterwards, as she lay in a cool bed in Acapulco, waiting for her third husband to claim her as his bride, Matille would remember that light and how, later that afternoon, the wind picked up and could be heard for miles away, moving toward Issaquena County with its lines of distant thunder, and how the cottonwood leaves outside the window had beat upon the house all night with their exotic crackling.

"You better not tell anyone about this ever, Shelby," Matille said, when she woke in the morning. "You can't tell anyone about it, not even in New Orleans."

"The moon's still up," Shelby said, as if he hadn't heard her. "I can see it out the window."

"How can the moon be up," Matille said. "It's daylight."

"It stays up when it wants to," Shelby said, "haven't you ever seen that before?"

It was Matille who made up the game now. They cleaned out an old playhouse that had belonged to Matille's mother and made a bed from a cot mattress. Matille would lie down on the mattress with her hand on her head pretending to have a sick headache.

"Come sit by me, Honey," she would say. "Pour me a glass of sherry and come lie down till I feel better."

"God can see in this playhouse," Shelby said, pulling his hand away.

"No, he can't, Shelby," Matille said, sitting up and looking him hard in the eye. "God can't see through tin. This is a tin roof and God can't see through it."

"He can see everywhere," Shelby said. "Father Godchaux said so."

"Well, he can't see through tin," Matille said. "He can't be everywhere at once. He's got enough to do helping out the Allies without watching little boys and girls every minute of the night and day." Matille was unbuttoning Shelby's playsuit. "Doesn't that feel good, Shelby?" she said. "Doesn't that make you feel better?"

"God can see everywhere," Shelby insisted. "He can see every single thing in the whole world."

"I don't care," Matille said. "I don't like God anyway. If God's so good why did he let Uncle Robert die. And why did he make alligators and snakes and send my daddy off to fight the Japs. If God's so good why'd he let the Jews kill his own little boy."

"You better not talk like that," Shelby said, buttoning his suit back together. "And we better get back before Baby Doll comes looking for us again."

"Just a little bit more," Matille said. "Just till we get to the part where the baby comes out."

August went by as if it had only lasted a moment. Then one afternoon Miss Rhoda drove Shelby over in the Buick to say goodbye. He was wearing long pants and had a clean sling on the finger and he had brought Matille the voodoo bone wrapped in tissue paper to keep for him.

"You might need this," he said, holding it out to her. He looked very grown up standing by the stairs in his city clothes and Matille thought that maybe she would marry Shelby when she grew up and be a fine married lady in New Orlenas.

Then it was September and the cotton went to the gin and Matille was in the third grade and rode to school on the bus.

One afternoon she was standing by the driver while the bus clattered across the bridge and came to a halt by the store. It was a cool day. A breeze was blowing from the northeast and the cypress trees were turning a dusty red and the wild persimmons and muscadines were making.

Matille felt the trouble before she even got off the bus. The trouble reached out and touched her before she even saw the ladies standing on the porch in their dark dresses. It fell across her shoulders like a cloak. It was as if she had touched a single strand of a web and felt the whole thing tremble and knew herself to be caught forever in its trembling.

They found out, she thought. Shelby told them. I knew he couldn't keep a secret, she said to herself. Now they'll kill me. Now they'll beat me like they did Guy.

She looked down the gravel road to the house, down the long line of pecan and elm trees and knew that she should turn and go back the other way, should run from this trouble, but something made her keep on moving toward the house. I'll say he lied, she thought. I'll say I didn't do it. I'll say he made it up, she said to herself. Everyone knows what a liar Shelby is.

Then her mother and grandmother and Miss Babbie came down off the porch and took her into the parlor and sat beside her on the sofa. And Miss Hannie and Miss Nell Grace and Overflow and

Baby Doll stood around her in a circle and told her the terrible news.

"Shelby is dead, Matille," her grandmother said. The words slid over her like water poured on stones.

Shelby had gone to the hospital to have his finger fixed and he had lain down on the table and put the gas mask over his face and the man who ran the gas machine made a mistake and Shelby had gone to sleep, and nothing could wake him up, not all the doctors or nurses or shots or slaps on the face or screams or prayers or remorse in the world could wake him. And that was the Lord's will, blessed be the name of the Lord, Amen.

Later the ladies went into the kitchen to make a cold supper for anyone who felt like eating and Matille walked down to the bayou and stood for a long time staring down into the water, feeling strangely elated, as though this were some wonderful joke Shelby dreamed up.

She stared down into the tree roots, deep down into the muddy water, down to the place where Shelby's pearl waited, grew and moved inside the soft watery flesh of its mother, luminous and perfect and alive, as cold as the moon in the winter sky.

NOTES ON FAILURE

by JOYCE CAROL OATES

from THE HUDSON REVIEW

nominated by THE HUDSON REVIEW, *Robert Phillips, Grace Schulman, and Barbara Thompson*

> To Whom the Mornings stand for Nights
> What must the Midnights—be!
> —Emily Dickinson

I<small>F WRITING QUICKENS ONE'S SENSE OF LIFE</small> like falling in love, like being precariously in love, it is not because one has any confidence in achieving *success*, but because one is most painfully and constantly made aware of *mortality:* the persistent question being, Is this the work I fail to complete, is this the "posthumous" work that will draw forth so much pity . . .?

The practicing writer, the writer-at-work, the writer immersed in his or her project, is not an entity at all, let alone a person, but some curious mélange of wildly varying states of mind, clustered toward what might be called the darker end of the spectrum: indecision, frustration, pain, dismay, despair, remorse, impatience, outright failure. To be honored in midstream for one's labor would be ideal, but impossible; to be honored after the fact is always too late, for by then another project has been begun, another concatenation of indefinable states. Perhaps one must contend with vaguely warring personalities, in some sort of sequential arrangement?—perhaps premonitions of failure are but the soul's wise economy, in not risking hubris?—it cannot matter,

194

for, in any case, the writer, however battered a veteran, can't have any real faith, any absolute faith, in his stamina (let alone his theoretical "gift") to get him through the ordeal of *creating*, to the plateau of *creation*. One is frequently asked whether the process becomes easier, with the passage of time, and the reply is obvious—*Nothing gets easier with the passage of time, not even the passing of time*.

The artist, perhaps more than most people, inhabits failure, degrees of failure and accommodation and compromise: but the terms of his failure are generally secret. It seems reasonable to believe that failure may be a truth, or at any rate a negotiable fact, while success is a temporary illusion of some intoxicating sort, a bubble soon to be pricked, a flower whose petals will quickly drop. If despair is—as I believe it to be—as absurd a state of the soul as euphoria, who can protest that it feels more substantial, more reliable, less out of scale with the human environment—? When it was observed to T. S. Eliot that most critics are failed writers, Eliot replied: "But so are most writers."

Though most of us inhabit degrees of failure or the anticipation of it, very few persons are willing to acknowledge it, out of a vague but surely correct sense that it is not altogether American to do so. *Your standards are unreasonably high, you must be exaggerating, you must be of a naturally melancholy and saturnine temperament* . . . From this pragmatic vantage point "success" itself is but a form of "failure," a compromise between what is desired and what is attained. One must be stoic, one must develop a sense of humor. And, after all, there is the example of William Faulkner who considered himself a failed poet; Henry James returning to prose fiction after the conspicuous failure of his playwriting career; Ring Lardner writing his impeccable American prose because he despaired of writing sentimental popular songs; Hans Christian Andersen perfecting his fairy tales since he was clearly a failure in other genres—poetry, playwriting, life. One has only to glance at *Chamber Music* to see why James Joyce specialized in prose.

Whoever battles with monsters had better see that it does not turn him into a monster. And if you gaze too long into an abyss— the abyss will gaze back into you. So Nietzsche cryptically warns us: and it is not implausible to surmise that he knew, so far as his own battles, his own monsters, and his own imminent abyss were

concerned, much that lay before him: though he could not have
guessed its attendant ironies, or the ignoble shallowness of the
abyss. Neither does he suggest an alternative.

The spectre of failure haunts us less than the spectre of failing—
the process, the activity, the absorbing delusionary stratagems.
The battle lost, in retrospect, is, after all, a battle necessarily lost to
time: and, won or lost, it belongs to another person. But the battle
in the process of being lost, each gesture, each pulsebeat . . . This
is the true abyss of dread, the unspeakable predicament. *To Whom
the Mornings stand for Nights,/What must the Midnights—be!*

But how graceful, how extraordinary these pitiless lines, written
by Emily Dickinson some four years earlier, in 1862:

> The first Day's Night had come—
> And grateful that a thing
> So terrible—had been endured—
> I told my Soul to sing—
>
> She said her Strings were snapt—
> Her bow—to Atoms blown—
> And so to mend her—gave me work
> Until another Morn—
>
> And then—a Day as huge
> As Yesterdays in pairs,
> Unrolled its horror in my face—
> Until it blocked my eyes—
>
> My Brain—begun to laugh—
> I mumbled—like a fool—
> And tho' 'tis Years ago—that Day—
> My Brain keeps giggling—still.
>
> And Something's odd—within—
> That person that I was—
> And this One—do not feel the same—
> Could it be Madness—this?

Here the poet communicates, in the most succinct and compelling imagery, the phenomenon of the ceaseless process of *creating*:
the instruction by what one might call the ego that the Soul "sing,"
despite the nightmare of "Yesterdays in pairs"—the valiant effort of

keeping language, forging language, though the conviction is overwhelming that "the person that I was—/And this One—do not feel the same." (For how, a scant poem later, *can* they be the same?) And again, in the same year:

> The Brain, within its Groove
> Runs evenly—and true—
> But let a Splinter swerve—
> 'Twere easier for You—
>
> To put a Current back—
> When Floods have slit the Hills—
> And scooped a Turnpike for Themselves—
> And trodden out the Mills—

The Flood that is the source of creativity, and the source of self-oblivion: sweeping away, among other things, the very Soul that would sing. And is it possible to forgive Joseph Conrad for saying, in the midst of his slough of despair while writing *Nostromo*—surely one of the prodigious feats of the imagination, in our time—that writing is but the "conversion of nervous force" into language?—so profoundly bleak an utterance that one supposes it must be true. For, after all, as the busily productive Charles Gould remarks to his wife, a man must apply himself to *some* activity.

Even that self-proclaimed "teacher of athletes," that vehement rejector of "down-hearted doubters . . ./Frivolous, sullen, moping, angry, affected, dishearten'd, atheistical," that Bard of the American roadway who so wears us out with his yawp of barbaric optimism, and his ebullient energy—even the great Whitman himself confesses that things are often quite different, quite different indeed. When one is alone, walking at the edge of the ocean, at autumn, "held by this electric self out of the pride of which I utter poems"—

> O baffled, balk'd, bent to the very earth,
> Oppressed with myself that I have dared to open my mouth,
> Aware now that amid all that blab whose echoes recoil upon me I
>   have not once had the least idea who or what I am,
> But that before all my arrogant poems the real Me stands yet
>   untouch'd, untold, altogether unreach'd,

> Withdrawn far, mocking me with self-congratulatory signs and bows,
> With peals of distant ironical laughter at every word I have written
> Pointing in silence to these songs, and then to the sand beneath.
> —"As I Ebb'd with the Ocean of Life"

Interesting to note that these lines were published in the same year, 1860, as such tirelessly exuberant and more "Whitmanesque" poems as "For You O Democracy," "Myself and Mine" ("Myself and mine gymnastic ever,/To stand the cold or heat, to take good aim with a gun, to sail a/boat, to manage horses, to beget superb children"), and "I Hear America Singing." More subdued and more eloquent is the short poem, "A Clear Midnight," of 1881, which allows us to overhear the poet in his solitude, the poet no longer in the blaze of noon on a public platform:

> This is thy hour O Soul, thy free flight into the wordless,
> Away from books, away from art, the day erased, the lesson done,
> Thee fully forth emerging, silent, gazing, pondering the themes thou lovest best,
> Night, sleep, death and the stars.

One feels distinctly honored, to have the privilege of such moments: to venture around behind the tapestry, to see the threads in their untidy knots, the loose ends hanging frayed.

Why certain individuals appear to devote their lives to the phenomenon of interpreting experience in terms of structure, and of language, must remain a mystery. It is not an alternative to life, still less an escape from life, it *is* life: yet overlaid with a peculiar sort of luminosity, as if one were, and were not, fully inhabiting the present tense. Freud's supposition—which must have been his own secret compulsion, his sounding of his own depths—that the artist labors at his art to win fame, power, riches, and the love of women, hardly addresses itself to the fact that, such booty being won, the artist often intensifies his effort: and finds much of life, apart from that effort, unrewarding. Why, then, this instinct to interpret; to transpose flickering and transient thoughts into the relative permanence of language; to give oneself over to decades of obsessive labor, in the service of an elusive "transcendental" ideal, that, in any case, will surely be misunderstood?—or scarcely valued at all? Assuming that all art is metaphor, or metaphorical, what really *is* the motive for metaphor?—is there a motive?—or, in fact, metaphor?—can one say anything finally, with unqualified confidence, about any work of art?—why it strikes a profound, irresistible, and occasionally life-altering response in some individuals, yet means very little to others. In this, the art of reading hardly differs from the art of writing, in that its most intense pleasures and pains must remain private, and cannot be communicated to others. Our secret affinities remain secret even to ourselves . . . we fall in love with certain works of art, as we fall in love with certain individuals, for no very clear motive.

In 1955, in the final year of his life, as profusely honored as any writer in history, Thomas Mann wryly observed in a letter that he had always admired Hans Christian Andersen's fairy tale, "The Steadfast Tin Soldier." "Fundamentally," says Mann, "it is the symbol of my life." And what is the "symbol" of Mann's life? Andersen's toy soldier is futilely in love with a pretty dancer, a paper cut-out; his fate is to be cruelly, if casually, tossed into the fire by a child, and melted down to the shape "of a small tin heart." Like most of Andersen's tales the story of the steadfast tin soldier is scarcely a children's story, though couched in the mock-simple language of childhood; and one can see why Thomas Mann felt such kinship with it, for it begins: "There were once five and twenty tin soldiers, all brothers, for they were the offspring of the same old tin spoon. Each man shouldered his gun, kept his eyes well to the front, and wore the smartest red and blue uniform imaginable. . . . All the soldiers were exactly alike with one exception, and he differed from the rest in having only one leg. For he was made last, and there was not quite enough tin left to finish him. However, he stood just as well on his one leg as the others did on two. In fact he was the very one who became famous."

Is the artist secretly in love with failure, one might ask.

Is there something dangerous about "success," something finite and limited and, in a sense, historical: the passing over from *striving*, and *strife*, to *achievement*—? One thinks again of

Nietzsche, that most profound of psychologists, who tasted the poisonous euphoria of success, however brief, however unsatisfying: beware the danger in happiness! *Now everything I touch turns out to be wonderful. Now I love any fate that comes along. Who would like to be my fate?*

Yet it is perhaps not failure the writer loves, so much as the addictive nature of incompletion and risk. A work of art acquires, and then demands, its own singular "voice"; it insists upon its integrity; as Gide in his Notebook observed, the artist needs "a special world of which he alone has the key." That the fear of dying or becoming seriously ill in midstream is very real, cannot be doubted; and if there is an obvious contradiction here (one dreads completion; one dreads the possibility of a "posthumous" and therefore uncompleted work), that contradiction is very likely at the heart of the artistic enterprise. The writer carries himself as he would carry a precarious pyramid of eggs, because he is, in fact, a precarious pyramid of eggs, in danger of falling at any moment, and shattering on the floor in an ignoble mess. And he understands beforehand that no one, not even his most "sympathetic" fellow writers, will acknowledge his brilliant intentions, and see, for themselves, the great work he would surely have completed, had he lived.

An affinity for risk, danger, mystery, a certain derangement of the soul; a craving for distress, the pinching of the nerves, the not-yet-voiced; the predilection for insomnia; an impatience with past selves and past creations that must be hidden from one's admirers—why is the artist drawn to such extremes, why are we drawn along with him? Here, a forthright and passionate voice, from a source many would think unlikely:

> There are few of us who have not sometimes wakened before dawn, either after one of those dreamless nights that make us almost enamoured of death, or one of those nights of horror and misshapen joy, when through the chambers of the brain sweep phantoms more terrible than reality itself, and instinct with that vivid life that lurks in all grotesques, and that lends to Gothic art its enduring vitality. . . . Veil after veil of thin dusky gauze is lifted, and by degrees the forms and colors of things

are restored to them, and we watch the dawn remaking
the world in its antique pattern. The wan mirrors get
back their mimic life. . . . Nothing seems to us changed.
Out of the unreal shadows of the night comes back the
real life that we had known. We have to resume it where
we had left off, and there steals over us a terrible sense
of the necessity of the continuance of energy in the same
wearisome round of stereotyped habits, or a wild longing, it may be, that our eyelids might open some morning upon a world that had been refashioned anew in the
darkness . . . a world in which the past would have little
or no place, or survive, at any rate, in no conscious form
of obligation and regret. . . . It was the creation of such
worlds as these that seemed to Dorian Gray to be the
true object . . . of life.

That this unmistakably heartfelt observation should be bracketed,
in Wilde's great novel, by chapters of near-numbing cleverness,
and moralizing of a Bunyanesque—a truly medieval—nature, does
not detract from its peculiar poignancy: for here, one feels, Wilde
is speaking without artifice or posturing; and that Dorian Gray,
freed for the moment from his somewhat mechanical role in the
allegory Wilde has assembled, to explain himself to himself, has in
fact acquired the transparency—the invisibility—of a mask of our
own.

   As the ancient legend instructs us, Medusa, the image-bearing
goddess of Greek mythology, could not be encountered directly by
the hero Perseus, for her power was such that she turned everyone
who gazed upon her into stone. (The Gorgon, Medusa, had once
been a beautiful woman who had been transformed into a monster—with wings, glaring eyes, tusk-like teeth, and those famous
serpents for hair.) Only through shrewd indirection, by means of a
polished shield, could she be approached in order to be slain—that
is, "conquered" by a mortal man.
   Medusa—Perseus—the polished shield: one is led to read the
tale as a cautionary parable, which tells us that the inchoate and
undetermined event, the act without structure, without the necessary constraint (and cunning) of the human imagination, is too

brutal—because too inhuman?—to be borne. Perseus, aided by
Athene, conquers the barbaric in nature, and in his own nature, by
means of *reflection*.

The demonic flood of emotion represented by Medusa is, then,
successfully subdued by the stratagems of restraint, confinement,
indirection, craftiness, patience—which is to say, by a kind of art:
the deliberate artfulness that substitutes intellectual caution for
the brashness of primitive instinct. So art labors to give *meaning* to
a profusion of *meanings:* its structures—inevitably "exclusive," and
therefore inevitably "unjust"—provide a way of seeing with the
mind's eye that is unquestionably superior to the eye itself.

(And if Medusa were not terrible of aspect, threatening both
sanity and life, who, one wonders, would trouble to gaze upon her?
It is precisely the risk she represents, the grave danger, that makes
her a Muse.)

Will one fail is a question less apposite, finally, than *can one
succeed?*—granted the psychic predicament, the addiction to a
worldly skepticism that contrasts (perhaps comically) with the
artist's private system of customs, habits, and superstitious rou-
tines that constitutes his "working life." (A study should really be
done of artists' private systems—that cluster of stratagems, both
voluntary and involuntary, that make daily life navigable. Here we
would find, I think, a bizarre and ingenious assortment of Great
Religions in embryo—a system of checks and balances, rewards,
and taboos, fastidious as a work of art. *What is your work-schedule*,
one writer asks another, never *What are the great themes of your
books?*—for the question is, of course, in code, and really implies
Are you perhaps crazier than I?—and will you elaborate?)

How to attain a destination is always more intriguing (involving,
as it does, both ingenuity and labor) than *what* the destination
finally is. It has always been the tedious argument of moralists that
artists appear to value their art above what is called "morality": but
is not the artist by definition an individual who has grown to care
more about the interior dimensions of his art than about its public
aspect, simply because—can this be doubted?—he spends all his
waking hours, and many of his sleeping hours, in that landscape?

The curious blend of the visionary and the pragmatic that
characterizes most novelists is exemplified by Joyce's attitude

toward the various styles of *Ulysses*, those remarkable exuberant self-parodying voices: "From my point of view it hardly matters whether the technique is 'veracious' or not; it has served me as a bridge over which to march my eighteen episodes, and, once I have got my troops across, the opposing forces can, for all I care, blow the bridge sky-high." And though critics generally focus upon the ingenious relationship of *Ulysses* to the *Odyssey*, the classical structure was one Joyce chose with a certain degree of arbitrariness, as he might have chosen another—*Peer Gynt*, for instance; or *Faust*. That the writer labors to discover the secret of his work is perhaps the writer's most baffling predicament, about which he cannot easily speak: for he cannot write the fiction without becoming, beforehand, the person who *must* write that fiction; and he cannot be that person, without first subordinating himself to the process, the labor, of creating that fiction . . . Which is why one becomes addicted to insomnia itself, to a perpetual sense of things about to fail, the pyramid of eggs about to tumble, the house of cards about to be blown away. Deadpan, Stanislaus Joyce noted in his diary, in 1907: "Jim says that . . . when he writes, his mind is as nearly normal as possible."

But my position, as elaborated, is, after all, only the reverse of the tapestry.

Let us reconsider. Isn't there, perhaps, a very literal advantage, now and then, to failure?—a way of turning even the most melancholy of experiences inside-out, until they resemble experiences of *value*, of *growth*, of *profound significance*? That Henry James so spectacularly failed as a playwright had at least two consequences: it contributed to a nervous collapse; and it diverted him from a career for which he was unsuited (not because he had a too grandly "literary" and ambitious conception of the theatre but because, in fact, his theatrical aspirations were so conventional, so trivial)—thereby allowing him the spaciousness of relative failure. The public catastrophe of *Guy Domville* behind him, James writes in his notebook: "I take up my *own* old pen again—the pen of all my old unforgettable efforts and sacred struggles. To myself—today—I need say no more. Large and full and high the future still opens. It is now indeed that I may do the work of my life. And I will." *What Maisie Knew, The Awkward Age, The Ambassadors,*

The Wings of the Dove, The Golden Bowl—the work of James's life. Which success, in the London theatre, would have supplanted—or would have made unnecessary.

Alice James, the younger sister of William and Henry, was born into a family in which, by Henry's admission, "girls seem scarcely to have had a chance." As her brilliant *Diary* acknowledges, Alice made a career of various kinds of failure: the failure to become an adult; the failure to become a "woman" in conventional terms; the failure to realize her considerable intellectual and literary gifts; the failure—which strikes us as magnificently stubborn—to survive. (When Alice discovered that she had cancer of the breast, at the age of 43, she wrote rhapsodically in her diary of her great good fortune: for now her long and questionable career of invalidism had its concrete, incontestable, deathly vindication.)

Alice lies on her couch forever. Alice, the "innocent" victim of fainting spells, convulsions, fits of hysteria, mysterious paralyzing pains, and such nineteenth-century female maladies as nervous hyperesthesia, spinal neurosis, cardiac complications, and rheumatic gout. Alice, the focus of a great deal of familial attention; yet the focus of no one's interest. Lying on her couch she does not matter in the public world, in the world of men, of history. She does not count; she *is* nothing. Yet the *Diary*, revealed to her brothers only after her death, exhibits a merciless eye, an unfailingly accurate ear, a talent that rivals "Harry's" (that is, Henry's) for its astuteness, and far surpasses his for its satirical and sometimes cruel humor. Alice James's career invalidism deprives her of everything; yet, paradoxically, of nothing. The triumph of the *Diary* is the triumph of a distinct literary voice, as valuable as the voice of Virginia Woolf's celebrated diaries.

> I think if I get into the habit of writing a bit about what happens, or rather what doesn't happen, I may lose a little of the sense of loneliness and isolation which abides with me. . . . Scribbling my notes and reading [in order to clarify] the density and shape the formless mass within. Life seems inconceivably rich.

Life seems inconceivably rich—the sudden exclamation of the writer, the artist, in defiance of external circumstances.

The invalid remains an invalid. She dies triumphantly young. When a nurse wishes to commiserate with her about her predicament, Alice notes in her diary that destiny—any destiny—because it *is* destiny—is fascinating: thus pity is unnecessary. One is born not to suffer but to negotiate with suffering, to choose or invent forms to accommodate it.

Every commentator feels puritanically obliged to pass judgment on Alice. As if the *Diary* were not a document of literary worth; as if it doesn't surpass in literary and historical interest most of the publications of Alice's contemporaries, male or female. This "failure" to realize one's gifts may look like something very different from within. One must remember that, in the James family, "an interesting failure had more value than too-obvious success"—as it does to most observers.

In any case Alice James creates "Alice," a possibly fictitious person, a marvelous unforgettable voice. It is Alice who sinks unprotesting into death; it is Alice who says: "I shall proclaim that anyone who spends her life as an appendage to five cushions and three shawls is justified in committing the sloppiest kind of suicide at a moment's notice."

In Cyril Connolly's elegiac "war-book" *The Unquiet Grave, A Word Cycle by Palinurus* (1945), the shadowy doomed figure of Palinurus broods upon the melancholic but strengthening wisdom of the ages, as a means of "contemplating" (never has the force of that word been more justified), and eventually rejecting, his own suicide. Palinurus, the legendary pilot of Aeneas, becomes for the thirty-nine-year-old Connolly an image of his own ambivalence, which might be termed "neurotic" and self-destructive—unless one recalls the specific historical context in which the idiosyncratic "word cycle" was written, between the autumn of 1942 and the autumn of 1943, in London. *The Unquiet Grave* is a journal in perpetual metamorphosis; a lyric assemblage of epigrams, reflections, paradoxes, and descriptive passages; a commonplace book in which the masters of European literature from Horace and Virgil to Goethe, Schopenhauer, Flaubert, and beyond, are employed, as voices in Palinurus' meditation. Palinurus suffered a fate that, in abbreviated form, would appear to cry out for retribution, as well as pity:

Palinurus, a skillful pilot of the ship of Aeneas, fell into
the sea in his sleep, was three days exposed to the
tempests and waves of the sea, and at last came to the
sea shore near Velia, where the cruel inhabitants of the
place murdered him to obtain his clothes: his body was
left unburied on the seashore.

(Lemprière)

Connolly's meditation upon the temptations of death takes the
formal structure of an initiation, a descent into hell, a purification,
a cure—for "the ghost of Palinurus must be appeased." Approaching forty, Connolly prepares to "heave his carcass of vanity,
boredom, guilt and remorse into another decade." His marriage
has failed; the France he has loved is cut off from him, as a
consequence of the war; it may well be that the world as he has
known it will not endure. He considers the rewards of opium-
smoking, he broods upon the recent suicides of four friends, he
surrenders his lost Eden and accommodates himself to a changed
but evidently enduring world. The word cycle ends with an
understated defense of the virtues of happiness, by way of a close
analysis of Palinurus' complicity in his fate:

As a myth . . . with a valuable psychological interpretation, Palinurus clearly stands for a certain will-to-failure
or repugnance-to-success, a desire to give up at the last
moment, an urge toward loneliness, isolation, and obscurity. Palinurus, in spite of his great ability and his
conspicuous public position, deserted his post in the
moment of victory and opted for the unknown shore.

Connolly rejects his own predilection for failure and self-willed
death only by this systematic immersion in "Palinurus' " desire for
the unknown shore: The Unquiet Grave achieves its success as a
unique work by way of its sympathy with failure.

Early failure, "success" in being published of so minimal a
nature it might be termed failure, repeated frustrations may have
made James Joyce possible: these factors did not, at any rate,
humble him.

Consider the example of his first attempt at a novel, Stephen
Hero, a fragmented work that reads precisely like a "first novel"—

ambitious, youthful, flawed with the energies and native insights of youth, altogether conventional in outline and style, but, one would say, "promising." (Though conspicuously less promising than D. H. Lawrence's first novel *The White Peacock*.) Had Joyce found himself in a position to publish *Stephen Hero*—had his other publishing experiences been less disheartening—he would have used the material that constitutes *A Portrait of the Artist as a Young Man*; and that great novel would not have been written. As things evolved, Joyce retreated, and allowed himself ten years to write a masterpiece: and so he rewrote *Stephen Hero* totally, using the first draft as raw material upon which language makes a gloss. *Stephen Hero* presents characters and ideas, tells a story: *A Portrait of the Artist* is about language, *is* language, a portrait-in-progress of the creator, as he discovers the range and depth of his genius. The "soul in gestation" of Stephen Dedalus gains its individuality and its defiant strength as the novel proceeds; at the novel's conclusion it has even gained a kind of autonomy—wresting from the author a *first-person* voice, supplanting the novel's strategy of narration with Stephen's own journal. Out of unexceptional and perhaps even banal material Joyce created one of the most original works in our language. If the publication of *Dubliners* had been less catastrophic, however, and a clamor had arisen for the first novel by this "promising" young Irishman, one might imagine a version of *Stephen Hero* published the following year: for, if the verse of *Chamber Music* (Joyce's first book) is any measure, Joyce was surely not a competent critic of his own work at this time; and, in any case, as always, he needed money. If *Stephen Hero* had been published, *Portrait* could not have been written; without *Portrait*, its conclusion in particular, it is difficult to imagine the genesis of *Ulysses* . . . So one speculates; so it seems likely, in retrospect. But James Joyce was protected by the unpopularity of his work. He enjoyed, as his brother Stanislaus observed, "that inflexibility firmly rooted in failure."

The possibilities are countless. Can one imagine a D. H. Lawrence whose great novel *The Rainbow* had enjoyed a routine popular fate, instead of arousing the most extraordinary sort of vituperation ("There is no form of viciousness, of suggestiveness, that is not reflected in these pages," said a reviewer for one publication; the novel, said another reviewer, "had no right to exist"); how then could *Women in Love*, fueled by Lawrence's rage and loathing, have been written? And what of the evangelical *Lady Chatterley's Lover*, in its several versions? In an alternative universe there is a William Faulkner whose poetry (variously, and ineptly, modelled on Swinburne, Eliot, and others) was "successful"; there is a Faulkner whose early, derivative novels gained him a substantial public and commercial success. Imitation Hemingway in *Soldiers' Pay*, imitation Huxley in *Mosquitoes*—with the consequence that Faulkner's own voice might never have developed. (For when Faulkner needed money—and he always needed money—he wrote as rapidly and as pragmatically as possible.) That his great, idiosyncratic, difficult novels—*The Sound and the Fury, As I Lay Dying, Light in August, Absalom, Absalom!*—held so little commercial promise allowed him the freedom, the spaciousness, one might even say the privacy, to experiment with language as radically as he wished: for it is the "inflexibility" of which Stanislaus Joyce spoke that genius most requires.

But the genius cannot know that he is a genius—not really: he has hopes, he has premonitions, he suffers raging paranoid doubts, but he can have, in the end, only himself for measurement. Success is distant and illusory, failure one's loyal companion, one's stimulus for imagining that the next book will be better—for, otherwise, why write? The impulse can be made to sound theoretical, and even philosophical, but it is, no doubt, as physical as our blood and marrow. *This insatiable desire to write something before I die, this ravaging sense of the shortness and feverishness of life, make me cling . . . to my one anchor*—so Virginia Woolf, in her diary, speaks for us all.

SONNET

by STANLEY PLUMLY

from THE MISSOURI REVIEW

nominated by Marcia Southwick

Whatever it is, however it comes, it takes time.
It can take all night.
My father would sit on the edge of the bed
and let the tears fall to the floor,
the sun the size of the window, full
and rising. He was a dead man and he knew it.

I think of him almost every time I fall in love,
how the heart is three-quarters high in the body.
—He could lift his own weight above his head.
—He could run a furrow straight by hand.
I think of him large in his dark house,
hard in thought, taking his time.

But in fact he is sitting on the edge of the bed,
and it is morning, my mother's arms around him.

MARCUS GARVEY ARRESTED AT THE 125th STREET STATION

by JOHN ALLMAN

from THE AGNI REVIEW

nominated by THE AGNI REVIEW *and Dan Masterson*

Squat, overweight, he's preening
like a diplomat. Is hope a fraud, because one man
receives an empty envelope? The train moves on to Grand
Central.
A bright manacle around his wrist; the fur collar of his overcoat
an open noose. Each
side, they crush him
into himself, into darkness of soul, the black light
like a wet flow of words, Black Cross nurses marching down
Lenox Avenue, memories
crowding like crayfish, mountain mullet,
the bats in Jamaica. Is he the boy with dust on his feet?
How many *darkies* complained to the Attorney General? There's
no good in quadroons, any
shade of white, captains who drink
in drydock while the cargo rots. His people do not straighten
hair, bleach their skins: lined up at the dock, waving to the first
Negro freighter
that ever left these shores.

"I would rather die
than be good, if being good means
extermination." What's war? Black factories. Black land.
Ethiopia fulfilled. Europeans annihilating each other, wrong
        color ants on a red
        hill. Isn't he a great man?
DuBois raving at him, while he vows to be "the wreck of matter."
That defector, Eason, shot down in New Orleans; the KKK
                                        wordless,
            sending someone a severed
            hand; cousins to men in East St. Louis
who nailed boards over doors and windows, poured kerosene on
                                        porches,
burned black families alive. He needs more than corroded boilers
        to float an army
        from Biloxi, to navigate a sea
already crossed by the dead. Can he raise a profit from ashes?
He's been in their tombs before, seen their fat fists, heard
        in a crowded courtroom
        the click of a judge's false teeth.

            Heat escapes between such
        bars. Dampness freezes along door-jambs.
All jailers have jowls. Nothing worth counting in his
pockets; scraps of paper, notes from Amy, ticket stubs, folded
            blank stock
            for shares in boats
that sink in the Hudson. Do the nations league against him
in Geneva, while he's banned from Liberia, and men who
                                        confiscate
            his land
            receive medals from France?
In Liberty Hall, plumes waving in his admiral's hat,
he took away the mop and broom: cashed in a people's
            dream of black sunrise,
            black navies; the SS *Yarmouth*
steaming past Ellis Island. Must he roll all his fingers in ink,
to make a mark? He hears the desk sergeant sigh. Keys jangling.
        The match put to the *Negro World,*
            his plump shadow hissing into the sea.

THE WEAVER

by ANN STANFORD

from NORTHWEST REVIEW

nominated by Louis Gallo

I am the weaver.
Before the last frosts I planted the seeds
covered with straw from the reeds by the river.
Green rising under the moon in springtime
the jagged long leaves lifting a tide around me.

In summer the blue seeds appeared
grew into harvest, and the blue of indigo
rose in the water when the cloth I had woven
took the color of sky, took the azure of evening,
took the darkness of blue night without stars.

Shining, the cloth that I carried
down to the river stones, carefully washing
the dross from the workroom, leaving blue
caught as the clear afternoon
looking down on the river.

The sedges dripped toward the water, dipped in blue
dropped from the sky, and the broad channel
ran from the cloth over the blue rocks
under the sky that would darken
into still ponds where the frogs turned
to blue statues in cold streams of midnight.

I have woven through springtime
at dawn at my shuttle; now the blue sky
dries in my yard. This blue will not fade.
It will darken to midnight. It will tell
of the river; it will speak of the weaver. It will
last you a hundred years
out of myself, out of the sky and river woven.

🔥 🔥 🔥

SAMBA DE LOS AGENTES

fiction by ANDREI CODRESCU

from THE PARIS REVIEW

nominated by THE PARIS REVIEW, *Gene Chipps and Louis Gallo*

My NAME IS José, I am Catholic and I was not a plainclothes policeman very long. In Argentina I wrote poetry and prayed to the Virgin every day for my mother who was a cancerous balloon grounded in the chicken shack behind the house and for my two sisters who tap-tapped their way past my window every hour drowned in lipstick and sperm. Here is one of my poems in translation:

> Every day is a long hallway to death
> Every night is an agony of lightning
> My heart lies in pieces at your feet
> My poor heart is a trampled field
> Bring down the rain, Mother of God

When I first came to New York I was taken under the wing of my uncle Pedro who is a cop. I became a plainclothes cop and roamed the city with two other cops, looking for crime. Because I was the first to spot the nervous, skinny young man playing with a gun in his pocket, I was the first to shove him into one of those doorways which in New York stand for nature, and whisper hotly into his ear: "If you move I kill you." I have whispered, shouted, mumbled and stammered that line ever since I remember enough times to get me in trouble. It never did; I think it is a very good line. Skinny didn't move so I slid out his gun like a rubber from a Trojan package and it turned out to be a toy. "What were you doing with this?"

"I was walking thinking up a poem," the man said in an accent as foreign as my own.

"What sort of poem?" I found myself unable not to ask although my next line should have been: "You robbed a liquor store, punk!"

"A poem about the Virgin Mary," he said shyly, beginning to cry. I saw the tear and knew that it was the tear said to perpetually exit from the statute of the Virgin in Fatima. "In it . . ." he pushed on, sensing my interest, "I was going to put my heart which is in pieces."

I took out the only piece of paper in his pocket, a poem to the Virgin by A. Alien, 54 Avenue C, 2 C, New York City, America.

"Where is your green card, punk?" I remembered my next line. "At home."

So I dragged him to his home to the address plainly written on the paper. There, we busted in the door and found ourselves in a room wallpapered with innumerable poems to the Virgin. The refrigerator door, which was open, contained tens maybe hundreds of carefully washed milk bottles, each one containing a rolled-up poem to the Virgin. "What do you do with these?" I asked.

"Launch them to sea," he said.

I arrested him on a charge of possessing a false pistol, a misdemeanor, and took him to jail. There, I visited him every day until the trial because A. Alien had no money for bail. When the trial came, I couldn't be found to testify. Reached finally at the Police Academy where I was taking classes, I refused to come to court because I was on my lunch break. The case was dismissed, I was fired from the force and I became a hippie and a film maker, and started writing short stories and a novel.

A prime specimen of the Nixon-Mitchell architecture of the early 70s, the Department of Justice, enfolding in its windowless interior The Immigration & Naturalization Bureau like a heart, bakes in the noon heat on the site of a former slum. The edges of the slum, like the extremities of a heart transplant patient, lie bloated all around it, dotted with idle young blacks lying on piles of rubbish, smoking at the sun. Parts of car bodies, only the useless parts, the unsavory entrails of animals rejected by the white middle-class rust, there too, scooped up from the inside. A child probes carefully the sides of a slice of watermelon, its inside, too, scooped up long ago. The freeway, a black incision still unfinished, stands over the landscape, its wire feelers extended toward the river. The earth too is hollow, hundreds of hardhats are digging below, one day trains will rumble through. Everything hollowed out and the sides rotten . . . this is the world to which allegiance must be paid by the poor alien disguised in a blue leisure suit like a bad lyric in a barely hummable song . . . and I go forth to pay it, green card clutched tight, an official shoot within a mannered walk—I almost said manured—my shiny wingtips narrow but properly wingless, my mask in place, the eyes almost fit my glasses which I wear as prophylactics. Today I am going to claim citizenship.

The guard runs his outstretched palms alongside my body glancing all the while at the metal detector needle which registers my keys with a slight tremor. With his palms on my hips I chuckle inwardly at the questions on the naturalization form in my breast pocket. Have you ever committed sexual perversities? Have you had any homosexual encounters?

The hands of the guard became the hands, crossed on a metal desk in fluorescent white light, of the immigration officer "in charge" of my request for citizenship. Hands progress, in institutional neon, from resting on hips to crossing on a desk. In the bureaucracies of hands, these are the hierarchies: the fist, impacting with the face as the immigrant, stumbling off the boat, appears ready to run off into the night past the guards; the index finger curled toward its owner, meaning come here, worm; the index finger pointing to the tubercular youth with two weeks' growth of beard, singling him out of line for shipping back; the vertical fist hitting the metal desk to make a point out of which, rage spent, could come forgiveness; the crossed hands, which I now face, ready to thumb through a greasy, fat file; the palms spread across the face of the man leaning wearily into them after a long day of silent hate and contempt for the Tower of Babel; the hands, finally, of the man, on the Bible, on his way up. All these hands, at no matter which stage in their office life, never lose the gesture of the guard, which they retain like a water mark.

Still crossed, the hands weigh me. Above them is the mustache of a man tensed between the incoming fat of middle age and the veneer of nearly gone muscle. They now uncross, these hands, to alert me that all has come to a point: the file. A mystery to both of us, the file is going to determine my status. My name, JOSE A., is embossed in red ink on it. The file opens. The man's eyes widen from the first page. So they know everything, I think. They know about the Virgin and the man I failed to jail because of Her. They know about Peggy, my agent. However, I am quite certain, they don't know a thing about me.

"Why have you been driven from the force?"

"For the love of the Virgin, by José!"

"In 1969 you were arrested for harboring minors. Suspicion of sexual activity. What was the deposition of the case?"

"Fiction."

"We shouldn't let your past stand against you. If you tell me the truth there is no reason. . . ."

"My past doesn't stand against me. It doesn't stand against you either. My past doesn't stand at all—I am another person now. I write novels. I have an agent. I am an American."

"There is no reason if you tell the truth why you should not . . . in time . . . become a citizen." He is generous with reason. After all, it isn't *his* reason he's being generous with. It is the reason of the founding fathers who wanted all the orphans. However: the world is full of orphans and he doesn't think the founding fathers meant *all* of them. Why, a man could come here, display his orphanism and be allowed to shake down the lemons off the first citizen. We must make sure he is a good orphan. Not orphan enough that is to *cry* for love, for chrissakes, not a pathetic fucking *ultimate* orphan . . . a reasonable orphan, a dignified orphan, a calm orphan.

"Your file raises questions. We will look into them. I see no reason, etc., if one day, etc., if the truth, etc., you may not, etc., one day, etc."

When I came home Madame Rosa Alvarez had a surprise for me: she flung open the door to my crusty rooms and there, in a circle reminiscent of a village dance, all embroidery, high-heeled shoes and black and red hair, were my mother and two sisters. The result of a miracle still much discussed in Buenos Aires, my mother had deflated and her cancers had been sucked out of her. The renowned psychic surgeon Xavier Urmuz had had his picture in many papers as a result, particularly the dramatic one which shows him stepping on wriggling brown spots pouring out of mama's body like hailstones through a grass roof.

My mama became a rapid American, so rapid I took her to Atlantic City. And for a moment there I panicked: I thought I'd lost her. Looking over the dazzling rows of madly whirring, bright slot machines, each one facing a wrinkled middle-aged woman in electric green polyester pants, I couldn't tell which one she was. It was a movement that gave her away: a jerky, spasmodic upward twitch of greed which made it seem as if she was pulling the machine off its black stem. Cherries whirled past and apples, and out of the tumbling fruit, something of mother appeared. Getting closer I noticed the fierce and familiar pursing of her lips in what was her unique and ancient quarrel with fate, or luck as she sometimes called it. Luck, luck, ran through her lips, in a flow of mixed syllables in various dialects, some have luck, some have all the rotten luck. She had already forgotten her miraculous cure when faced with the evidence of her machine-neighbor, her identical image, her fellow bus-passenger, pulling showers of silver out of the air. Before the coin she proffered to the secret quarrel with her destiny had even reached the insides of the machine, she pulled it hard and stalled it. Every time, she had to duplicate her movement, as the arm of the one-armed bandit would not comply the first time around. This double movement, notwithstanding the miracle, running as it did through her whole life, divided her days and nights. Her days were now dedicated to achieving the semblance of an American woman with whom she competed for blandness in endless shopping sprees which were fast draining my sisters' hard-earned whoring money, and which yielded the same plastic colors as the stuck slot machine. Her nights were occupied by the dead. Useless to resist, unresponsive to medication, contemptuous of doctors, the dead came to her every night to converse, ask and answer questions, as much at home in her dreams as they had ever been. Her grounded years in the chicken shack had been crowded with dead people, her shack had been the coffee house of the necropolis. They had all come with her to America now, happy like all new immigrants, a dream come true. For the past two weeks, I had been sleeping around, unable to listen to the wild cacophony of my mother's dreams. My sisters, who were used to it, said that it was this constant dead talk which had driven them from home at night in Buenos Aires. By the time they had had her removed to the chicken shack it was too late: they liked what they did. For the past two weeks, my mother had been teaching her dead English until dawn. When the last of her quarters brought forth a mixed bag of grapes and cherries, she turned to me and sighed with the satisfaction that I, at least, looked exactly like everyone else, an investment which she had made earlier and which had, unlike the *pure* operations of luck, paid off. She had no way of knowing that the blue suit of which she was so proud—she had sent it to me by boat—had only been worn once before, when I had gone in to ask for citizenship. In her mind I was always clad in the blue suit, and when I wasn't she didn't see me. Invisible in my childhood, I was still partly invisible. Unfortunately, I *was* partly visible. This is the part which writes prose.

I made small talk with the man ahead of me, No. 15, on the bench at the Immigration & Naturalization Bureau. He was Romanian. He told me that, contrary to popular belief, Dracula was a man of the people. He was man enough to impale them. He boiled people. He stuck a lid with holes for heads over the cauldron people were boiling in. He ate in front of the boiling with relatives of the boiled. He nailed people's hats to their heads if they didn't remove them fast enough. He made dishonest merchants swallow their money. He nailed thieves to one another and impaled them horizontally on the dotted line. He poured poison into people's ears. He saved Christianity from the Turks. He invented nationalism. His portrait hangs in classrooms all over the country. He has been maligned. Then his number, No. 15, was called, and I was next.

"We have perused your file, José. We have half-looked into your soul and found good things. We know that you are a writer. What have you written, José?"

"A guide to fucking in the great cathedrals. A guide to gargoyles in ten great cities. A spiritual guide to gambling. A Transylvanian in Disneyland."

"How do you make a living?"

"I am a philosophical fashion arbiter. I decide what colors the ideas should wear."

"Do you make enough to eat?"

"Enough for Shrimp Imbecile for two. Sizzling flied lice, too. Flied polk! Oystels! Egglolls! Watel! Evelything! I am a well-fed American who doesn't even moan in his sleep . . . though the silence was terrifying at first."

"I sense a bit of resentment. An old wound, perhaps?"

"Yes. The wound winds all the way around my body, through the air. My aura is unzipped. A kind of spare lyricism attends my movements. Sometimes I am Spartan and hemophiliac at the same time."

"That sounds like a paradox."

"To find a true paradox you must dig at least six feet. I sense nothing of the sort. True, I have had many serious, late night discussions with people in the know. The world is dying."

Getting up from his desk, the Immigration agent looked furtively around then closed the door. He winked. I understood from his automatically lowered voice that his inner police ear had been activated. He implored me to listen to his position. He spoke cautiously, as if behind every word someone or something waited for him with a slingshot. He tested each word in his mouth, prodding each letter with his tongue. Even to himself he appeared as a conscientious consumer making sure of each tomato before buying. But his words, when finally released, turned over and bought, came out tired, boring and insipid settling in their reasoned predictability on me like flies on the summer sweat of a bald pate. I have no idea what he said.

"What do you mean?" I asked.

"I can't tell you that. Suffice to say that under the circumstances we will have to keep working on your file until every shadow of doubt is erased. The whole world comes through this door: Vietnamese peasants, Cambodian spies, Cuban killers. And writers, you know . . . I have here something a writer once wrote, I flushed it out. . . ." He handed me a dog-eared mimeograph pamphlet entitled DIALECTIC OF TERRORISM OR THE PLEASURES OF EXILE. Leafing through it I saw underlined: *Rely on your basic transparencies*. On the margin, a hand had scrawled: *Pictorial key to terrorism*. I saw also *Happiness is a loss of integrity,* and on the margin: *Psychological milieu*. On the back cover was a picture which looked like random meat after a TNT blast. The caption said: *Fragments of a Comrade*. "Needless to say, we had the author deported. . . ."

"Why?"

"Anarchism. Subversive milieu."

"I have arthritis of the milieu," I confessed.

"On the other hand," he continued without hearing me, "we have a writer who not only deserves to stay, it is a pleasure keeping him." He handed me a poem. Here it is:

COUNTERREVOLUTIONARY SONG SUNG BY THE
WHITE GUARDS IN THE UKRAINE 1921 IN PRAISE OF
THE UNITED STATES—A NEW TRANSLATION BY name
deleted

At the small arms seminar
Vera and I whispered about Lenin's bananski
There isn't any said Vera
He left it behind in Indianski

The mountains are covered with manna
We have only just begun to fight
Like the corn in far away Indiana
We will conquer the Bolshevik blight

At the small arms seminar
Aliosha inserted the firing clip for Anna
A snow drift came from the mountains
As beautiful as the hair of Fata Morgana

We will stomp each Bolshevik with our boot
Like a wiggling scarlet piranha
The mountains will be free forsooth
And we will be famous in far away Indiana

I handed it back.

"You know," said the agent, carefully folding it in four and
putting it back in his suit pocket, "to this day the Cossacks are very
famous in Indiana. In my little town we have the Cossack Inn, a
White Tower, and we have a corn ritual where we sing Cossack
songs."

"How long then?"

"No one knows. Form's just benign content, as the doctors
say . . ." he said, waving my application, "but content may well be
malignant form. . . ." He pounded my file.

My sister Tabita's boyfriend gave her the crabs and now she can't
work. She's been told by everyone, myself included, to get rid of
them but she demurs. Crabs, she says, are jewels from Venus. She
clings to them as if they were ideas, she says that at Lourdes

Christ's tears fall on his toes and turn to gelatin and then his greenish fungoid feet soft and wobbly walk over the minds of His worshippers. Would you remove his tires? she screams. I am no less attached to the ancient rottenness of my whimsy! she hollers. I try to talk sense into her:

"If Christ would think of us as fondly as you think of your crabs, Tabita, we would all be in Heaven!"

But there is no talking to Tabita and now there are crabs everywhere: in my hair, in my eyelids, under my arms. I didn't even sleep there and I got them. Just by sitting down. And as I get up I can't make up my mind if the little beasts have colonised or inhabited me. Likewise, our earth must at times ponder this question. I know it is not an appropriate moment, at the very beginning, nay, before the second chapter of *The Queen of the Morgue* (as I retitled my ghost job), to ponder this, but nevertheless: when writing, am I colonising or inhabiting the language? Until Peggy, I would have laughed this question off as utterly stupid. Until then I had been sure that words came to inhabit me, little astral spores in search of a mouth. Shortly after I thought well perhaps I am inhabiting them though Lord knows *what* inhabits them if that's the case. Bad enough as that proposition was it can't compare to the criminal magnitude of colonisation. And yet, as a still honest—though barely—ghost I must ask. That this sort of inquiry is utterly inappropriate in a ghost was made abundantly clear to me by my ghost agent who having just read the first chapter of *The Queen of the Morgue*, tells me that my "love affair" with the American language is somewhat one-sided: as if I'd persuaded her to give me an unreluctant hand job and then lost her phone number. There are true ways of writing a story, you little prick, even if I have to—as you never tire of pointing out— make the old bag look like Mary Queen of Scots and her ghoulish departed hubby like Sir Galahad, ways of making it believable at the very least. Truth is like rooms one looks for in strange cities. You don't know the neighborhood but you have to trust your idea of a room even if it's only the fact that it's got to have walls. But try fighting conformity with your feet in the goo: the material is like a rubber tree. No one is ready for the slightest bit of truth. But don't worry, it isn't you who points the gun at my head. The hand that types is the hand that squeezes the trigger. And rocks the boat that rocks the cradle, as Tabita says when her boyfriend implores her to be normal. I must remember, in whatever twisted fashion, to allow language to breathe, ah, ah, scratch scratch.

Tabita's crabs and mama's poltergeist have turned my habitat into Luna 4, I can't even eat lunch there without drama. The poltergeist, a recent escapee from her nightly cafe for the dead, turns chairs over. If I look away from my bowl it turns the soup into my lap. On a mild day, it's only Tabita's feather hat floating around the room and the dead flies in mother's Inca Cola swaying from side to side and the glasses in the cupboard toasting each other in an intimate sub-tinkle. I can live with that, but on bad days it breaks windows, snaps legs off chairs, breaks mirrors, twists doorknobs, lifts up the couch, aims knives and forks at the flesh. On days like that interpretation wears thin, the severe diet of faulty premises begins to show itself as ribs, I see the skull under the peachy skin, I feel like Little Red Riding Hood and the Wolf all rolled in one, my face half in shadow.

Tabita's boyfriend, who plays guitar, plants his mournful physique and his untuned instrument a few steps over my sleepy head and lets go fortissimo all night with such classics as DON'T WAIT FOR THE SHRIMP BOATS HONEY I'M COMING HOME WITH THE CRABS or THE ALBINO SEX POT BLUES which, when added to the amplified gravel of mama's soccer-crowd-sized company and the poltergeist crashing the furniture, and the wailing of New York City in heat, seriously put language on the block. And they say America is running out of energy! Bring on the Argentines! I'm having so much fun I can't remember my name. And Madame Rosa Alvarez threatens to evict us.

The Red Square in Moscow is full of people looking up expectantly to Brezhnev as he is about to speak. Suddenly: a sound like that of a field full of grasshoppers in August breaks the silence: a million men are pulling down their zippers at once! And another time, when the lack of meat drove everybody crazy in Russia, the crazed Russians poured across the borders into Romania and ate raw all the cows grazing there. And those are just some of the things that go on behind the Iron Curtain, No. 15 told me.

No. 15 was ensconced in my former bed in the middle of my

apartment, tended to by my mother with wine, and by Raquel with rhythmic brushes of her breasts across his chest.

"What about Dracula? And did you ever become a citizen?" I asked him.

Dracula, he said, was Gutenberg's son. After Gutenberg printed his Bibles he printed a book on Dracula's atrocities. This was the first mass produced book in the world and the world's first taste of literacy. Dracula made print successful and the vogue it has enjoyed ever since was rooted in him. The ink of that early tale about the blood he spilled is indelible. The content of cultural democracy is a horror tale. The blood he spilled issues forth from the source of the modern mind like sperm from a bull. "I am not a citizen yet," he concludes.

Raquel had broken the house rule. Even Tabita was not allowed to bring johns in, she had to work wherever the light was dim and the place deserted. Tabita is obsessive and therefore certain things are forgiven her, like her fondness for dwarves and her passion for crabs but even she does not work in front of mother. Raquel, on the other hand, is a murderous fury clad in outward calm who glows like a brilliant panther when aroused. She has been known to murder and mutilate and will no doubt do it again when the moon is full. I am afraid of her because she is full of intricate canals through which flows a crimson substance which isn't blood. So instead of throwing her on her ass out the window followed by her john, which everyone tells me I must do if I hope to assert my authority, I prefer to make conversation. Authority to me is like sleep linguistics. Words in dreams, awkward flights over rooftops.

"But you must ghost Dracula's autobiography," I tell No. 15. "If direct violence is unadvisable, you would do well to sell the object of your distaste to the devil. But he is not stupid, this foreigner. He sips his wine like a fox, intent on citizenship. Dracula, who was the father of the modern state and the inventor of nationalism, stands firmly behind him, with one hand on his skull and the other on the book. "Justice," he says, "cannot be established without terror. Ivan the Great copied Dracula. As did Machiavelli. The fatal flaw of Western democracies, the United States chief among them, was to transform Dracula from a voice of the State, which he has always been, into a private citizen with a taste for blood. You can stake an individual through the heart, bury him at the crossroads, lop his head off with an axe, transfix him with a hawthorn bough and quarter him, but there will always be another individual ready to rise and take his place, or another movie. No wonder he's bigger than Christ! Where Christ merely offers his blood like a wimpy liberal, Dracula takes it!" No. 15 became so excited he stood in bed and lifted his wine glass high over his head. His swollen member fell through his spidery genitals like a monkey through ferns, touching the red top of Raquel's hair. My mother took her pulse compulsively and I saw large drops of blood on the ceiling. In the tiny film of light winding through the blood drops, history marched in rags, endless waves of men covered with wolf hair. Yes, his tale had to be written and I said so again but mainly to recover my body which has a tendency when excited to rise up on a flood of adrenaline and leave me stranded among dictionaries. But No. 15 was drunk and making doleful sounds of wooden instruments, his hands—he had dropped the glass and crashed it to the floor— drumming on the ceiling from which protruded two boars' heads covered at the neck by tight skins, his feet pumping two wolves' clawed feet which operated an accordion-like contraption formed partly by Raquel's bosom, and his cock banging solemnly my sister's echoing skull.

This is when Madame Rosa Alvarez burst into the room, her flat yellow mug streaked by orange tears, her hands in the air:

"Tabita is dead!" she screamed.

"She is not dead!" No. 15 screamed back at her. "She has gone to marry the sun! The moon and the stars will be her bridesmaids and the heavens will look on her wedding! The moon will wear a red velvet dress and the angels of God will hold their gold mirrors to her face so she could see how beautiful she is! The angels of God are blind but their mirrors see for them! She will marry the sun and the sun will shine on earth to tell people how happy he is with his bride! On beautiful summer days you will be able to see her sitting beside her husband the sun greeting you!"

"She is dead I tell you!" She has been positively identified!" shrieked Madame Rosa. But at the moment the room was flooded with light and the sun which had been in the clouds for the past few days came through the crepe curtains and put roses on everybody, so we all knew that the old landlady had been lying. Tabita herself came in a few minutes later to say that she had been stretched naked on the roof hoping the sun would come out because she was "white as milk and freckled as a general's map," when Madame Rosa had burst into tears over her and ran off screaming "I knew it! I knew it! The bugs have killed her!" Madame Rosa shook her head adamantly and declared: "You were dead! I saw it with my own eyes! If my husband was still alive, God bless his soul, he would throw you all out like rabbit bones from the stew!" She shook her head violently from right to left, Tabita shook hers from left to right, mama began to shake hers, Raquel shook hers and No. 15 shook his up and down—only I, in midst of the storm that shook the tree, kept mine still because I needed it to think with.

It is a cliché, I know, but within the confines of a policeman's uniform there often beats a huge, trapped moth, the tips of his wings brushing frantically against the sides of the ribcage. In my old police soul this butterfly beat so furiously it burst its cage and that's how I came to beg for lemons and film. It's an old story, made complicated by the fact of police love which is that the euphoric sadism of power can never have enough to feed itself. Policemen, like the rest of us, want boundless love, and they die for lack of it: they want to bind, be bound, beat, be beaten, piss on and be pissed on, and more than anything they want the butterfly to stop the agony of its thrashing. And like the rest of us, they eat to still the ache, and eat, and eat, spaghetti, sausages, egg foo young, cheese, meat, pies, candy and bacon. The more they eat the more insatiable they become: the spirit is a bottomless hole. Cops have been known to aim their service revolvers at their chest where they imagine the head of the moth is and fire deliriously. Often, this wild firing does no more than enlarge the hole into which they then pour redoubled portions of pasta, tomato sauce and leftover casserole, until they become so large they have to be given an official reprimand and ordered to trim down. The fat cop is a tragic creature, the victim both of a furious desire for the world and of a crazed butterfly in his chest.

I am telling you this so that you may understand the spirit in which I am teasing my Immigration agent who, frozen with terror and suffering in his chair, faces me, his butterfly wild and out of control, fluttering visibly and ruffling the hair on his chest. My butterfly, freed long ago, calls and sings to his butterfly, trying to lure him out to mate. I am being cruel, nay, sinister as I improvise the prettiest canzones ever hummed and ever woven, as I dive and circle and pirouette and shoot golden pollen. Come, my darling, I sing, let's make a four-winged being, enter each other until no one can feel the seam, let's be utterly crazy and demonically deliberate, let's give the horse space a whack with our wings until it shoots through time, obscurity is hateful, let's proclaim the approximate clarity of feeling, let's whip out of the sordid history of the police body into the coolness of the night, let's create en route the solid delights we can't imagine!

"Level with me, José! I have no time any longer for shots in the dark!" he pleads.

"Yes," I agree, "The dark is bigger than all the rifles."

"Once, I too . . . considered being an artist. . . ."

"Oh . . . what happened? Did she leave you?"

"How did you know?" He is surprised, but in pain.

How did I know? Because she is written all over him, just the way she sprawled that afternoon on the Peruvian blanket with cones and spirals everywhere, ready to make him into an artist, a devotee and an ecstatic until, later that evening, she left for the jungles of the Americas with two men she found sleeping in a bus station with their heads on motel Bibles and chains around their necks. Yes, my sweet judge of citizenship, you still reek of her, her smell is indelible, she was the only one who knew the secret of stilling the butterfly. And your idea of the kind of art you were going to make wasn't bad either. You had noticed—thanks to the vision she lent you for one week—that people made all sorts of involuntary gestures: a pat on the hair, a fingernail in the crotch, a wink, a grimace, a gentle tug at a stray hair, a knee jerk, an opening or closing of hands or buttocks, raising one shoulder or another, a tip of tongue darting out . . . and you conceived, in a reverie, the possibility of having these involuntary mannerisms replicated in stained glass. You saw a church rising out of the floor, composed entirely of representations of coincidental movement arranged by you in classic religious scenes: the wedding at Cana, the stations of the Cross. After the vision you saw, for the week she gave you, people's willed and ordinary beings were framed entirely by their unconscious gestures. You even saw though too briefly for understanding that a great deal of devotional faith inspired people to move in ways which they knew not.

"What sort of artist?" I asked.

"Oh . . . stained glass . . . nothing much. More of a crafts thing really."

"That makes you almost a foreigner. If you would like to emigrate to art I will be happy to look into what I can do to get citizenship for you," I said. "Artland has stricter entry require-ments than the United States of America. To come to the U.S. you need merely a clear anti-communist conscience, proof that you always screw on top if a man and on the bottom if a woman, a mouth clear of boy cock, alas, a whole mind in shock over the mere fact of cock if a man, cunt if a woman, no aristocratic titles, not even Discount, no hidden hate of taxes and no authorship of even minor crimes like drinking hootch at fourteen, am I right? But to gain admittance to Artland, ah! You must, first of all, remain vague while the circumstances are attacking or circumstantial when vagueness does, then you must be nobody, you must divest yourself of your person, your class and your property not to speak of your so-called mind and your opinions, you must allow yourself to lapse unexpectedly into metaphorical Corinthian, let no one take you for granted, you must make sure that everyone knows including yourself that you are capable of perpetrating any enor-mity at any given time, and never under any circumstances must you finish your sentences, you must never know how a sentence will end, you must escape confinement continuously, that is, you must never serve your sentence, you must brutally uneducate yourself, the world is a speech malfunction, the simplest things must be a complete mystery to you and you must approach them with the eternal idiot questions like a child bearing flowers to the enormous tractor leveling the old cemetery, you must live veri-fiably in the huge emptiness between possibilities and decisions, loving the former, amusing yourself with the latter, and above all you must always be amused, you must destroy agents, editors, censors and representatives of the state as often as possible, all dirty tricks permitted, and you must approach the universe in a militant fashion because you make it up as you breathe, also you will allow yourself to be kidnapped by all and sundry forms of whimsy and will refuse to follow plans, you will not set foot where anybody wants you to but you must visit Plato's Republic as often as you can so that you can be thrown out of it, you must not above all believe in art or any other forms of confinement, you must inspire madness, impossibility and confusion, and on the ladder of discarded negations, with a mouth full of grass, holding a lit bomb, you must climb at all times into the movies which you must trust are being shown in their entirety, any questions?"

"No" he says, "only one. Can I visit your place of residence? It is routine."

"Sure. Put your coat on, man, and let's go. My mother and sisters will be delighted, I'm sure, they love doctors, lawyers, engineers and the rest of the middle class. In fact, there may be some already there so you won't have to feel out of place. . . ."

"No, not now. How about tomorrow?"

"Fine, but I don't think you'll get into Artland with an attitude like that. But who knows, maybe the moth will bust out . . . if properly coaxed, goodbye, goodbye."

When I say that mama cleaned up . . . well, maybe you know what happened to the two girls who every morning swept up dust into the eyes of the sun. The sun turned them into the stars with the broom, up there by the Southern Cross. Well, if the sky had been in the mood he could have turned mama and my two sisters into meteorites, moon vapor and echoes, because the three of them swept dust into the rising sun and the milky moon, sweep sweep sweep all day and all night . . . and when they were done sweeping they tore open mama's collection of liquid, gaseous and solid cleansers, everything advertised on TV since they had come to America, boxes and boxes and bottles and bottles which until then had been piling up in pyramids behind the bed, dresser and in front of the full-color poster of the Virgin, covering up her robes and the left foot of the Holy Infant. Simultaneously, grainy blue powers foamed on the walls and liquid plumbers burrowed through the pipes. Bombs exploded causing roaches to migrate, long sorrowful lines of refugees leaving under the door crack for the neighboring apartments. The windows became transparent for the first time in memory, letting in a view of dirty windows across the street behind which startled fat nudes watched early morning television. The mattresses were beaten savagely, stains cracked and springs moaned. The floors vied with the boots of old-fashioned sergeants in reflecting our faces. The ceiling could be read like a coloring book through hundreds of exposed layers of ancient paint. "Now if I could," mama said, "I would like to clean up the street of all these dirty houses, this one first of all, get rid of all these people, wash the sidewalks, suck all the dirt out of the air and move New York out of New York."

"Ugh, look at this!" Tabita exclaimed, pointing to the screen of the old TV she had just finished scrubbing and sponging. "Now you can see what people are wearing!" Indeed, the game show host and his guests shone with new-found details. Ties and shoes stood out distinctly. Tabita touched one of her breasts fondly but exclaimed mournfully: "All these freckles. . . ." We were all naked because our clothes were boiling in the kitchen, spewing clouds of steam. Our bodies, dissimilar only in the distribution of skin, loose like a crumpled wino bag on mama, taut and stretched over breasts and hips on Raquel and Tabita and pinned niggardly to my pointed bones, were otherwise and for all theoretical purposes, the same body, particularly in the pubic area which was stamped by four identical pyramids of red hair. Known as "the Amazonian forests of First Avenue," my sisters' bushes were legendary where such legends circulate. It would have been inhuman and unnatural for these lush growths to contain no life and here was the rub . . . they teemed with it. Mama had tried to pour a bottle of A-200 on Tabita while she slept but she'd awakened screaming genocide and hadn't calmed down yet. "You might as well kill me too. . . ." she repeated every five minutes. Raquel tried to talk sense to her: "They are just like roaches, only smaller . . . you don't seem to speak up for roaches, do you . . . no one else is either. . . ." "That's tough!" screamed Tabita. "I can't champion all the bugs in the world!" I saw her point: the roaches had no apologist, no house critic, but they could take care of themselves. The crabs needed Tabita the way corporate publishing needs *The New York Times Book Review*. The only concession we were able to extract from her was a solemn promise that she would not scratch herself during the Immigration agent's visit. I don't think a visit by the Pope would have caused such a promise from her. Only Immigration had such power and I never understood why until later events revealed that Raquel was in love with No. 15 and No. 15 had twice attempted suicide when denied citizenship, and Tabita loved Raquel more than anyone else in the world. Our household was a household of love and one person's beloved crabs were the others' beloved crabs no matter what we happened to think of them. And that is how it came to pass that amid the shining cleanliness, an oasis of purity in the heart of New York, only a few crabs, the more visible for being the sole survivors of a truly American cleaning binge, made their accustomed rounds in the forests of our beings.

But just when it appeared that all was in order and in pristine readiness for the visit, tragedy struck. The lush use of Lysol, bleachers, Clorox, detergents and soaps in the water, destroyed our clothes. Every last piece of cloth has boiled irretrievably away and there wasn't another garment in the apartment. The water in the cauldron had turned into purple paste. My blue suit had merged with my sisters' lingerie and my mother's polyesters had merged with our Argentine flannels.

Only four hours remained until the visit, a time mother had deemed sufficient for the clothes to dry but now we were in trouble. Raquel picked up the telephone to call No. 15 to ask him to purchase anything he could find but the telephone was dead. It seemed that in scrubbing the walls Tabita had dislodged the connections. Either that or one of the powerful detergents had corroded the apparatus. There was only one thing to do and what was for me to wrap myself in the plastic shower curtain with the Hobobken angels on it and go to the store, and this I did.

Roaming the streets in transparent plastic, o bards, is no big deal in our city. I noticed many hundreds maybe people in similar attire . . . I had never seen them before which confirms my law of New York which is that you only see your own sort of humans in our great city . . . depending on the speed of your walking and the demands of your eyes . . . rapid businessmen with swinging briefcase see only their own kind . . . parallel to them but slower is another world and parallel to that is a yet slower one until you arrive to the motionless bums who see only the motionless . . . and parallel to the worlds of speed are the worlds of tweed, cotton and plastic likewise aware only of each other . . . so it was no surprise really to see thousands of Hoboken angels dancing on grayed plastic around the bodies of an entire social subclass. But when I got to Orchard Street where all the affordable clothes are I saw that I had no money. In our haste to boil our clothes we had boiled away our wallets and purses also.

One thing to do then. I walked into the crowded offices of the Manhattan Chemical Bank and stood in line. When my turn came I advanced on the teller, a spry Puerto Rican blond standing on 20-inch platforms, and said: "Lean over the counter as far as you can and look down . . . you will see a weapon pointed at you! Take all the money in the drawers and put it in a blue deposit bag or these are the last words you hear!" To make my weapon as visible as possible I filled my mind with the curves and buttocks of my filming days and I bent in memory over the deliciously spread body of the adrenaline-filled love of my Buddhist-burning days, and helped these images with my hand, up and down. The teller leaned far over the counter and looked down and saw the weapon grinning at her and pointing straight at her ruby-lipsticked heart-shaped mouth. "All right," she mumbled, and filled a bag with cash.

Loaded with clothes and feeling not a little crinkley and quite a bit squeaky in my brand new striped green suit and tight wingtips I flew up the stairs of our apartment, convinced that a rush of bank robberies by penis awaited our mimetic city in the next few days as soon as the *Daily News* hit the stands. I had purchased lush silks and expensive shoes and exotic perfumes and Persian rugs. I opened the door, dropped the huge parcels and saw that I was too late.

Sitting stiffly in the better of our two wooden chairs, was the Immigration agent, his eyes riveted to the square tips of his shoes, which slipped on the waxed floor back and forth, while facing him, on our other chair, was my naked mama, making conversation. On the bed, with their legs crossed, and their arms around each other, my two little nude sisters smiled large fixed smiles like birds about to attack a ripe plum tree.

"Yes, you should have seen my little son in Buenos Aires. Always praying to the Virgin, always reading . . . reading and praying, he was an angel he really was . . . would you like to see some pictures?" Mother got up and removed from a trunk the carefully dusted photo album, exposing, as she bent over, her ancient wobbly buttocks atop her jiggling old thighs.

"Here he is at ten, in our parish church. . . ." Mother moved her chair closer to him so he could look. She put part of the album on his knees while another part rested on hers. "Here he is with the statue of the Mountain Virgin of the Eight Miracles when she came through our town . . . little Joselito didn't sleep for many nights before she came . . . he prayed and cried until his eyes were red . . ." Page by page, the devoted little boy went on his knees from icon to icon and statue to statue, crying rivers of tears.

"I brought you some clothes" I offered, directing their attention to my bundles. "I hope I got the right sizes. . . ."

"Ah!" said the agent, "I'm glad to see *you*! Your mother and sisters were kind enough to entertain me but it is you I have business with. Could we go into another room?"

"I am sorry, there is no other room. We could sit out on the steps. . . ."

"No, that's fine. We can sit here I suppose, if your family doesn't mind. . . ."

"No, no," they all hastened to reassure him, moving off the chair and beds to examine my purchases. They tore open the packages and a storm of underwear, skirts and blouses broke over the room as they lifted their legs and their arms to slip them on, and bent and shook to adjust them.

"You have an understanding family," said the agent, "We place great value on harmonious family life. The family is the base of our way of life!"

"Yes, I have been blessed that way. I am lucky, I really am."

"I like your mother very much. She is a fine lady," he said, but what he meant was he liked Tabita very much because his eyes were glued to her hips. "Are your sisters married? Do they have young men?"

At this point, the door burst open and No. 15 rushed in, one of his arms in a sling and the wrist bandaged. "You!" he exclaimed, when he saw the agent. "I almost died because of you! Where is my citizenship?" He took a menacing step, holding up his wounded arm.

"Regulations . . . forms . . . it isn't up to me . . . procedure . . . ." he was visibly alarmed. "We never determined how you came to this country. . . . Where is your green card?"

"I told you how I came. I flew, that's how. I lost my green card in the parking lot in Hollywood! What more do you want from me?"

"There was no record of your flight!"

"Of all the nerve! Every bird between here and the Black Sea can vouch for me! I even smiled at the stewardesses on a transatlantic Pan Am jet and they waved at me! Jerk!"

The Agent stood as if to leave.

"No, you don't" grinned No. 15, a large blackened and calloused paw on the official's shoulder. "Not until I tell you what we do to tax collectors in Transylvania."

In Transylvania a tax collector was lacerated bit by bit, until his reason was destroyed. Often, he was attached to a chair or a bed hung from a horizontal arm attached to a pillar in the middle of a

damp dungeon or a cave: by means of a system of gears the
machine was set for any degree of speed. The rotatory machine
gained speed slowly until it looked hell-driven and the sufferer's
pockets shook loose all the pillaged taxes while his reason fell away
in spasmodic chunks. The inventor of the rack, a Transylvanian
nobleman named Baron Von Bruckenthal, refined this machine to
such heights of perfectability that in 1731 an imperial tax collector
was completely dismembered by the centrifugal force and pieces of
him were found as far as Vienna sticking in the weather vanes of
some of the finer houses on Elisabethstrasse. Later, it seems, new
techniques came into use, including the infamous "tax collector
music machine" which was inserted into the body through what
was called "a rigorous system of organic and moral penetration." It
consisted of tiny disks resembling roll music for the player piano
which were put inside the intestines, the brain and the spine.
Seven strong fellows with wooden hammers hit the wooden keys of
the machine a little distance from the tax collector who then began
to fill up with music and start to hum and reverberate louder and
louder until all his internal organs started dancing madly. The
music eventually attained such frenzy that all the whirling and
waltzing organs exploded, merging inside the man in a furious and
indistinct sea which rose in a single wave and lifted the body into
the clouds, pulling him off the disks. "And that!" shrieked No. 15,
"is only part of the story!"

There was only one way to anesthetise No. 15 so he wouldn't
harm my fragile link to citizenship, and Raquel took it. She
dropped one of her large breasts into her palms where it fell with a
heavy plop and she introduced the nipple into No. 15's angry
mouth which closed immediately and began to make baby noises.
"There, there," she said, patting him on the rough black brillo pad
most Romanians seem to wear on their heads. "There, there," and
he closed his eyes and fell asleep.

When the agent saw he was out of danger he became indignant:
"That man!" he grunted. "To every simple question I asked him he
replied with riddles! Fairy tales! Vampire bats! I said 'Have you
ever been arrested?' and he gave me the history of his twelve
cousins' cardiac arrests! He probably doesn't have any cousins! He
doesn't even have a mother I'm sure of that! He's a down and out
orphan with a big mouth!" The agent half stood, shaking his finger,
while Tabita nodded gravely, agreeing with every word. He now

addressed himself entirely to her: "Some people think we are robots! No respect at all for what we represent! And then they want to be citizens! Sometimes I think I'm being punished with this job for sins from another life but of course I don't believe in that nonsense! Believe me after a day of the strangest gibberish in one thousand different accents I'm ready to hang my hat!"

"Hang it! Hang it!" cried Tabita, falling into his arms, "Hang it on me!"

He had no hat to hang but he held on to her as they both fell on the floor and wriggled there utterly penetrated, he by red-haired Argentine heat and she by compassion and a big man. I prayed No. 15 wouldn't wake up and he didn't. Mama got up to fix some snacks because she knew they would be mighty hungry when they got up off the floor. I was rather hungry myself—emotions render me famished—and I rocked back and forth on my heels, abandoning myself to the familiar and lovely sounds of my now wordless household, No. 15's snores alternating with the contented suckling sounds of his lips, the agent's and Tabita's ahs ohs madres dios gods oh my gods oh fucks, and the sizzling heavenly aromas of frying hot peppers, thin slices of marinated beef, bubbling beef bones and fresh bread coming out of mama's pans and ovens. Ah, yes, even everloud New York appeared to have been stilled outside the window in hot afternoon sun. All was peaceful, quiet and safe.

Sometimes, not often enough, the world is like this, gently immobile in an eternal Sunday afternoon. We stop our banging and clanging for long enough to taste the sweetness of things at ease, their hard edges softened, harshness gone or out of focus, something dimly remembered flows sluggishly through the body. A gaucho, asleep on his horse, stands still in the pampas. There is no wind, the animals sleep. On the half-eaten head of a cow the flies stop buzzing. The maggots too take time off for a nap, stretched lazily in dark tunnels of food. Sudden peace illuminates the eyes of the man dying in the house next door; he falls into it like a fat snowflake on a white field. I am six years old and I am watching him, not moving. Later, when the adults come back, I tell them how the Virgin came in softly and took his soul with her. They too can feel the peace. This peace is a gift, you cannot buy it and nowadays for the people my age it comes more and more rarely. Only violence can at times bring it up briefly, often with death in tow. And there are many to whom it never comes. It never comes to dreamers who have become cops. The price for re-entry into the society which hated them is half the hate, which they must take into themselves to lighten society's burden. A true Sunday afternoon comes only to those able to make their experience public and this they are forbidden to do by the self-hate with which they bought their way in. The prodigal son is an anomaly, he fits nowhere, he has denied his past but has no taste for the present, his parents do not want him now, they want him then, the labor market will only take him grudgingly and then at a substandard wage, he suffers all the agonies of a turncoat and none of the pleasures of forgiveness except money and money is garbage so the only place short of death which he has also forsaken in favor of old age is Tabita's pussy and in it he goes, up and around, up and up, up and out, unaware that myriad-legged swarms of Venusian jewels are migrating onto his body, riders of the storm awakened by heat. The content of his revelation, the fleeting beginning of his abandoned art return briefly in orgasm without the mushy edges of political hysteria and they are public for the first time in his life because I am watching carefully and mama too, her pan full of sizzling red peppers held in suspension briefly, because this is one of the few moments that bear watching, being both incomprehensible and totally true. But we aren't newspapers, of course.

No. 15 woke up mythological, throwing his startled body out of sleep with a stream of curses invoking fabulous beasts and was about to strangle the agent who was struggling to his feet with pants around ankles, when mama served the food. We ate it and each dish we became sadder. No. 15 remembered the food of his country and began in low monotone to recite the names of all the dishes of yore. It was a litany of the dishes of Transylvania as beautiful as a funeral dirge, and it seems that indeed, at funerals the people of that country recite the names of all their best dishes over the body of the departed in order to remind the angel of death that the deceased is on that special diet and will not have anything below par in the next world. Mama became sad because the peppers and the tomatoes were not the way she remembered them: they tasted limp and airless not at all like the robust vegetables of Argentina. Raquel was sad because every time she ate she got a little fatter and one day would come when she would be too fat for love. Tabita was sad because in reaching inside the agent she had found only a terrifying and whistling emptiness and now she wasn't hungry. And I was sad because the world is sad and my loved ones were very sad but my sadness was happy like rain in the fall. I was sweetly sad and not at all unhappy. The agent, of course, was sad because he didn't know what he wanted from these people and worse he didn't know who he was anymore, and the food was foreign and it didn't warm him.

He left with his report unwritten, the first time it had ever happened. He strolled aimlessly through the river front park. At one point he felt what he took to be a prick of his conscience but it was only an itch in his chest hair. Soon another false prick of conscience which again was only an itch below his abdomen. As the pricks began to multiply he thought well, maybe it is my conscience after all, I was derelict of duty. Soon his entire hairy body seemed to be on fire and the passersby slowed down to take a long look at the madly scratching bureaucrat set on fire by his conscience. By this time he had almost ceased looking human as he leaped and jumped like a shaman deer-dancer trying to pull off his skin. He ripped up his shirt and drew long bloody lines with his nails. They went up and down his body, deep and crimson like railroad tracks. Trains of maddened guilt ran on them at great speeds. His pants and shoes and socks came off next as he contorted and rolled into balls of pain attempting to tear open parts of his body he had never touched before. It was not much later when the moth in his chest, temporarily stilled by Tabita and by the hot peppers, began to flutter frantically inside him. This redoubled itching from the inside awoke in him what can only be described as the collective guilt of world bureaucracies. The unfulfilled nationalisms and sadistic racisms of all the buried strains in the dream of the uniform attacked him with the fury of their incompletion. Every new itch said "We counted on you!" and every letter of that reproach was a line of red ants berserk in his body. I could barely keep up with him from the distance I was following. But I knew he couldn't recognize me any more. So I came closer.

"Don't move or I kill you," I again quoted myself.

I killed him. I pushed him into the river where, instead of swimming, he continued to roll and tear at his insides until a long rubber object the likes of which float only on the East River and nowhere else, wrapped itself around his neck and squeezed the air out of his lungs. He sank rapidly and I knew that it had been a mercy killing.

𝅘𝅥 𝅘𝅥 𝅘𝅥

CRANE AND CARLSEN: A MEMOIR (1926-1934)

by LINCOLN KIRSTEIN

from RARITAN: A QUARTERLY REVIEW

nominated by RARITAN: A QUARTERLY REVIEW *and Robert Boyers*

For John Unterecker

IN 1927 as a sophomore at Harvard, I started *Hound & Horn*, a "little magazine," with Varian Fry, classmate and classicist. We were seconded by Richard P. Blackmur, then working as a salesman at the Dunster House Bookshop run by Maurice Firuski, a Yale bibliophile and patron of fine printing who published lavishly designed editions of George Santayana's "Lucifer" and Archibald MacLeish's early verse. *Hound & Horn's* model was the recently deceased *Dial*, edited by Marianne Moore, but more particularly T.S. Eliot's *Criterion*, then very much alive. We strove to attain an elitist progressive tone and stance through the late twenties and early thirties. We set our aesthetic on traditional nineteenth-century values as extended via the nineties by Ezra Pound, who provided our name from a poem in his *Personae* (1906): " 'Tis the white stag fame we're hunting,/bid the world's hounds come to horn." We began publication as "A Harvard Miscellany," but within a year, aided by the immediate interest of Pound and Eliot, grew into something wider than undergraduate enthusiasm. Our growth depended greatly on Dick Blackmur, whose solid and persistent intellectual application more than compensated for his lack of formal academic education. Later he became famous at Princeton as a licensed pundit.

Pound wrote us almost weekly tyrannical letters, called us "Bitch & Bugle," considered he controlled the quarterly, and

quarreled with us when we bridled at his demands for the publication of Ralph Cheever Dunning, Louis Zukofsky, and Adrian
Stokes. We did not take ourselves very seriously, except in the
several departments of our special interests. Blackmur, and later
Bernard Bandler II, a student of Aristotle who eventually became a
distinguished psychiatrist, took care of the Big Ideas. My own
interests were painting, architecture, American history, and films.
At the time, I was even more preoccupied with the Boston of
Beacon Hill, Mrs. Jack Gardner, the friends and heirs of Henry
Adams and Henry James, and what remained of the Cambridge of
Charles Eliot Norton and William James. I had the enormous good
fortune of a roommate whose grace of person, name, and character
embodied the numinous race of Cabot and Emerson. An alien, a
Jew, and an ageing child, I was welcomed into what then remained
of the world of Brattle Street and Beacon Hill where seventy-five
years before Henry Adams had commenced the triumphant failure
of his education, the story of which Dick Blackmur was already in
love with.

Perhaps a note on the background of our inherited philosophy
may clarify the peculiarity of the following account. It may explain,
and in part apoligize for the editors of *Hound & Horn* in their
refusal to print Hart Crane's "The Tunnel," seventh and penulti-
mate canto of his masterpiece "The Bridge." We did accept a mass
of mediocre and much more forgettable verse, among a small
amount of distinguished poems by well-known names. How could
ostensibly sensitive young men with notions "advanced" (for their
time), with some aquaintance with advance-guard French, English, and American poetry, reject Crane's evocation of the power
and grandeur of Manhattan's mystical bridge and mysterious subway? It was not refused out of hand, but after discussion, led by
Blackmur the purist, Varian Fry the Latinist, and myself, who was
entranced by the poem's epigraph:

> To find the Western path
> Right thro' the Gates of Wrath.

I had had as my Freshman Advisor S. Foster Damon, who had
just published the first important American explication of William
Blake's symbols and story. To Harvard's everlasting shame he was
denied tenure and was let go to Brown; Providence then was

considered provincial exile, and it was this proprietary attitude of
Harvard's Department of English that *Hound & Horn* sought to
contest. Blake's beautiful painting of "Glad Day," a brilliant nude
youth seen against the dazzling spectrum of a full rainbow, was my
personification of Melville's Jack Chase and Billy Budd, and Walt
Whitman's comrade. In arguments over the acceptance or rejection of Crane's poem, I felt he had not lived up to the oracular in
Blake's lines. I was a victm of Blackmur's compensatory stringency
and my own snobbery derived from my recently earned arcane
knowledge on Blake's true cosmology, derived from Foster Damon. This was an early example of the academic deformation we
thought we were trying to avoid—competitive vanity based on
subjective attachment.

In extenuation, I've always considered that I was born in the
nineteenth century, although the actual date was 1907. The twentieth, in my mind, didn't start until the 1913 fanfare of Stravinsky's
Sacre du Printemps, followed immediately by the First World War.
I entered Harvard College in 1926, which was still redolent of an
epoch before the institution of the House System. Our Freshman
Class was addressed by Charles William Eliot, editor of the once
famous five-foot shelf of the world's "best" books, but now a
doddering ancient on the brink of his grave. He advised the young
aspirants of the class of 1930 to "avoid introspection." This synthesis of a long life's experience puzzled some of us at the moment,
but Harvard would indeed offer many diversions, academic and
social, to avoid both conscience or consciousness.

In 1927, the more energetic Americans were writing books
which would provide capital for future Departments of English
Literature—mainly in London and Paris. Harvard's imaginative
aura lingered in a prior generation, with veterans of the recent war
(Cummings, Virgil Thomson, Dos Passos) providing the exuberant
foundations of our future hegemony. London seemed closer to
Cambridge, Mass. than Paris, because T.S. Eliot's own teachers
were still ours. Irving Babbitt lectured on Rousseau, Chateau-
briand, the sources of French romanticism, and his own brand of
humanism. Still in residence was J. L. Lowes, whose *Road to
Xanadu* became a bible, and there was Grandgent for Dante, A.N.
Whitehead for Plato and Pythagoras, A. Kingsley Porter for the
Romanesque. We had French and some German, but compared to
Christchurch or King's small Latin and less Greek. For us, at our

stage of development, Baudelaire tended to be primarily a Roman Catholic, Rimbaud an anarchist, Joyce a lapsed Jesuit, and Valery Larbaud more "modern" than Corbière or Laforgue. The Germans were Rilke and Thomas Mann; Goethe and Heine were largely ignored.

I had met Dick Blackmur the year before I entered college. He advised me on what most recent books I should buy and what I should think of them. He regretted that he knew no Sanskrit (yet). His reading was enormous in fields I had no notion were even available, from symbolic logic to the Nicomachean Ethics, from Origen to Gerard Manley Hopkins, Crashaw, Hegel, Jeans, and Eddington. When he first married I asked what he wanted as a wedding present: it was a pretty new four-volume edition of Herrick. He had contempt for many of my limited roster of masters. I would race down to his shop, comfortably housed in what was once an eighteenth-century tavern, eager not to miss the latest arrival from Faber & Gwyer or the Nonesuch Press. He had asked me what I had "learned." Maybe I told him that Professor Babbitt had said something astonishing about Sainte-Beuve; Dick's thin lips would curl: "Oh, that. It's just his usual inane reply to M. Tel-et-Tel's theory in the May number of *La Nouvelle Revue Française* (or *Le Mercure de France*)." This goes some way to define the attitude or atmosphere in which we felt free to refuse an important poem by Hart Crane.

Perhaps I might have felt less guilty if I had known that there were other more eminent rejectors of Crane—Harriet Monroe of *Poetry: A Magazine of Verse*, Marianne Moore at *The Dial*, Edmund Wilson at *The New Republic*. And in reviewing the published "Bridge" in *Poetry* (June, 1930), Yvor Winters, with Allen Tate, Crane's most useful literary correspondent, turned on his entire achievement. I might mitigate my own responsibility, evoking the authority of our editorial board, which indeed exerted a common authority. I was much involved with verse, daring to print some of my own. I had no interest in politics or social theory. *Hound & Horn* would increasingly be taken over by Southern Agrarians under the captaincy of Tate, and finally by a mixture of Anglican Marxists(!), Trotskyites, and "humanists." When poetic contributions came into the office I chose "the best" for Blackmur's severity. Unlike myself, he was not chastened by seeing his own verse in print, which was far more professional and justified than mine. He thought Crane's "Tunnel" was "promising, confused, self-indulgent, inchoate, etc." It had some "good lines"; Crane would be better next time around, doubtless after a long letter from Dick, written on his thick six-by-four-inch blocks in his small, square, immaculate orthography. Perhaps a script exists; it was my duty to abstract refusals from his too extensive text.

In *Hound & Horn's* summer issue for 1931, the excellent poet and discerning critic Yvor Winters reviewed a French study of the influence of *symbolisme* on American verse, analyzing Crane's presumed debt to Rimbaud, which was then discounted since Crane could only read him in translation. The first writing of Crane's I happened to have read, mainly for its subject matter, was dedicated to Stanislaw Portapovich, a dancer in Diaghilev's Ballets Russes who elected to stay in the United States after its disastrous 1917 season. In this poem Crane used as a rhyme "Chloe" (from *"Daphnis et Chlöe"*) as a monosyllable. This was enough to demonstrate how shockingly ill-lettered and pretentious was Crane. And Yvor Winter's analysis of Crane's beautiful "For the Marriage of Faustus and Helen" complained that

> The vocabulary of Mr. Crane's work suggests somehow the vocabulary of Rimbaud's prose and of a very little of verse, in its quality of intellectual violence and of almost perverse energy. . . .

"Perversity" and "violence" indeed. If there were any two elements lodged in my head to justify the rejection of unworthy or uncomfortable material, unorthodox or unfamiliar, in spite of our ostensibly pro-"modern" bias, they would have been violence and perversity. We were "educated" (in a strict sense, as editors); we were sustaining humane values, traditional though progressive, against mindlessness, anarchy, and chaos. We were mandated by Eliot ("Tradition and the Individual Talent") and Pound ("Make It New"). Blackmur, severely traumatized by his permanent lack of a *summa cum laude*, used overkill. I had taken received ideas as scripture and wasn't to be budged against instruction I'd absorbed with awe. Later, listing errors of commission and omission, one could be partly consoled by the names of those who got, and didn't get the Nobel Prize for Literature. Pearl Buck, John Steinbeck did. Marcel Proust, W. H. Auden didn't. As historic compensation, up to a point, Allen Tate reviewed "The Bridge" (*H & H*: summer, 1930) under the heading "A Distinguished Poet." (For those curious about Crane's worried if deeply appreciative, yet far too troubled reaction, it is fully covered in John Unterecker's monumental biography, *Voyager*.)

I was also at this time a companion of John Brooks Wheelwright, who helped us with his very professional if eccentric analyses of architectural styles. A properly improper Bostonian, an authentic Puritan combining extremes of High Episcopal liturgy, proto-Trotskyite metaphysic, and post-Ruskinian taste, he was both monk and dandy. An important, now ignored writer of ethical verse, he was kin to Henry and Brooks Adams; he wrote a beautiful threnody on Crane's death after a tense confrontation, entitled "Fish Food," which I came to wish I had been able to write myself as my particular personal apology. I was also a friend of Walker Evans, the photographer; with Wheelwright, we found a hundred fine nineteenth-century houses in the Greater Boston area and published some in *H & H*. Evans was living in quarters near Crane alongside the Brooklyn Bridge, and he had contributed photographic illustrations to the deluxe first edition of Hart Crane's poems published in Paris and reproduced, I never knew why, in the format of postage stamps. A little later I shared a house with Archibald MacLeish, then writing for *Fortune*, who had the happy and generous idea of commissioning Crane, who badly needed a job, to describe the construction of the George Washington Bridge. I also knew Estlin Cummings; he and MacLeish had not met, and I brought them together. They spoke of Crane's difficulties. "eec" said flatly that Crane was incapable of finishing anything; Archie should be warned.

I never knew Crane personally. I bumped into him a few times when I came down from Cambridge to New York. He never failed to frighten me. His reputation, of course, preceded him, a negative fame of lurid pyrotechnics, at once alluring and repulsive. He surely could have had small use for a supercilious college kid, some ten years younger, with firm poetic prejudices.

On March 28, 1931, I went to a party thrown by the editors of *The New Republic*, in a big penthouse above Fifth Avenue. Present were Edmund Wilson, Paul Rosenfeld, C. D. Jackson, Dwight MacDonald, and Walker Evans, among others. e.e. cummings's second wife, a termagant, baited me, deservedly, for being gratuitously rude to Crane at another party at the MacLeish's a few weeks earlier. Cummings said that Crane's mind was no bigger than a pin, but that it didn't matter; he was a born poet. The one person present I knew at all well was Walker Evans, then about to embark on a south-seas voyage to make a film on a yacht chartered by Oliver Jennings. It was through Walker that I encountered Crane's friend, Carl Carlsen, who was signed on as an able-bodied seaman.

The New Republic's party sticks in a befogged memory, illuminated by a brief thunderclap. The air was subdued, with the usual self-enclosed groups in a haze of cigarette smoke and alcohol. Abruptly, in a far corner of the high big room, angry voices and motion. I had not noticed the spark of the fracas; now there were fisticuffs. Two men traded punches. The taller seemed in control; he held the other at arm's length and hit him, hard. Someone had called somebody else something. Whatever the source of the rumpus, music-under swelled into gathering general irritation. "Chuck the son of a bitch out!" A door onto the elevator outside opened as of itself, and Crane, slight, with rumpled shock of pepper-and-salt hair, helped by hands other than his own, was chucked out. Quiet resumed, drinks were drunk; nobody paid much mind to an interruption which scarcely had had time enough to come to serious trouble.

About half an hour later there were blunt bangings on the door. Kicks, knocks, yells; it was opened. Crane bounced back into an unastonished assembly, pursued by a small but furious taxi driver. Crane had hailed him for a run to a Sand Street sailors' bar under the Brooklyn Bridge. Having arrived, Crane had no cash. Driver had pushed him into the gutter, but was persuaded to drive back to the party where friends would take up a collection and pay for three trips. Crane, filthy, sodden, and desperate, was remorseful but morose. Cabbie, given a couple of drinks, was mollified. Crane proclaimed what a marvelous character he was; he would hire his taxi to take him to Mexico on his recently awarded Guggenheim. They left, quietly enough, together.

This eruption, which probably seemed abnormal mainly to me, was no great event for those foregathered. To others, on similar, more or less familiar occasions, this was not rousing behavior. For those who lived by the lyric imagination, whose craft and career was the play of words and imagery, Crane was not over-distressing or disagreeable—except possibly to himself, when he sobered up. When he came back with the cab driver I was struck and humbled by his patient penitence, muffled apologies, a small boy's pathetic, instinctive good manners. At first I was inclined to be, or tried to be, surprised, horrified, and outraged. Actually, I longed to have had the guts to get drunk and pick up a character who much resembled Jimmy Cagney in *Taxi*, a brilliant Warner Brothers film. I idolized Cagney and had written an extended appreciation of his genius for *H & H*. I studied his films assiduously as they appeared, and saw each one half a dozen times—from *Public Enemy, Smart Money, Blonde Crazy, The Crowd Roars*, and *Here Comes the Navy* to Max Reinhardt's beautiful *Midsummer Night's Dream*, in which he starred as a marvelously inventive Warwickshire Bottom. Cagney, for me, provided a postgraduate course in heroic lyric realism in opposition to Harvard good taste. Cagney liked my article and we became intermittent friends for fifty years. I aimed to delete the conditioning of my schools and class, costumed myself from cut-rate Army-Navy stores, and was not wildly successful as a male impersonator. In Brooklyn bars Walker Evans taught me to keep my mouth shut, and so I penetrated the safer areas of some charming jungles where there was no real threat or risk except of an exotic landscape. I deceived no one; denizens of such urban areas can spot a stranger on sight. I smelled different, but I was kindly tolerated for my curiosity and adulation. It was not exactly cross-pollination, but there was some exchange in encounters between mutually bizarre tribes. In this ambiance I met Carlsen.

If he had any professional calling it was the sea, but his real ambition was to be a writer, with the sea as his subject. Walker Evans had met him through Crane's great friend, Emil Opffer, a merchant seaman, and Evans had told Carl to send some of his stories to me, an editor of *H & H*. Three duly arrived, each neatly typed in its own spring-binder. None of them made much of an impression. Walker pressed me concerning them. I found it hard to say anything definite. Although we were small fry compared to big-circulation magazines, we printed the first or early stories by Katherine Anne Porter, John Cheever, Erskine Caldwell, Kay Boyle, Stephen Spender, and others during seven years of publication. I read the greater part of the fiction contributions, and what I deemed best was passed on to Dick Blackmur and Bernard

Bandler for final judgment. As for Carl Carlsen's quite unmemorable pieces, they had passed without comment, or at the most gained an impersonal rejection slip.

Then, one day when I was lunching at the greasy spoon near *Time-Life* with Walker Evans and Jim Agee, Evans brought me a scruffy bundle of typewritten yellow sheets, the rough draft of another story by Carlsen. I think its raw presentation and obvious travail attracted me, since it was so unlike the shipshape typescripts previously sent. It concerned the stoker in a boiler room of a merchant freighter. An important piece of a machine, overheated or lacking lubrication—perhaps a piston—had split and snapped. The stoker or other mechanic immediately substituted his forearm for the broken part. For some minutes the man's flesh and bone was a working replacement for steel and oil. The tragedy, while not convincing as written, obviously derived from vivid memory. The prose was by someone who knew more about metal and machinery than short-story composition. However, I could not be entirely disdainful of its stiff primitive energy, small as its wick might glow. Its strained rhetoric was influenced by Melville and his masters; it was overwritten, rhapsodic, and rhetorical. Yet somehow pretentious it was not, nor even synthetic. There was too much detailed observation to betray contrivance. The narration could not read as exactly naive; there was the taint of absorption in Melville and Conrad. The notion was powerful, but the prose was without practice; we couldn't bring ourselves to accept so primitive a piece. I wrote its author the kindest rejection note I could manage and sent him a volume of Rudyard Kipling's riveting short stories, including "The Ship That Found Itself," in which the intransigent components of a newly commissioned steamer, after an agonizing launch run, grew to have its stubborn separate parts finally work together. It was this that brought Carlsen to our office at 10 East 43rd street (we were newly transplanted from Cambridge to Manhattan). He did not come in person; I was thanked by a letter slipped under the door. Carlsen found the Kipling tale unreal; its author obviously had been no merchant-seaman. Fame did not forgive the fable, but his strictures made their point.

Who was Carlsen? I never discovered as much as I wished to know. Walker Evans could or would not elucidate: only "a chum of Emil and Ivan Opffer's, Gene O'Neill's and Hart's." In 1930, Crane wrote Caresse Crosby in Paris that Carl was "a former sailor who has got tired of office-work and expects to hit the deck again for a while." Crane drowned before I had real contact with Carl. Eventually, after some timorous urging, Walker took me around to Carlsen's home. This was an oversized doll's house, a picturesque miniature semisecret habitat, awarded him by the guardian angels of Walt Whitman and Herman Melville. One passed through an all but unmarked gap in a row of mid-nineteenth-century brownstones in the middle of a block somewhere between far-West 16th and 20th streets; I can't now say exactly where, since I've not been there in fifty years. Between the two blocks survived three tidy two-storeyed unpainted clapboard buildings with a joined narrow porch and pairs of gabled dormers. Built by 1840, these were freshly shingled, old, but without decay. In the middle house dwelt Carlsen. The single downstairs room was bare, spotless, shipshape tidy. It might have been comfortable as a whaler's cabin anchored in Nantucket, New Bedford, or Sag Harbor. The only intrusion from the twentieth century was a small shiny upright piano with stacks of music on top. A narrow stair with a rope banister led above. Later, I would find a common lavatory in a back courtyard which served the three buildings, and there was a hand pump. Gas was laid on, but there was a total lack of heat and hot shaving-water.

Evans introduced me as the man from *H & H* who had judged his offerings. Carl was a stocky thick-trunked man, thirty-five to forty, clean-shaven, leathery, no extra flesh, and apparently hard-bitten. He had coarse, untrimmed bushy eyebrows fairer than his ash-blonde, close-cropped hair. The piano obviously belonged to a stolid, self-contained woman, maybe ten years older than Carlsen. Her hair was in a stiff orange pompadour. She nodded to Walker and me without enthusiasm and abruptly disappeared up the stairs, as one might say, in a marked manner. This didn't seem to bother her companion. He wore well-worn, crisply-laundered old regulation U.S. Navy bell-bottoms, with a drop fly and thirteen buttons, in honor of the thirteen original colonies. Next to the small gas range was a wooden icebox, maple, with nicely turned legs, unpainted—perhaps a recent addition. In the icebox were cream and lemon; on the stove water, boiling. Tea was made; the master of the house took rum from a cupboard and set the full bottle before me. The—to me—exotic purity or clarity of the local weather bemused me. Speech was slow in coming. Soon enough,

Walker made desultory politenesses. I studied the room. On the mantle above the wood-framed fireplace were three brass candlesticks, all different. Next to them was a portrait of Crane by Walker in an old cork mat. Inside a foot-long green bottle was the model of a full-rigged sailing vessel. I asked how it managed to get inside the bottle, which couldn't have been blown around it. Carlsen explained that the mast and rigging had been laid flat; the hull was thin enough to slip by, and a thread pulled the masts upright.

From upstairs came grunts of furniture being moved; something slammed. Carl rose from the tea table to investigate. I tried to signify to Walker in Carlsen's absence how abjectly fascinated I was by this quaint home; there was hardly enough time. Some manner of abrupt exchange was heard from the top of the stair. Walker winked. Carl came down; there were no apologies; we were dismissed leaving warm tea in mugs and rum untasted. He smiled without embarrassment; hoped he'd see me again "sometime"; slapped Walker on the back, firmly shook my hand, and we were out in the courtyard. There had been not a word about his manuscripts.

I was loath to leave, troubled, as if, somehow, I'd done the wrong thing, for I had been enchanted. Here was a human situation, a concentrated mystery of class behavior which I might have read about or suspected, but never touched. I was torn as to what further contact I might seek. How could I warp a half-uttered invitation into some story *H & H* might print? Walker was no help. On the walk back I bombarded him with questions, but his thin answers told more of Crane than Carlsen, whom he claimed to have met only in passing. Evans had a collector's passion for ephemeral American artifacts: matchboxes, baseball and cigarette cards; old valentines; tobacco boxes; trademarked paperbags, and twine. Somehow, Carlsen and his ambiance was connected with such collecting.

In my idiosyncratic mythology, those whose fortunes followed the sea had solemn significance. The first dress-up clothes I'd been given to wear were when my father brought me (aged seven) the midget uniform of a Royal Navy rating (from Rowe of Gosport), complete with a silver bosun's rope and whistle, in which I was duly photographed. At bedtimes, he read to my brother and me Dana's *Two Years Before the Mast*. His steady affairs in Britain supplied the *Illustrated London News*, with their splendid extracolored souvenir editions celebrating the coronations of Edward VII and George V. Portraits of Princes of Wales disguised as midshipmen were linked in my mind with Mark Twain's *The Prince and the Pauper*. The role of sailor, ordinary and extraordinary, seemed to be that of classless, or de-classed prince. As a freshman at Harvard, Foster Damon, my tutor, gave me *White-Jacket* and *Israel Potter* to read. The reputation of *Moby Dick* was at the crest of its recognition. The manuscript of *Billy Budd* lay in Widener Library. I paid a classmate to transcribe Melville's illegible handwriting, since Damon told me that the recently published Constable "complete" edition was full of errors as printed. I had been on my brother's small boat in Marblehead Harbor, but never on the open sea. In 1925 in London I had fallen in love with the Russian Ballet. Léonide Massine's *Les Matelots*, with Georges Auric's early jazz, had among its three sailors an American, borrowed from Jean Cocteau's memories of the U.S. Mediterranean cruises with gobs ashore in the bars of Toulon and Villefranche. The jolly sailors Massine choreographed for Diaghilev's Russian dancers in exile were domesticated acrobats, hardly sailors at sea, but players ashore. Like Carlsen.

My image of him, presumably fictive, had little enough to do with any essential self; but for me, he incarnated legends. The fact that he was approachable, on the beach, and hence both estranged from his proper province and yet accessible, made his vague presence all the more exhilarating, for surely "he knew the name Hercules was called among the women and held the secrets of the sea." Perhaps he only existed between voyages, likely to ship out at any moment. How would I ever find him again unless I were able to conceive a stratagem which, so far, I had not the slyness to imagine? Here, again, Walker Evans was no help; he had gone as far as he could pushing Carl towards "literature"; he wasn't particularly generous, or amused by my fascination. If I wanted to see the guy again, no big deal. Drop in on him, just as we had today. After all, as yet there had been no mention of his ambitious writing, nor my dubious thwarting of it.

So, breathless and in some dread, I did risk it. On my second visit, he was alone. Now, my self asserted its typecasting as college critic; my sincerity was clear even if suggestions were limp. But perhaps I was almost the first to take him seriously as more than a mechanic, and thus I advanced slowly, solemnly into a hesitant friendship. Steps from cautious contact to relative intimacy were propelled by the abrupt arrival of his brother, a second officer on a coastal freighter on regular runs from San Diego, through the Panama Canal up to Portland, Maine. Every three or four months Nils Carlsen enjoyed a few days liberty from Hoboken. Carl took me over to explore his command. First climbing aboard, there seemed to be no one anywhere. It was deserted. One custodian tended pilot fires in the furnace room. Here was surely the site of the split piston rod and a stoker's shattered arm. Carl drew no special attention to any single piece of machinery. I was about to ask the function of every obvious object, but realized this was his private time and sacred place, not to be profaned by idle or overeager curiosity. If I, indeed, had the wit to feel awe, then let this jungle of polished brass bandings, glistening serpentine coils, and tigerine furnaces purr its hot breath. My cautious questions were answered by his ready brother. The latent power in the engines seemed to swell, filling Carl's fixed, riveted silence, in which his complete comprehension of mineral potency was haloed in a scent of oil, the slumbering, acrid fragrance of coal-fire; an incandescent bluish gloom through thick-glazed furnace doors. A brutal but delicate mechanism was alive, grossly asleep, lovingly tended, waiting to be ignited into full flame. An unfired weapon, immaculately maintained, called for its own ration of love, and love is what burnished it through Nils Carlsen's professional concern. He apologized for the inadequacy of active operation. Here was power at one remove; his ship slept, not to be aroused until it met open sea. As we left, Carl astonished me by saying evenly that if we ever should ship out together, then he would let me learn what hot metal meant as the measure of energy in motion.

Initiation in the boiler room was revelation, but this abrupt personal inference of interpolation, tossed out so lightly, exploded that vein of incendiary excitement which is the rapacious flare of first love. While I realized only too well I could never bet on any specific date for a joint voyage, the fact that he had uttered so vague a proposal diffused small logic. After all, his brother was bound to this boat and could probably arrange everything easily. Why shouldn't we, some time in what glorious future, ship out together? I would teach Carl how to write as he taught me how to live.

For two good reasons, among tides of unanswerable others. First, Carl was in retirement from the sea, by will or chance. He was fixing to be "a writer." He took writing seriously; he wrote mornings, he said, every day: eight to eleven. What he wrote, Bertha, the piano teacher, his consort, typed afternoons. I could imagine that while she typed, he wandered around, did chores. She was the real hindrance for me. I never knew whether or not they "slept" together. It would have been impossible to have guessed otherwise, yet in public there was little contact. Carlsen never talked dirty, nor made the exciting, outrageous, or forbidden raw jokes or reference which might have been expected, and for which I knew men of his class were famous. This further distanced me from a full unveiling of the many secrets he seemed to hold. Bertha cooked; she kept their house in its pale immaculate rigor. As I ventured to drop in more often and stay longer, she made fairly polite efforts to speak, but sooner or later, she retired, upstairs. She even tried to make it appear that she knew Carl and I had serious things to say by which his career might be furthered. Perhaps she somehow knew his "writing" was more or less of a fantasy, but at least it was an alternative to his going back to sea, which certainly she did not want. She kept him on a loose chain; he had his "freedom." I hoped he was free enough to include me somewhere in it. He seldom spoke of her, but his perfect manners precluded such folly.

However, eventually I felt close enough to Carl to risk mentioning that I sensed that "Bertha didn't like me." I dared this presumption, risking a connection to which I had precarious right. All he admitted was: "You don't bother her." This was no resolution, but I knew enough not to press it. At the time when one is breaking out of postadolescence, fright, insecurity, apprehension encourages an appetite for adventure dared. Everything I had previously experienced or felt about people seemed now on the other side of a glass wall, and my "education," *pace* well-beloved Henry Adams, was a half-conscious attempt to eliminate the self-protection from a "real world." Carlsen was my real world, and his isolation was at once nearer and farther than any one or any thing. Unfleshed imagination flickers, a vast amorphous void, filled with rainbow possibilities and doubt. Carl exploded in my life, bringing to the exercise of heart and mind the chance for a three-dimensional existence, released from the prison of prior habit. While he strove to make art out of a half-life, I tried to make come alive what heretofore I had only read of in books, which were now the models which stopped him dead.

As for any actual contact with Hart Crane, the poet, heir of Poe, Whitman, and Hopkins, this was tenuous in the extreme. Encounters with Crane were negligible; yet I depended on Crane's immediacy to certify my contact with Carl. I knew Crane would not have recognized my face. But I was rather close to those who did know him very well: Evans, Allen Tate, Katherine Anne Porter. I was not really drawn to his gift; I barely connected the man with his poetry. Both seemed outrageous and unmannerly, although I was not ready to face the blame for fearing its obscurity. After all, there was Modern Art, and what a success that was becoming! And I was forced to feel, in spite of prejudice, that there was some irreducible courage, both in art and life, a defiance, however gross or unseemly, of which I could not help being envious. Carl was slow to speak of him; if they had been drunk and disorderly together often enough, he volunteered little that was revelatory or proprietary. He shied away from mention of violence of perversity. For these there were no apologies; he inferred such was the fibre of genius that Crane was licensed to play as he pleased. Crane was above praise or calumny. As for Carlsen's own preference or promiscuity he let me hear nothing; when he dealt out rum, it was the classic brace at the capstan. I was forced to assume his deliberate moderation was the result of some possible earlier excess now monitored by a lady piano teacher. Yet I was eager to bring Carl into "my" world, to exhibit him to Muriel Draper and Carl Van Vechten. But he disdained entrance into alien areas, and was not eager to be exhibited as a picturesque trophy.

On April 28, 1932, I was invited to Muriel Draper's for cocktails. I wrote in a diary:

> I learned of Hart Crane's drowning. A sickening feeling, but I never really cared for him or his work, except for "Hurricane" which I thought magnificent.
>
> Rock sockets, levin-lathered!
> Nor, Lord, may worm outdeep
>
> Thy drum's gambade, its plunge abscond!
> Lord God, while summits crashing
>
> Whip sea-kelp screaming on blond
> Sky-seethe, dense heaven dashing—

Thou ridest to the door, Lord!
Thou bidest wall nor floor, Lord!

After this, I began to hesitate in asking Carl to show more of his writing, since my early response had been so unwelcoming. With the removal of much compulsion to connect the two of us through "literature," he grew less shy, and our relations went from friendliness to something approaching friendship. One of the impersonations requiring considerable craft is that of feigning enthusiasm about the disappointing labors of one liked or loved. Carl was never going to be much of a literary man; if his attempts had been high school student work by a sixteen-year-old, it might have proved promising. Apt phrasing, careful observation, genuine emotion, and brief bursts of oddly personal intonation there may have been, but since he had read so little, and what he had found on his own to read—Marlowe and Melville in particular—were such monstrous models, and since his own vital experience was both so very deep and narrow, one could not hope for much quality beyond the primitive. There was yet a further, more profound impediment. From inherent shyness, good manners, or instinctive discretion he excluded from his narrative much approaching vivid personal comment. He wrote about the sea and its mariners in terms of popular magazine illustration confused by "literary" rhetoric, avoiding psychological insight, as if such realism might dull a "beauty" in expression. Carl, like Crane, his idol, was a rhapsodist, not a precise analyst. The exalted rhetoric of Marlowe and Melville derived in great part from traditions of the spoken word—drama or pulpit, the heightened accents of vocal utterance. Carl's prose, like Crane's verse, was written to be read aloud, yet I have yet to hear any speaker give voice to Crane as satisfactorily as one mouths it in the mind with closed lips. Carl's opacity and stumbling richness was hard enough to read and would never be printed.

He came to the world of books late in his development, receiving the key to his furnished library from a poet who canonized four overwhelming masters: Marlowe, Melville, Whitman, Rimbaud. Before almost anyone in the United States, through Yvor Winters, Crane came upon Gerard Manley Hopkins, and strove earnestly without much effect to make him better known. Crane's power was more verbal than metrical; Hopkins' shackled ferocity combined word, measure, and music with far more discipline, despite the short-circuits and elided metaphors of which both were masters. Just as Hopkins adored and was terrified of Whitman's barefaced carnality, so Crane concealed the immediacy of his sentiment in an almost hysterical chromatics of language and compressed imagery. The alchemy of the word was a hazardous science; Carlsen, with his slight talent and less familiarity with his betters, was doomed as a writer. His awe of the potential in the English language betrayed him. Carl's longing to make literature was a means of touching magic he couldn't make. Crane came into his life as some Prospero, transforming Manhattan and Brooklyn into enchanted islands. Did Carl have much notion of what Crane was trying to say? We had once been reading, together, from "The Bridge":

> Whose head is swinging from the swollen strap?
> Whose body smokes along the bitten rails,
> Bursts from a smouldering bundle far behind
> In back forks of the chasms of the brain—
> Puffs from a riven stump far out behind
> In interborough fissures of the mind . . .?

Carl stuck on "swollen strap." Why swollen? Now "interborough"; he could see the subway connection, but he asked: "Why in hell can't he say what he means?" In the summer of 1926, Crane had written to Waldo Frank, one of his first professional enthusiasts:

> . . . work continues. The Tunnel now. I shall have it done very shortly. It's rather ghastly, almost surgery— and oddly, almost all from the notes and stitches I have written while swinging on the strap at late midnight hours going home.

In 1932, writing after the suicide, introducing the first American edition of "The Bridge," Waldo Frank explained:

> "The Tunnel" gives us man in his industrial hell which the machine—his hand and heart—has made; now let the machine be his godlike Hand to uplift him! The plunging subway shall merge with the vaulting bridge. Whitman gives the vision: Poe, however vaguely, the method.

Now, fifty years later, Carl's innocent objection irritates like a stubborn hangnail. Here as elsewhere Crane said something less than what he hoped to mean. Rather, he relied on Rimbaud's *alchimie du verbe* to make magic more than morality or meaning. "The Tunnel," with its random mosaic of subway-mob vernacular quotations, could too easily be read as a gloss on Eliot's "Game of Chess." To the editors of H & H, hypnotised by that poem and its author, any similarity would have seemed more weakening then than it does now. Perhaps it was this very likeness, or homage, which prompted Eliot to print it in his *Criterion*, for August, 1927.

But, partly as a devil's advocate, partly in my role as professor of Modern Poetry, I tried to particularize for Carl what I conceived Crane's method proposed. I had been struck hard by an arresting image in "For the Marriage of Faustus and Helen" (part III), which mentions "Anchises' navel, dripping of the sea—" wherein I saw some ancestral demigod, striding towards a surfbound Tyrrhenian shore, Giovanni da Bologna rather than Praxiteles, an ancient marine divinity, model for a baroque fountain, one of Bernini's gigantic epitomes. Carl asked: "Who the hell's Anchises?" Making it easy, I might have said Anchises was another name for Neptune, the sea god Poseidon, brother to Zeus, enemy of Ulysses, author of his misfortunes—or possibly merely a trisyllable Crane happened to have come across, which like so many fortuitous findings fired his prosody. There seem to be two mentions only of Anchises in the Iliad; he was father to Aeneas, lover to Aphrodite born of sea-foam, second cousin to Priam, King of Troy. In Book III of the Aeneid,

> When old Anchises summoned all to sea:
> The crew, my father and the Fates obey. . . . (Dryden)

Years later, a young Harvard scholar told me that in the Homeric "Hymn to Aphrodite" Anchises mates with the goddess, who bears his child in secret. Later, he is punished for presuming to couple with divinity. Mortals suffer who dare touch the immeasurable. Crane could have had something concrete in mind by naming Anchises—an autodidact, he read widely. But with Carlsen it was useless for me to pursue all this; it reduced a marvel to the academic. I did my best by trying to suggest the taut muscular belly of an ancient athlete brimming with saline, not very wine-dark liquor, chill and glistening as from some celestial shower bath.

*   *   *

Meditating on Hart Crane's life, death, and residue is sobering exercise. Now enshrined, he has his niche in the mortuary of dazzling self-slayers. He's been well served by friends and students whose sympathy and industry have restored what failed ambition must certainly have granted. Before crisis framed him, his was the treasure of a small, closed audience of passionate if troubled admirers. Now widely available in paperback, griefs forgiven or forgotten, he is redeemed in posthumous sovereignty. This came without any compulsion as the inevitable slow but logical recognition of genius. To regret or complain that there are not more relics to worship, or that his legacy might be other or superior, begs the question. Crane handled, mishandled, and manipulated words, warping heard speech into an electric recalcitrance as no American has done before or since, and which few Englishmen have equalled since Father Hopkins. Nevertheless, Allen Tate, one of his closest friends, wrote in the obituary for H & H (July-September 1932) a judgment of "The Tunnel," which he saw as Crane's attempt to write his *Inferno*, and which is still hard to refute:

> At one moment Crane faces his predicament of blindness to any rational order of value, and knows that he is damned; but he cannot face it, and he tries to rest secure upon the mere intensity of sensation. . . . It [The Bridge] is probably the final word of romanticism in this century. When Crane saw that his leading symbol would not cover all the material of his poem, he could not sustain it ironically in the classic manner. Alternately he asserts it and abandons it because fundamentally he does not understand it. The idea of bridgeship is an elaborate metaphor, a sentimental conceit leaving the inner structure of the poem confused.

Pondering the brief span of Crane's performance, one risks deciphering roots of dysfunction, tension, torment, terror, and hysteria. There are masterful studies of his times and temperament, notably Unterecker's huge *Voyager*. Crane's catastrophe can be reduced, perhaps simplistically, to two afflictions: Cleveland and Christian Science. This middle-American town early in the century stands for the basic provincial Philistine criterion, the Protestant work ethic of crippling but mandatory somnambulistic success as the guarantee and habit of salvation. C. R. Crane's candy business cannot be assigned the worst level of hell, but purgatory of the paralyzed imagination, particularly when genius is at stake, is as sad. Attempts to benevolently strait-jacket his only son and heir into the patterns of industrial health were wounding and drained Hart's energy at the very moment it asserted itself towards invention. C. R. was no villain, neither ungenerous nor entirely insensitive. He loved his boy, wished him well, even when wife and mother did her damned best to kill any mutual contact.

She was and is, alas, by no means an unfamiliar American darling. "Science," for her, was true magic. And as too many others had proved, material suffering, physical and mental, was wholly imaginary; *it did not exist*. Mary Baker Eddy stated: "Nothing is real and eternal; nothing is spirit, but God and His ideal; evil has no reality." Since God is pure Good, He cannot have created, or have been responsible for aught that is not Good. Man is God's personal notion, and belongs by essence to an order in which there may be no disease, ugliness, hate, sin, sorrow, or death. Such are mere errors of Man's mortal mentation, without "reality" save as man's mortal mind admits them. Disdain them! *They do not exist!* There is only True or False with neither degree nor choice. To the neurotic, this banishes neurosis; what we do not wish to credit, asks no credence. But this denial precipitates a terrible burden on the vulnerable lyric mechanism through the solipsism of un-measured fantasy. The constricted, stoic self tries to force free association into passive courage, but creatures of Crane's tempera-ment, torn between the duel of his parents' feuding, rushed roaring through the barriers of genuine suffering to drown in the only harbor he could imagine: oblivion. As Crane's wise counselor, Yvor Winters, wrote of Hart as Orpheus:

> Till the shade his music won
> Shuddered, by a pause undone—
> Silence would not let her stay.

He could go one only way;
By the river, strong with grief,
Gave his flesh beyond belief.

Yet the fingers on his lyre
Spread like an avenging fire.
Crying loud, the immortal tongue,
From the empty body wrung,
Broken in a bloody dream,
Sang unmeaning down the stream.

As a gesture of filial devotion to Grace Crane, now divorced and in lonely anguish, Crane himself tried to "practice" Christian Science, but with little confidence. He recommended his mother be more assiduous in her own practice—the amateur psychologist suggesting placebos. But she was infected, corrupting both herself and him. If human disease does not exist, there is no need to seek the means to face it, endure, handle, or use it. However, since suffering does indeed exist in omnivorous constancy, deliberate ignorance of its presence is an error majestic in consequence. Crane suffered more than most, in the depth, delicacy, and intensity of his sensibility. The pain that sprang from it, the energy taken to resist it and at the same time to bury it, somehow justified it, and absolved him from it. His short life was drained on two incompatible levels: Chagrin Falls, a well-to-do Cleveland suburb, and Sand Street, Brooklyn, a nirvana of sailor bars. Alcohol was a benison; it was as if Mrs. Eddy had handed him her witches brew. Alcohol obliterated and at once inspired—a distillation of alchemical ink. Unraveling accomodation with his furious progenitors, patched up by his want of and need for love, plus sheer poverty, took more of a toll than bathtub gin or harbor adventures. Random encounters were seldom successful as enduring affection and became hateful payment to his "curse of sundered parentage." One-night stands are for a single night; love of one's mother, however torn, is lifelong, endless, stoked by an overkill of anguish. Physical absence may split son from father, but the tie binds. Maleness is the criterion, and Crane took sides against his own. Only the wavering is constant and consistent; wild nights are blessedly discontinuous; to make small matters better or worse, there's always tomorrow with its luckier midnight. To solve the dreadful problem—freedom, talent, genius—one can embrace a stupendous falsity: Cleveland, Chagrin Falls, according to Christian Science, don't exist.

But psychic energy nurtured by self-deceit only accelerates the false and irrelevant. The old heresy which proclaims Resurrection without Crucifixion as a material fact consoles generations of fairly affluent middle-class vulnerability in its competitive mass. While there may be unemployed Scientists, there are few born and bred as working-class folk. Carl Carlsen could never have been a practicing Christian Scientist, but I was to discover that Bertha, his piano teacher friend was, on the side, yet importantly for her, a Christian Science healer.

My short connection with Carlsen was through Crane alone, and this was a weak link. Carl spoke little about the person, whom he knew well, but always with awe about the poet, whose lines he could barely grasp. To him, they were disparate identities, never twins. They seemed to have seen less of each other than formerly. Friends that lasted—Tate, Malcolm Cowley, Waldo Frank—were those to whom, finally, Crane could speak of ideas, the matter of his primary labor. But in some deep way for Carl, Crane was faultless; his behavior, his aberrations, were simply routes to a level of fame or feeling which was destiny.

Nevertheless, in meetings with Carl, Crane was an invisible third, spectral but manifest. I could understand well enough what he meant to Carl, but what did I mean—to him, or anyone? I was a rich college kid, twenty-three years old, whose surfeit of "education" had misprized Crane's Pindaric ode to the tunnel beneath the bridge:

> O caught like pennies beneath soot and steam,
> Kiss of our agony thou gatherest;
> Condensed, thou takest all—shrill ganglia
> Impassioned with some song we fail to keep.
> And yet, like Lazarus, to feel the slope,
> The sod and billow breaking—lifting ground,
> —A sound of waters bending astride the sky
> Unceasing with some Word that will not die . . . !

Perhaps this fixation on one of Crane's buddies was an attempt to compensate for my stupidity, my wickedness. But the truth was,

Carl didn't connect me with either Harvard, *Hound & Horn*, or Crane. By then the magazine had been taken over by Dick Blackmur, Allen Tate and his Southern Agrarians, and other intellectuals with political or metaphysical preoccupations. My postgraduate studies were centered in Manhattan. Carl was amused that I was in love with him.

It wasn't easy to find him. He had his work, which I had to assume was dogged, daily typewriting—moonlighting sometimes as handyman, janitor; certainly he didn't type all day and all night. Money never seemed a problem. Maybe piano lessons paid for his drinks, because he was scrupulous about paying for them. But he was not someone I might feel free to drop in on any old time, particularly if Bertha was likely to be at home. Possibly I made more of her as a problem than she actually was. Most days, having learned to estimate his working habits, I would go over with the excuse of asking if he'd want to go for a walk. If he didn't feel like it, and if she were in, she promptly vanished upstairs. Her presence was pervasive. Some nights Carl might even walk me home to my own room on Minetta Lane, where I made him tea and a drink. I was then sharing the place with Tom Wood, an ex-cowboy who, having been trained as a blacksmith, turned into a craftsman of forged iron. He made handsome firescreens with carefully cut out silhouettes of animals, stubby andirons, and pleasant shop signs. Carl and he shared the experience of handling metal; there were also the unspoken bonds of class and manual labor. Their immediate cool rapport made me objectively happy and subjectively sad.

One night, a clear September evening in 1934, I went around hoping to catch Carl in, and on the way bet myself he'd be out—insurance against disappointment. The city street-sounds were diminished and clarified, the darkening air all the more transparent from the thin punctuation of fragmentary voices. The courtyard in front of his house was swept clean; three garbage pails were in a neat triangle, coverless and empty. Carl was alone. I expected Bertha to return shortly and spoil my fun. He was wearing a crisp pair of regulation white navy ducks. Rum was on his table-desk; typewriter on the piano. It was almost as if he had been expecting me. Bertha had gone to Chicago to care for a sick sister (through prayer?). How long would she be gone? Don't know; you want tea or grog?

The abrupt luxury of freedom felt then I can still feel. It's a shrunken residue, and although the intensity of the explosion was a once-in-a-lifetime thrust of luck which can only erupt in youth, it was a real joy by which others would later be judged and found wanting. For the first time, I had Carl to myself, in his place, his tavern, forecastle, island. Now I could discover everything—how he felt, what he thought, who he was. It didn't turn out like that. We drank quietly for some time, in a rather oppressive silence, speaking of nothing in particular. What I wished to say rushed far and fast ahead of what I could actually say. Inside, my curiosity boiled, but he seemed perhaps even more self-centered than usual. My first wild manic propulsion subsided into apotropaic depression. I asked what he'd been up to. Writing. Evening was leaking away with each sip of rum and water. It would have been ordinary for him to have been drinking alone. I was an intrusion, whatever his placid courtesy; yet I couldn't bring myself to quit. Talk unraveled. Finally, I had to say: "Carl; you're bushed. I'd better go," and pushed my chair back to stand up. So did he. He put a hand on my shoulder: "Stay here, kid, if you like."

We had nightcaps. I stayed. Thus commenced a brief domestic interlude in which I played substitute housekeeper, enjoying the closeness and coolness of a creature whose mythical image was then for me no less mysterious than a unicorn or a manticore. Carl's quest for quiet, his spareness in motion, his quizzical softness which was also a tender firmness, his nicety in consideration, his dispassionate attention or friendliness, could easily be translated into terms of love. In him, and not far below the surface, were layers of reserve that denied me any very profound exchange. He was not concealing himself; his nature, either from its poverty, discipline, or good manners, secreted some unchallenged dignity, possibly fear, but of what? Such witholding or denial was of course for me an accumulated provocation. He was not teasing; he was just Carlsen. When I too earnestly discussed all this with Walker Evans, he said only: "Oh, that Carl. He's just another one of Crane's characters; a sphinx without a secret."

Despite cold water and intermittent doubt, he remained an enthralling riddle, never more so than when he got up early, made his kettle of shaving water, washed from a wooden bucket, and set out breakfast. I stayed in bed, partly to seem to let him have his house to himself for a little; partly to observe and enjoy his singularity. I don't know whether he wandered about bare-assed when Bertha was there. With me, he never dressed until he was ready to go into the street. This wasn't "narcissism." He never drew attention to himself, nor was he particularly graced in the flesh. He might have been any age, twenty-five to forty-five, a sleek, hard, almost hairless male; easy, self-confident, and deliberate. Nakedness was this creature's kind of clothing.

Questions intruded. I couldn't accept my situation for whatever it was on his part. I must worry it, "make sense" of it. Where, and who, after all, was I? Soon, Bertha must be back; she might walk in at any moment—tomorrow morning, tonight; now. . . . Each time I noticed her stubby upright piano with its sparkling black-and-white keys, its pile of music stacked neatly on top, I felt a looming adversary. Yet why should her pervasive if fragile absence cloud my present since it in no way seemed to disturb Carlsen? How greedy can you get? We both knew she was inevitably expected; ours was no marriage, nor was it a one-night stand. If I strained trying to make myself useful, to justify proximity by offering some "contribution," Carl didn't notice. This was my business. He wouldn't have asked me to stay if he hadn't felt some need. Guilt was nowhere near, as far as I was concerned; only delight. I had hoped to have helped him with his "work," his writing, but he never seemed to have finished a story to the degree he thought it ready or worthy of being criticized. He kept his papers in progress in manila binders. Sometimes when I was in his house alone, I was moved to glance at a page or so, but this was a disloyalty for which I might be mortally punished. Then, about a week after I'd moved in, something prompted me to start reading one of the folders straight through. There were some ten or a dozen pages, a few typed, others handwritten. Then, halfway down a page, words stopped in the middle of a sentence. This was true of all of his stuff. Nothing was finished; the fact that every one stopped seemed an odd coincidence. I suddenly realised that Carl longed to be "a writer," but couldn't write. Perhaps this was due, in some way, to the refusal from the editors of H & H. I guessed that he knew I knew his secret, but mutual convenience prevented it from being betrayed. He had a rare reserve of emotional energy without any sentimental taint, and I recognised him as a classic stoic. Self-aware, in control, with Carl you hit his core, if at one remove. Perhaps this is why Crane chose him. In an untidy universe, here was order, magic, however miniature, a clipper-ship in a bottle.

Quiet consciousness of self, a centered, inexpressed self, trying to comprehend what is done while doing it. For myself, at the age of nineteen, I had by chance begun to engage in similar self-instruction, through the means of one system of analytical method. Hart Crane himself only touched on his astonished impression of a dramatic, then much-publicized demonstration of the corporal manifestation of this same discipline. On February 2, 1924, he had written his mother back in Ohio that he had witnessed a performance of dancing organized by George Gurdjieff, which although executed by amateurs "would stump the Russian ballet." In 1917 when Crane had first come to New York, aged eighteen, he had seen Diaghilev's company at the old Metropolitan Opera House, and later became friends with Stanislaw Portapovitch, to whom he dedicated an early poem:

> Vault on the opal carpet of the sun.
> Barbaric Prince Igor:—or, blind Pierrot,
> Despair until the moon by tears by won;—
> Or, Daphnis, move among the bees with Chloe.
>
> Release,—dismiss the passion from your arms.
> More than real life, the gestures you have spun
> Haunt the blank stage with lingering alarms.
> Though silent as your sandals, danced undone.

Crane came to know a number of people who had been close to A. R. Orage, whom T. S. Eliot called the best editor of his generation. Orage was designated by Gurdjieff as his first American representative. Some twenty-five students performed movements derived from Near-Eastern and central Asian sources in Manhattan, Chicago, and Boston. These drew considerable attention and had some issue. On May 29, 1927, Crane wrote from Patterson, New York to Yvor Winters in California about his total disagreement with Gurdjieff's proposals, which claimed to impose instruction towards a "harmonious development of man" in its trinity of physical, mental, and moral capacities. He told Winters the aim was

> . . . a good idealistic antidote for the hysteria for specialization that inhabits the modern world. And I strongly

second your wish for some definite ethical order. [Gorham] Munson, however, and a number of my other friends, not so long ago, being stricken with the same urge, and feeling that something must be done about it—rushed into the portals of the famous Gurdjieff institute and have since put themselves through all sorts of Hindu antics, songs, dances, incantations, psychic sessions, etc. so that now, presumably the left lobes of the their brains respectively function (M's favorite word) in perfect unison. I spent hours at the typewriter trying to explain to certain of these urgent people why I could not enthuse about their methods; it was all to no avail, as I was told that the "complete man" had a different logic than mine, and further that there was no way of gaining or understanding this logic without first submitting yourself to the necessary training . . . Some of them, having found a good substitute for their former interest in writing by means of more complete formulas of expression have ceased writing now altogether, which is probably just as well. . . .

On December 21, 1923, Crane wrote from Woodstock, New York to his mother in Cleveland a letter replete with patient sympathy for her maddening complaints, her self-martyrizing, her distaste for his way of life.

I, too, have had to fight a great deal just to *be myself* and *know myself* at all, and I think I have been doing and am doing a great deal in following out certain natural and innate directions in myself. . . . Suffering is a real purification, and the worst thing I have always had to say against Christian Science is that it willfully avoided suffering, without a certain measure of which any true happiness cannot be fully realized.

Crane might have been paraphrasing Gurdjieff himself. Ultimately, the essence of his teaching proposed means to utilize that suffering which is the common lot, not by avoidance, but by its positive and negative energy. Certain temperaments or "personalities" have found themselves predisposed to the magnetism of the recension of esoteric and exoteric exercises in the residue of post-Pythagorean notions. Like Crane, not a few have been moved by the apparent magic in the organization of corporal action in the Gurdjieff exercises, but have been put off by the ensuing demands of his metaphysical lucubrations. My good fortune, for I consider it the greatest luck that ever hit me, was that I encountered this cosmology when emotionally I was an adolescent, without any essential experience, and hence lacking prejudice but not appetite. I was hardly more than a child, with few "ideas" good or bad. Crane, early on, had ceased being a child. His physique, gifts, affective life were forced into prematurity. Due to over-aroused psychic activity, the furious problems of domestic tension stoked raw habits of antagonism and escape long before the boy had any capacity to diffuse them. The anguish in his prepotency withered him. He quickly became an old youth in an unresisting body and settled for a hysterical persona, laminated to his true center—brilliant, irascible, corruscating, and electric—a rocket launched towards a magnetic relief in extinction.

When, in the summer of 1927, I was in Fontainebleau for a short stay at Mr. Gurdjieff's priory, I met a Scandinavian-American ex-farmer who might be placed (or rather, I chose to place him later) in a similar category to Carlsen. I revered him for his undemanding straighforwardness, his unblinking devotion to the feckless jobs which Gurdjieff assigned as muscular extremities of conscious coordination or self-discipline. I had barely reached that limit where I could distinguish between positive and negative energy, but I was able, instinctively, to realise that in the superficially boring, chaotic, but exhausting games that we played there was, somewhere, somehow, a key for conduct to a life I hoped to lead. Hauling big rocks from one pile in the garden to another hole a hundred yards away for no purpose I could decipher was not the most enchanting way to inherit wisdom from the ancients, but due to my proximity in this "work" (rockpiles) to Swede, the sweat (his and mine) was more than tolerable. He took orders unsmiling but uncomplaining. His lack of visible protest or question somehow bespoke genuine need. If he wanted something so clearly undefined, I could borrow whatever it must be. Mr. Gurdjieff, marking our companionship, grinned and said: "So. You and Swede." I was delighted at such attention. He said evenly: "Swede. Honest workman."

Honest workman. This phrase had a stubborn resonance. When I was posing for Gaston Lachaise, the sculptor, some five years later, he instructed me in his personal criteria for "modern art," in which, at that time, I was obsessively interested. I mentioned Aristide Maillol, who in the twenties had that mandatory ubiquity now enjoyed by Henry Moore. Lachaise said: "Maillol; not great *artiste;* honest workman." Hart Crane had been friends with Lachaise and his wife since 1923 and owned a fine alabaster dove. On March 5, 1924, Crane wrote to his old friends, the Rychtariks, whom he had left behind in Cleveland: "This afternoon I went around to an exhibition of sculpture by Maillol (who is an honest workman, but not very creative)."

Perhaps Gurdjieff's nomination had been transmitted through Orage, Gorham Munson, Caesar Zwaska, Wim Nylan, or others in G's first New York "Group." As I received it, the appellation "honest workman" did not imply peasant, day laborer, or mechanic. It was a judgment not only of a particular artisan but also of the condition and quality of art and craft in general. Here a basic integrity is not always foremost, whatever the currently accepted reputation for excellence may be. I feel certain that Crane borrowed this from Lachaise; the identity with Gurdjieff's epithet was fortuitous. There were other odd linkages to Crane in my remote contact with him. Years later I came across two irrelevant facts which further diminished my superstitions concerning chance. The first art work I collected (given me by a favorite cousin) was a Maxfield Parrish color print of "Cleopatra." It portrayed a flapperish serpent of old Nile in her barge, lounging on what appeared to be an American "colonial" four-poster bed, bowered in dogwood, and attended by three high school athletes. It had been commisioned as the first of a series by C. R. Crane to adorn his five-dollar *de luxe* gift chocolate boxes. This was in 1917; I was ten years old. In 1923, Crane moved into 6 Minetta Lane with his friend, Slater Brown. In 1933, I moved in there with Tom Wood, with no notion of what was a meaningless coincidence.

Crane's appreciation of art, for which his parents had prepared him, though primarily in the interests of commerce, was real. His admiration for William Sommer's undistinguished painting was inspired by his first encounter with a working artist. He adopted and adapted opinion, as also in his verse. But as to "honest workman," the simpler it sounded, the more recalcitrant the inference. Merely, honest. Only, a workman. As for Swede, his absolute health, sanity, sense, and sweat that I imagined smelled of raw wheat—his massive softness and ready acceptance of whatever had to be practically done—were these the normal attributes merely of honest workmen? And why should such try to be any more than that—why also "creative," like Ezra Pound or T. S. Eliot, who then governed the lending-library I fancied as my "mind"? Why should unadulterated animal magnetism or sweetness of spirit be allied necessarily with the capacity to paint tremendous pictures or write extraordinary poetry? What is the pay potential on a humane level? Honest work was to be judged on what range of imagination, lyric fantasy or the responsibility which kindles the heroes and martyrs, makers or failures?

Carl Carlsen had strayed into an adventurous and dangerous area of electrical transformation which has come to be called "creativity." He had stumbled unequipped and unendowed into the field of imaginative play. His will to write, to become "a writer," licensed desire and gave it an illusion of spirit and ability which was little more than echoed promise. This honest workman had been lent a vision of unlimited possibility. He might have pursued a more profitable existence by schooling himself in physics, chemistry, or navigation, and insured an alternate future, but the words, the fearsome sorcery of words fixed him in a situation which held only the recognition of ultimate weakness. Crane launched himself on an inevitable trajectory only to be arrested at its peak. Carlsen never got within sight of a start.

I lost sight of Carlsen; perhaps he went back to sea as a purser, or shipped out with his brother. Maybe he married Bertha. Walker Evans didn't know. When I went around to call after I came back from abroad in 1933, there was a for-rent sign tacked to his front door. My conscience had been assuaged somewhat by printing in the twenty-eighth and final number of *Hound & Horn* two letters of Hart Crane to his patron, Otto H. Kahn, telling him of the progress of "The Bridge," with a letter of Kahn's to Grace Crane thanking her for a photograph of David Alfaro Siqueiros's portrait of her son, the original of which he had razored to ruin some days before he sailed from Vera Cruz. In the same issue we printed three large, evocative photographs by Walker Evans of downtown Havana, Crane's last port of call.

I don't think that the academic or literary renown that was

beginning to collect around Crane meant much to Carlsen. To him, Hart was buddy and model, beyond any question of worldly status. Yet the ferocity of suicide must temper earlier memories, a sequence studded by signs, big or little, of ambiguous destiny. After the fact of threats, rehearsals, and the big event itself, was there, could there have been much doubt that he could have ultimately put an end to his agony? Were there no other alternatives here than with Ralph Barton, Harry Crosby, Randall Jarrell, Hemingway, John Berryman, Sylvia Plath—or even Dylan Thomas, Robert Lowell, or Ted Roethke? (And while Thomas and Lowell do not strictly fit into the coroner's casebook as self-slain, they were as much destined, self-centered victims as Delmore Schwartz or Scott Fitzgerald.) Is it only rationalizing to believe that Crane, like others, enriched language, enhanced its rhetoric while the magnitude of negation was an exact equivalent to the intensity of talent? As to why there was not more positive energy, why suffering could not have been bridled or used, or why there was not enough spirit to exist while being consumed, perhaps the answers lie in the nature of romantic solipsism. One might wish that the dynamics of affection and revulsion that tore his parents apart, and him in the bargain, might have blessed Crane with Walt Whitman's patience, benevolence, or detachment. Whitman, whose family situation was even more disastrous (with the exception of an ignorant but loving and loyal mother), survived extreme illness, madness, and poverty into his seventies. Crane's residue was achieved in a term of some fifteen years; yet it had its own febrile harvest. His synapsis, "the conjugation of homologous chromosomes, of material and paternal origins respectively," exploded into electrical short-circuits which kindled magnificent verbal sparks, flares and ever-burning torches in their positive bursts and, on the negative coil, brawls, despair, self-pity and self-loathing. There was never to be

> My hand
> in yours,
>   Walt Whitman—
>   so—

It does not take much special pleading to propose Whitman as an "honest workman." He cast himself in a role of which the mature image was a grandiose version amplified from an impersonation of a youthful original. Cocteau said that another bard, Victor Hugo, was a madman who imagined he was Victor Hugo. Whitman invented "The Good Grey Poet," complete with a photograph of a paper butterfly wired to his fingers. He had begun as plain Walter Whitman, journeyman typesetter, printer, school-teacher, Free-Soil editor. One has no feeling that Crane ever cared or plotted to be or impersonate anyone other than his haphazardly given self. As far as his work went, he felt himself one of a band of brothers which included Poe, Rimbaud, Whitman, and even Gerard Hopkins, hoping his voice was a vatic conduit rather than a conscious and governable identity. His legitimate claims to join the company of Marlowe and Melville are his sensational elisions and impacted fireworks, so tightly compressed that the shock of their implosion lasts longer than the time it takes to scan his pages. His is a high style, an extension of the grandest rhetoric, and could only have been achieved by the most abject expenditure of sense, sentiment, and skill. Whitman's easygoing, lounging prosody betrays few hints of rewriting or emendation; he constantly altered his texts from edition to edition, but this was almost careless correction. It is hard to think of Whitman drunk or Crane sober. Crane failed as apprentice candy salesman, journalist, and professional literary man. Whitman lived as a civil servant, reporter, and lecturer: a career by pittance, but he survived.

While I was living in Carl's house, he took good care that I had my own towel, tumbler, and tar soap; he didn't like to share his old-fashioned straight bare-blade razor, and anyway, I would have cut myself. Everything was shipshape, and the days passed without memorable event. Sooner or later I would leave. Either there would be a letter or telegram from Chicago announcing Bertha's return, or she might surprise us. Carl didn't think so; she had her own sort of consideration, which is why they got on so well. The delicacy that linked them need not be broken by resentment on her part, although she of course had no notion I was temporarily taking her place.

So, her special delivery letter arrived: Bertha's mission in Chicago was a complete success. The sister was entirely recovered, although she made no boast of her "Scientific" ministrations. She planned to take such and such a train, could be expected at such a day and hour. There was no big deal about goodbyes; in the few days of grace left we pursued our amiable routine without apprehension.

The best place to call it a day was in bed. I loved sleeping with Carl; this was no euphemism. We learned to sleep like spoons; if either had to get up in the night it was no problem to reverse positions and sleep more soundly. Vulnerability transcended? Something like that. Alone, together; cosy and quiet. What I felt most was the gravity or power of his light treatment of my fascination with him. He knew I loved him. As for him—he liked me; I was a pet or mascot.

To make a neat end to this story I could say: "You smell so good." Tar soap? Any less oppressive farewell would have been unseemly. "Yeah; that's vinegar-water—but not from vinegar. Crane liked that stuff." I told him how much I had enjoyed this vacation. Abruptly, and for the first time, there was an edge to his ease. "Why didn't you like Hart?" I'd hardly known him; he scared me; I wasn't up to him. His disorder; my envy. Guilt. "Funny. You didn't like him, but you like me." I heard myself say: "Carl. Why the hell do you always have to bring Crane into it?" "Why, you silly son of a bitch. If it wasn't for Crane I wouldn't have given you the sweat off my ass."

CAROLYN AT TWENTY

by PATRICIA DOBLER

from THE BELLINGHAM REVIEW

nominated by THE BELLINGHAM REVIEW *and Raymond Carver*

One hand on the trailer door, one holding
your baby, you turn to watch the oilrag sun
swipe down the sky. All Middletown knows
the father: string-muscled briarhopper
your mama says you *chose;* and he's decamped.

You sit like a stump outside town
or hang out the diapers like flags;
you bury the trailer wheels in cement sockets,
oh thorn in your mama's side. Judgment,
she says, that gray streak in your glossy hair,

but standing under the fuming sky,
your son's fist in your hair, you name it:
joy, the dark rooms of your mother's house
exploded at last, the caverns of a man's body
shot with light, as beautiful as you suspected.

THE HOUSE THAT FEAR BUILT: WARSAW, 1943

by JANE FLANDERS

from CHELSEA

nominated by CHELSEA

*The purpose of poetry is to remind us
how difficult it is to remain just one
    person,
for our house is open, there are no
    keys in the doors . . .*
> —*Czeslaw Milosz
> from "Ars Poetica"*

I am the boy with his hands raised over his head
in Warsaw.

I am the soldier whose rifle is trained
on the boy with his hands raised over his head
in Warsaw.

I am the woman with lowered gaze
who fears the soldier whose rifle is trained
on the boy with his hands raised over his head
in Warsaw.

I am the man in the overcoat
who loves the woman with lowered gaze
who fears the soldier whose rifle is trained
on the boy with his hands raised over his head
in Warsaw.

I am the stranger who photographs
the man in the overcoat
who loves the woman with lowered gaze
who fears the soldier whose rifle is trained
on the boy with his hands raised over his head
in Warsaw.

The crowd, of which I am each part, moves on
beneath my window, for I am the crone too
who shakes her sheets
over every street in the world
muttering
What's this? What's this?

HIDDEN JUSTICE

by GERALD STERN

from THE GEORGIA REVIEW

nominated by THE GEORGIA REVIEW, *Jack Gilbert, Linda Gregg, Grace Schulman and Marcia Southwick.*

This is my forest now, this Christmas cactus,
stretching out leaf after leaf,
pink blossom after pink blossom.
This is where I'll go to breathe
and live in darkness
and sit like a frog, and sit like a salamander,
and this is where I'll find a tiny light
and have my vision
and start my school—
in this dry and airy place
beside these trunks
in this fragrant mixture.

I will put my small stage here
under a thick leaf
and I will eat and sleep and preach right here
and put my two dogs there
to keep my two guards busy
with prayer and feeding.
I will live completely for the flowering,
my neck like a swan's,
my fingers clawing the air
looking for justice;
year after year the same,
my fingers clawing the air for hidden justice.

🔥 🔥 🔥

JUDGMENT

fiction by KATE WHEELER

from ANTAEUS

nominated by Sarah Vogan

W HEN MAYLAND THOMPSON dies he wants to be buried with the body of a twelve-year-old girl. "A fresh one," he says. "Huh! Just toss her in there and let her keep me company till Jesus gets here."

As for his wife, Linda, he'd like her to wait for judgment in a mass grave with all of her boyfriends. He threatens to write their names in his will: two deputy sheriffs, a detective, a railroad switchman, bartenders, motel owners, pavement repairmen, drunks.

"You'll have some real winners to cuddle up to," he tells her. "They're bad enough alive. Just imagine what they'll be like, full of worms."

She holds up a dead mouse by the tail. "There was three of these in the basement. Reminded me of you. Time I get old enough to die, you won't be able to make me do nothing."

His hair turns a shade grayer in the afternoon light. It's just that he wouldn't want her to be lonely either, he tells her.

Her expression is blank, the muscles of her face completely relaxed. She has Indian blood, and Irish. Once a month, she uses a special wax to remove fine black down from her upper lip.

He's known Linda since she was eight and her mother used to roll with him naked on the musty box spring in the attic. Right on this very porch, he would sit the two of them on his lap, Felicia Biggins and her daughter; they would each put an arm around his neck and fill his ears with tongues. He pinched here and there, gave them sips of Schlitz. The three of them were the talk of Rampart City, Kansas. At least once a week there would be a preacher or a

juvenile officer or a member of the Ladies' Benevolent knocking on
Felicia's door, until she borrowed Mayland's Goose gun and
started to wave it around. That stopped them. She was his kind of
woman.

The day she died of the liver, Mayland felt a natural responsibility arise in his heart, so he kidnapped Linda away from her uncle
Clyde and the custody girls. Through one moist night he drove,
Linda curled snoring beside him, her face stuck to the plastic seat.
At dawn, a sleepy Mormon gave him the key to Room 206 of the
New Paris Motel outside Provo, Utah. Three weeks he hid her
there, feeding her ice and double cheeseburgers. She took two
baths a day and watched the TV news in color. She cracked the
enamel of her molars and grew plump as a broiler.

They were married, which made Linda the third Mrs. Thompson. He waited six months, until she was of age, before bringing
her back to her mother's farm.

Did marriage agree with her? She was as silent and distant as the
moon. Each night as she lay under him in bed, she seemed
plumper and more mysterious than the night before. By the end of
the year, she was pregnant.

Wild with joy, Mayland bought two used pizza ovens at the
auction and resold them to buy her a color television set. It had no
knobs; he placed it on the coffee table and turned it on for her with
a screwdriver. It refused to turn off again, but Linda didn't mind.
She watched it for two days straight, changing channels with a
wrench, until one morning the tube burned out in the middle of a
program. Then she sat up on the couch and announced she
couldn't stand the feeling of being overweight. Hitting her stomach with her fists, she walked out into the dusty yard, climbed
into Mayland's pickup and drove to town for diet pills. That night,
and for two days afterwards, blood came out of her in clots that
filled Mayland's two cupped palms.

The doctor shook his head. He gave her a shot.

When Linda woke up, she would eat nothing but celery and
carrots.

Now she won't let Mayland touch her, so what has he got? A ninth-
grade graduate with a magazine figure who sleeps in cotton
underwear, and a hundred and twenty acres of her land to take
care of. He has done as much as he can, as much as his wife and the
farm will let him, but in four years he hasn't scraped together a hill

of beans. How much can you do with forty acres of river bottom full of dead trees and another eighty oversprayed? What can you do for a girl twenty years old who can't make change for a dollar?

These days he wakes up, the backs of his legs red from the heating pad, and he has the feeling that there is something he doesn't want to remember. He leaves the house quietly, very early, and goes to talk to high school girls waiting for the morning bus. If he can't get any of them to play hooky he'll spend the rest of the day in town making deals.

In the river bottom, another man's horses graze, standing with their tails to the wind. On the northwest corner of the property, Roy the sharecropper sweats over the broken windmill. Mayland wants to get somebody out there with a metal detector: one of the milo fields is supposed to have been an Indian battleground.

Noon. Linda straightens her legs under the electric blanket. Sunk in the mattress, her body seems boneless. Blue veins show through the skin of her neck; she is no longer asleep.

Behind the toolshed, in a square plot Mayland made by wiring four yellow gates together at the corners, there is a tablet of slate over Linda's mother and a small aluminum marker that says "Baby" but doesn't have anything buried under it. Linda keeps the weeds out, and she's collecting rocks from every state in the union to decorate the graves.

Rummaging in the bottom of the closet, she finds a pair of blue stretch pants and a T-shirt with a silvery photograph ironed onto the front. She dresses, puts on her eye shadow and goes out to stand on the road. The man in the red car sees her from a distance and takes his foot off the gas.

Wednesday Mayland traded a hundred junk cars to the dealer for eighty dollars in cash and a purple boat with an inboard motor. Thursday he traded the boat for twenty dollars and a four-wheel-drive truck that was missing one wheel. Today he is making arrangements with his pal Frank about the metal detector: they'll split anything Frank finds, fifty-fifty.

"It don't matter who holds the title when it comes to something buried more than a foot," Frank says. "This'll be in your name for a change, how do you like that?"

The two men smile at each other across the counter of Frank's Shoe Repair Salon.

"How is that wife of yours, anyway?"

"Oh, you know her," Mayland says. "Pushing the legal limit. And you know me. When the two of us comes to town . . ."

In that white Lincoln or the blue pickup: Frank knows all about it. "The mothers lock their girls in the closet and they push their sons out the back door."

"You got it."

"No, you all's the ones that's got it." Frank pushes away the display of rubber heels and leans across the glass. "And you deserve every bit of it you get." He slaps Mayland's shoulder and the two of them laugh. "It's just too damn bad you can't sell the place till she's twenty-one. I hate to see a friend scratching in the dirt like that."

"You bring that machine out and it's finders keepers." Mayland tells him. "Anyway, we'll sell it next year and be in Florida with water skis on our feet."

As Mayland gets ready to leave, Frank says, "I'll remember what you said. If you can sell that dump I'll have a pig roast for you."

"Pigs is free at the 4-H farm. If you go at night."

Walking out in the thin autumn sunlight, Mayland wishes he were in Florida. Some of his children are there, including Junior. The only one of Mayland's kids ever to try to walk the straight and narrow: turns Jehovah's Witness and a week later he gets shot in the head at a rally. Junior's alive, but he'll never be the same. Some things just go to show you, Mayland thinks, they just go to fucking show you.

He decides to check at the bar to see if Linda and the sharecropper are having a beer. But she's not there.

It is too dark to see. There is a smell of frying onions.

Mayland comes up the steps and sees Linda inside, standing in the yellow light of the kitchen, slicing. The tip of her tongue is out, she is concentrating on a potato. He bangs the door and she looks up.

She flicks a strand of black hair behind her ear. "You left the refrigerator open this morning," she says. "I could have drank the spread, it was that runny."

"I want you to tell me where you was this evening and this afternoon."

"Roy came over and we went down for a beer. You said that was all right, Mayland."

Roy the sharecropper, Mayland thinks disgustedly, she's named eighteen guys after him just because she knows I know she thinks he's ugly. And Roy will usually tell me whatever she says to. But today at six o'clock, Roy told Mayland there was a red car parked all day in the driveway, and Roy didn't know whose it was.

" 'Went down' might be the truth," Mayland says. "But you wasn't at the bar and you wasn't with Roy either."

She smiles faintly at the cutting board. "How come you know so much? You been following me?"

He wants to hit her. "No, it ain't worth my time. I want to know where my three-hundred-dollar ratchet set is and my seventy-five-dollar power saw."

"Ask somebody else. I ain't touched nothing of yours."

"You had somebody over and they took it." He steps closer to her and she shrinks back against the wall, her lips shaking open to show her teeth.

Now she's scared of me, Mayland thinks, damn it. That's all we need for her to think. I never hit a woman in my life. He turns away and walks back toward the bedroom, clicking on light switches as he goes. There are three beer bottles on the table, and an ashtray. As he tears the sheets off the bed, he notices Linda standing in the doorway, watching.

"The trouble with you is that you don't know how to judge people," he tells her. "You might be real pretty, but that ain't going to stop you from getting a disease. You might own a farm, but you'd get yourself in a lot of hot water real fast if it wasn't for me."

"But all my blood relatives is dead except for Clyde, and he hates me because of you."

"I got a lot more dead relatives than you do. That don't mean you can't make something of yourself." He throws the sheets on the floor. "Better make sure them onions don't burn."

She runs back to the kitchen. Look at her, Mayland says to himself. Pounding through the house like a three-year-old. I guess I can't leave her out here by herself no more to moon over them graves and attract the low-life.

"I got you a job," he says as the screen door slams behind him.

She is standing in the middle of the kitchen, staring out the window. "Somebody ran over that spotted horse," she says. "It's in the road."

"I saw that this morning while you was still asleep." He walks around in front of her, hoping she will say something.

Linda looks down at the floor. Her small bare feet look cold, bluish against the dark linoleum; there is fresh persimmon-colored polish on the nails of one foot. "It screamed," she says finally. "Before the sun came up."

"I'll sell it to the dog food factory tomorrow," he says. "Now listen up. I'm taking you to town at seven o'clock a.m. tomorrow morning. You're going to wash dishes at the cafe for three-fifty an hour."

"You just want to make me pay you back for that saw," she complains. Turning her back on him, she walks past the refrigerator into the living room. "I guess I better get some rest then, huh."

There is nothing in the refrigerator except fifty-two-percent oil spread and an empty cardboard box. The first time he tries to close it, the rubber cord they use to keep the door shut snaps back; the metal hook flies past his ear. He goes in to look at his wife on the couch: she has covered her face with a sheet of newspaper which blows gently up and down with her breath.

She can sleep more than any human being, until four in the afternoon sometimes. In his opinion she's still suffering from that brain fever she had when she was two, three years old. At least she reads. She reads the newspaper every day, and she pays attention to the radio.

"There's a man in Colorado who was teaching his dog how to shoot a gun," she will say, excited. "It picked it up off the table and it fell out of its mouth and onto the floor and now he's in the hospital!"

No way would Mayland let her near his guns. The ones that aren't at the pawnshop are locked in a closet in the basement.

At the table, her mouth full of store-bought chicken, she tells him she doesn't want to go to work in the morning. She'll do something wrong the first hour and then she'll want to quit. He answers that he'll lock her in the woodshed and hustle her to niggers if she wants to stay home.

Linda giggles. "It wouldn't be no worse than nothing to eat but this greasy fucking chicken," she says. "But I tell you what, if you do that, I'll get one of them niggers to kill you and then I'll bury you with a goat!"

"Greasy chicken is your own fault," he says. "You should have asked that guy to take you to the grocery store at least."

Both of them laugh. After dinner, he tries to give her a lesson in case Mrs. Folsom wants Linda to work the register.

"Here's a dollar. Coffee's thirty cents," Mayland says. "Plus tax."

She counts the change in brown coins, big silvers, medium silver, one small silver coin.

"Good," he says. "Now, pie."

She throws the money on the floor.

Her breathing is slow and quiet, her back curves away from him like a train track. He watches her body rising and falling, its edge against the dark. The October moon is cold in the window; a shaft of its light falls across the rumpled blanket, the gray carpet, the gray wallpaper with its gray roses, once pink.

His arthritis is bad tonight; his legs stick to the heating pad. If he touches her now she will roll away, even in sleep. She will mutter in her sleep and roll away.

He tries it anyway. She lets his arm stay for one second and then says, "Quit." For a year now she's been saying he's not her style in bed. It was never good except for once upon a time when she had a couple of other guys on the side, who paid her probably. She was hot for Mayland then. It lasted one month. He didn't understand anything about it, but it was nice while it lasted. Nowadays they have an understanding about sex. She's not jealous about Mayland's little girls and he doesn't ask her questions very often. She will even call the girls' houses sometimes and say she is a classmate when the mother answers.

If you consider the difference in their ages, Mayland figures, if you consider everything together, they are two people who can live with each other.

He'd like it to be different.

It's not as though he is the type to be found on the bottom of the cage with his feet in the air. When he was her age there were women who would pay him fifty, a hundred just to feel his body heat. He rubbed up against a woman eighty and a girl thirteen, Linda; he spent himself on a pool table, in church and in the Sears furniture department.

He used to pick locks with the ace of spades—snap, like he

owned the place, that fast, Like he was John Doe, picking up the mail from the mailbox and going inside to read it.

There are at least eight of his sons and daughters scattered over the nation. Rosalinda, his Mexican ex-wife, Junior's mother, still sends him religious postcards from Florida. His first wife, Belinda, is dead. Funny how he ended up with three Lindas. The other ones had longer names, but this one's as complicated as half the letters in the alphabet.

"Linda," he whispers.

"Huh?"

"Once for old times' sake?"

She groans. He remembers the horse outside, its brown legs stiff as an inflated toy's.

"A man has his needs," he says.

"I'm trying to sleep, please."

He stands back and sets fire to a whole book of matches.

It lands on the horse's shoulders. For an instant he can read the words "Purina Feeds" printed in red on the white cardboard. Then there is a thumping sound and a huge yellow flame. It smells terrible, the gasoline and burning hair, and Mayland yells in delight. He sees Linda's white face at the bedroom window, then her white fluttering nightgown as she runs along the driveway toward him.

"See!" he shrieks. The carcass is burning ferociously. Several yards behind it, out of range of his jerking shadow, Linda comes to a stop. Lifting one foot, she shakes a stone from her slipper.

The two of them stand in awe until the burning stops. This happens sooner than Mayland would have liked. In the dark, the dead horse hisses and crackles like a doused campfire. Mayland can tell that only the hide is really burned; but the horse's lips have broken and stretched back horribly, so that its teeth gleam in the moonlight.

Linda covers her eyes. A small cloud of black smoke drifts eastward across the stars. "What did you go and do that for?"

"Saturday night's all right," says Mayland. "That's what we used to say in Texas."

"Texas," she says. "You're out of your mind." She giggles. "Let's go to Texas. Then I won't have to work tomorrow."

"The dump's as far as I guess either one of us is going unless you sell the farm for me in town."

"Guess so."

Later, as they lie in bed staring up at a string of water spots on the ceiling, he feels Linda's fingers brush his shoulder.

"Look," she says. "A crocodile trying to eat a duck."

The water spots on the ceiling. Mayland chuckles, air pushing through his teeth. Thick fingered, he touches her hair where it lies dark against the pillow.

"That plaster needs to be fixed or it'll fall in on us," he says. She turns halfway toward him, so that he can see the moonlight gleaming on her teeth, in her eyes. Suddenly he rolls his big body on top of her and kisses her, holding her arms down. She squeaks a little, tries to bite him, but he doesn't give up and soon she is just lying there, staring past his face.

"Fuck you. Fuck you," she says as he begins to grunt. He thinks he feels her spitting. "Fuck you, old man."

A crocodile that ate a duck, he thinks afterward.

The walls of the house dissolve in moonlight.

After some time there is the sound of running water. The radio's digital clock says 6:38. Through the window, the plains are a mild gray-blue; the huge loneliness of the sky is disguised by a thin ceiling of clouds. He has dreamed, he suddenly remembers, that Linda's mother was in the attic calling for cake and ice cream.

His body aches.

Wrapped in towels and a cloud of steam, Linda appears in the doorway to announce that she can't find any underwear. "I guess nobody's going to know the difference."

"I bet you tell six people, time I come get you. I bet you let them look."

"Shut up," she says. "Pig."

"Sorry," he says. Then, "Do whatever you want."

She stares at him.

Ahead, on the road, they can see the dark silhouette. Two buzzards are walking around it in the dust. The birds look awkward on the ground. Linda peers down at the carcass as Mayland drives around, his left wheels almost in the opposite ditch. The buzzards fly up. He accelerates to forty-five.

Linda pulls down the visor and leans her head back on the seat, narrowing her eyes against the sunrise. "I didn't get no sleep at all," she says. "I don't know if I can work today." The muscles of her neck tighten as the truck bumps up onto the highway pavement.

When they reach the cafe, she won't let Mayland come in with her. He doesn't insist; he watches as she inspects herself in the rearview mirror, tucks her purse under her arm and is gone.

As she walks into the building, she waves at a long-faced young man who is eating an iced doughnut at the window table. Mayland recognizes him as the operator of the truck scales at the Pearsall grain elevator, the half-brother of a fat girl named Minnie who once let him kiss her breasts.

In the window, Linda holds up three fingers. Three o'clock. He makes an okay sign with one hand and she disappears into darkness behind the counter.

The young man's name is Gene, and he changes seats so that he can watch Linda's head and shoulders through the foot-high opening in the wall behind the counter. He orders another doughnut; when it's gone, he wipes his mouth with a napkin and goes to the cash register to ask Mrs. Folsom for a loan of her ballpoint pen.

On a napkin he writes: "Winter coming. Last chance to get out! Meet me at 2 p.m. at Fast Gas, reg. pump if you want a ride to sunny Arizona. Yr pal, G. Friddell."

He folds the napkin and waves it at Linda; he points out the window at a black Pontiac with fiery wings painted on the hood.

Some in jeans, some in Sunday clothes, half a dozen teen-agers are sitting on the city park benches near the monkey cage. They smoke, and look Mayland up and down.

"Playing hooky from church?" Mayland calls to them in a friendly tone.

"What's it to ya?" asks one of the girls. Her hair is dyed blonde, showing black at the roots, and it stands out in pointed wings on either side of her face.

"Want some beer?"

The teen-agers drift over. They know him, Mayland Thompson, lives out west of town on Route Six. Mayland invites them out to his place to see the ugliest thing in the world, but first they have to stop at the hardware store to get some kind of pulley rig. The blonde and a red-headed girl sit with Mayland in the cab, along with one of the boys. The redhead's arm is squashed against the side of Mayland's chest. Her name is Diane; Mayland tells her she's a little fatter than he likes them, but he bets she'd be a whole lot of fun if she'd just relax.

He tells them the whole story about the horse: about lying awake in bed, about his old lady cold as a piece of liver out of the icebox until he did something to light a fire under her. They would see it in a minute.

The boy named Fuzzy makes a joke about barbecue.

"We had some of it for breakfast, yeah, but we left the rest for company like you," Mayland says as the carcass comes into view.

"That's the rudest thing I ever say," Diane observes.

"You bet, honey," Mayland says. He turns the truck around in the road.

Diane stays in the cab, playing the radio while everyone else goes out to sit on the tailgate and look. A tall boy takes out a pack of cigarettes and offers them around. Fuzzy pokes at the carcass with a stick.

"Believe it or not," says Mayland, "that thing right there used to be spotted. A spotted horse. That was even its name, Spot." He wants to put his hands on the blonde, but she is sitting on the tall boy's lap. On her arm is a homemade tattoo, the initials E.G. inside a heart. The horse smiles hugely at Mayland, making him feel uncomfortable. Something ain't right here, he thinks, checking his fly. No problem.

The beer is gone. "Okay, boys," Mayland says. "Time to load up. We've got to take this sucker to the dump."

"Listen, old man," Fuzzy says. "Not so fast." He puts his hands on Mayland's shoulders. "We got our good clothes on, man."

"I was wondering if you'd say that," Mayland says. He smiles slowly. "You can walk back to town if that's how you feel."

Fuzzy's not a bit surprised. "We don't want to start no fight here. Give us ten bucks each and everything's cool. Okay, Grecian Formula?"

Mayland sees all the boys' legs arranged in a loose arc in front of him. One of them could hold my arms and then the rest knock my teeth out, he thinks. I should have seen it coming. "Fifteen bucks for the four of you boys."

"What about the girls? You a chauvinist?"

"Twenty."

It's a deal; Mayland pays in advance: a ten, a five, five ones. The boys take off their jackets, roll up their sleeves. Mayland lets down the tailgate.

In ten minutes the horse is loaded, covered with newspapers and canvas, and tied firmly down.

"You can drop us off at the pinball parlor," Fuzzy says. "Everyone in front this time."

The teen-agers sit on top of each other; no one talks. Diane has changed all the button settings on the radio to rock stations. Sharp bones press against Mayland's arm. Once, he is obliged to wave and smile at the driver of another truck, who has pulled off the road to let Mayland by.

Finally they stop across the street from the Balls of Steel.

"See you around, man," the teen-agers say as they untangle themselves. They dance through traffic and away.

Two-thirty by the clock on City Hall. A new rattle in the engine. Mayland decides to stop at the cafe on the way to the dump. If Linda isn't finished with work, he'll have a lemonade and figure out what to tell the owner of the horse. He hopes Linda's not going to be mad at him still.

"I bet you can't guess my secret," Linda says as Gene's car reaches eighty miles per hour.

"You ain't got any underpants on."

"You're too smart," she complains. Her bare feet push against the dashboard, her right hand dangles against the window. She starts to tell Gene about her rock collection: she's got a lot from Oklahoma and one each from Texas and Arizona, but none from New Mexico.

"Rocks," he says. "That's a new one on me. Well, where we're going they have all the rocks you want." He laughs. "All the rocks you want."

Mayland never noticed before that the crickets still sing in October. They make a crazy sound in the trees as he stands at the foot of Linda's mother's grave, telling the whole story out loud and asking Felicia for advice.

Yes, he wanted Linda to pay for those tools. But there just wasn't any other money for it. Yes, he made her do a lot of things she didn't want to: made rules, gave lessons. Partly he did it because he thought it would have made Felicia happy, partly because he thought Linda needed it. She wasn't smart enough to get along by herself but maybe she knew her own mind better than he did. Maybe she was too old to have a husband who acted like her daddy. About what happened last night, he guesses it was the last straw for her. He can't say why he had to set that horse on fire, but he knows he couldn't stop himself. He couldn't stop himself from rolling over on top of Linda either. He still can't keep from feeling like her husband.

"Tell her I ain't going to chase her down," he says. "If this was the old days I would. But tell her I'm right here. Bring her back if you can." This seems to be the end of what he has to say. His arms hang loose and heavy at his sides. He starts to cry. The crickets keep making their screamy noise. Finally he goes back to the house, careful to step over Linda's curving rows of colored rocks.

Everyone, even the bartender, is out on the sidewalk. The squad car is making a right turn into the parking lot; the siren dies suddenly, with a strangling sound. The car stops and three Oklahoma state troopers get out.

Grim, pale, silent at the center of a fury of sparks, Linda is ripping the neon off the front of the Sportsmen's Lounge, by hand.

No one wants to get close for fear of being electrocuted.

Chrome stripping hangs crazy and twisted from the side of the black car. Gene Friddell stands under the blue mercury lights of the parking lot, drunk, telling the trooper it's not his fault. Yes, he pushed over the chair. Yes, he called her a whore. But it was only because she kept talking about her dead mother. No, he didn't slap her, she slapped him.

"The witnesses say different," the trooper says. "Put one hand on your head. Good. Now the other one." Handcuffs click twice.

"I got business in Arizona," Gene says.

"Too bad," says the trooper, leading him to the black-and-white squad car. He locks Gene inside and goes to help his buddies subdue Linda.

The three of them tell her she'll set her hair on fire if she doesn't stop, but she won't listen. Suddenly they are holding her arms in a grip she can't break. She goes limp. The troopers call for another car.

Mayland is at the county jail by midnight with two hundred dollars' bail money he borrowed from Frank. Linda comes out of her cell in an orange jumpsuit that flaps around her ankles. She looks happy to see him.

"It was cold in there," she tells him. "I didn't have any socks."

"You don't look so good," he says.

The jailer gives Linda her clothes and she goes into an empty cell to put them on while Mayland pays the bail.

"Drunk and disorderly," the jailer says. "Destruction of property. You got a handful there, mister."

"There's going to be some new rules around the house starting tomorrow," Mayland says, without knowing what they will be. The jailer tells him that Linda will probably get off with a light fine because it's a lady judge and because of Gene hitting her.

When she comes out in her clothes, the men in the big cell whistle and wave good-bye to her, sticking their hands through the bars. Except for Gene: Mayland sees him reading a magazine at the cement table in the middle of the cell.

Outside, in the parking lot, Linda hugs Mayland. She still smells like beer. "You know what?" she says. "I knew you wouldn't like it when I ran off. I was going to come back anyway in a couple of weeks."

"You should have left me a note," he says.

WHAT LITERATURE MEANS

by CYNTHIA OZICK

from PARTISAN REVIEW

nominated by PARTISAN REVIEW, *Louis Gallo, and Sherod Santos*

AT A PARTY ONCE I heard a gifted and respected American writer—a writer whose prestigious name almost everyone would recognize—say, "For me, the Holocaust and a corncob are the same." The choice of "corncob"—outlandish, unexpected, askew— is a sign of the strong and daring charge of his imagination, and so is its juxtaposition with the darkest word of our century. What he intended by this extraordinary sentence was not to shock the moral sense, but to clarify the nature of art.

He meant that there is, for art, no such element as "subject matter"; for art, one sight or moment or event is as good as another—there is no "value" or "worth" or "meaning"—because all are equally made up of language, and language and its patterns are no different from tone for the composer or color for the painter. The artist as citizen, the writer explained, can be a highly moral man or woman—one who would, if the Nazis came, hide Jews. But the artist as artist is not a moral creature. Within literature, all art is dream, and whether or not the artist is or is not in citizenly possession of moral credentials is irrelevant to the form and the texture of the work of art, which claims only the territory of the imagination, and nothing else.

For that writer, a phrase such as "a morally responsible literature" would be an oxymoron, the earlier part of the phrase clashing to the death with the latter part. To be responsible as a writer is to be responsible solely to the seizures of language and dream.

I want to stand against this view. The writer who says, "For me, the Holocaust and a corncob are the same," is putting aside the moral sense in art, equating the moral impulse only with the sociologically real, or perhaps with the theologically ideal. In literature he judges the moral sense to be an absurd intrusion. He is in the stream that comes to us from Greece, through Walter Pater and Emerson: art for its own sake, separated from the moral life. He is mainly Greek.

For me, with certain rapturous exceptions, literature *is* the moral life. The exceptions occur in lyric poetry, which bursts shadowless like flowers at noon, with the eloquent bliss almost of nature itself, when nature is both benevolent and beautiful. For the rest—well, one discounts stories and novels that are really journalism; but of the stories and novels that mean to be literature, one expects a certain corona of moral purpose: not outright in the grain of the fiction itself, but in the form of a faintly incandescent envelope around it. The tales we care for lastingly are the ones that touch on the redemptive—not, it should be understood, on the guaranteed promise of redemption, and not on goodness, kindness, decency, all the usual virtues. Redemption has almost nothing to do with virtue, especially when the call to virtue is prescriptive or coercive; rather, it is the singular idea that is the opposite of the Greek belief in fate: the idea that insists on the freedom to change one's life.

Redemption means fluidity; the notion that people and things are subject to willed alteration; the sense of possibility; of turning away from, or turning toward; of deliverance; the sense that we act for ourselves rather than are acted upon; the sense that we are responsible, that there is no *deus ex machina* other than the character we have ourselves fashioned; above all, that we can surprise ourselves. Implicit in redemption is amazement, marveling, suspense, even the suspense of the didactic, wherein the next revelation is about to fall. Implicit in redemption is everything against the fated or the static: everything that hates death and harm and elevates the life-giving—if only through terror at its absence.

Now I know how hazardous these last phrases are, how they suggest philistinism, how they lend themselves to a vulgar call for an "affirmative" literature in order to fulfill a moral mandate. I too recoil from all that: the so-called "affirmative" is simpleminded, single-minded, crudely explicit; it belongs either to journalism or to piety or to "uplift." It is the enemy of literature and the friend of coercion. It is, above all, a hater of the freedom inherent in story-telling and in the poetry side of life. But I mean something else: I mean the corona, the luminous envelope—perhaps what Henry James meant when he said, "Art is nothing more than the shadow of humanity." I think, for instance, of the literature of midrash, of parable, where there is no visible principle or moral imperative. The principle does not enter into, or appear in, the tale; it *is* the tale; it realizes the tale. To put it another way: the tale is its own interpretation. It is a world that decodes itself.

And that is what the corona is: interpretation, implicitness, the nimbus of *meaning* that envelops story. Only someone who has wholly dismissed meaning can boast that the Holocaust and a corncob are, for art, the same. The writers who claim that fiction is self-referential, that what a story is about is the language it is made out of, have snuffed the corona. They willingly sit in the dark, like the strict-constructionist Karaites who, wanting to observe the Sabbath exactly, sat in the lampless black and the fireless cold on the very day that is most meant to resemble paradise. The misuse of the significance of language by writers who most intend to celebrate the comeliness of language is like the misuse of the Sabbath by the fundamentalist Karaites: both annihilate the thing they hope to glorify. *What literature means is meaning.*

But having said that, I come to something deeply perilous: and that is imagination. In Hebrew, just as there is *t'shuva,* the energy of creative renewal and turning, so there is the *yetzer ha-ra,* the Evil Impulse—so steeped in the dark brilliance of the visionary that it is said to be the source of the creative faculty. Imagination is more than make-believe, more than the power to invent. It is also the power to penetrate evil, to take on evil, to become evil, and in that guise it is the most frightening human faculty. Whoever writes a story that includes villainy enters into and becomes the villain. Imagination owns above all the facility of becoming: the writer can enter the leg of a mosquito, a sex not her own, a horizon he has never visited, a mind smaller or larger. But also the imagination seeks out the unsayable and the undoable, and says and does them. And still more dangerous: the imagination always has the lust to tear down meaning, to smash interpretation, to wear out the rational, to mock the surprise of redemption, to replace the fluid force of suspense with an image of stasis; to transfix and stun rather than to urge; to spill out, with so much quicksilver wonder, idol after idol. An idol serves no one; it is served. The imagination, like Moloch, can take you nowhere except back to its own maw. And the writers who insist that literature is "about" the language it is made of are offering an idol: literature for its own sake, for its own maw: not for the sake of humanity. *Literature is for the sake of humanity.*

My conclusion is strange, and takes place on a darkling plain. Literature, to come into being at all, must call on the imagination; imagination is in fact the flesh and blood of literature; but at the same time imagination is the very force which struggles to snuff the redemptive corona. So a redemptive literature, a literature that interprets and decodes the world, beaten out for the sake of humanity, must wrestle with its own body, with its own flesh and blood, with its own life. Cell battles cell. The corona flickers, brightens, flares, clouds, grows faint. The *yetzer ha-ra*, the Evil Impulse, fills its cheeks with a black wind, hoping to blow out the redemptive corona; but at the last moment steeples of light spurt up from the corona, and the world with its meaning is laid open to our astonished sight.

In that steady interpretive light we can make distinctions; we can see that one thing is not interchangeable with another thing; that not everything is the same; that the Holocaust is different, God knows, from a corncob. So we arrive, at last, at the moral purpose of literature: to reject the blur of the "universal"; to distinguish one life from another; to illumine diversity; to light up the least grain of being, to show how it is concretely individual, particularized from any other; to tell, in all the marvel of its singularity, the separate holiness of the least grain. *Literature is the recognition of the particular.*

For that, one needs the corona.

A VALEDICTION

by W. D. SNODGRASS

from PLOUGHSHARES

nominated by PLOUGHSHARES, *Philip Dacey and Elizabeth Spires*

Since his sharp sight has taught you
To think your own thoughts and to see
What cramped horizons my arms brought you,
    Turn then and go free,

    Unlimited, your own
Forever. Let your vision be
In your own interests; you've outgrown
    All need for tyranny.

    May his clear views save you
From those shrewd, undermining powers
That hold you close just to enslave you
    In some such love as ours.

    May this new love leave you
Your own being; may your bright rebirth
Prove treacherous, change then and deceive you
    Never on this earth.

    Now that you've seen how mindless
Our long ties were, I pray you never
Find, all your life through, such a blindness
    As we two shared together.

    My dark design's exposed
Since his tongue opened up your eyelids;
May no one ever lip them closed
    So cunningly as I did.

I KNEW I'D SING

by HEATHER MCHUGH

from KAYAK

nominated by Seamus Heaney

A few sashay, a few finagle.
Some make whoopee, some
make good. But most make
diddly-squat. I tell you this

is what I love about
America—the words it put
in my mouth, the mouth where once
my mother rubbed a word away

with soap. The word
was cunt. She stuck that great
big bar in there until there was
no hole to speak of, so

she hoped. But still I'm full
of it, the cunt, the prick,
short u, short i, the words
for her and him. I loved

the things they must have done,
the love they must have made
to make an example of me.
After my lunch of Ivory I said

vagina for a day or two, but knew
from that day forth which word it was
that struck with all the force of sex itself.
I knew when I was big I'd sing

a song in praise of cunt. I'd want
to keep my word, the one with teeth in it.
And even after I was raised, I swore,
nothing, but nothing, would be beneath me.

REMEMBERING TITIAN'S MARTYRDOM OF ST. LAWRENCE

by JORIE GRAHAM

from IRONWOOD

nominated by IRONWOOD, *Jack Gilbert, Grace Schulman and Sarah Vogan*

The glistening black
   armor
in which the men
   resemble
great feeding birds
   catches the light

of the torches, the light
   of the moon
and blurs them
   furiously.
It would have them be
   indistinguishable,

blue light, red light. See how
   to that end
something like a heart
   flickers in the convex
of the breastplate
   and reaches out

296

towards us, lost souls
　　and citizens.
The fires soldiers have built
　　to keep warm
along the river live
　　over the riverskin,

over their limbs
　　and spears,
though even the meanest
　　twig or
fingertip is branded
　　by that blue

intelligence the dress
　　of smoke
these men have made
　　around their deed
must open for. See
　　how the two lights

twine, over my face,
　　my hands.
Every pocket will be
　　found out,
every hollowness
　　forgiven,

and yet it's not the light
　　of saints,
this mixing of rivers.
　　Where the man Lawrence
is burned alive,
　　where the twigs

beneath him invent or steal
　　that quick red flesh
out of thin air
　　he is not touched.
He grows
　　into what he is

under the steady blue-white light
   that means him.
Even the excitements
   of the smoke
glide over him
   unshadowing . . .

Meanwhile what's alive
   all round him—firetenders
spectators, even the stone
   of the steps
they have descended, even
   the wet brown

paint, the folds of the small
   brushstroke—
becomes a ground
   on which these two
negotiate—the light
   we make, the light

we receive. I would not be
   that man
illuminated wholly
   by the heavens.
I would not be that man
   in the fire

unable to feel the fire, the acrid
   ancient
smell. What blue river
   does he think
courses through this world?
   Is there a stream

whose banks don't
   come away
into its muscular spirit,
   whose love
doesn't scour its own bed,
   roil its mud

with sky? You who
   rise up
into the flawless sky
   the face of this river owns
on a still night
   in a free world,

how can you know
   when you see us
from your high fearlessness
   running our fingers
through the flames
   as if demanding

reimbursement
   by the felt
pain, how can you know
   what you see,
the terrible deficit
   we work into,

how can you judge us, how
   can you stand
for us among
   the elements?

𝖎 𝖎 𝖎

ROBO-WASH

fiction by JEAN DAVIDSON

from MISSISSIPPI REVIEW

nominated by MISSISSIPPI REVIEW *and Elizabeth Inness-Brown*

I'M LEANING AGAINST A Coke machine outside Magic Mart and watching several Rock Bridge High students wash my old Chevy, when a woman wearing harlequin sunglasses and a yellow motor-cycle helmet comes up.

"You're comparing the properties of water to those of metal," she says.

"Me?" I say, pointing a finger at my head.

"You're as see-through as this tumbler here," she says. She holds up a clear, plastic tumbler so the sun can shine through it.

"It's Sapphire from the Robo-Wash commercial," one of the students says, and he and the other car washers crowd past me and surround Sapphire. She reaches into a large brown bag and pulls out purple and pink ROBO-WASH bumper stickers which she distributes to the students.

"Grand Opening at Robo-Wash," she says. "Rust inhibitor, poly silicone weatherguard, computerized. Two for one with a sticker."

The students get into a red van with a minotaur mural painted on the side and drive off without finishing my car. Sapphire raises her eyebrows at me and shrugs her shoulders, then walks around my car to the passenger side and gets in.

"I need a lift," she says, as I slide in behind the wheel and drop a wad of wet chamois onto the back seat.

"Do I know you?" I say, not knowing what else to say.

"Not necessarily," she says. "I'm Sapphire from the Robo-Wash commercial. And you're Miss Martin, science teacher at Rock Bridge."

"Ophelia," I say. "Miss Martin sounds like an old maid's name. Don't you think?"

A man in an orange jumpsuit comes running across the parking lot towards us. He's carrying a pink fish-shaped ceramic lamp that's almost as tall as he is.

Sapphire raises the upper half of her body out the window and calls, "Muhal, hey Muhal." She sits back down and glances at me. "My cousin, Muhal," she says. "He and I are co-owners of Robo-Wash. He's technical, I'm PR."

Muhal comes up to Sapphire's window and holds the lamp up for her to see. "It's still there," he says. Then he opens my back door, shoves the lamp into the back seat and gets in next to it. "You don't mind giving me a lift over to Komfort Furniture Store, do you?" he says to me.

"You'll have to give me directions," I say. "I don't get out in the city much."

"You're as see-through as this window here," Muhal says, knocking on the window next to him. We are driving somewhere in the city, fifteen miles from where we started and not yet at the Komfort Store.

"I was just like you not long ago," Sapphire says, "always avoiding people, afraid of complications."

"Tell the truth," Muhal says. "You'd secretly love to put on a slinky number and go down to the Astoria Bar for a nightcap. But you won't go alone. It wouldn't look right. You secretly wish you had friends you could call up and go out with. Isn't that right, Ophelia?"

"You won't find friends any better than us," Sapphire says, looking at herself in the rearview mirror. She takes another pair of rhinestone harlequins from her brown paper bag and puts them on me. "Wear these," she says. "You'll be surprised."

I have poor vision anyway, and the sunglasses make it difficult to see dogs and pedestrians. After a couple of close calls, I stop the car and trade places with Muhal, who switches on the radio as he pulls the car out into traffic without signaling.

I've never ridden in the back seat of my Chevy before and find the familiar space suddenly changed. I sit back, an arm around Muhal's lamp to keep it from falling over, and consider the orange jumpsuit and the yellow helmet in front of me. My dark lenses tend to join the colors together without any sharp boundaries, making everything look like a reflection in a store window instead of the real thing.

"Ice to liquid to what? To gas? Surely not," I say, drowned out by the radio. I lean forward and fold my arms on the back of the front seat between Muhal and Sapphire. "It's fun being a passenger for a change," I say.

"See, I told you," Sapphire says, sticking a Top Value stamp on the lower right corner of the windshield.

"Why fight it?" Muhal says, "Why not be a 'both/and,' instead of an either/or?'" Muhal and Sapphire have been having a heated discussion for the last half hour, ever since we left Komfort where we picked up Sapphire's houndstooth check birdbath. Muhal is still driving, somewhere in the city, taking us and the birdbath to Sapphire's apartment. I am completely lost by now and doubt that I'll ever find my way back home.

Muhal puts on a pair of narrow, rectangular, tortoise-framed sunglasses and pulls down the visor to look at himself in the visor mirror. "It's the vision," he says. "It changes with the shape and size of lenses, windshields, TV screens, portholes, peepholes. But it's all the same."

"You've got it wrong, Muhal," Sapphire says. "The changing vision does not depend upon the shape and size of all those things. The shape and size of all those things depends upon the changing vision."

"Change is change," Muhal says, "no matter what does the changing first. "He makes a sharp turn into the parking lot of an apartment complex called Tiger Village.

Sapphire's apartment is at the end of a long, third-floor balcony. An assemblage of cement frogs, gnomes, and benches flanks the sliding glass door.

"You really have your own personal style," I say to Sapphire, tapping a planetarium chime made from can lids that hangs by the door.

"It changes all the time," Sapphire says. "I call it Pod. I live Pod."

"You mean eclecticism?" I say.

"No," Sapphire says, unlocking her door. "Well, you could call this Komfort phase eclectic-eccentric, I suppose; but I'm talking basic pods here. Like peas. Inductive progressions. You live one at a time. Then, at some point, you look back and see it all for what it was instead of what it seemed to be. Last week I was neocolonial, Ethan Allen, and I wore wrap skirts and polo shirts just like you. Next week or next month, I don't know, I may be Park Avenue or Papago Indian. This week Muhal's talked me into trying Komfort. Komfort is Muhal's permanent style."

"She separates things on her plate, too," Muhal says. "First, she eats all the beans, then she eats all the baked potato, then she eats all the steak, then the Texas toast. It's all the same. Why not mingle?"

"Recreation," Sapphire says.

"Why ask why?" Muhal says. "It's a matter of what's sexy. Now, to me, Komfort is sexy."

Muhal fills the birdbath with milk, out on the balcony. Then he, Sapphire, Sarge (Muhal's barber who lives next door to Sapphire), and I stand around the birdbath soaking our hands and listening to Thelonious Monk's greatest hits. From time to time Muhal improvises on trumpet; Sarge improvises on alto sax. They're showing me how to live Komfort.

" 'Straight, No Chaser,' " Muhal says, then leans over and sticks his face into the birdbath and blows bubbles.

Sarge, who's wearing a red skullcap and tortoise-rim sunglasses like Muhal's, shuffles around us blowing a single note on his horn, spins around, then blows two more notes in rapid succession.

"Take it, Sapphire," Muhal says.

Sapphire sticks an elbow into the birdbath, then looks at my elbow and nods. I stick my elbow into the birdbath.

Muhal does a run, then hands his horn to me and says, " 'Hackensack.' "

I blow a note. Rather, I make a sound into the horn like blowing my nose. Muhal nods, struts around us, still nodding, takes his horn back and does another run. "You got it," he says, then lapses into vocal improvisations with Sarge.

Sapphire and I stand across from each other and put our hands back into the birdbath.

"Good for your skin," I say.

"Men have all the fun," she says. "Pod is better than Komfort. At least there's some order to it."

"One thing about Pod," I say. "How do you know when to look back?"

"We're a great deal alike, you know that?" Sapphire says.

On my way home I stop at a yard sale and buy two large turquoise ash trays and a sunburst clock. That evening I try to capture the essence of Komfort decor in my living room.

I'm adjusting a fan-shaped arrangement of *True Confessions* on the coffee table when two of my sophomore biology students stop by.

"Where are the shades?" Donald, the tall, red-headed one, says, touching one of my eyelids. Then he picks up a magazine and flips through it.

"I could go for a chilli omelet and some chocolate chip cookies," Kevin, the short one with braces says.

"Where's the checkered mushroom?" Donald says, hitting the TV's ON button, then going down the hall to my study.

"We saw you today, down on Rampart," Kevin says, slouching on the sofa and taking off his tennis shoes. "You're so straight in class. No one would guess."

"Guess what?" I say, walking back to the study where I find Donald looking into my microscope and shaking his head.

"I don't get it," he says.

"Time for you boys to go home and read up on genetic progressions," I say. "Pop-quiz tomorrow."

"Let's go," Donald says to Kevin, who has followed me into the study and is flipping through a wildlife stamp album. "It's a full moon."

"Moon-lighting, huh?" Kevin says to me as I pass his shoes out the front door and wave good night.

The next day at school, Donald and Kevin move up to the front row and take turns giving dissertations on vampires, werewolves, and the multiple uses of the crowbar. I recognize their uncharacteristic vocalizations as a delaying tactic (I give the quiz anyway), but usually they don't go to the trouble. I interpret this transformation as a good sign, although the reason behind it is a bit fuzzy. I assume that the boys have categorized me by association and that they find my new image more appealing than my old one.

During the last few minutes of first-hour biology, I suffer a lapse in concentration. I interrupt the genetics quiz by saying, "Scramble them, tin soldiers. You'll never know what hit you." During second-hour chemistry lab, while demonstrating the properties of potassium bitartrate (cream of tartar), I suddenly yield to the urge to pour everything down the drain and poke it with my pointer. "Blend it with lemons," I say. "It's all the same."

During my free hour I'm sitting at my desk wearing my rhine-stone harlequins and grading papers when Mrs. Perkins, my department head, walks in. I take off the glasses and stick them into my pencil jar, but Mrs. Perkins takes them out and tries them on.

"Miss Martin," Mrs. Perkins says, looking around the room, up at the ceiling lights, "you seem distracted. But that's not why I'm here." She takes off the glasses and puts them back into the jar. "Mrs. Watt was in this morning."

Mrs. Watt is my problem parent. We have frequent conferences concerning reading material given to her daughter, Julie. Most recently, Mrs. Watt took issue with the aquatic mammals unit.

"I sent the anatomy charts home with her," I say.

"Mrs. Watt thinks you're involved with Mr. Watt," Mrs. Perkins says. She reaches inside her dress through the "V" in her collar and pulls up a strap. I wonder if she's ever considered Komfort.

"Involved? What's involved?" I say.

"So you've thought it over," Mrs. Perkins says, pulling brown leaves off my philodendron, then jabbing her finger into the wet dirt.

"Root rot," I say.

"Tell me about it," Mrs. Perkins says and sits on a corner of my desk.

"Did you ever feel as if you were not yourself but someone listening in on yourself, Mrs. Perkins?" I say.

Donald and Kevin came back to my next hour's advanced biology class to watch the film on cell division. Kevin sits on my desk reading the dictionary while Donald helps me thread the projector.

"Random House, unabridged, 1966," Kevin reads. "Undines: female water spirits get souls when they marry a man and have a kid."

"Paraphrased, of course," I say over my shoulder.

"Of course," Kevin says. "Listen to this: a sylph is an imaginary girl who lives in the air. Oh, this is great. Salamanders are imaginary girls who live in fire."

"What does it say about gnomes?" I say, pushing the projector's ON button.

"Interphase, prophase, metaphase, anaphase, telophase," a metallic male voice says. Diagrams of each phase flash onto the screen. I freeze the frame and pick up a ruler.

"Interphase," I say, "environmental change, no visible nuclear change." I'm sitting on my desk between Donald and Kevin trying to get the shadow of the ruler to match up with the diagram. First I'm too far left. Then I'm too far right. Donald takes the ruler from me and walks over to the screen where he points as I talk.

"Prophase," I say, "we have these little fibers reaching out, pole to pole, pole to equator. Metaphase, we have this little unit here that can be shaken loose and moved around by sounds too high for us to hear. Anaphase, the little unit becomes two sisters who go their separate ways. Telophase, pop, bang, whatever, each sister is a new cell. Then back to interphase, up to telophase, back to interphase, ad infinitum, hopefully for mankind, anyway." I release the HOLD button and more diagrams, accompanied by Donald's fingers, scramble around on the screen. Kevin is lying on the floor in front of my desk asleep. His head rests on the dictionary.

When I get home from school, the phone is ringing. Sapphire wants me to meet her at Robo-Wash for a free wash and guided tour.

"I had to get a cop to show me the way out of the city last night," I say. "I'll never find you."

"Get out your compass and drive north to the first Junior Food Mart," Sapphire says. "They'll have a map."

Robo-Wash turns out to be a pyramid of purple glass bubbles with a skylight dome that flashes the time on the hour and half hour. Sapphire and I walk around in the lobby, a brightly-lit, central bubble, for a while. Other people mill about drinking from styrofoam cups and watching small TVs hung from the ceiling.

"Most people prefer to watch from that viewing window over there," Sapphire says, pointing to a large, rectangular window in the lobby wall. "But I prefer to drive through." She waves to a man dressed in an orange jumpsuit like Muhal's and a yellow helmet like Sapphire's. "Richard, bring Ophelia's car around. We're going through." She tosses a silver dollar to him, which he catches and sticks under his watch band.

"This won't chip my paint, will it?" I say, stopping my car at a red light that flashes STOP in white letters. We're just inside the tunnel that passes by the viewing window.

"Computerized," Sapphire says. "Sonar. Knows Cadillacs from Volkswagens."

The light says TURN OFF/PARK, which I do, and my car creeps forward.

"I don't see the exit," I say.

"Muhal's design," Sapphire says. "Enhances the reflective qualities of the bubble and heightens the quality of the expectation."

"So Muhal's the catalyst here," I say.

"He's technical, I'm PR," Sapphire says as two giant orange
brushes spin down from the ceiling and flatten against the windshield.

"Sapphire? Ophelia?" It's Muhal's voice over a loud-speaker.
"How you like it so far? Wait until the light show, Ophelia. You'll
really like that."

"I thought you agreed to stay out of this one, Muhal," Sapphire
says into her watch. "I'm the PR person here, remember?"

"Old habits and all that," Muhal says. "Watch for the blue light,
Ophelia," he says. "That's suds. You'll like suds."

"There you go again, Muhal," Sapphire says. "If you don't stick
to your job and let me stick to mine, we'll never have any
organization around here." She takes off her helmet and lays it on
the seat between us. "I'm sorry, Ophelia," she says. "Muhal
doesn't know the meaning of rules. Sometimes I wonder. I really
wonder."

Sapphire and I appear to be trapped inside the Robo-Wash. The
brushes have been rolling over the car for more than an hour.
Water, suds, water, suds. It can't seem to kick into the dry cycle.
Now and then, through gaps in the bristles, I see a pair of blue and
yellow jogging shoes running back and forth, finally joined by a
pair of black rubber boots. A monkey wrench falls by the boots and
a yellow glove picks it up. The boots run away, followed by the
jogging shoes.

"There's a built-in trouble-shooter," Sapphire says, "but Muhal
disconnected it.

"Sapphire? Ophelia?" It's Muhal's voice over the loud-speaker
again.

"No reason to worry," Sapphire says.

"No reason to worry," Muhal says. "We've called the Fire
Department. Listen, the boys and I are going to play a little
something for you, just to pass the time. Can you hear me? Turn
this thing up, will you, Richard? Okay, Sarge, Amadee, T.J. One
and two and take it and."

"Muhal's arrangement of 'Round About Midnight,'" Sapphire
says.

When the brushes finally raise back up into the ceiling and the steam around us clears, I look over at the viewing window where Muhal, Sarge, and a dozen or so other people lean against the glass looking at us. Muhal raises his thumb like a hitch-hiker.

"Heating coils," Sapphire says, rubbing her harlequins with a wad of tissue.

"There's an inescapable perversity to all this," I say. "Here," Sapphire says, picking up her helmet and fitting it on my head. "Try this on."

"Adjustable chin strap," I say. "Nice."

"Keep it," Sapphire says. "I have another one just like it."

My car rolls forward and the exit door swings open. We stop halfway through the door.

"Maybe we can go see a drive-in movie later," Sapphire says. "You don't mind using your car, do you?"

"Hey, unlock your door," Muhal says, pecking on my window. "Look at you," he says to me as I scoot over next to Sapphire and he slides in behind the wheel. "First time I laid eyes on you I knew you'd look just fine in Komfort. Here. Let that strap dangle."

🔥 🔥 🔥

THE STENCH

fiction by JILLIAN BECKER

from SOUTH AFRICAN JEWISH VOICES (Micah Publications)

nominated by MICAH PUBLICATIONS

THEY WERE BOILING A HORSE.

That, the schoolmaster was to discover eventually, was the cause of the stink which rose from the mud-hut village half-way up an adjacent hill to his own house on the top of the higher rockier one; and also sank into the valley where the road wound, forcing the rare passing drover or rider to narrow his eyes, pinch his nostrils closed, twist his head this way and that but without escape, while his oxen plodded and swung on imperturbably, their noses too close to dust and perhaps too full of it to be irritated by anything else; but the ponies and hinnies snorted, nodded, and stamped harder in the warm powdery margins of the stony track. The occupants of the car which bumped along in the late afternoon of the second day since the stink had begun were less exposed, but could not have missed it.

The schoolmaster Schwallendorf—a bald, stout, heavy-jowled Saxon—did not make the discovery himself. He had hesitated to venture down among the huts—the presumable source of the stink—into its density and to its very nidorous epicentre. But then a directive came, tactful, amiable, but unmistakable; in the form of a request but nonetheless compulsory; from District Commissioner Bertel Maria Pik, a small Afrikaner in black serge forever troubled by facial impetigo and hay-fever, who, with respect to his hay-fever, shirked the task which should have been his immoveably. He climbed to Schwallendorf's house—four rondavels united by a central square kitchen roofed with pleated tin—by a steep, circuitous path, in an effort to get round the nastiness he had had to drive through: leaving his official blue Chevrolet in the charge of his Xhosa driver, who parked it in the bedraggled shade of eucalyptus, within sight of the store where the tribeswomen came and went.

Schwallendorf was sitting in creased white clothes on the stone step outside his back door, the cooler but hardly less smelly side of the house, and rose to greet his visitor as Pik reached the level pressing a white handkerchief to his wet, erupting face, and poking it down under the high collar of his shirt.

'Good evening, Meneer. How goes it?'

Meneer Pik had no breath to answer. He slumped into a bamboo chair on one side of the small table on which a whisky bottle stood and two glasses as though he had been expected, or been seen approaching.

'If you please,' he panted as Schwallendorf raised the bottle, and he stuffed the crumpled handkerchief into a trouser pocket, took a fresh one from his jacket, unfolded it, wound a corner over the tip of a forefinger and dabbed gingerly at his nose.

'Fiff! But what a stink, hey? You'll do me a favour Schwallendorf. If you please. I cannot go and see myself. This nose of mine. You would oblige me. Or do you know what it is?' He bubbled as he breathed. His nostrils red and damp, his eyes brimming over.

'I've asked the washgirl and the houseboy,' Schwallendorf assured him. 'But they pretend not to know. So I'll go and see what I can find. Of course. Certainly.'—As if to oblige and not obey. And they toasted each other with a raising of their glasses.

Pik fastidiously refolded his handkerchief to dry his lip with its sore spot or two. 'It's this nose of mine, you must see. It's an allergy, you must understand. A lot of people are allergic to something. But I am allergic to everything. Alles.' He swung his infected head to indicate all; and closed his eyes on the long-suffering of all; enflamed western clouds, abrasive gravel, pungent leaves of eucalyptus, a black mote of a bird in the exposure of blue.

'Shall we move into the house?' Schwallendorf suggested. 'It's not so bad with the windows shut.' And he puffed out his lips and cheeks as he waited for the answer.

'No! I cannot stay here any longer under these circumstances.'

'Oh!' The schoolmaster's lips remained open and round on the syllable, his eyes wide, but his cheeks falling flaccid again; a foolish expression, not as if he were disappointed but as though he had been rebuked.

Pik drained his glass and rose. 'I must go. I should never have come up.' He plied his handkerchief again. 'I should have gone on home and telephoned you. Even with the windows up it filled the car like a poisonous gas. I've borne as much as I can. But we'll get to the bottom of this thing. Find out what those kaffirs are up to.' (For men as much as nature plotted against Pik.) 'I can't bear it much longer,' he warned, standing there and dabbing.

It was as if Pik were waiting for Schwallendorf to confess—that he had had a hand in starting the smell, or had carelessly allowed it to erupt, or had tolerated it when he might have stopped it. Schwallendorf felt guilty for having postponed investigation—but the smell had been even more intense then than it was now.

But Pik reassured him. 'I regard,' he said, narrowing his eyes as though what he regarded might sting, 'your co-operation. I must go, I must go.' He hurried off. 'Ring me up in the morning, ja?' He stared down. 'Obliged,' he called. And again after a moment, 'Obliged!'

Schwallendorf felt the ambiguity of it, and looked unhappily after Pik as he sidled away down the rocky path, handkerchief over nose; and plodded along a dry stream-bed past yellow-blossoming thorntrees which could only torment him with their sweetness.

Now the screendoor of the kitchen groaned as it was opened behind him, creaked as its tendency to bang shut was curbed, so that it rejoined its jamb without violence; from which Schwallendorf knew without turning round which of the several possible persons who might be coming out of the house this was.

He said, 'That was the D.C. He wants me to find out what's causing the stench. I can't blame him for shirking it. I'm not sure I can stomach it myself.'

'I'll go!' The peremptory announcement was made. '*Ich werde gehen!*'

As the man who said this with such finality came to stand beside him, Schwallendorf turned to him with the look if not the words for 'Are you sure you want to?' The words had been forbidden by that tone. But the younger man was deliberately looking away, and the schoolmaster could not see much of his face, only the firm-set line of the jaw, at the end of which a ball of muscle was thrust out by the clench of determination, and was throbbing and quivering a denial that this man was made of anything harder, less vulnerable, than other mean are—and so also a plea that his resolution go unquestioned.

The schoolmaster grunted.

He believed that he understood: nasty as the stink was, it was not such a challenge, and the grit with which it was being met was less a response to the occasion than a habit of resolution and self-discipline.

'So—if you will,' the easy-going schoolmaster accepted. 'But there is no hurry. Tomorrow will do. By the morning it may have cleared a little.'

That was most probable. Which could have been the reason why the other man said, 'No, I'll go now.'

The large surface of Schwallendorf's face was flattered by the softening light.

And the other's face was also flushed. Its skin was of that sensitive thinness which quickly reddens on exposure to the sun. It was a face in which the bones showed, not gauntly but distinctly enough. Unlike Schwallendorf's, this face—and body—had no redundancy of flesh. Because of its physical hardness it was not a face which changed much with the shift of thoughts or feelings in the man. It might have been unexpressive, set to the point of impassivity, had not conflict—of the will against weaknesses—revealed itself through that quiver in the muscle. No—the hardness was itself an expression, conscious and consciously maintained; so much so—and so plainly to anyone who observed or talked to the man for more than a moment—that even the narrow nose, the cheekbones, would seem to have been willfully achieved rather than naturally endowed: and further evidence could have been found in the hair, for although Konrad Reitzger was not yet twenty-six, his black, thick, short-cut hair was turning an iron-grey at its edges. His eyes were pale as steel, deep under black eyebrows, but there was no animosity in them. They were clear, questioning, open. Not, they would seem, the eyes of a self-obsessed introvert, but of a man who would probably look well before he judged: a man more interested in seeing a thing clearly than in expressing a quick reaction to it.

'As you prefer, Reitzger,' the older man consented—or gave formal permission to the volunteer. He added, 'Danke!'

Schwallendorf watched the rather strange young man, in conventional white shirt and grey trousers, go off round the house to make his discovery.

Schwallendorf's oldest friend, Max Feuchthaber, had sent young Reitzger to him. The letter had arrived a month ago. Barry Theobald had brought it over from the store as soon as he got back from meeting the train at Butterworth. It looked important, he said, coming all that way, and could he have the stamps for his step-son who was at the T.B. hospital in the Transvaal, yes improving thanks, but very slowly. Theobald knew that Schwallendorf had been waiting some months now to hear whether he'd be granted a pension if he went 'home' to the Bundesrepublik where in fact he had never set foot except to sail from Bremerhaven.

'Dear August—'

Disappointed, and simultaneously pleased, Schwallendorf read the letter from his friend.

'We were at school together,' he told Theobald. In Leipzig, the Gymnasium, and then the University; where he had studied Theology, and Feuchthaber had studied Physics and laughed at God, so their intimacy had begun to lessen. Then Schwallendorf had come to Africa, and they might have lost touch altogether, but their mothers too were friends: and during the war—when August himself was in the internment camp—his mother had moved to the south to live near her sister in Augsburg, and old Frau Feuchthaber had also moved to some small town near Munich where she had relations. Both were widows, both lonely, and they visited each other from time to time. So from his mother, after the war, August heard news of Max. He heard he had become Professor at Heidelberg. He wondered if Max was less lonely than he. Ten years ago his mother had died, and he had heard no more of his friend, until now.

'If you receive this, write at once so that I can give your address to a former student of mine who is coming to "investigate" Africa . . .'

Feuchthaber had used the English word, perhaps because *untersuchen* or *erforschen* could equally well mean 'explore', which is what anyone might do who was coming to Africa. Schwallendorf had wondered about this, and now he thought that Feuchthaber had cleverly caught, with that one word, something of the character of young Reitzger. He could see exactly what Feuchthaber—whose affection for Reitzger had also, *nichtsdestoweniger*, been suggested—had meant to imply when he said 'investigate'. Or was it perhaps a word that Reitzger himself had used, when telling Feuchthaber his plans? Reitzger spoke excellent English, at least as good as Schwallendorf himself.

'Investigate.' Yes. In three days this Reitzger had asked more questions about the country, its climate, its people, its past and present, its birds, beasts and plants than Schwallendorf had learnt the answers to or even thought to ask in thirty years.

Well, this appetite for information might be useful now. Reitzger was not the man to miss whatever was happening down there, and if the reasons were not obvious he'd do his dogged best to find them out. And yet, even if he persuaded some of the villagers to use their English, they were unlikely to tell him much. Not enough to satisfy Pik. He should have thought of that. He'd have to go himself, after all.

But then again, Schwallendorf had to admit, they were not likely to tell any white man more than they had to—certainly not Pik. Only last week Pik had taken away one of the men—Johnjohn, whom everyone knew was the headman's son and who'd come back from the mines a year ago to his home village. But Pik had maintained that he had no right to be here, and had 'endorsed' him out of the territory, no one knew where. The headman had asked him, Schwallendorf, to intercede—and he'd gone at once to Butterworth, but who on earth could make Pik change his mind? 'I'm sorry, Meneer Schwallendorf, the law is clear and I do my duty.' Then the headman had ridden off to Butterworth himself, as if he could succeed where a white man failed. Perhaps he hadn't even believed that Schwallendorf had done his best. For the sad thing was, they didn't trust him either. This was the tragic *Ausfall* of his whole life. Though most of them had been or were still his pupils, they no longer trusted him with their secrets. In the last five years he seemed to have lost what he'd gained so patiently and conscientiously in the twenty-five years before. Now there was an atmosphere of disgruntlement, if not rebellion: or building up of storm clouds in the minds of men—that's what they were achieving, Pik and his kind! And though it wasn't through any fault of his own—he was sure of that—it amounted to a personal failure all the same. There was no reclaiming the lost ground now. He had wanted to stay in this job for their sakes, but what good was a man to those who didn't trust him? 'Co-operation' with Pik might keep him his job for a while yet, though most of the other white Protestant teachers—and all the Roman Catholic missionaries—had been sent away. But if that co-operation meant his losing the trust of the very people he wanted the continued chance to serve, what was the use of his staying on anyway?

He sighed. A stout old man getting fuller of doubts and shorter of the spirit to deal with them. Feuchthaber had laughed at God, and yet became Professor at Heidelberg, and had many friends. While he—Hadn't he wanted to be a father to them, no matter his colour and theirs?

He was feeling particularly dejected this evening, as though something were missing that he depended on: yes, it was like nostalgia, but not for anything he could name; not for lost friends, or youth, or Germany; but for something the past had always contained until recently. Hope for something perhaps. But for what exactly, he could not grasp; though it wavered about him, inapprehensible but pervasive, like the stench—which was probably, he concluded, itself the actual cause of the unpleasant mood.

He went into his house, seeking some refuge from the pervading rotten smell.

As Reitzger descended into the stronger zones of the smell, he reminded himself that squeamishness was easy to overcome. He had wanted to make this investigation since he had woken up to the foul stench on the second morning after his arrival, but Schwallendorf had insisted no, they would wait, he would ask, there was no need. Reitzger liked answers. He wanted all the phenomena of this country to be identified and explained. The impact of Africa was strongly physical; it appealed immediately to the senses. It could hardly be expected to stimulate the imagination as old cities and man-worked landscapes did. Rather, it assailed a man: these primitives of heat, wilderness, mountain and valley and plain, of intense colours in a generally unrelenting sunlight under a ceiling of hard even blue, harsh sounds of birds shrieking and chattering and purring but not singing, the tastes of things distinctive but not subtle, and now this penetrating smell, roused mood, distracted the mind with irritation and offence, if one didn't keep hold. It could distort one's view—in the atmosphere of sunset and stench the whole landscape might seem warmed to the point of decay: gangrene of the bush; the sulphur-yellow of fever-trees. But his eyesight was extraordinarily good. He saw, as red rocks crumpled in the deepening—at last relenting—light, each ridge defined; and grasses burning out individually.

He reached the valley, where the stink seemed less intense: but as he climbed up again towards the village it thickened. And when the path brought him to a level where he turned off to walk among the huts he was enveloped and filled with it, he could have choked on it, but refused to of course.

Women long skirted and bare breasted continued to pound with pestles into deep wooden mortars—but they watched him pass, and the babies on their rocking backs gazed at him. Men dressed in togas of blue cotton with matching turbans, and girls in little more than beads, appeared from all sides, and as they passed they turned their eyes towards him, but none of them stopped or spoke to him. They surely knew why he had come. There was curiosity and perhaps amusement in their glances, but not fear. The pounding went on, the walkers passed him, this one with a tin of water on her head, that one with a bundle of sticks across his shoulders. And Reitzger said nothing to them. He did not even nod at them. His nose directed him.

He came out beyond the last of the huts into a stony space. There was a fire in a square shallow pit; and over it, balanced on logs, a huge tank with a scaffolding erected on one side providing a ladder and a platform. One man was pushing branches down into the pit. Another stood on the platform and was using a branch to stir the contents of the tank. A woollen scarf was wound round his nose and mouth. He was smoked and steamed, but persisted. The job must be very important to keep a man at it in such discomfort. Women approached him, one hand pressed to mouth and nostrils, and he would let go of his huge spatula to lift the tins from their heads and empty the water into the tank. The smoke came round and billowed over Reitzger. He did not move away but waited for it to be shifted again by an otherwise undetectable current of air. His eyes watered and stung. The slow procession of water-bearers continued to advance towards the platform, and the attendant up there to empty the tins and stir. His presence did not apparently perturb them. Whatever it was they were doing was calmly proceeded with, as with any normal occupation. He could look on to his heart's content, no one minded in the least. But the smell was abnormal, terrible. And in the red light, in the stench, in the smoke, the silent business seemed lurid and sinister.

Reitzger stood watching, and prepared himself for what he

might see when he climbed the ladder. Prepared himself, that is, for the worst, that experience, which had exceeded imagination, could warn him of: a scene which came back to him vividly from his first day at the University of Heidelberg. In a large hall of the Medical Faculty, a rectangular pool, wide and long enough to be a swimming-pool, but full of mustard yellow water. He had gone to the edge and peered down into it, expecting what?—fish?—lilies and reeds?—and found it was full of floating human corpses; with swollen green-white flesh, streaming hair, bulging eyelids. He had felt his gorge rise, but stood still and ordered it down, closed his eyes, drooped his shoulders; and though sweat had broken out on his forehead he had been able to walk steadily down a busy passage among bustling white coats, and vomited when he reached the lavatory. So his shame had not been public, but in any case severe. He was aspiring—had intended since childhood—to become a surgeon! Before the war he had dissected animals without a qualm. What had reduced him to this then? The cold eye of the dissector, the detached mind of the science-student had surely not been changed by hunger or fear. Fear had been overcome, by grit, which was the product of willpower and intelligence. So why should not an augmented courage, which had helped him face the near possibility of his own death and the actual deaths of others who if not exactly friends were by then in any case familiar, help him to look calmly at a tankful of cadavers? What was this—was it pity, or was it revulsion? Neither was called for. And as for why—though a question one did ask—a man cannot take a scalpel to himself!

One had not changed one's course then, or at least not for some time, and not for that cause; and one would not now, when one was quite prepared.

He climbed the ladder of rough split eucalyptus logs, tatty with peeling bark, to stand beside the cook who paused in his stirring but did not look at him. The reeking steam made his eyes sting, and at first he could see nothing through the billows of vapour and the scum and the bulges of heaving water at the boil. Then it swam up, the horse. Stiff legs, enormous hooves, open bulging eyes, streaming mane and tail, split skin, the bowels floating out. A scene by Hieronymous Bosch, he thought. And he stood steady, and steadily looked down, breathing in the sickening stench without nausea or even disgust.

He climbed down unhurriedly, and went back among the huts.

'Pardon,' he said to one of the busy villagers, and stepped in front of him to make him stand still.

'Boss?'

'Is Walter here? Walter? Is he still here? I want to speak to him.'

The man stared at him stupidly.

'Walter,' Reitzger repeated, louder but not impatiently.

The man tipped back his head as he understood, and then he pointed. Round there and straight on, his hand told the stranger.

Reitzger went the way he was shown, and soon saw the person he was seeking, standing in front of a hut. It was as if he had been standing there waiting for Reitzger to appear, for he promptly raised one hand and smiled in greeting.

'Mr. Reitzger!' he called, pleasantly, familiarly; 'Welcome, my friend!'

Reitzger had found Walter for the first time three days earlier.

Two cranes, huge awkward birds with gold crowns; grey, white bellied, with tails of butter and mauve, soared up and slumped upon the top of a tree in full blossom of scarlet, but with no leaves. The tree grew beside a river—of water, not a dry bed. Still water, in a valley at noon. On the other side a cornfield, wrecked by its harvest; pale bent sticks in stony furrows of the red earth. And in the middle of the field, in the sun, on a high chestnut horse, a hefty black man in a yellow shirt, smooth polished riding-boots with silver buckles, a crop in his hand.

Reitzger had crossed a bridge made of heaped stones. Then over the hard red earth through the devastation of the sticks. And called out, 'Good morning!'

The man raised a hand in salute, then lowered it to the pommel of his saddle and leaned forward graciously to enquire.

'Yes sir. Can I be of some assistance to you?'

Reitzger asked for directions.

'It happens,' the equestrian replied, 'that I am proceeding there myself immediately. It is unfortunate that I cannot procure an-other horse for you to accompany me.'

How far was it? Could one not walk?

'It is not too far. In nine-ten hours you could be at your destination. But you would conclude your journey in a state of exhaustion, even if you did not lose your way.'

They considered the problem, which both placed at a distance from themselves where the valley flowed away into the sky. One of the cranes rose, circled widely, returned to its mate. It took time.

Reitzger turned back to look up at the man again.

'My name,' he said, 'is—Konrad.'

'Conradie?'

'Not Conradie. Just Konrad. It is my first name. The other is hard to pronounce.'

Reitzger had been told by two or three women—one of them his mother—that he lacked not only 'charm', but, more seriously, 'tact'. He was intending to achieve tact now, but as he spoke became uneasily aware that he was falling short of it again.

The man said, in the same clear, strong but quiet tone as before, and without straightening again with any bridling movement, 'I have been through High School, and I have matriculated. I was in the war as a medical assistant. I can read and write three languages. In particular my spelling of English is exemplary.'

Exemplary. Reitzger gave in.

'Reitzger,' he said. 'Konrad Reitzger.'

'Mr Reitzger.' The man pronounced it impeccably. And went on, 'You are German then. Which means that once you were officially my enemy.' This time the two men in the middle of the red and plundered field made their considerations while looking at each other's eyes: the one straightened now on his height, looking down; the other on stiff legs planted apart in the red dust, looking up. Waiting. The valley held the heat in stillness. But then the horseman smiled, widely, showing his white teeth. 'But not necessarily my enemy now. What would your opinion be on that question?'

'Not necessarily,' Reitzger agreed, who was however in no hurry to reassure or befriend, and saved his emphasis for what he must insist on—his own determination. He would not plead. He would not make strenuous efforts to convince. He was the last man to smile foolish smiles and stutter in efforts to create goodwill.

'So,' the other went on, content enough with this answer, 'you can call me Walter. Yes. That is my English name. My Xhosa name clicks, and white men have difficulty with clicks. You, Mr Reitzger—' again he repeated it just as he had heard it, with the guttural German 'r'—'would not be able to pronounce it.'

Touché!

Reitzger moved his eyes from the dark ones of the mounted man to the tail of the horse which was flicking at horse-flies on its haunches. The same idea was growing in both of them. But neither was in a hurry to tell it. They looked away to the birds, one of which raised its wings in a restless half-rise, then flopping and wing-rowing scrambled again for a claw-clutch.

Reitzger's awkwardness, his shyness, was concealed—or divulged—by stiffness. 'Walter,' he said, looking at the cranes, 'could let me ride on his horse—'

Walter did not move or speak.

'—behind him, on the haunches.' He put a hand on the wide flanks of the animal. Another man might have slapped it.

'You mean,' Walter corrected him, 'if it would not make me uncomfortable, would I consider such an arrangement?'

'I could pay—'

But Walter raised his voice to stop him. 'With pleasure. And if you were to offer me recompense, Mr Reitzger, I should definitely refuse.'

And he smartly removed foot from stirrup on Reitzger's side, and held the leg forward and one arm rigidly down, so that Reitzger could use stirrup and arm to swing himself up, to sit astride the horse close to the broad yellow back of its master.

'Forward Ukuthula!' Walter commanded, and tapped the hefty shoulder with his crop. Ukuthula curved his neck and paced through the field, stamping down the sticks, the bent and the straight, and some still with papery leaves, which stood in his way, crackling and faintly rustling, and starting up small spurts of the soft red dust. Over the bridge, past the tree with its reflection, scarlet and scarlet, and the four cranes, two high in the heat and two low in the cool brown water.

Konrad Reitzger did not like to entrust himself to another person. Equally he would not like others to entrust themselves to him. Not because he shirked responsibility but because, on the contrary, he believed that everyone should accept full responsibility for his own actions. Men should meet on terms of equality. Respect yourself and respect others—unless they should prove themselves unworthy.

As, in his opinion, his father had. Who had demanded the respect of his children as a duty, denying their right to judge what he was or what he did. 'A weak man, a moral coward, afraid of authority, inclined to be servile, kowtowing to his bosses,' was the conviction he had confided to Professor Feuchthaber, one of those rare people whom Reitzger found it possible not only to respect but even to like. 'I know the type well,' Feuchthaber had said. And yet, while Konrad had no doubt that these qualities belonged to his father, he was not convinced that having said that he had said all there was to say about the old man. As a boy he had been puzzled by him—why was he so grand and grave with the family at dinner, and so different, loud and laughing, winking and whispering, when there were visitors? What was it about him that made the younger children hang their heads and answer in whispers when he spoke to them, and made Konrad, though he would stand straight, and look into his father's eyes, and speak up, feel his face grow hot as if he had something to be ashamed of, or was lying when he wasn't?

Kurt Reitzger was a thick man, not fat but solid, who sat and stood and walked in a rigid manner, with the straight back of an old Prussian officer—though he came of a Bavarian burgher family none of whom had ever been in any regular army. He had worked for a chemical company, one of the biggest in the world. His position was secure but not eminent. When he found out that Bernhard Kuhn, the son of his chief and classmate of his eldest son, often invited Konrad to the palatial Kuhn house on the other side of the river near the Schloss, he summoned Konrad into his study ('in that pompous way he had,' Konrad recalled), to inform him of his approval of such a 'respectable association' and hoped it would 'blossom' into a 'close and lasting friendship'.

For years Konrad had squirmed for his father's sentimentality and vulgarity; though he only put the names to these things when he was quite grown-up. In the evenings after dinner they all had to sit together for an hour 'to show that we are a proper loving family'. If there were guests, his father would tell his Joke. It didn't matter to him if he'd told it to the same guests a dozen times before, it must be told again because it proved him an amusing fellow. It was about a stutterer walking inadvertently into a cow-pat, and exclaiming Sch- sch- schon reingetreten! When this joke stopped being one of the great adult mysteries because he came to understand it, Konrad wondered why his father bothered to tell it, and why the visitors pretended to find it funny.

On Sundays they had all to go to Mass together. When he was fifteen he had asked his father, 'How can you be a scientist and

believe in God?' To which he received a long, solemn and uncon-
vincing reply. The expression of disbelief or even contempt on his
son's face roused his father eventually to red-faced anger. And it
may have been out of a desire for revenge that a few days later he
refused Konrad's request for a set of scalpels of his own. Konrad
had been staying late after school in the laboratory to investigate
the quadrate bone of the snipe, and write a paper on it under the
supervision and encouragement of his new but very old biology
teacher, who had been called back from retirement now that the
war was absorbing the young men. Konrad wanted to carry on at
home after the school had to be locked up. He wanted to finish his
paper in time to enter it for a national competition, and now his
father was too mean to help him. '*Scheiss!*' he hissed, as he left his
father's study. He was called back at once. 'What did you say?' the
old man demanded, his eyes bulging. 'I said, *schon reingetreten*,'
Konrad said, stiff with defiance. The old man stared helplessly, his
mouth opening and shutting silently, and Konrad marched out of
the room.

Perhaps old Reitzger was afraid of losing his son's respect. He
took him once to Ludwigshafen, to the laboratories of the Company. There was a fat woman there, some kind of secretary. His
father called her Lili and patted her bottom. She had metallic
yellow hair wound up in plaits, and wore a dirndl. She giggled
when the old man whispered to her. He looked stupidly pleased
with himself, but became serious, pompous as ever, as he showed
Konrad how to filter chemicals and how to mix them by shaking
them in a test-tube. Still the boy looked unimpressed. 'Ask me
anything you want explained,' he said. But it was obvious that he
didn't really know the answers to the boy's questions. He filtered
some more chemicals, and shook them in the test-tube. Konrad's
face remained wooden, and they drove home in silence.

Konrad won a prize for his paper—an ornate certificate which he
soon lost, and more importantly an exemption from service as an
anti-aircraft gunner which would otherwise have been compulsory
when he turned sixteen. He was allowed to stay at school until he
was seventeen. In that year he began to investigate genetics,
breeding generations of *Drosophila melanogaster*. Then, in the last
year of the war, he had to go into the army. 'Now be careful you
don't catch syphilis,' was all his father could think of to say in his
jocund bar-room manner the day Konrad left for his training.

The regiment was sent by train into the Battle of the Bulge. 'I may die soon,' Konrad thought, 'and I hardly know anything.' What was there, he wondered, that he could learn at this late hour? Perhaps he could learn to drive a locomotive. He went to ask the driver to give him lessons, and drove himself into battle.

He was wounded, not severely, but hospitalised at Mannheim. His father came to see him.

'You just get better, my boy, and when all this is over you won't have to worry. With the contacts I've got you'll get a good start up the right ladder. That I can promise you. You know you can rely on me,' he said. 'When peace comes —,' he kept saying. '*Kommt der Friede. Hab' keine Angst* — don't worry!'

And very soon after Konrad was sent back to the front, the peace did come. He was captured in a town called — he appreciated — Misery.

The prison camp was an open field enclosed with barbed wire, without shelter of any kind. A perpetual drizzle and the piss of thousands of men turned it to slush. The prisoners, wet and hungry and itching, sat or lay in the mud and scraped at it with their hands in the hope of reaching firmer ground. The young pink Americans watched suspiciously from the wooden towers at the corners of the field from behind their machine guns. Sometimes a prisoner, soaked and mind-wandering, would get up and try to run through the mud towards the fence, and the fingers of a frightened Pinkface would fly to his trigger, and the gun would rattle and bullets spray the running, the digging, the sleeping, a whole line of bewildered men. Once one of the guards shot his counterpart in the diagonally opposite tower. But despite wild and frequent rumours few of the prisoners believed that their extermination was intended. Each was given a bar of chocolate — his only rations — per day. Konrad Reitzger wondered if his bowels had lost their capacity to function, but after three weeks, an hour's labour, and a contribution of blood to the communal bog, he shat a rock.

In the fourth week — it was early March — some officer conceived the idea that it would be better to intercept and reason with those men who lost their nerve and squelched towards the fences than to shoot them down, especially as this method of dealing with them had proved so hazardous for the guards themselves. They needed an interpreter, and enquiry soon brought them to Reitzger, who thereafter spent his days sitting high on the back of a jeep, being driven round and round the mudfield, spotting, shouting at, explaining how things stood to those who'd had enough of mud and chocolate and lice and rain and thought they might prefer bullets. His padded uniform was so torn that all over it the padding hung out in little clotted mudballs, reminding him of a costume hung with bells that he had seen on Papageno when his mother had taken him to the opera in Salzburg on his tenth birthday.

The jeep was an improvement on the mud — to which however he returned to sleep. And it wasn't long before his English took him to the green pastures of a bed, regular meals, clean clothes, water and soap at the American base, for he was handed over to a priest who needed an interpreter who was also Catholic and educated. Reitzger hid his atheism and his contempt. 'The Mess was worth a Mass,' he was to explain to those who would agree, like Feuchthaber.

His usefulness delayed his return to civilian life, but one did not starve as long as one stayed with the American army. Home in Heidelberg that winter of forty-five to forty-six he found out how scarce everything was. Or would have been, even for him, had not the American High Command set up its headquarters there. And of course the intelligent man would survive if survival was possible. And not only survive, but survive well. And the real test of intelligence (Konrad Reitzger said) was life itself.

He became a waiter at the American Club. One took one's tips and commissions in cigarettes. A 'bar' of them was a bar of gold. Clumsy money, but it bought food, clothes and even books.

The Americans themselves organised a lending library for civilians. As 'Now the war for the minds begins,' the padre had been fond of saying who had been Reitzger's patron, and to whom he had therefore restrained himself from answering with his own opinion — 'Nazism — Catholicism — one irrational faith or another — is a poor choice if any at all.' And when he searched the library he found nothing there either — mostly the conqueror's naive and misplaced faith in Steinbeck and O'Neill. The first time he went in there a woman kept trying to catch his eye and smirk at him. On a later visit she said, 'Don't you remember me? I remember *you*. My name's Lili — I used to work at — ah, now you remember! And tell me, how is your father these days? He used to be very amusing your father, very good company!' Lili's hair was shorter and darker, and no longer plaited and wound. She was thinner and usually dressed in a red suit; and her lips and nails were red. She told him she was engaged to an American called Al. When he told her that he was working as a waiter at the Club she became cooler. Yet she couldn't have earned as much in a month as he did in a single night.

The Club was smoky and noisy with a piano and singing and frivolity, and full of women with square beaded shoulders and hair in sausages on top of their heads. At four in the morning Konrad would go home to sleep. At eight he would go to the apartment of two stout old ladies, the central exchange and chief agents of the Black Market.

Little pearl earrings pressed into their lobes. One wore a tangled wig like beige coir; the other's white hair was pinned in a tight knot with big black hairpins. The skin of their necks looked like grey used chamois. They smelt as musty as their apartment. The wigged one had been married, and the broad gold ring pressed into her flesh. The other had a big watch chained to her belt. Their feet were squeezed into schoolgirl shoes, on each a cushion of flesh between the curve of leather and the strap. Their many high dark rooms were crowded with enormous articles of polished furniture, and silent motionless clocks, antimacassars, a multitude of ornaments—bucolic china children with faces like buttocks, orange dogs with blunt muzzles and blank round eyes. Rugs worn to the jute. Canvases of cracked oil paint in pompous frames. Crowds of portrait-photos on an upright piano. The Goethe, the Schiller, the aspidistra. Torn velvet curtains with fringed valances. The windows nailed shut. The chandeliers in calico bags, grey and lumpy and bulbous as wasp-nests. One waited and waited, so often and so long, in the dining-room or a drawing-room or a music-room or a bedroom or even in the kitchen, that one became familiar with the objects and the atmosphere. In each room someone waited. And the two old ladies came and went between them, arranging the deals. Buyers and sellers never saw each other. No doubt the old ladies took the biggest profit, but nobody did badly who had patience.

Socks, twelve pairs of, whisky, pens, watches, wool-tweed a bale of, one overcoat. How many bars for the overcoat? Wait. A cut-glass vase on a painted cloth in the middle of the oval table had grey dust in the bottom. Things taken no notice of, no longer admired or used. As though the ladies were only tenanting lives which their former selves had built and owned.

Sixty bars for the overcoat? Very well, I'll take it.

The cold air of the street was welcome then. A thick white light. Agitated grey river, grey light-stained river. Harsh rattle and sparks of the trams. Hungry intent faces, mufflers across mouths as if people were deliberately gagging themselves. Once, a man standing on a bridge, his bare red-raw hands held out in front of him like a sleep-walker: a cap so low over his eyes he could surely not see, and its flaps tied down over his ears, and a muffler across his mouth—I have seen no evil, heard no evil, spoken no evil, but what have I *done?* A cloud on others' spirits as on the mountains compressing the town. Pigeons, grey flocks of. Sorrows, other people's. For oneself there was a new warm overcoat, and one knew where one could go and buy Russell on Einstein in the original English.

And then there was still one bar of cigarettes left over.

'Ach, Konrad! Is that you?' the old man would call from his study, putting on surprise, when he'd been watching from the window, craving what he would not ask for—'You've brought cigarettes for me? That is very lucky!'

Konrad would reach round the door, drop the bar of ten packets on the desk without glancing at his father and retreat without a word.

'I must pay you back!'—the old man hurrying out into the hall and following him to the foot of the stairs, brandishing a few useless Reichsmarks, pretending that these cigarettes were some sort of extra ration that his son was somehow regularly awarded by the new authorities. As if he were deaf, the son would go on up, to his room at the top of the house, with his new book.

There had always been English books at home, belonging to his mother, who had gone to school for a time in Sussex. He and his sister and two brothers had been brought up to speak English by a nursery-governess named Miss Baldwin, who claimed relationship with the Prime Minister of Great Britain. She had never learned to speak German well, but had gone home in nineteen thirty-nine very reluctantly, having become so fond of the children and their mother.

Konrad's mother was stern and practical, but witty and intelligent. She was much younger than his father and, the adult Konrad realised, scornful of him. At this time she used her cleverness at cards which she played twice a week, with ladies who came in from the country. Their debts were paid in eggs, chickens, ducks, potatoes, which stocked the otherwise empty larder of the Reitzger house in Handschuhsheim, though occasionally Frau Reitzger had to part with pieces of her family silver. Her books were mostly novels, some poetry. Her son had no use for them any more. Nobody had. And they were less likely to recover value one day than the silver was.

The old man, home all day now with nothing to do but complain, had always enjoyed food and wine. He had kept a good cellar before the war, and had tried to teach Konrad about wines. And the boy had been interested enough, but found that his father could make any subject boring. Now he was boring them all with his complaints. His children not only refused to sit and listen in the hour after dinner, but Konrad, always the most recalcitrant of them, wouldn't even come to the dinner table. When he was in the house at all he kept to his own room. And 'the Lord knew where he got to the rest of the time,' old Reitzger groused to any of his other children who might be provoked into answering.

But he did know where Konrad got to.

Visitors, of whom there were few enough, but at least the farmers' wives—'not unrespectable women' he would have it known—who came to play skat with his wife, would be told: 'My son is working for the Americans, you know. Yes, I arranged—that is to say, I encouraged him to offer his assistance to the officers—'

To his son he said: 'A waiter! With your education. With that science prize you won. Surely you can get yourself a better job than that. Have you spoken to the right person at the right level?'

The son would mount the stairs away from the voice, shut the door on it. His room contained nothing but a bed, a table, a chair and a bookcase. There had been a wardrobe which he'd moved out on to the landing. Bare floor. No heater: though he would leave his door open at night to let in the warmer air rising from the rooms below. Konrad thought of himself as an ascetic scholar, cleanly occupied with science, the opposite of his father who was weak, soft, ineffectual, a sensualist. He could imagine how his father would behave in the Club with all those women: the coarse jokes, the bottom-slapping. Of course his mother must despise such a man.

—About whom, however, there was something elusive. What had he now to be so proud about? He still strutted, he still tried to dictate—the useless, snobbish ignorant old ninny! Konrad dismissed him from his thoughts to concentrate on algebra.

The time for real study came at last.—But on the very first day, the shock of the bodies in the tank. Of course he had not allowed that to deflect him from his intention of studying Medicine. Not, at least, until he was sure, and reassured by all his teachers, that his talent was really for Mathematics and theoretical Physics after all.

'Mathematics!' old Reitzger had protested, peevish because he had not been consulted, and barely informed. 'What is the use of Mathematics? It never earned a living at the best of times!'

But he wasted his breath, and he knew it.

The two men on the horse swayed through the valley.

'What do you call those big birds?'

'That bird? In my language? We call him i-Hem. It is the noise he makes. It is good that he is here—he brings the rain.'

Soon Reitzger wanted to change the position of his dangling legs, shift the weight of his shoulder-hung bag from left hip to right, but instead sought distraction. He asked, 'Are you a chief?'

'No sir. But I am a chief's son.'

'Will you be Chief when your father dies?'

'My father has many sons. My personally becoming Chief is a matter only of possibility.'

'Do you want to be Chief?'

'I would be glad to have the opportunity to govern my people. Or rather, let me say, to help them in the government of themselves. You understand, that is a different thing from being Chief of a people under the government of foreigners?'

The foreigner asked, in his direct way, 'For the sake of power? Or because you wish the good of your people?'

'That,' Walter granted, 'is an important question. It is a necessary question that a man must ask himself. And I can answer it. I say, because I wish the good of my people.'

'I've heard that the Government talks of letting this land of yours become self-governing.'

' "Self-governing"? Now please, I ask you for your opinion sir, as a man of the world. What sort of freedom will we get? All the big country—it will be their Republic. They say that soon—five years, ten—it will be their Republic. No more English Kings and Queens over the water. They will divide it. Yes sir. We must live in the parts they call our "homelands". But they will be our guardians, because they say we are like children and not yet civilized enough to look after ourselves. Paternalism, Mr Reitzger. I have just been to see a white father. He told me he knows better than I do what is good for my son. He does not mean good for my son, of course. My son Johnjohn is a big man already among my people, although he is only young like you, Mr Reitzger. The white fathers fear Johnjohn because my people listen to him and believe what he says. So they send him far from his land of the Transkei, far away among strangers.'

'What does Johnjohn say?'

'He says, this division of the land of which the white fathers speak, it will not at all be equal. They are very few and have very much land. Very good land, where the rain falls. We are very many and will have little. Look, Mr Reitzger. Look all about. Look down there, at those big holes in the earth.'

They had come out between the narrowing hills, on to a winding road along a ridge. The land dropped away on either side, dry rocky hill after hill to both horizons, where the red of earth met the blue of sky. An ox as thin as if constructed of sticks grazed the margin of the road. There seemed to be no other grass in the land, in all the billowing dark plush of dust.

Walter pointed with his crop, a wide-armed gesture.

'Dongas, that is all we are rich in, sir. Look at our cattle. Are your cattle in Europe like that, sir? They say it is our bad farming which makes the dongas. Look there on that hill—that is where the government agricultural expert showed us how to plough. Last September month. Where did the seed go? What will be the harvest? You can see the furrows but you cannot see the crop. The man said, do it this way and when the rain comes your crop will not be washed away. The soil will not be washed away. But where was the rain, sir? Where was the rain?'

'Yes, I see.'

They proceeded for a while in silence, through the barren but beautiful land. Only the deepening light enriching the red hills.

'Not even,' Reitzger enquired, 'the hope of freedom then?'

'No hope? How can you say that? How can a people live without hope of freedom?'

'How then?'

'Men can live without hope for themselves if they can have hope for their children. We hope for good land, and we hope for freedom. Perhaps we must have freedom before we have good land.'

'How will you get it?'

'Ah Mr Reitzger sir, we have much to learn. Now we will rest for a short time.'

They dismounted in the shade. The African stood looking over his plains. The European sat against a thin tree trunk, his knees bent, an ache in his thighs.

'If your friend Mr Schwallendorf,' Walter said, 'had been my teacher when I was a boy, I would have asked him to teach me German. Do you know why? Because if any man has anything to teach you that you do not know you should try to learn it from him. Europeans have very much they can teach us Africans. What they know makes them very strong. Very powerful. So we must learn from them.'

'I think so too, that one must learn whatever one can,' the European said.

A pair of small black birds dipped and went. What were they called? Beans dangled on the trees. What sort of tree was it? Pink-spotted seeds lay scattered in the shade. Were they edible? The sun bloomed as a poppy. The earth-holes brimmed with shadows. They mounted again and proceeded. Reitzger dozed and woke, to find that his head was pillowed on the warm wet yellow back of the big African. He felt too sleepy to lift his head. He had dozed like this on the back of his grandfather, who had carried the infant Konrad up and down in the shade of his garden when the boy had had his terrible headaches, which the doctors had said he might grow out of, and which he had in fact seldom suffered from in the last ten years or so. Again he shut his eyes, and again he woke. Red of earth and red of sky were infusing each other until their meeting-line could no longer be distinguished. Slept again, woke again. The sun was on a level with his own bent head. An orange disc sunk into, and cutting, as the horse jerked up and down, like a round saw, through the red earth. And slept again.

'Mr Reitzger, we are here.' The man's voice resonated through his back.

The horse had stopped.

Dark hills. Big bulging stars and splinters of stars, the alien configurations. Orange window-lights from a house on a hill, the shapes of huts dancing in firelight on one another.

He climbed stiffly down.

From among the stars Walter bent down and held out his hand.

'It was my pleasure, Mr Reitzger,' he said.

'It is good you have come to visit me.'

They were sitting facing each other, on flat-topped stones.

'I came,' Reitzger corrected, 'to find out what is causing the smell.'

'I hope you are well sir.'

'I am well. I have been living further from the smell than you. I am surprised it has not made you sick.'

'I found it very bad at first, but now I am used to it. And it is diminishing, I think?'

'I came to find out.'

'Ah,' Walter said, not 'why', but perhaps Reitzger thought he had, or meant to. So he answered, 'It is always interesting to know what is the cause of something.'

'And you have completed your investigations? You know what is the cause?'

'Yes. I know that the cause is the boiling of a horse.'

'The curiosity is satisfied sir?'

'It would be interesting also to know *why* the horse is being boiled.'

'Ah.'

Walter's eyes were bloodshot. So were the others, of the men and women and children who came and went near the stranger, looking at him but not stopping. It seemed that everybody's business took him along this route past Walter's hut.

"You will drink some beer with me, Mr Reitzger?'

Reitzger bent his face to the stuff in the tin; tipped it until it showed yellowish white, and smelt it. Not too bad. Nothing like the smell from the horse-cauldron. He glanced at Walter, who was watching him, and as he looked up Walter said, 'I drink to the coming of the rains.'

'The rains,' Reitzger agreed, and tasted the stuff. Gritty, flaky, sour.

'Do you like the taste of our beer, Mr Reitzger? It is different from yours, is it not?'

'It is completely different!'

'Do you like it?'

'No.'

Walter laughed. Perhaps he enjoyed the man's candour. Or perhaps he intended to tease him. 'Some white men are afraid to drink it. They are afraid that we brew it with harmful or disgusting ingredients.'

'And do you?'

'No sir!'

'Where is your horse?'

'My horse? *Ukuthula?* Mr Reitzger!'

'Where is he?'

'My horse? You think I would kill my horse? I will tell you how much I have paid for my horse. Six cows, Mr Reitzger. It is more than some men give for their wives. *U-ku-thu-la*. It means Peace, Mr Reitzger. What is that in your language?'

'*Der Friede*. But why are you boiling the horse?'

'*Derfriede*. That horse,' Walter said, 'died. One, two weeks ago, he died.'

'Two weeks ago? Where was he found?'

'He died here, near here, on the grass beside the road, where he was eating.'

'Why?'

Walter shrugged. 'He was old.'

'He died a natural death?'

'Yes, sir.'

'And then?'

'And then what, Mr Reitzger? What is "and then" for a horse after he has died?'

'What did they do with him? They weren't boiling him the day you brought me here. It started up the next night, the smell. Had he just been left lying about?'

'No sir, Mr Reitzger. He was du-ly *buried*.'

'Buried.'

'Yes sir. Buried in the earth. And now I am going to ask you a question if you will permit.'

'Go ahead.'

'You say it is only out of interest that you have come to see what is the cause of the smell?'

'That is so.'

'I see.'

'You and your friend received a visitor this afternoon, I believe.'

'A man came. I did not meet him.'

'You did not have the pleasure of meeting the Commissioner of the District? The Grootbaas? Meneer B. M. Pik, *E*squire?'

'No.'

'But your friend has told you what an important gentleman is this Grootbaas?'

'No.'

'Ah. So you are making these enquiries entirely on your own behalf.'

'Yes. I have come only because I wanted to come. But Mr Schwallendorf has also been disturbed by the smell. He would also like to know about it.'

'We have no wish to disturb Meneer Schwallendorf. On the contrary sir. He has been our friend for many years. We have much respect for Meneer Schwallendorf. And poor Meneer Pik— he has such a weak nose! He would like to know about us here in the village. He asks us questions, questions, questions, all the time. But he does not believe what we tell him. He believes only what he can understand. And what does Meneer Pik understand? He understands that kaffirs are liars. He knows we are dumb kaffirs and liars. He knows. But you are a visitor, Mr Reitzger.' (Was there a slight mockery now in the way he said the name?) 'You may come, you may ask. I will tell you about the horse. And please— you will inform Meneer the Teacher. He will be very pleased to know why we are boiling the horse. We say to each other, we must listen to what the Teacher tells us. He is a white man who knows many things we do not. He knows how we must plough our fields. He tells us and we do not listen, and when the rain comes it will wash away our crops. We are dumb kaffirs, so we must listen. He tells us about hygiene. He tells us how we must boil to kill the goggas that jump a sickness from one to another. So maybe this horse did not die from just being old. Maybe he had a bad sickness. We must dig up this horse and boil him. That is what we say to each other. I am giving you this information, Mr Reitzger, and if you will tell Meneer the Teacher he will be very pleased.'

And the 'dumb kaffir' reached for his beer. The matriculant whose spelling of English was exemplary, and who believed one must learn from the white man, learn from any man whatever he could teach! He drank deep, but kept his eyes on his confused visitor, and when he lowered the pot, he laughed. The laughter spread. Reitzger looked about at the villagers, who had stopped at last and were all showing their teeth. As Walter laughed his eyes narrowed and almost disappeared, but now and then as he opened his mouth for a loud guffaw, his eyes opened too, very wide, to take in the sight of his serious visitor, and then shut deep in their folds again as his shoulders shook and his hands thumped his knees. He stopped at last. The others too.

Reitzger did not mind the mockery as much as the disappointment—in the explanation, but also more importantly in Walter himself.

'It's sheer nonsense,' Schwallendorf spluttered. 'They can't have gathered from me that they must dig up dead animals and boil them for reasons of hygiene! If it's some dreadful medicine they're brewing, I only hope they pour it on the lands and not down their own throats. Well, Pik will have to make what he can of it. He's suspicious enough to invent some fantastic reason for anything.'

All the windows had been shut against the smell. But the house was unbearably stuffy. So Schwallendorf opened the two leaves of the dining-room door, leaving the screen closed against the insects which flashed out of the darkness into the light and left bits of their wings and bodies stuck to the wire. A glow on the hill opposite and below marked the village, the source of the air's sepsis, and the persistent doubt.

'They and I,' Schwallendorf mourned. 'We built the first school-house together, with our own hands. I worked with them, I didn't just give the orders. We made it out of galvanised iron. Just a great shed, yes? You should have heard it when the rain came down. Like being inside a drum! We used to try and sing above the noise.'

Schwallendorf swallowed his whisky and looked down glumly upon the red glow on the other hill, his cheeks hanging heavy as if from the habit of disappointment.

Reitzger wanted to ask him about Walter. But he did not want to be questioned about him. So he did not even mention his name.

'But there must be a reason,' he insisted. It bothered him more than it did Schwallendorf, who was soon asking him, as he had on the previous nights, about what it was like 'at home' nowadays. But he seldom listened to what Reitzger told him. Instead he would interrupt to explain how it used to be, as though it had not only been better then, but right. He didn't ask about the war, not Reitzger's war, though he did mention that his father had been killed, as Feuchthaber's had too, in France in nineteen-seventeen.

But tonight, as he drank more, he began to describe the past differently. A childhood cold, obscure, in a greyness of weather and closed houses, snow and rain; shame of body, guilt of sin; autocratic, devout parents; joylessness. And then he had come here—to a four-roomed house on a hill and a piece of ground in the valley where his school was yet to be built: but to a country which seemed new from the Creator's hand, sounding out, scented, shot-from-the-dye! And tall people, in bright blue cloth, riding over the hills. He had succeeded in making friends with them. Why had they become his enemies? Why had his achievements rotted away?

'From Ezekiel—do you know—?' His hand shook as he poured more whisky. ' "Wearing clothes of blue, captains and rulers, all of them desirable young men, horsemen riding upon horses." '

'Goodnight, Herr Schwallendorf!' Konrad said.

'Goodnight, Max!'

Another sentimental old fool, the young man thought. Feuchthaber had certainly sent him to this man only because of where he was, not what he was. Feuchthaber could not have remembered, perhaps, just what his friend was really like. Or had he lost respect for him—Reitzger—since he'd had to leave the University after the currency reform, and take up journalism? No! Feuchthaber knew that he had every intention of going back and taking up the struggle again, with relativity, and the quantum. It was hard to be young, and to know what potential you had in you, while no one else knew it and you had to be patient, and prove it.

And yet he could not think of a reason for the boiling of the horse.

He left Schwallendorf, who was still drinking; and as he lay in the dark in his rondavel he could hear the old boy bumping about, still muttering to himself. '. . . *alle junge, liebliche Gesellen, Reisige, so auf Rossen ritten.*'

Reitzger felt the sort of throbbing which used to come before a headache, but he fell asleep, and dreamt of his father.

Kurt Reitzger had had some of his wealth restored to him when his shares in the company, which had been wound up after the war, became valuable again as new companies were made from remnants of the old. But the gloom which had settled on him did not leave him. It had started when his chief, Friedrich Kuhn, had been tried for war-crimes at Nürnberg. Old Reitzger seemed to have been disturbed both by the fear that he too might be called to answer for having worked in the department that first made and patented the Zyklon-B crystals for the gassings in the extermination camps, and a strange humiliation that he was not considered important enough. Or so his son had interpreted him.

The old man died one night in his sleep. In the morning, in the darkened room, by candlelight, the son reviewed the father, whose skin was beige now and blobbed with blue. Konrad had waited to feel what emotions would come to be instantly quenched—remorse, regret, guilt, or painful realisation of his own mortality: but all that came was a thought, in English (a language the old man had never spoken well): 'Old Gorgonzola—there he lies!'

Now, in his dream not his memory, his father was being lifted out of the bed by his mother and Feuchthaber. They heaved him off and away in his crumpled white nightshirt. Then Konrad himself, against his own will, protesting but compelled, climbed into the bed, laid his head on the pillows and was covered with the eiderdown. The stench filled his nose, his whole head, which swelled as if to split; and it went down his throat into his lungs to choke him.

He woke suddenly, fully and perfectly understanding what the boiling of the horse was for.

Exactly what it had achieved—that was what it was for. It made a stench, and the stench kept Pik away, because Pik suffered from an over-sensitive nose. So someone or something was there which Pik must not find. Something which, however, Schwallendorf might come looking for on Pik's orders. So the secret must be of a kind which Schwallendorf would probably not betray to Pik. And the secret of who or what this was which Pik must not discover in the village was clear to Reitzger beyond all doubt.

In the morning, before Schwallendorf was up or the table laid for breakfast in the largest rondavel, Reitzger went out through the front door, not letting the screen-door bang behind him. It was past six o'clock, but as he went down into the valley he could hear the cocks of the village still crowing as lustily as if it were dawn. The cool air was spoilt by the smell, which had not lessened much if at all. And as on the evening before, it was worse in the village itself.

The bare-breasted women were stirring pots over fires. Again they watched him pass. There were a few men about, dressed only in loin-cloths and blankets worn as shawls. Some of them followed him at a distance as he made for Walter's hut. In front of it there was a young woman feeding a fire with sticks.

'Is Walter awake yet?' he asked her.

The girl looked up at him and then returned her attention to the fire. The men who had followed him drew nearer.

'You want me, Mr Reitzger?' Walter came out, dressed in trousers only.

'Yes.'

'You have something you want to ask me, or tell me?'

'Both to ask and to tell.'

'You still wish to know why the horse is being boiled?'

'No. I know why. That is what I have to tell you.'

Walter said nothing. Everyone was still.

'At least,' Reitzger went on, 'that is part of what I have to tell you. I must also say that I shall not tell anyone else, not even Meneer Schwallendorf.'

Still Walter said nothing. The girl watched the fire. But the other men, young and old, edged forward, and more appeared between the huts on either side.

Reitzger raised his voice so that all might hear him. 'Now I shall ask my question. Walter, which of these young men is your son, Johnjohn, who had been endorsed out of the Transkei?'

Nobody laughed at him this time.

'I believe,' Walter said, 'that your curiosity may be satisfied without the answer to that question, Mr Reitzger.'

His curiosity, yes. And his need to solve this problem. But the great problem which the solution revealed, Walter's problem, Johnjohn's problem, the problem of all these people and millions more, that was not within his power to solve even in theory. Men like Pik made such problems, out of beliefs which Reitzger scorned: beliefs he was all too familiar with: beliefs which stank much worse than a dead beast.

'In the end,' he said loudly but sadly, looking round at the men, 'you'll have to fight.'

'We know that, Mr Reitzger,' Walter said. 'When we met, you

and I, sir, I told you we had been enemies once. The truth is, sir, that we were enemies still, we are enemies now, and we will be enemies for a long time. Sir.'

'You and I? Why? I am not your enemy. I am the enemy of Pik and what you call the white fathers.'

'You are white. I am black. That is enough reason, Mr Reitzger.'

'What nonsense!' Reitzger said, the way Miss Baldwin used to say it. But that way was not strong enough. '*Stinking* nonsense,' he shouted. 'The sort of nonsense Pik believes.' He turned round, glaring at the faces round him. 'You'll rot your noses with stinking ideas like that. You—you'll be another Pik, Walter, another Pik, that's all.'

He walked away. The men parted to let him through. He walked on to the edge of the village, then he tried to run, stumbling among rocks and tufts, slipping on stones, down and up again, to reach the other survivor of the spreading, rising, inescapable stench, in the ark on the top of the hill.

PROCESSION

by PHILIP BOOTH

from THE HUDSON REVIEW

nominated by Dan Masterson

A white-throat flicked into the sunset window.
How small a thing to bury: his short neck limp,
eye perfectly blank, the feathers warm in my hand.

Nothing left now to whistle *Old Sam Peabody,*
Peabody, Peabody . . . The rest in their thickets,
knowing to go. The winter stars coming. Out early

this morning I see Orion, the first time this fall,
Aldebaran brilliant in Taurus, the Dipper's
handle tipped down toward daybreak. As sun-up

dims Venus, I walk the first frost out into ground fog,
as it happens. Slowly, it comes to me: today
would be father's 85th birthday. I hear

today's birds in the cedars, woken, knowing to go.
I think of a boy years beyond me, back in Council Bluffs,
a boy with father's name, out on a third-floor porch

after midnight, without knowing why, watching (he must
have told me hundreds of times) against his own horizon
these same winter stars beginning to show.

LINING UP

by RICHARD HOWARD

from GRAND STREET

nominated by GRAND STREET and Grace Schulman

Pasadena: the museum vestibule

Better stay where we are: here at least
we have, however odd, what passes
   for a roof over our heads,
and even if the walls are nothing
more than glass, they will be nothing less;
   how else take in so clearly
these citizens coming upon us
in radiant raiment, the motley
   of Southern California?
Where else but in Eden could we find
our freedom only by losing it—
   such nakedness, and such clothes!—
leathers "treated" to be tractable
as silk and velvet supplanted by
   aniline facsimile,
shades of medieval shades, louder
than the flaunts of Florence! Our neighbors
   add themselves to the straggling
file we stand in, parti-colored lives
clustered, strung-out, singular, alone,
   these burghers of L.A., some
eager to sample what is promised them,

others uncertain why they have come—
    not turning back but turning
aside, as if reluctant to face
engagements they suspect are lying
    in wait for them up ahead,
although disinclined to loiter long
over an obstacle in their path,
    avoided and already
behind them: *The Burghers of Calais*,
such more-than-life-size Others looming
    monochrome and lame, naked
bronze which has gained a life of its own
—green and grisly, but a life of sorts—
    by merely being outside . . .

We are safe here; you feel safe, don't you?
for all the sudden menace of a sky
    variable to the point
where no one evidently knows how
to be prepared for what is in store . . .
    Well, no one alive; *they* know,
the Six made over to their ruin
by Rodin, who a hundred years back
    (before there was a museum
in Pasadena) found them waiting
for him in the chronicles of his
    fellow snob and countryman
Froissart, recorded without favor
or much fear (five hundred years before
    there was a Pasadena),
men who brought themselves to break the siege,
"stripped, barefoot, ready for the hangman":
1) Jean d'Aire offering the keys
which drag his muscles down to string,
ecstatic as he moves, Calais saved,
    to a death an hour away;
2) Andreu d'Andres encircling his despair
within both arms as if the body
    were the pain it knows will come;

3)   Jacques de Wiessant striding, neck outstretched
to let his eyes see *how* it will come
     before the lean flesh can learn;

4)   his brother Pierre beckoning—to what?—
under his crooked elbow he looks
     back to find the angry stars
knotted into new constellations;

5)   Eustache de Saint-Pierre wearing the rope
     as though it might prevent him
from falling before he falls for good
and God, huge hands already hanging
     open, helpless, curled to find
comfort in their own unreadiness;
and to complete the invisible
     cube sealing them together,

6)   Jean de Fiennes spreading his arms to let
rags that must once have been finery
     fall open to manifest
a nakedness fiercely young again . . .

Yes, they know what is in store, six men
     shambling to the English camp
where the English queen will save them all,
though they do not yet know about that.
     And maybe they are with us,
always with us, lining up—maybe
we deserve a share of what they know
     and don't know . . . Take any six:

1)   the tall man, for instance, in tight jeans
and a ginger turtleneck, the one
     cupping his hands in order
to look straight into the museum—
is he discovering that to be
     bewitched is not to be saved?

2)   Does the black girl—the one behind him
in unforgiveable (and unforgiving)
     cerise stretch-pants know we live
as ruins among ruins, rendered lovely
by staring at ourselves in the glass?

3)   One man encased in plastic
       has turned around to face the statues,
       buttoning his coat against the wind—
           does he guess what he appears
       to know: where all is bad it must be
4 & 5)   good to bless the worst? And the two
           who move so much like ourselves—
       do they know what we know: that the great
       pleasure in life is doing what people say
           you cannot do? At the end
6)   comes a fat woman with a tattoo
       on her left wrist—I hear her sighing:
           "God, You have appointed me
       from the first day to fall at the feet
       of the living and to stand at the head
           of the dying . . ."

                    Do they come
like this to their reprieve? Will there be
at the end a forgiveness ready?
    Rodin himself could not show,
how can *I* tell these six the good news:
"You have been chosen, you will be spared"—
    I am standing first in line.

Cats and dogs out there any minute . . .
and in here, now and forever, death
    of a kind, as if a man
needed a diamond and was given
the moon: desire is a relic here,
    Venus becomes a document;
or to put it still another way,
inches of Vermeer can mortify
    massacres by Delacroix
and acres of subsequent carnage
(only the Dealer Takes All), so that
    even before we get in,
futility bears down on fatigue

in irresponsible foyers where
    a man can know everything
but nothing else. The omnivorous
package waits, and our riches blind us
    to our poverty . . .

                        Bundle up
against the weather and wait your turn;
we are standing where the burial-
    places of our memory
give up their dead. MUSEUM OPEN
SUNDAY UNTIL FIVE. ADMISSION FREE.

THE LONGING

by JOHN DANIEL

from CUTBANK

nominated by CUTBANK

Death is the supple suitor
That wins at last—
     Emily Dickinson

When he slipped on the mountain
I would have held him
but he chose the jolt of the rope

when the raft overturned in the canyon
he was confused   he went up
instead of down to my arms

I wait to the right   he turns left
I am on time   he is early or late
I whisper when he lies awake at night
he turns on a light   he pretends
he does not know me

I cannot forget his face
every day he becomes more beautiful
and my longing becomes harder to bear

but I wait
I know him better than he knows himself

I watch him walk in circles
lift his feet in the same worn tracks
all the time he comes to me
like a moth in love with the moon

I watch him read books
scratch words on paper
he will understand nothing
until he looks in my eyes

I watch him build his heap of things
find friends and lose them   couple and part
I am the one
always beyond his reach

I was with him in the darkness of the womb
they took him out screaming   he promised
   to come back to me

when I step from behind that final tree
he will throw down everything   even his name
and before we lie down together
he will hold out the handful of blood
that remains from his birth   crying *here*

I carried it all the way for you

THE TIME, THE PLACE, THE LOVED ONE

fiction by SUSAN WELCH

from THE PARIS REVIEW

nominated by THE PARIS REVIEW

I SPEND A LOT OF TIME ALONE NOW. It doesn't bother me. The others took up too much time. I am glad that they are gone. But it is January and now and then I think of January in Minnesota, how in late afternoon a rusty stain appears along the rim of the sky and creeps across the ice. The stain seems to stay there forever, spreading beneath the banked tiers of white sky, until it fades suddenly into the snowbanks and is gone. It is bleak then, as if the sun has just slipped off the edge of the world. Then there is only the ice and the freezing wind on the ice as the sky gets blacker and blacker through the long, deep night.

I hardly ever think of Minnesota now that I am content in Florida. There is a garden with a trellis and orange trees. The branches bend to me as I pluck the fruit, then spring back. As I bite into an orange I can taste the juice of the tree still in it, all its green leaves. The thorns on the rose bushes tear my skirt. The house has pillars and a courtyard; it is not far from the sea. Mal has given me all he promised. When Mal comes home he picks up my daughter at her school and she drinks lemonade while we drink scotch, sitting in the gazebo. By the time my head is clear again we have gotten through dinner and put the little girl to sleep and are upstairs, lying on the bed.

So I hardly ever think of Minnesota, how dark and still the winters are there. There was an apartment once, but I don't miss it, I just think about it sometimes when I consider how completely I have gotten out of the cold. From the street you could see a pale lamp shining through the window of the apartment, and the reflection of the lamp in the window; it was high up on the second floor above a store. Signs hung beneath the windows: Grimm's Hardware, Shaak Electronics—and together with the streetlights they cast a white glow into the big room all night long. Sometimes, coming home, we would see the snow falling silently in the beam of the streetlight, as if it were all a stage set.

Across the street was an all-night restaurant and sometimes people would leave there late, and yell to each other before they got into their cars. The first night I saw Matthew he was rushing down the stairs of our apartment building to confront some boys on the sidewalk near the restaurant. If I hadn't pressed against the railing he would have collided with me in his descent. I stood watching him through the glass of the door as he told the boys to be quiet, people were trying to sleep. They hooted and snickered as he turned to leave. As he came in the door, almost in tears, the boys were screaming in a mocking, falsetto chorus.

"They laughed at me," he said, bewildered, shutting the door against them, staring out. We started up the stairs together. He was tall and very thin, stooped even, pigeon-breasted in the t-shirt he wore in spite of the cold. His hair was a mass of ringlets and golden curlicues and it seemed full of its own motion like something alive at the bottom of the sea. For a moment, standing in the hallway, he looked very beautiful and strange.

"I live here now," I told him. "In that apartment, there."

His face was haggard, lantern-jawed, but his eyes were gentle as he stared at me. "Come over and visit me tomorrow night," he said. "I'll bake you some brownies."

All day long I thought I wouldn't go. I stood for a long time in the hallway, looking from Matthew's door to mine, before I turned to knock on his. When he called "Wait a minute," I thought he was a girl, that's how light and high his voice was.

His apartment was immaculate. The wooden floor gleamed. There was a rug made of swans' heads and necks, dark and light, facing in opposite directions—the neck of a dark swan provided the relief so you could see the neck of a white swan and so on. It was impossible to hold both the white and dark swans together in your mind at the same time. There was a bed at one end of the large room, a table with two chairs, and windows that faced the street all along the wall. There were no pictures up, just plants on a shelf, purple passion, jade plant, wandering jew, and a bulletin board studded with funny clippings, cartoons, a picture of a bald woman in a long smock.

"I see her all the time at school," Matthew said. "She goes to all the rallies and concerts and just walks around the university."

He was wearing a t-shirt that said "Minnesota" and a pair of jeans that hung on him. I saw that he was not handsome at all. He was bony and long and his joints, his elbows and wrists and probably his knees, were huge, like a puppet's.

"How old are you?" I asked.

"Twenty-one," he said, but he looked sixteen or seventeen. "You?"

"Twenty-five."

"I couldn't imagine what your age was," he said. "People are always drawn to you, your looks, aren't they?"

"My mother was beautiful. She's dead," I said.

I looked out the window and saw how the dark was settling in. When I was eighteen I won a beauty prize, Princess Kay of the Milky Way at the Minnesota State Fair. They sculpted my face in a thirty-pound block of butter, put the bust in a refrigerated glass case and ran it round and round on a kind of merry-go-round so people at the fair could look at it. I liked it and went every day to see it, standing on the dirt floor near the glass, wondering if anyone would recognize me, but they never did. My father told me I looked like my mother in the sculpture, but he thought it was dumb of me to stand around there all day. He made me come home.

"What in the world brought you to this place?" Matthew asked, and then I told him how I had come to be there. I must have been lonely, or starved for someone so nearly my own age, I know that's what made me pour out my feelings to him so. I told him how I had met Mal when I took a job in his publishing company, and how he had left his wife and children for me, and how he had taken me to live with him five years ago, right after my father died. I told him how Mal called me his suburban Botticelli and how he took care of me and taught me all he knew. Now Mal had sold out his interest in the Minneapolis company and we were moving to Florida, where he had a new business. But I had never been out of Minneapolis, my parents had died here, it was all too sudden. I begged him to let me have a couple of months here, work in the business as it changed hands, get used to the idea of leaving as he got our new life settled. I had found this apartment in a familiar area, near the university, where I, too, had gone to school. Matthew was looking at me so hard his jaw hung.

It was late autumn, just before Halloween, and Matthew and I watched out the window as the sky went down from copper to livery red to mother of pearl. The streetlights blinked on and so did the signs above the stores. The room darkened with the sky but the signs and streetlights shed pools of incandescent light on the bed, on the floor.

"What kind of person would leave his wife and children?" Matthew asked.

I sat with my head in my hands. "I don't know, he felt so awful about it. They'd been married twenty years. He told me not to think about it. He said it was my face; he loved my face." I pressed my fingers into my cheeks. The flesh gave like wax. But suddenly I was asking myself, what kind of person was Mal, to leave his wife and children. I had never thought of him in that way before.

Then slowly Matthew began to tell me about himself. It was hard for him to talk, he didn't charm me with what he said or the way he said it, no, not at all. His voice was a whisper and sometimes it cracked as it came out, no, not a man's voice at all. He had been in love with a girl and she hadn't loved him, but still he kept loving her and loving her and finally he had gone crazy.

He told me what it was like to be crazy. Everything seemed to have a secret meaning, cracks on the sidewalk, a phone that rang once but not again, the world was full of hidden messages.

"It sounds wonderful," I said. "I would love to feel that everything had a secret meaning."

He shook his head and his curls bounced. "You don't know what you're saying. No, it wasn't wonderful at all. It was horrible."

"And the girl?"

"She's gone. Gone a long time ago."

It was hard to talk to him, I had to strain to hear him, his murmurs. It was as if he were used to talking in whispers to himself. His father was a doctor, his mother wanted him to be a doctor, but he couldn't do it, his grades weren't good enough, he couldn't concentrate. So instead he was taking this degree in psychology, maybe something would come of that.

I don't know what it was, I didn't want to leave him. After a while he got up and turned on the lamp by the window, then he put on a record.

"I like that a lot," I said. "Mal and I don't listen to any rock, just classical. Bach. Vivaldi. Telemann. A lot of baroque."

"Don't you know any people your own age?"

I looked at him. "Hardly any. There are a few girls at work but I don't see them much."

It was late when I got up to go. I walked along the shiny dark floor to the door. The lamp shone on the green leaves of the plants and reflected white in the window. I could feel the cold on the street below seeping in around the window frames.

Matthew followed me and stood with me by the door. I thought I had never seen such a delicate-looking man. I could almost see the blood beating in his temples. He took my hands in his huge bony hands. I felt it only for an instant but my hands were throbbing where he had touched them.

A few days later I found a copy of the album we had been listening to wrapped and pushed under my door. When I walked over to Matthew's apartment I could hear the bass pounding in the record he was playing. I stood in the hall for a moment but the door opened.

"I heard your footsteps," he said. But how could he have heard me over the music? We stared at each other. He looked gawky and stupid. I wondered why I had come. "Listen, I've got a coupon for a pizza," he said. "Do you want to go?"

As we walked he took my hand in his. I couldn't take it back, his own hand trembled so.

"They removed a rat's memory surgically today," he said. And all through dinner we talked about how the rat experienced everything for the first time, every time.

When he himself had gone crazy, Matthew said, he thought about the same things over and over again. He had thought then that he was refining memories, getting down to their essence and their core. Now he realized that that was impossible.

His way of talking was innocent and strange. He thought differently from other people and I had to listen carefully to catch his meaning. Neither of us ate much. We pushed the pizza back and forth between us.

"Do you want to come back over?" he asked as we walked out into the bitter cold. He took my hand again. I just wanted to be with him, I don't know why. Perhaps I admired the sculpted, jutting angle of his cheekbones. He made some coffee and got out a box of fresh pastries from the bakery downstairs. He sat across the table from me, staring down at the coffee, his long legs stretched out until his feet nearly touched mine. The white light enclosed us in a long oval. He shook his head and ruffled his fingers fiercely through his curls.

"Your hair is so unusual," I said.

"I was helping my father give EEGs last summer," he said. "One lady saw me and wouldn't let them put the electrodes on. She thought that was what had happened to me."

We laughed. At that moment, I looked at him and he looked at me. I felt a dizziness, a tightness near my heart. I was snug, safe in his apartment against the cold—I'm sure that's what it was. I have thought about it since.

He put a record on and we were silent, sitting in the pool of light.

After a while he came over and knelt beside me and wrapped his arms around my waist. I could see the top of his head, his bobbing curls.

"Matthew, I have a lover."

He ignored me and put his cheek next to mine, holding my head. I could see the fine grain of his gold skin, how tight it was on the bone.

"Do you want to go lie down with me?" he asked and I nodded, yes.

I looked into his face as he undressed me and saw that his eyes were all pupil. For a long time he stroked the place where my hip met my thigh, running his fingers over the pale blue traceries of the veins.

"I love you," I said. Yes, I remember I said it, and I said it many times, I don't know what came over me. And I thought, this is the most wonderful night of my life, nothing will ever be this sweet again. We stared at each other in the light of the streetlamps and the Grimm's Hardware sign and we made love. All night long we looked into each other's eyes, He was so young I could see that his eyes were brand new, just budded in their sockets.

Sometimes even now I fancy I can feel Matthew's tongue, scratchy as a cat's, and the way he wrapped me up in his long, long arms. But I scarcely think of him at all now. In fact, I have entirely forgotten him. If it weren't for the little girl, considering her as much as I do, and the way the days are so long for me here, I doubt that I would think of him at all.

Three days later I went to work again. The phone was ringing as I walked into my office and I picked it up, knowing it was Mal. There had been a short circuit in one of the stereos in the electronics store and all night music from a rock station had pounded up to us through the floorboards. Elton John, Matthew told me they were playing. "Love Song." "Come Down in Time."

"What are you telling me?" Mal asked. "You were walking along, just minding your own business, and you got hit by a freight train?"

Light from the apartment flooded into my eyes and behind them as I held the receiver, the pure light on Matthew's face as he twined me with his legs and arms.

"I never should have left you alone, I knew it was a mistake," Mal said. And when I didn't answer he said: "I'm coming up there."

He was waiting for me in the office the next morning. For a long time he wouldn't believe that I was serious, that I wasn't coming down to Florida.

"I suppose his teeth are all white, not stained like mine," Mal said. "And I suppose he has all his hair and a flat belly, that's what you're thinking when you look at me, isn't it?"

"No, it's not," I said, but now that he'd said it it became true. All I was worried about was that he would kill me, and then I wouldn't be able to be with Matthew.

I wanted to tell him how fond I felt of him, how grateful I felt, how it hurt me to see his eyes glaze as he slumped against the window. But I stood speechless.

"I gave up everything for you. I can't let you go," he said.

For a moment I thought of the filthy warped floor in the hall of my apartment building, the way the brown paint on the floors bubbled and peeled. "I was a child then," I said. "That was for then."

I turned my face away as he held me.

"There's nothing I can do," he said. "I can't live without you." For an instant I prayed, begging that Mal would not die.

Then, miraculously, he was gone. He had me fired from my job but I found another where I just had to type. I bore no grudges. I was walking on love's good side. I had Matthew.

From our first night together Matthew was always in my thoughts. I suppose you could say I lived for him. He wanted us to be twins.

"One consciousness in two bodies," he said. "That's what we are." He looked at me in a way that made me feel holy. No one had ever paid this kind of attention to me, no, never. He painted our toenails the same color, green with silver dust. When I got a pimple he would often get one himself, in a similar spot. We wore each other's clothes, bought matching shoes. We copied each other, walked alike, talked alike. How I loved imitating Matthew. It was no longer lonely being me. We could be each other.

We had been together two months when I found out I was pregnant. Matthew had told me not to get another diaphragm, there could be no mistakes between us. Anything that happened was right.

When I told him, he smiled. "That's wonderful," he said. "I can't wait to tell my family. Now we'll get married."

We drove out to the suburbs for dinner so I could meet his parents. He had told them about me but they had resisted meeting me, until now. We drove to a ranch house with a swimming pool behind it, big as a gulch. His father was a tall, silent man who left in the middle of dinner to go to the hospital. His mother had Matthew's jagged features but none of his softness. She hated me on sight.

After dinner she took me aside.

"Do you realize what a sick boy he is?" she asked. "You're a grown woman, you should see these things. He's been institutionalized for long periods."

"I love him," I said calmly. "He loves me. He knows exactly what he's doing. And it's medieval to think of mental illness as a permanent condition. You get over it, like a cold."

"What do you know about it?" She stared until I dropped my gaze. "Have you ruined your life, eating your heart out over him?"

We left before dessert.

"Cheer up, honey. We have to go out and get some sour cream cherry pie, some cheesecake," Matthew said as we sat in the car in his mother's driveway. He started kissing me, digging his fingers into my thighs. "There's a great place near here. You'll love their hot fudge cake," he said. "I can't take my honey to bed before she has her dessert."

We went to a delicatessen where cakes and pies dipped up and down on little ferris wheels. "It tastes as good as it looks, too," Matthew said. We held hands and fed each other hot fudge and cherries on heaping spoons. The rich goo dripped like wax. We nudged and stepped on each other's feet the whole time, pressing each other's soles and toes till they hurt.

"Why doesn't she like me?" I asked. "Is it because I'm older?"

"She'll get over it, don't worry about her," Matthew said. "All she knows is her Bible. That time when I got sick—she thought it was God's rebuke to her. She's just going to have to get used to it."

I scraped some hot fudge on my plate with my spoon. It dried fast, sweet cement. "You're so old for your age, Matthew. I'm surprised she can't see it. I've always known I could depend on you."

He fed me the last bite of hot fudge cake. "How about some more?" he asked. "Come on, honey, you know you want it."

"Let's have the hazelnut torte," I said.

"Great," Matthew said. "Great. My mother would die. She believes in minimal sweets."

"Mal too," I said. "Seaweed and spinach. He made us eat seaweed and spinach every stupid day." We both grimaced, wrinkling our noses.

Matthew stared into my eyes and jammed my feet tight between his. "Hi, baby." I saw his mouth move but no sound escaped his lips. The waitress put the torte before him. Shrugging and rolling his eyes at me he plunged his fork into the crest of hazelnut lace.

We got married and I moved all my things into Matthew's apartment. Our lives went on much as before.

How did those days pass? They went by so quickly I swear I can't remember. We had everything in the world to find out about each other.

He took pictures of me with an expensive camera his parents had given him for his birthday. He gloated over the prints. "Look how you're smiling," he said. "How happy I must make you." He set the time adjustment so we could be in pictures at the same time, hugging or kissing or with our heads together, staring at the camera. "What a beautiful couple," he said.

He played his guitar as we sang duets of rock songs. He was charmed by my flat singing voice. He even admired my upper arms which had started to get pudgy from all our desserts. He flapped the loose flesh with delight. "That's one of the things I love about you most," he said. "Chubby arms, just like a little baby."

One freezing night as we walked home after a movie our boots crunched into the moonlight on the snow. Our gloved hands fitted into each other like the pieces of a puzzle.

"What should we name the baby?" he asked.

"I don't know," I said.

"If it's a girl how about Phoebe, after the moon," he said. "The moon is so beautiful, look how we're walking on silver, baby. And it always seems to have so many secrets."

"But we don't like secrets, Matthew," I said. "We don't believe in secrets."

"I bet she'll look like the moon," he said. "You'll get round like the moon and then the baby will come out and look like the moon."

I woke up once during the night. He was sleeping with his arms around my neck. He slept silently, like an infant. How could he be so quiet? The lights outside flooded his bulletin board, the shiny wooden floors, the carefully arranged cabinets. The radiators hissed then fizzled to stop. Outside the window the full moon shared the secret of the shadows on the dark street, his beating heart. I almost woke him up to tell him. I wanted to say, I could die now. I am so happy I could just die.

For Valentine's Day he wrote me a song. I sat on the bed while he played it for me on his guitar. He didn't need to breathe with my lungs filling his, the song said. He wanted to die from drinking my wonderful poison. I listened, filled with wonder.

As he played I watched his hands. For the first time I saw tiny scars on his wrists, fine and precise as hairs. When he finished playing I put my fingers to his pulse.

"Your wrists, Matthew," I said. "Look. Where did all those little marks come from?" He had never told me, yet he said he told me everything.

He withdrew his hands, fixing me with his long stare. "Let's stay in the here and now. Why talk about things that happened a long time ago, things you can't remember right anyway. What did my honey get for me?"

I had forgotten Valentine's Day. The next day I bought him a shirt and an expensive sweater. He thanked me but seemed disappointed. His mother could have given him the same. He had been involved in his gifts, mine were clichés.

The next day I got a valentine from Mal, forwarded from the old office. He loved me, he was thinking about me, he wanted me to come back to him. As I put it in the waste basket I found the valentine I had given Matthew folded at the bottom.

In the dead of winter it was fifty below for days at a time. We would sit on the bed and watch the smoke rise out of the chimneys in timid frozen curls. When we came home late at night, walking across the huge U of M campus, we would have to kiss and hold each other for twenty minutes before our noses and fingers thawed.

On Sunday mornings we would have breakfast at the restaurant across the street. We sat facing each other, our legs locked, talking about what was happening in our lives. I treasured my separate life for it provided me with stories to tell him. Nothing was real until I told Matthew about it.

After breakfast I walked him to his part-time job at the laboratory where he was working on a hearing experiment. Chinchillas were made deaf in one ear and then trained to jump to one side of a large revolving cage or another, on the basis of certain sounds. If the chinchillas didn't perform correctly they got a shock. That was Matthew's job, running them through tests and shocking them if they made mistakes.

I went with him once and saw the little animals in their cages. They were furry and adorable, bunnies without ears: how could Matthew, the gentlest of people, stand to shock them?

"They have to be shocked when they're not doing their job," he said. "It's horrible, but that's the way life is."

"Since when do you believe life is that way?"

One evening he came home shaking. A chinchilla had died when its eardrum was being punctured for the experiment.

"Matthew, why don't you quit that job?" I asked, looking up at him from where I sat at the table. "Don't you see what it's doing to you?"

"It's not doing anything to me. I'm fine," he said, standing there trembling. "Do you think you're better, that you wouldn't do that job?"

I stood up and rushed to him. "Matthew, are you angry at me? Please don't be angry at me. I just want you to be happy." I hugged him tighter, tighter. "Do I give you everything you want?" I whispered into his shoulder. "What can I give you?"

"You're everything I want," he said.

"But is it enough? You're so much better at being somebody's lover than I am."

"Yes, I am good at that, aren't I," Matthew said, and I could feel him thinking about it, there was a hum in him like currents in fluorescent tubes.

Then he held my shoulders and looked deeply into my eyes. "Come here, baby. Let me tell you about this experiment I've been thinking about all day."

We sat down at the table holding hands. "When they fasten electrodes to the pleasure centers of a rat's brain the rat will do nothing but push the bar that activates the electrode. It won't eat, it won't drink, it won't sleep, it just keeps pushing the bar for the pleasure sensation until it dies of starvation and dehydration."

We sat silent. "That's interesting," I said. I watched his hand as it moved slowly up my arm, to my shoulder, then curled around my neck.

"You," he said. "You."

Late afternoons Matthew would go to the bakery downstairs and come back with boxes of sweets. Then we would sit at the table, listening to the voices on the street, feeling how the winds lightened and the air became less bitter as spring blew in our windows. We watched the sun on the grain of the table. We cut eclairs with knives and fed them to each other. When Matthew ate chocolate he was in such ecstacy he had to close his eyes. I could see him shudder. It was like when we were in bed. Being around all those sweets made me greedier for them, it was strange. The more I ate the more I wanted. It was like being in bed.

I got fatter and fatter from the sweets.

"If you can't get fat when you are pregnant, when can you?" he asked, feeding me another pastry. Yet Matthew never got fat.

I ate cakes, petits fours, upside down tarts. At the soda fountain around the corner he fed me hot fudge sundaes.

"Eat, baby," he said. "I love to see your little tongue when you lick the syrup."

My breasts became huge. I swelled like an inflatable doll. All night long Matthew would lie in my arms as I lay there puffed with life and the splitting of my own cells. When we woke up he went downstairs and got doughnuts, filled and frosted pastries called honeymooners, pecan rolls.

Before long it was spring verging on summer and we took long walks along the Mississippi, breathing the crisp shocking air that rose from the torrents of icy water that came with the thaw. Sometimes we took sandwiches and stayed out till two in the morning. On one walk a pale, ovoid form approached us. It was the bald woman whose picture was on Matthew's bulletin board.

She stopped Matthew, held on to his arm, mumbled to him. She had been at the zoo, she said, and fed the elephant peanuts. It had lifted them out of her hand with its trunk, she said, holding up her palm, showing it. Its soft trunk had tickled and nudged her hand, gentle, tender. She could feel its hairs.

"Do you know her?" I asked Matthew, watching her as she disappeared. But Matthew wouldn't answer.

One afternoon after a rock concert we followed the path along a cliff near the river; below us the Mississippi glimmered like diamonds. We walked hand in hand but I was waddling fast to keep up with Matthew's long strides.

"Let me catch up," I said, and he stared at me, his eyes hard.

"You know I've been thinking," he said, walking faster. "We're really not that much alike."

I couldn't catch my breath. The air was freezing my fingertips even where Matthew held them.

"Like how so?"

"Like make-up," he said. "Like you wear make-up and I don't."

My eyes watered from the wind. "But I've always worn make-up," I said. "I'll stop wearing it if you don't like it."

"That won't do any good," he said. "And you take up a lot of the bed. It's hard for you to keep up with me when I walk."

"But I'm pregnant, I've got fat," I said, nearly in tears. "If I weren't pregnant and if you didn't force all that food on me, this wouldn't happen."

Tears were streaming down my face but Matthew was walking fast, not seeming to notice.

"I don't make enough to support a baby," Matthew said. "It's all going to be different. It seems cruel. Sometimes I think I can't do the job."

"You know I've got savings. And your parents will help." Now I couldn't stop crying. I halted in my tracks, jerking my hand out of his. The Mississippi roared below us. I waited for long moments by a tree, waiting for him to come back. And suddenly I knew that we would never again be as happy as we once were.

Finally he came back, retracing his steps, and looked at me.

"I'm sorry," he said. "I never want to hurt you."

I looked into his eyes and saw how young and frightened he was. I will never leave you, I said to myself. You need me and I will always take care of you.

That night in our room rainy air billowed the curtain inward on our long embrace. There was the smell of skin, warm salt flesh, clean.

"Please baby, whatever you say, never say you stopped loving me," Matthew said.

"Oh, never. I would never say that."

"You would never start hating me, would you? You would stop long before that."

Stop? He had never said anything about stop. "No. I would stop before that."

"We would stop while we still loved each other. And now . . . are you going to hug me all night long?"

The next day, on impulse, I called up Mal from work.

I couldn't even wait for him to get over his shock. I rushed into it. "You won't believe this, but I've just got to talk to someone. About Matthew. It's just interesting, you won't mind? He's absolutely terrified of getting fat. He is the skinniest man you've ever seen, yet he's worried about fat. Once he went on a fishing trip with his father and he ate a whole pound bag of M & Ms and he was so appalled he didn't eat anything else the whole trip. And by summer he had got so thin he could see the sun shining through his rib cage. Can you imagine anything so stupid?

"He loves sweets, you know, we live near a bakery, and sometimes he'll get so many good things and eat them, then do you know what he does? He sticks his finger down his throat and throws them up. Really, I've seen him do it."

Mal listened, silent, until I was done. "Why don't you leave him?" he said.

"Because I'm happy, that's why," I said, suddenly desperate to be off the phone. "Besides, I'm very fat, do you think you could like me fat?" He didn't answer. "I was just kidding about him throwing up. Do you believe me?" Mal was silent. "Well, maybe he did it once or twice when he was drunk."

"Do you know why I'm fat?" My voice grew shriller in the silence. "Because I'm pregnant. I'm going to have a baby in two months."

I pressed down the button, hoping he would think we'd been disconnected.

I came home from work one afternoon and found Matthew lying naked on the bed, his stereo earphones on, one leg propped straight up against the wall. He was so absorbed in the music he didn't see me coming up to him, see how I was staring at the long red marks on the inside of his thigh. As I sat down beside him he took his leg down quickly and removed the headset, smiling.

"It's spring," I said. "It's gorgeous out, Matthew."

"It's pretty," he said. "Have a good day?"

"Did you?" He said he hadn't been out and, leaning back again, he pulled me down with him. I moved away.

"Matthew, let me see your thigh." He watched me docilely as I lifted his leg. It was as if it were a specimen we were both going to examine.

"What are those red marks from?" I asked.

"Me."

"How did you do it?"

"With my own little fingernails," he said.

They weren't scratches, they were deeper than that. The gold hairs on his thighs spoked up innocently around.

"Matthew, why did you do it?" He took his leg down.

"Don't worry about it. It's nothing. It's something I do sometimes. I put iodine on it, it won't get infected."

"But why did you do it?"

"Because I was having evil thoughts."

"About what?"

He shook his head. "Don't worry about it." He eased me back

down. "Don't worry your little head," he said. "Baby. Double baby. Baby to the second power. Baby squared." He started moving his hands up and down my body.

I pulled away. "Wait."

"What's the matter, baby?" he asked, touching me all over. I felt his tongue in my mouth and I closed my eyes.

One night he came in late, very agitated.

"There was this guy following me down the street just now for about a mile. He was this weird, juiced-up black guy even skinnier than I am. He was muttering, calling me sweet cakes, doodle-bug, boney maroney. Can they tell about me?" he asked, looking into my face. "Can they tell I've been crazy? Do I give out special vibes?"

I thought of the tense air he always had, the speed of his walk on those long legs.

"He followed me all that way. He kept saying, 'Think you're pretty hot stuff, you creep, you creep.'"

And the bald lady, had he seen her? Matthew wouldn't answer.

"People can't tell," I said finally, but he wouldn't stop looking at me.

"Why are you staring?" I asked.

"Because you're so nice and fat," he said, still staring.

Behind that gaze there was an intensity that had nothing to do with me. I felt something ungiving in him, the tightness of his skin on the bone. "Stop making me eat," I said. "You're turning me into a monster."

"But honey," he said smiling. "I likes you fat." Then his expression changed. It was a dark look he gave me. "You're eating with your own mouth," he said.

I called up Mal again. "Can you imagine?" I said. "He washes his hair every morning because he doesn't want dirt to accumulate too close to his brain. He's afraid it will penetrate and sink in. And scratches himself with his fingernails when we have a fight. When I told him to stop buying me so many sweets he thought I hated him and you know what he did? He put a long cut down the top of his arm with a knife."

"He's crazy," Mal said. "Don't you know you've got a mental case on your hands? Why don't you get out before he does something to you?"

"He won't do anything to me," I said, but it was a long time before I could hang up the phone.

When I came home that night Matthew was sitting at the table with a stack of pictures. I sat down beside him.

"What are they of?" I asked.

He looked annoyed but said nothing. I slid the pictures over and started going through them. They were all of him. He had taken twenty-four pictures of his own face: laughing, smiling, stern, pensive, in profile, in three-quarter view, from the back.

"These are really good," I said. "When did you take them?"

"I've really changed a lot," he said. "I suspected it, but I can tell from the pictures how drastic it is."

"How have you changed?"

"In ways." He put his hand over his mouth, staring at me and then staring at nothing.

"Why are you so indifferent to me?" I said.

"I'm not indifferent." He took the stack of pictures and began looking through them again, humming to himself.

"Why don't you take my picture?"

He continued to sort through the pictures, humming.

"Why don't you take my picture, Matthew?"

There was a long silence. "Sure, I'll take your picture some-time," he said, and I saw how his hair flared out in the photo-graphs, like a sea fan.

I remember every detail of the next few days. It was the hottest part of the summer in Minnesota. Night after night I went sleepless in the motionless air, hanging over the side of the bed so Matthew would have more room. I was so huge and moist my nightgown clung to me like a membrane. I had to take it off and lie naked on top of the sheet. When I tried to meet Matthew's eyes he looked away.

"It will all be different after the baby comes," I whispered to him, but he pretended to be asleep.

One evening I could hardly walk when I got off the bus after work. With every step my fat thighs rubbed against each other.

They had become so sore and chapped they had begun to bleed. As I walked past the bakery the heat rose in waves; behind the window, a sheet of sunlight, I saw wedding cakes, gingerbread men, cookies with faces, shimmering.

I heard music coming from our apartment. I twisted my key again and again in the lock. Surely Matthew could hear me? I punched my knuckles against the door. I tried the key again and the lock gave suddenly.

The room was filled with smoke. Matthew was sitting on the bed with the bald woman and a short black man who was even skinnier than he was.

"We're tripping," Matthew said. "But there's nothing left for you."

"Who is that?" said the bald woman.

"She lives down the hall."

"I do not live down the hall and you know it, Matthew," I said. "I live here and I'm his wife." I stood there awhile and nobody looked at me. I put down my purse and sat down next to it on the floor.

"These are my friends. They're like me," Matthew said. He looked at me with the eyes of a little animal, eyes that were all pupil, the color black, absorbing everything and giving nothing back.

"He's a cabdriver," Matthew said. "You wouldn't think of having a cabdriver for a friend, would you? Or a busdriver? I like cabdrivers."

"I would so have a cabdriver for a friend," I said, but I couldn't think of a single friend I did have. Matthew was my only friend.

"You wear make-up and you're fat and you only want to be friends with editors," Matthew said. "Oh, yes, and friends with Uncle Mal." The bald woman edged closer to Matthew on the bed. Her hand brushed my pillow, the pillow I had brought to Matthew from my old bed. She whispered in his ear, moving her hand to his hip, to the front of his pants.

"We're going now," Matthew said, standing up.

"Wait a second, I'll come too," I said.

"Do you want her to come?"

"No way," said the bald woman.

"See? They don't want you to come," Matthew said. "They're my friends and they're like me and they don't want you to come."

I stood still as they passed, stupefied by my pain.

"Matthew, please don't go!" I said. "It's just a tough time now, baby. Isn't it?"

He stopped in the doorway, staring down at me. A vein like a root throbbed in his temple. His face blurred in my gaze and I saw his eyes staring wide at me as we made love on that bed, silver ghosts in the wash of pale neon. I saw the snow falling silently as we hurried home in the cold, looking high up for the glow of the lamp in our apartment.

He put his hands on my shoulders. His palms and fingers cut into me like brackets. "Stay here," he said.

I watched him from the window but he did not turn to look back up at me.

I lay on the bed watching the ceiling change as it got darker and darker. I don't know how long I lay there or when the pains in my back and stomach started, they blended so imperceptibly with the other things I was feeling, staring at the ceiling, lying on the bed. Then I lay down on the floor, on the rug of swans' heads and necks, hurting so much I imagined I felt them moving under me, nudging me with their bills. I waited and waited there for Matthew to come back, but he didn't come back. It must have been a couple of days later that I called a cab to take me to the hospital.

The baby was tiny. She was born feet first, the wrong way. They gave me a drug that put me in a twilight sleep, that turned everything pink until I saw her after she was born. She came out curled like a snail and stayed calm in her crib sleeping all the time. She fit over my shoulder like a chrysalis, a tight little cocoon.

It was Matthew's father and mother who came to see me at the hospital and who took me home. I wanted to go back to our apartment, but they wouldn't let me, they said Matthew wasn't there and I needed somebody to take care of me. They took me to the house in the suburbs, but Matthew wasn't there, either. He had taken too many drugs and hurt himself, they had to send him away somewhere, they wouldn't say where. His mother gave me the Bible to read.

He came to see me once, I was still lying down most of the time. He came and sat down beside me near the big swimming pool. He had seen the baby. "She wasn't like the moon," he whispered, or did I dream that? He sat down on a chair next to me in the sun for a little while and he cried.

He got up and started walking toward the house, muttering something.

"Matthew, I know you didn't mean to hurt me," I said, but he kept walking, shaking his head.

"He didn't even recognize you," his mother told me later, glaring at my face in the sunlight.

"Then why did he cry?" I asked. "If he didn't recognize me then why did he cry?" Words from her Bible swam in my head, he whom my soul loveth. We could do anything, be anything, with what we had. Hadn't he always told me that?

I rushed into the house, hoping I could still find Matthew, but he was gone. I took the keys to his mother's car off the kitchen table and ran to the garage, before she had a chance to stop me.

Then I went out to look for Matthew. I looked everywhere nearby, up and down the streets, and when I couldn't find him I drove back to our old neighborhood. I parked in front of the old apartment and went upstairs and knocked and knocked on the door but no one answered. I tried my key but it wouldn't fit into the lock. I pushed at the lock until the key had scratched my fingers and made them bleed. Then I sat down by the door on the floor in the hallway and remembered how there had been heaven in that apartment, time had stood still. No matter what he did, Matthew knew. We had made love all night, in the light of the streetlight and the Grimm's Hardware sign. If I put my cheek to the wood I could feel the vibrations of those nights, still singing in the floorboards of the apartment.

Mal came to the house in the suburbs after I called him. He cried when he saw me and I saw how his cheeks were now cross-hatched with tiny red veins. Matthew's mother wanted to keep the baby for herself, but Mal wouldn't let her. He took me, and the baby, and brought us to this beautiful house where we have been so happy. It is not far from the ocean and we go sailing a couple of times a month if the wind is not blowing too hard. I am thin again and Mal has bought me wonderful new clothes. The little girl calls him Daddy and has never known another father.

I thought Mal would ask me to explain a lot of things, but mostly he hasn't.

"I know you've never loved anybody but me," he said. "I knew you'd come back. That's why I waited." That was four years ago. And more and more I think Mal was right.

Once we were sitting under the trellis and Mal asked me what I was thinking about when I looked so preoccupied and far away. I told him an apparition gripped my mind sometimes.

"It's a picture of man who looked like a boy and a girl at the same time, a man with hair like a sheaf of golden wires, with eyes as black and shiny as lava chips. You remember, it was a man who confused me, a man who studied the memory and even tried to look into his own head. I must be making it up, don't you think? For no real person could be anything like that."

Mal was annoyed, he said it was certainly something I had made up. I'd made a mistake and had altered the memory to turn it into something more compelling, so I didn't seem like quite such a fool. It was basic psychological theory, he said.

That was a long time ago. I am content with my life and light of heart. I know how evening rises up in the blue noon and I know every moment by the angle and quality of the sunlight spreading on my lawn and on my courtyard. I stand in the courtyard and watch the days and walk through my garden and wait for my daughter and Mal. For surely, as Mal tells me, I am the happiest of women. But it is always summer here and sometimes I remember how the winter was in Minnesota, how dark and drear. And it is just occasionally, as I watch Phoebe's copper hair growing into tighter and tighter curls with each passing year, that my mind strays back to that dead and gloomy time.

🔥 🔥 🔥

AVANT-GARDE MASTERY

by THOMAS LECLAIR

from TRIQUARTERLY

nominated by TRIQUARTERLY *and Louis Gallo*

THE AVANT-GARDE in American fiction is now a topic for loud noise. While the critical conservatives John Gardner, Mary Mc-Carthy, Gerald Graff, Alfred Kazin, Robert Alter, and, most recently, Bryan F. Griffin in *Harper's* (Aug. and Sept., 1981) attack the avant-garde—whatever they say it is—for causing the parlous state of contemporary fiction, some vocal novelists who consider themselves avant-garde—Ronald Sukenick, Raymond Federman, Jonathan Baumbach—and their critical boosters Richard Koste-lanetz and Jerome Klinkowitz reply in conventional *épater les bourgeoise* fashion with exaggerated claims for experimental or surfictionist or disruptivist works more often distinguished by their differences from traditional narration and their similarities to one another than by intrinsic merit or substance. Our writers, says Kazin, are weak in the legs, "part of the drift instead of exercising some mastery."[1] "The dynamics of artistic change," says Koste-lanetz, "invariably sabotage the masterpiece-mentality."[2] Let mastery of the new define the avant-garde, artistic conclusiveness as well as experimentalism, and one finds in the last few years a number of important counterexamples to both Kazin and Koste-lanetz, novels that imaginatively comprehend complex areas of American life, specifically the commerce, technology, media, and politics Kazin believes frighten writers into self-reflexiveness and game-playing. The books that I think represent our avant-garde—Joseph McElroy's *Lookout Cartridge*, Don DeLillo's *Ratner's Star*, William Gaddis's *JR*, Joseph Heller's *Something Happened*, Robert Coover's *The Public Burning*, Thomas Pynchon's *Gravity's Rainbow*, and John Barth's *Letters*, all published in the last eight years—may not be as technically "advanced" as the never-repeated experiments Kostelanetz is fond of describing (concrete fictions, one-page novels made of numbers, showers of word-rain); but these novels do take advantage of new stylistic and formal possibilities, and they are more intellectually advanced, more informed by truly contemporary systems of thought outside literature, than much superficially innovative fiction.

The seven I've mentioned are published by commercial presses, several have won prizes, a few were harshly received, some are largely unknown or unread by academic, as well as general, audiences, and all are their authors' best work. Written before the latest outbreak of the Ancient/Modern argument, they do not constitute a movement or program, though a couple of them might be mistakenly added to other recent signs as evidence of a current withdrawal from experiment. Barth says his writing students are no longer interested in "formally innovative writing"; an editor of this magazine wonders why he's receiving little explicitly experimental work, and many of the avant-garde novelists mentioned or included in Joe David Bellamy's *The New Fiction* and Klinkowitz's *The Life of Fiction* seem to be pulling back in their latest novels. Walter Abish's *How German Is It?*, Russell Banks' *Jamaica*, Donald Barthelme's *The Dead Father*, William Burroughs' *Cities of the Red Night*, John Hawkes' *The Passion Artist*, Jerzy Kosinski's *Blind Date*, Ishmael Reed's *Flight to Canada*, Gilbert Sorrentino's *Aberration of Starlight*, Kurt Vonnegut's *Jailbird*, and even *The Tunnel*, the novel-in-progress by William Gass, the most-quoted aesthetician of the new, are less experimental than their authors' earlier fiction. However, the novels I have in mind as an avant-garde of mastery are not withdrawing from experiment. They are the next stage forward, synthesizing experimental forms, employing technical innovations to defamiliarize the materials of realistic fiction and not just the literary text, a limitation of much academic and small-press avant-garde writing. The books are large, ambitious, syncretistic systems, neither traditional imitations nor pure inventions but imaginative models, integrations of original abstractions, new information, and old narrative purposes. "Systems," too, because each of the seven authors has been influenced, in one of its manifestations, by systems theory, the contemporary epistemology that searches orders and patterns where the early modern science that influenced many modern and post-modern avant-gardists was a mine for relativity and disorder.

Two new studies of the avant-garde in music, art, and literature—Christopher Butler's *After the Wake* and Ihab Hassan's
remarkable *Right Promethean Fire*, both published in 1980—agree
that much avant-garde energy has been expended in deconstruc-
tion and negation of old modes, what Hassan calls "unmaking,"
rather than in original creation. This self-reflexive reductiveness is
found, for example, in Raymond Federman's proposal that new
fiction be "deliberately illogical, irrational, unrealistic, non sequi-
tur, and incoherent."[3] We understand the creative anxieties that
underlie this proposal for "Surfiction"; they come from the atmosphere of "indetermanence," Hassan's portmanteau of indeter-
minancy and immanence, to which have been added the radical
literary skepticisms gathered around structuralism. But now,
eighty years after Nietzsche's death, sixty years after Einstein's
Nobel Prize and surrealism, and thirty years after the beginnings
of structuralism, this kind of program for disintegration of the
medium seems not advanced but aged, old-fashioned, produced by
the disappointment of naive assumptions about certitude. The
concept of entropy, a much-discussed rationale for imitative decon-
struction, offers an instructive example of some avant-gardists' use
of dated science. Entropy has a malign and fixed rule in mechanistic, closed systems—the heat machines of late nineteenth- and
early twentieth-century physics—but systems theorists of our day
show that man, nature, the universe, and, I think, literature are
open systems, circular networks of disintegration and adaptation. I
don't mean to suggest that transcendence is making a comeback, or
that doom isn't crouched in missile silos or diffused in the exhaust
of a hundred million automobiles, but that theoreticians in many
scientific disciplines are now moving beyond the fragmentation
produced by specialization and the infinite regresses of experimental sciences to propose new orders, some elegant in their simplicity
and useful in their explanatory power. There is not space here to
summarize the work of Ludwig von Bertalanffy, the initiator of
systems theory, or some of his more notable followers—Gregory
Bateson in anthropology, Kenneth Boulding in economics, Buckminster Fuller in ecology, R. D. Laing in psychology, Ervin Laszlo
in biology, Norbert Weiner in cybernetics, Anthony Wilden in
literary and cultural criticism—but I can briefly list some qualities
of systems thinking that carry over into the work of the novelists I
call the avant-garde of mastery—or the reconstructive avant-garde.

Systems theorists accept relativity, fragmentation, and the artifices of knowledge as givens, then proceed to make new intellectual maps. Their method is more like that of mathematics than of physical sciences: hypothetical, imaginative, comprehensive, highly abstract. Some of the emphases of systems theory are illustrated in this table of contrasts with mechanistic science:

Mechanistic Science	Systems Theory
phenomena	relations
functions	formal properties
sequences	homologies
linear	hierarchical
causes	processes of communication
effects	constraints
one-way	reciprocal
isolation	collaboration
closed systems	ecosystems

The conclusions offered by systems theory are models, or what Thomas Kuhn termed paradigms, new ways of organizing and seeing the world. Systems theorists seek mastery of bewildering multiplicity and communication with nonspecialists.

How are these general characteristics of systems theory, in skeletal form similar to the principles of formalism, adapted for a fiction specifically different from both the deconstructive avant-garde and Gardner's traditionalism? Barth and the others included here practice an art of excess: their novels begin as conventional literary types (the sequel and epistolary novel in the case of *Letters*) which, by overloading, deforming, or otherwise exceeding, the writers change into large constructs whose governing principles are different from the novels' initial conventions and are derived from systems theory or one of its associated disciplines. Vestiges of characterization, recognizable settings, physical action, and probability are retained to invite traditional narrative interests. But by working extremes of the concrete and the abstract, the writers crowd their narratives with information—scientific, historical, commercial—left out of realistic fiction, then offer homologies and hierarchies that give that information new contexts for understanding. Novels of excess are highly rhetorical; they examine themselves and they deconstruct various literary expectations with innovative techniques, but they also reconstruct an old literary value: comprehension of the world. Their intent is transformation—of the work and of the reader, who is solicited, confuted, and released into a new system of ideas. The novelists vary in their views of the world, their judgments about the possibilities for human value and survival, yet in their mastery of their culture and form they imply that comprehension of the world is worth the effort they give it. While their characters may fail to solve or even recognize the systems they occupy, the novelists' loyalty to both internal coherence and communication compensate for their characters' limitations and make these novels—contra Gardner—the moral standard of the decade. How the novels work, what they contribute, and why their mastery is more advanced than recent writing usually considered avant-garde can be outlined through contrasts with several dominant themes of the deconstructivists.

The unmaking of language: With Wittgenstein, linguistics, and semiotics as theoretical bases, and with Beckett as exemplar, deconstructive avant-gardists have been much concerned with reducing the symbolic quality of language and demonstrating the limitations of their medium. In *Out*, Ronald Sukenick replaces the word as symbol with the page as symbol as he rushes language into the open space and silence of blank pages. In *Alphabetical Africa*, Walter Abish illustrates the arbitrariness, circularity, and emptiness of signs with a schematic, alphabetical arrangement of his narration. These books are Exercises in Style, as Raymond Queneau called his contribution to linguistic permutation: they are language written, self-enclosed, and programmatically diminished. In contrast, the reconstructive avant-garde remembers that language is also spoken and, whatever its duplicities, referential; that the languages of technology are new creative sources; and that language limits—or enables—all human beings, not just itself and the artists who choose it as medium. Heller in *Something Happened*, a book whose intellectual seriousness is yet to be recognized, and Gaddis in *JR* place their characters in communication industries to illustrate that, along with its intrinsic limitations, language also carries in contemporary America the pervasive and negative effects of the business world's obsession with entities, quantity, and prediction. In these novels, unlike the shrinking works of the deconstructivists, the difficulties of communication do not decrease speech acts but rather increase their number. Gresham's Law becomes linguistic and practical as well as economic and speculative.

Begun respectively as another ad man's confession and as an Horatio Alger parody, *Something Happened* and *JR* employ techniques of "unmaking"—typographical experiment, lexical flatness, redundancy, fragmentation, noise—as well as the "recording" of natural speech, to give the reader local discomfort and, finally, to lead him into recognition of the global forms being created as alternatives to plot—positive feedback systems, influenced by Bateson and Laing (Heller) and by Weiner (Gaddis), and characterized by growth without control, a tendency toward the infinite regress of the question "What happened?" and the infinite expansion of J. R.'s "the more you have the more you get" business practices. As informed about communication processes as their deconstructive colleagues, Heller and Gaddis choose to combine theoretical knowledge with the closely observed "real-time" of commerce, thus manifesting the reciprocal relation between language and the world, not just between language and the writer. In these two novels and in the five others I've mentioned, language is unmade but also replaced by or included within a system which, understood, could help reverse the process of linguistic waste.

The unmaking of mind: From the elegant modernist paradoxes of Borges, we descend in some post-modern American fiction to the simple contradiction of theory-based novels that disallow the formulating mind within them. The gratuitous acts of Kosinski's books and the digressive consciousness of Federman's improvisational surfictions are representative reactions against mind as mechanism, psychological cause and effect, the intellectual enclosures of plot and character; but their reduction to the aleatory, the irrational, and the personal is at odds with the dominant fact of science and technology: that the rational and creative mind expands outward through the methods and machines it invents. The deconstructivists' isolation of mind and their metonymic techniques are replaced in the reconstructive avant-garde by the collaborative intellectual processes and the extended homologies of systems theory, exemplified in two works that should be more widely known, Don DeLillo's *Ratner's Star* and Joseph McElroy's *Lookout Cartridge*.

Ratner's Star first appears to be a science-fiction adventure, but DeLillo transforms story into naked structure and character into abstract voices, turning the book into fictional science, a past and future history of mathematics that derives its method of conceptual connections and its intellectual integrity from its subject. From the number mysticism of Pythagoras to Godelian undecidability and beyond, the novel traces a boomerang form, a large and learned metaphor for the advance of mathematics into uncertainty. And like the best speculative science, *Ratner's Star* is a system both internally rigorous and capable of being used to measure heaven and earth. *Lookout Cartridge*, like *Ratner's Star* and the others briefly noted here, is also a book for measuring. Beginning as a tale of detection, overloaded with the materials, formats, and language of information science, the novel becomes a fictional imitation of the analog computer, demanding that the protagonist and the reader perform the high-speed, simultaneous, and collaborative processes necessary in "the great multiple field of impinging informations" where we live now.[4] As complete and original an achievement as any novel published in the seventies, *Lookout Cartridge* is a planetary vision, the world seen through the microscope of massed details and the telescope of inclusive ideas. Kazin has said our writers lack mastery because they are unable to "imagine the impact of the technological storm on our mental life."[5] But this is exactly the strength of the writers considered here: turning what the old-fashioned humanist sees as a "storm" into a source of energy, language, and concepts that expand our mental life. Full of new theory and facts, formed to exceed expectations and create new homologies for their subjects, innovative in their uses of abstraction and precision, these novels are a remaking of the literary mind along lines with a future.

Unmaking the book: Attracted by the malleability of the visual and performing arts, some avant-gardists have substituted for the print, permanence, and scale of the book collages (sketches, pictures, scrambled typography) and experiments in short forms (miniature stories, found language, pieces in series) usually published in magazines or small reviews. There are good aesthetic reasons for crossing strains of media, and there are the practical difficulties of getting experimental novels published, yet the brevity of much experimental work suggests grafting without fruition, satisfaction with gestures rather than mastery. Although often original and witty, sometimes profound, and certainly much-copied, Donald Barthelme represents in his less inspired work and in the following quote from a recent review that failure of confidence or ambition that separates many deconstructivists from the makers of large wholes I call the reconstructive avant-garde: "In earlier times people could attempt to explain everything. Today there is too much to explain. The effort would be fruitless. So you have to try and do something else. For me it's more attempting to deal with parts instead of attempting to deal with the whole."[6]

What Barthelme's fiction has in common with other small works called avant-garde, as well as with the short stories of Barth and Coover of the writers here, is performance: parodies, tours de force, games, metafictions that ask for recognition from the audience but not at the risk of communication or emotional affect. They are what J. L. Austin termed "illocutionary acts" to which one responds "I see what you're doing" rather than "I believe you," the perlocutionary response.[7] Nabokov had the power to extend these games, both in space and in meaning; and two recent books—Sorrentino's *Mulligan Stew* and Alexander Theroux's *Darconville's Cat*—have some of Nabokov's distinctly literary range. But I think the real avant-garde is found in performances with perlocutionary force, the epic theater of *Gravity's Rainbow* or the three-ring circus turned sacrificial festival of *The Public Burning*, novels that use the alienation effects familiar from the deconstructivists—multiple perspectives, baring of devices, confusion of fact and fiction, combination of the foolish and serious—to first disturb, then revise the reader's notion of his culture—its media, politics, history, religion, and science, to name a few subjects of these two works. Pynchon and Coover know the constraints of print, as well as the limits of language and mind—they too are subjects of their novels—yet with their knowledge of systems through anthropology, mathematics, cybernetics, and other disciplines they have the confidence to take advantage of the book, the mode in which analogies for the excesses of our history can be created, in which the creative mind can achieve some mastery of the "everything" that frightens Barthelme. About *Gravity's Rainbow* perhaps too much has already been said, annotators turning a powerful book into a dead scroll. Equally concerned with the processes of which human beings are but one instance, but harsher, more willing to exceed and repel in order to affect, *The Public Burning* has been less successful, has run afoul of the hazards all these novels take—the risks of mass and mastery that are neither familiar nor altogether new, yet insistent, forceful, both disorienting and reorienting.

The remaking of everything: The avant-garde of mastery is summarized by Barth's *Letters,* a system of systems that is and is about reconstruction, or what Barth has named "replenishment": the remaking from alphabetical letters a language both artful and referential, the remaking of mind through the information and reciprocity of mailed letters, the remaking of the book from "exhausted" forms in belles lettres.[8] Barth's definition of plot—"the incremental perturbation of an unstable homeostatic system and its catastrophic restoration to a complexified equilibrium"—suggests in a sentence the pervasive presence of systems theory in the book, especially in its formative principles.[9] As an epistolary novel, *Letters* accepts print as its medium and takes full advantage of two meanings of "correspondence," making it refer both to the processes of communication exchange and to the homologous relations with reality emphasized in systems theory. As a sequel to Barth's first six books, the novel recycles their disparate materials into an ecological whole, a large, collaborative, literally open system in which entropy is everywhere mentioned and everywhere combatted by the negentropic patterns of order and growth Barth formulates. *Letters* is full of hierarchies, isomorphs, encompassing abstractions, and the language of systems theorists—computer talk, boundaries, constraints, codes, frames, recursion, mapping. But like the other reconstructivists, the author is also an "editor" of realities: the radically interdependent revolutions in business, media, history, politics, and everyday life of the other six novels I've discussed. Barth is willing to risk excess—"To get enough of anything in nature," he quotes William James in *Letters,* "one has to take too much"—to create a new naturalism. Not Dreiser's naturalism with new information plugged in, for *Letters* has a full supply of deconstructive games, self-reflexiveness, and foregrounded language to remind the reader that he's not reading the newspaper, that systems knowledge is an artifice like any other knowledge, but a sophisticated naturalism of form as well as content, a synthesis of "algebra and fire," a model of the world as conceived by contemporary science. Like other novels of excess, *Letters* is "about" the world in various ways: it gathers or invents unfamiliar facts, describes processes through which the fictional "data" can be understood, and provides as a whole—in its collaborative forms and styles—a manifestation of "organized complexity" (Bertalanffy's phrase) that exceeds the simplifications of novels usually considered realistic and calls us to awareness of the new, larger reality of systems science.

Magnifying with its comprehensiveness and ambition the qualities of other novels I believe are avant-garde, the mass of *Letters*— 772 small-print pages dense with information from the Maryland tide-pool to the Burlingame gene-pool—also manifests some of the difficulties attendant upon their accomplishments. "The Closer You Get The Less You See" reads a bumper sticker in *Letters*, and it's true of these seven: one needs patience to read them, willingness to find out what they know, tolerance for deconfirmation, puzzlement, even boredom while large and, finally, instructive and original wholes are being created. The rhetoric of excess aims for mastery but may seem masochism to the readers of consumable fiction or the readers of experimental fiction written by an author who, in Raymond Federman's words, "stands on equal footing with the reader in their efforts to make sense out of the language common to both of them, to give sense to the fiction of life."[10] Or the resistance to reading may seem, as it sometimes does in the classic text of reconstruction, *Finnegans Wake*, authorial self-indulgence. But once understood as systems, validated and just maybe verified as well, these novels have the integrity of the Ancient Mariner's tale: a long and difficult story because it had to be for both truth and effort, for mastery.

1. Alfred Kazin, "American Writing Now," *The New Republic*, October 18, 1980, p. 29.

2. Richard Kostelanetz, "New Fiction in America" in *Surfiction*, ed. Raymond Federman (Chicago: Swallow, 1975), p. 86.

3. Raymond Federman, "Introduction" to *Surfiction*, p. 13.

4. Joseph McElroy, *Lookout Cartridge* (New York: Knopf, 1974), p. 465.

5. Kazin, p. 29.

6. Michiko Kakutani, "Donald Barthelme," *International Herald Tribune*, September 25, 1981, p. 20.

7. J. L. Austin, *How to Do Things with Words* (Cambridge: Harvard University Press, 1962).

8. John Barth, "The Literature of Replenishment," *Atlantic*, January, 1980, pp. 65-71.

9. John Barth, *Letters* (New York: Putnam, 1979), p. 767.

10. Federman, p. 14.

ZOË

by DIANE ACKERMAN

from THE KENYON REVIEW

nominated by Herb Leibowitz

Ultimate immigrant,
who passed through the Ellis Island
of your mother's hips,
with a name slit loose
from its dialect of cell and bone:
welcome to the citadel of our lives.
We listened for the hoofbeats
(your heart) for nine months
and then your mother nearly died,
hospitably, to give you light.

Like an Hawaiian princess,
you are carried everywhere,
on a litter, in a carriage,
by the arabesque of one's arm.
Your feet have never touched ground.
You, who can't even roll over
when you want, creamy little tyrant,
control the lives of all around you.

Sound leaps from your face
and your ribs quake
each time the downy world chafes.
Last week, you first smiled
because grownups acted silly.
Things elude you, but you can grasp
absurdity already.

By mistake, you suck your wrist
instead of mother's nipple.
We laugh. With your operatic cries,
and Michelin-man pudge,
and seepages from below,
and eyes alert as twin deer,
you have no sense of self whatever.

Zoë Klein, goddaughter
with a hybrid name,
living in the soft new crook
of your mother's arm,
with a face like a Dalai Lama's
or a small Neanderthal's,
born out of a dream by two,

you live a dream by halves now:
slumbrous, milky-breathed.

In time, love will answer questions
you didn't raise. A belled marvel,
the cat of your inquiry, will stalk
through a world brighter
and more plural than you guess,
where a baby's fingerprints,
loopy weather systems, one for each tip,
will leave you spellbound

that matter could come to this.

HAMLEN BROOK

by RICHARD WILBUR

from POETRY

nominated by Michael S. Harper

At the alder-darkened brink
    Where the stream slows to a lucid jet
I lean to the water, dinting its top with sweat,
    And see, before I can drink,

A startled inchling trout
    Of spotted near-transparency,
Trawling a shadow solider than he.
    He swerves now, darting out

To where, in a flicked slew
    Of sparks and glittering silt, he weaves
Through stream-bed rocks, disturbing foundered leaves,
    And butts then out of view

Beneath a sliding glass
    Crazed by the skimming of a brace
Of burnished dragon-flies across its face,
    In which deep cloudlets pass

And a white precipice
    Of mirrored birch-trees plunges down
Toward where the azures of the zenith drown.
    How shall I drink all this?

Joy's trick is to supply
    Dry lips with what can cool and slake,
Leaving them dumbstruck also with an ache
    Nothing can satisfy.

THE MAN OF MANY L'S

by MAXINE KUMIN

from THE SEATTLE REVIEW

nominated by Maura Stanton

My whole childhood I feared cripples
and how they got that way: the one-
legged Lavender Man who sold
his sachets by St. Mary's steeple,
the blind who tapped past humming what they knew,
even the hunchback seamstress, a ragdoll
who further sagged to pin my mother's hems
had once been sturdy, had once been whole.
Something entered people, something chopped,
pressed, punctured, had its way with them
and if you looked, bad child, it entered you.

When we found out what the disease would do,
lying, like any council's stalwarts,
all of us swore to play our parts
in the final act at your command.

The first was easy. You gave up your left hand
and the right grew wiser, a juggler for its king.
When the poor dumb leg began to falter
you took up an alpenstock for walking
once flourished Sundays by our dead father.
Month by month the battleground grew thinner.
When you could no longer swallow meat
we steamed and mashed your dinner
and bent your straw to chocolate soda treats.

And when you could not talk, still you could write
questions and answers on a magic slate,
then lift the page, like laundry to the wind.
I plucked the memory splinter from your spine
as we played at being normal, who
had cradled each other in the cold zoo
of childhood. Three months before
you died I wheeled you through the streets
of placid Palo Alto to catch
spring in its flamboyant tracks.
You wrote the name of every idiot flower

I did not know. Yucca rained.
Mimosa shone. The bottlebrush took fire
as you fought to hold your great head on its stem.
Lillac, you wrote. *Magnollia. Lilly.*
And further, *olleander. Dellphinium.*

O man of many L's, brother, my wily
resident ghost, may I never spell
these crowfoot dogbane words again
these showy florid words again
except I name them under your spell.

🔥 🔥 🔥

UNCLE BALT AND THE NATURE OF BEING

fiction by WILLIAM GASS

from CONJUNCTIONS

nominated by CONJUNCTIONS

WHY SHOULD I BOTHER to remember Uncle Balt. He's dead now. I'm half. He never meant much to me; though back then, I suppose, he meant something. People often have value for you when you're ten. And for a lot of odd reasons. Ten is not an even age.

We had a huge storm the other day—a Great Plains wind—and it churned up the cornfield behind the house like a shallow lake. I told Martha once more about the time a bolt of lightning struck a landing-window at the very moment my mother was descending the stairs, and how powdered glass had filled her hair so it looked like the head of a fall weed, the bolt blowing away her blood, too, like foam from a beer, and leaving her faint. Later, after she had had shock treatments and her hair was white with alcohol and age, she would be disoriented again as she was then. Anyway, it took a long time to comb the glass out without scratching her scalp. I remember Uncle Balt had been calling to her about the wind, warning her, telling her to come down.

I always thought of him as a deep, unreadable, hole of a man—a well of loneliness. There you are: of course I didn't think of him that way when I was ten or twelve, a tiresome time, or at nine either, the neuter's age. Maybe, by the year I reached thirty— thirty-five—and I had read the novel, dreaming the little excitement I didn't receive, I'd have come to the conclusion that for anything that befell him there would be a long fall before one heard—I heard—or thought I heard—the plop. But, as I say, my mind rarely entertained his figure, offered him anything but forgetfulness and silence.

Yet that was what he fed on. So it seemed. He was *dasein's* quiet cancellation. *Dasein* indeed. More achery into the infinite. And there I go again.

Tall, thin, slightly cadaverous, Uncle Balt's voice issued from his body as from a length of pipe. He was completely and supremely "an uncle." I saw him rarely, so he retained a foreign flavor for me, an exotic far-offness that his moustache—two droopy loops of thin black rope—did nothing to diminish. He had an immense stride, and a posture like his gaze: straight, unbending, blunt. Work had pastured his face the way weather wears a field. Past burning, beyond tanning, not even any longer leathered, it seemed the sorrowful smoothing out of some angrily wadded paper, his bones like the shadows of bones behind his skin, a gift from the butcher for the dog.

I marveled, I remember, at his hands, with their huge knuckles hard and round as the wooden spools in my set of Tinker-toys. These knuckles nearly made him up: his wrists, elbows, Adam's apple, cheekbones, nose, were knuckles. I called him Uncle Knuckle for a while.

He wore overalls over long underwear, even to the dinner table, where he insisted on saying grace, his O LORD like a bull's bellow. He took more time over the saying of grace than he did in eating. He did say a good grace, though: full of very particular gratitudes, intensely meant. He ate very swiftly, very neatly, with both hands; they flew at his mouth like bees; and then his napkin would cover the chewing like a biscuit basket. Still, from the side where I sat, I could see his jaw moving as rapidly as the treadle on Granny's sewing machine. When he had chewed his food, the napkin would be withdrawn like a curtain, and Uncle Balt would look at us all with stern amusement. WELL, WHAT HAPPENED TODAY? NO HOEIN, NO ROWIN, NO PLANTIN, NO WEEDIN OR PINCHIN BACK, I BET. NO SEWIN, NO BAKIN, NO RUBBIN AROUND WITH RAGS, I GUESS. Our first forkfulls still in our mouths, he would wait for an answer (or at least that's what I supposed he was doing), and not immediately receiv-

ing any, his head would bob once like a bird's. YOUNGSTER?
WERE YOU A LOT OF HELP CREATIN CRUMBS? YOUR
GRANDMA, NOW, DID SHE NEED SOME ASSISTANCE
WITH THE GABBLE-GABBLE? I dunno. I went walkin. OH?
WELL. WALKING IS HARD. HARD. YOU MUST BE CLEAN
BLOWED OVER. Or sometimes it was HAILED FLAT and
THRESHED OUT. He used these farm-life terms like a sailor. It
kept him safely in his world and you quite firmly out. Uncle Balt
would pour cream in his coffee and watch the pale stream curl, the
coffee cool as it clouded. SO MUCH ALMIGHTY HENNIN
GOIN ON, THE SUN STOPPED TO TALK TOO. This was a sign
for my Uncle Balt to fold his napkin and rise, tall as a tower, I
thought, the oat and wheat stems, the corn tassel he'd tucked in
the tiny pockets of his bib (I guess to check the progress of the
crop), shuddering as though back in the field. Then he would bring
his coffee in a swoop to his mouth and toss it down his throat like
dipper rinsing. All of a sudden he was through the kitchen to the
yard where we knew he'd be checking on granny's vegetable
garden and grumbling deep in his throat.

He folded over like a ruler from the waist. His knobby hands
would flicker through the bean leaves. He would sometimes carry
a caterpillar to me on his arm—a swallowtale often—from the
parsley. His forearm alongside and overwhelming mine, we would
watch without a word the caterpillar crawl gingerly down onto my
reluctant wrist.

At ten you can't compare those many light steps to the passage of
a lover's lips.

The bugs Uncle Balt discovered on the beans he would crush
against his thumb, or cut in two with a yellowed nail—sharp, I
thought, as a stone knife. He liked to rub a tomato leaf near his
nose as I do mint—better smell than marigold, SNIFF THAT, he
said—and then his fingers would be thrust in the soil where they
made a fist the way I always wanted my steamshovel to take hold,
grab and grip. TOO DAMN DRY, he'd shout, though I suspect he
wasn't shouting, simply stating, giving voice to a fact. MARGA-
RET. GET OUR MOTHER TO HOE THIS ROW. MORE
WEEDS THAN WORRIES ALONG HERE. He would eat a bean
or pea pod whole.

There were a few more hours of light—till nine, sometimes—
that's what he meant by saying the sun had stopped to talk with the

wimmin—so Uncle Balt was off on some chore or other, disappearing down rows where I wanted to follow him, scared I'd get lost in the corn otherwise; or he'd stride through the orchard like that Rodin statue—so complete in his walking he had no arms, and too fast for me to keep up. He liked to stop on a little rise just beyond the hawthorne thicket where you could see a stand of wheat like ten thousand German arms salute their leader. Except they hadn't their leader then. There I go.

MARGARET! I was flat beneath the dining room table, held there by my fear of the heavy air. I heard my mother's footsteps, even in those days irregular and indistinct as if she had a limp in both legs. Maybe it was just the wind—the tornado—which blew the window in. MAR and suddenly she had her halo and her glistening head of glass.

Uncle Balt wasn't deaf. I think he was loud because he was alone. He was a silo . . . sunk in the ground like those missiles would be. His words came, it must have seemed to him, from so far away they needed to be bugled.

He owned the farm. It was his land, and he knew every dirty inch exactly the way those men who farm in films are supposed to. He never displayed any tenderness toward it, no particular affection; yet he tended it, all right, strode over it winter and summer, rode over it spring and fall; always in the fields alone, without any kind of companion, dogless even when he went gunning for pheasant or grouse; outside like one of his few trees . . . a root released from the ground.

His wife had died before I was born (I never even knew her name), and my grandparents, who weren't grandparents then, came to live with him and help on the farm. *Help out* is how they put it, but I suspect (though just when I began to suspect it I certainly can't recall) that it was my Uncle Balt who had done the helping. It was my mother's myth that her parents were gentry, but whatever they'd had was gone without a crazed plate or piece of lace or the ruin of a chair to reminisce the loss when I knew them. Then Uncle Balt's one joke suggested that he felt unhappily re-related. Maybe he had some long-standing resentment of his sister. It is discouraging to leave the past behind only to see it coming toward you like the thunder storm which drenched you yesterday. Anyway, the joke was that the women never worked, only left droppings about like pigeons: pecked and cooed and preened. They kept company with coffee cups and a few cookies as though they were engaged; they sat around kitchen tables and chatted continually, now and then picking up a crumb with a moistened fingertip or underlining something they were saying by indenting the oilcloth with the edge of a spoon or a knife. If he had lived in the city, Uncle Balt would have described how women shopped or played bridge; and if he had lived on into my time, he'd have shouted about their eternal tennis and their golf. In any case, the joke went on and on, in this version or that, past boredom into cruelty, scaring away any other kind of conversation like a school-yard bully.

Uncle Balt would have called it *joshing*. LESS SOUL THAN A CROW. His head would bob. NO KNITTIN, JUST NATTERIN, is one way he put it. On Sunday it was CHITCHAT IN A HAT; it was DITHERIN AMONG THE DUSTY DOILIES: on weekdays it was BUTTERIN THE BEE'S BUZZ; it was GOSSIPIN A GUT FULL, or GETTIN FAT ON CHAT; it was CHICKIN PICKIN and FRYING GAB. I gathered he could become obscene, but something about trading tit-milk was the worst I heard. I knew a line of some kind had been crossed when granny would suddenly say, shut. A bob, as if to say, "yup," would follow instantly, but I never knew what the "yup" was a yes to. THEY'LL HOPPER A MAN IN HALF, GRAZE YOU TO THE GROUND. Now and then he was explosive. THEY'LL MAKE YOU INTO **MAN JAM** AND SERVE YOU ON **TOAST.** He'd maybe give me a small smile. DAMN IF THEY WON'T. IS THEY BACK THERE MUNCHING AWAY LIKE MOTHS IN A CLOSET, he wanted to know one day when he caught me trailing him. BEST YOU'RE HERE. I DON'T WANT YOU ADDIN TO THE TATTLE RATTLE. YOU BE AROUND WIMMIN LONG, BOY, AND BONES IS ALL YOU'LL BE. BONES WITHOUT ANY MARROW, BOY, STRAWS WITH ALL THE SUCK OUT, BONES BOY, THEY PLAY SONGS ON, THE DEVIL'S DITTIES. He seemed himself a pure translucency, the sun shining through to him as though he were a saint all of a sudden.

None of what he said was so, of course—not close. My grand-mother slaved. That's how everybody had decided to speak of her life. She scrounged; she scrimped; she saved; she slaved. Uncle Balt didn't see a slave, naturally enough, in her sturdy square shape, but he knew she was all the standard things: god fearin, hard workin; she grew a good kitchen garden; she cooked solid starchy things; she canned and preserved and put up; she washed and cleaned and darned and made her own clothes—a regular pioneer, my father said, though I remember it was said sourly. Uncle Balt found it fun never to say so; never to acknowledge anything positive from her presence; to shout precisely the opposite right into the wedge of pie he would soon be nuzzling under the flap of his napkin. I remember being told that Uncle Balt had false teeth. Maybe they came loose when he chewed.

Well, Uncle Balt toiled too. It was life itself—to Uncle Balt—to work. Daybreak to sundown. Season to season. But Uncle Balt (I'd say now) worked for himself, and owned what he made; gave away what he chose; while my grandmother had a few clothes and some fat and a faraway brat to show for her labors: a dress for buttering a bee's buzz, a dimpled butt for softening a wagon's seat, a dipsomaniacal daughter to disappoint her life. Uncle Balt enjoyed her stove, her iron, her hoe; but Uncle Balt (I guess I must mention) hadn't asked for her help, her sacrifices, her moist eyes, her resigned sighs, her patience, her pallid personality, her folded soul. My grandparents were strays he'd taken in, and now he had to suffer their services, their suffering, their simple presence, their bulk. There were no more empty rooms or silent days; there were my grandfather's night-groans, his uncomfortable cough, his tromp, my grandmother's darning egg or embroidery hoop in Father Bear's Chair; there was pipe ash and stale smoke and one more car, unaccountable coming and going, squabbling behind doors, silly chitchat, glooms; there was no calm; there was instead that kid, Margaret, with a gaze as loose as a pond leaf, her skinflint husband, anger like a scar disfiguring his face; and then there was the kid's kid, too, come to visit—me—running after him even out of doors, breaking the peace.

To lose a wife and regain a sister + husband + ... is to multiply the loss.

Uncle Balt had apparently resolved to grouse only in areas where there was no real room or reason for it; in that way his crabbing would be like a standing joke, and my grandparents could never argue ingratitude, or complain of his complaining themselves; and in fact it might have been a shy man's thank you, an inverted acknowledgement, the tease's praise; for he would insist a row be hoed only when it had been; a bed be made only when a dime danced on the coverlet; that food be prepared only when the sideboard sagged from bowls and platters of it; that a room be cleaned after the floors were carefully swept; but **by god** and nevertheless, his actions insisted, I have much to complain of, and complain I shall; I have violated rights; I have onerous duties; I shall not niggle or nag about it; I shall give orders even though my orders are empty; I shall rail and rage; I shall shout. I want you a hollarsworth away, these shouts said.

So he held them at bay; he remained remote, out on his own, with a lunch he would pack at breakfast in a pail, when he didn't drive off with a couple of the hands he hired on to harvest because they were working the north and the north was near town. Then he ate pancakes and drank whiskey in a big booth and bar so dark you couldn't see the sunrise, the new men grinning because Uncle Balt had insisted I take a taste, and I'd stuck the tip of my tongue into the shot glass as if it were a snake's mouth, making the expected face. I'd been taken along because—what the hell—he'd be working with these other men anyway, so there'd be no solitude to shatter, pleasure to spoil. Why not, if the kid wants to come. But I now know it was because the storm's blam had blown my mother's wits away, it seemed, and she was being taken off to a hospital somewhere in that road-rulered emptiness . . . to a bed by a cornstalk was how I saw it.

Strange he should drink the day they argued the drunk up out of his house; and she never did darken his door again, as they say, because that wind put a period to our visit. I was stood in a corner with some cousins for a while, so we never did return to the farm, though I saw Uncle Balt now and then at various family get-togethers . . . that is, always—though alone—alone with relations; dragged there by what compunctions I can't imagine; still protected by his formulas WE ARE BEIN SMOTHERED BY A HAY-LOAD OF SKIRT SKITTER! HOW CAN A MAN REMAIN SANE WITH ALL THIS GABBLE AND GEESE HISS GOIN ON AROUND him like a fence, silent inside his shouts as a cyclone. EVER SEE THE WAY IT COMES OUT OF A TRAIN? LIKE LIVIN IN LIVE STEAM!

I wondered how he would get to granny with my mother gone, since he had always addressed himself either to me or Margaret, never said his sister's name to my knowledge, left granddad strictly alone as if he didn't exist, which was almost the case; so with just the three of them what would he do? call out to the weeded rows directly, yell at the tidy rooms and clean bare halls? He didn't refer to my father either, but the circumstances of my father's life had turned him into a tight coil of fury and frustration, and who wants to stir up a snake? Uncle Balt hollared MARGARET instead, and spoke to her as if she were a crowd. The wind had torn her name in two like a ticket. There was glass in the pocket of her blouse and her·lashes glittered.

The dust ruined him, the hoppers grazed him to the ground, the hail threshed him flat, and finally my grandparents left to find work with some corn flake company in Minneapolis—the both of them— in an office full of hum and florescence. It was rumored that granny was a char. The farm became as isolated as my uncle then. Even the dirt died. And the deep life inside him, what did it do when the wind blew across him: hooo like an owl?

Anyhow, Uncle Balt has yielded me a metaphor for Being, makeshift maybe, but an image in the form of a tall dark column of damp air, hole going nowhere—yes—wind across the mouth of a bottle. At dawn, dusk and dinner—about as often as the barnyard cat—that's when I saw him. He really was a man shaped of absence, and must have made love, when he had to, by continued and fervent uncoupling. One saw he had the intangible integrity of a hollow, a well's heavy wet deficiencies. Yet at ten, that morning hour of my life, what could I have seen but the exotic: his shoelace moustache, his great gruff voice, that stern amused glare in his knuckled face, those giant strides which took him, always, away. Did he think he was an early pioneer, and hadn't he realized how the settlers were imprisoned in space, crowded together in sod huts, rude shacks, as though on rafts, the hostile ocean everywhere?

Naturally, no well can exist apart from the firm walls which round it—stones wedged in place like city neighbors—nor those walls without their usual moss and mildew, either, their ancient echoes, small frogs; so I suppose we were necessary too, otherwise Uncle Balt would simply have been at work in the fields, not in flight from his family; and I feel sure that, while his muscles were lost in their labor, his consciousness considered us and how we hemmed him like a hankie; because his crabbing had calculation; it was composed like a headline; it even somewhat artfully alliterated; it had a little of the ringmaster's rodo-montade (I have had,

myself, to take some thought about the capitalized recomposition
of his complaints); so of course it couldn't exist, I'm compelled to
think: such independence, such isolation, such chosen loneliness,
such transcendence; but imagine emptiness uprooted, air rising
like drawn water, a desperate turning as one beset by many
enemies might turn and whirl in self-defense—a furious energy,
then, containing a calm and silent center . . . from nothing,
nothing coming like the climax of an ardent woman.

Uncle Balt desired the impossible, all right. He wanted to live
like a mountain man on his endlessly level plain, as out of place in
his hopes as a Mongolian. Later on in my life I would come to
understand the difference between a term and a relation. Uncle
Balt was a term.

To have her hair combed, my mother sat on a chair in the middle
of newspapers the way mine was placed when mine was cut. A faint
smile had been bled on her face (by granny, I suspect), but it was
Uncle Balt, to my surprise, who was drawing the comb carefully
toward him, the glass accumulating in the tines like the finest sand.
It wouldn't be long before dust would invest him too, coat the
whole house—land, crops, grass—as though the sky had exploded.
In her last years my mother would powder her face, lay pallor upon
pallor until it was as white as it looked then, a character in Ka-
buki . . . ah, there I go. Upon my mother's face that day he placed
his wide and knobbled hand to steady her head while he pulled the
comb one final time through her already thinning hair, and I half
expected his palm to come away white as if it had been put down in
a patch of paint.

Uncle Balt used to disappear after dinner, but occasionally he'd
dawdle in the garden or go to the barn for something before
walking off toward the applause of the wheat as he usually did, and
I would sort of hover; but I never saw him do anything really
interesting, maybe cut from his plug a thin slice of tobacco to slip
in his mouth, which he certainly wasn't supposed to do (filthy
habit, granny said, let the hoppers spit if they must, it sits well
with their needs and nature); and that also might be why he held a
napkin in front of his face at table: either the stains showed on his
false teeth, or he felt guilty now when he chewed anything at all.

What else?

Once, while I was hiding in the barn loft from the Secret Agents
of the Underworld, or some similarly diabolical enemy, Uncle Balt

came in and carefully selected a burlap bag from a stack he had collected; but what was odd, and it was the only thing, was the loud monotonous hum I heard.

There's nothing to be made of it, really. I might have wondered whether, out of the depths of the man there rose from time to time the sound of a soul singing . . . but oh boy there I go . . .

Yesterday, before the rain arrived, the wind began to rattle furiously through the cornfield. I could hear it in my study like hundreds of snapping flags. Out there, in that world—that life— one stalk, like the one I had imagined standing by my mother's bed, counts for nothing, only in the mass is it fruitful, and the dust, only in clouds containing trillions is it murderous and terrifying; ants, bees, baboons, live in families for similar reasons; and I remembered, upon hearing that jingonizing sound, how Uncle Balt, pulling the silk down to examine the quality of kernel his corn bore, had stood inside the field like a Self . . . or so it seems to me now in my search for a symbol, some sense for my silly situation: SEEKS SOME SENSE IN HIS SILLY SITUATION, yes, good god.

Let the hoppers spit if they must, granny had insisted, they masticate enough, it sits well with their needs and nature. It sounded to me as though a terrible thing had been said. At ten, I don't think I had ever encountered the word, *masticate*, before, so I was surprised to hear that sentence coming from grandmother with the force and intent of a judgment, for it *was* a judgment. Whatever it meant.

Suddenly I see a dab of warm brown juice in one corner of Uncle Balt's mouth as if tucked in there and the tip of something larger the way the wheat and oat heads poked out of the little pockets of his overalls.

My mother sat up stiffly enough through the combing although she looked faint and her red smile didn't move. Then she went slowly up the stairs on my Uncle's arm with scarcely a glance at its boarded window.

In my memory, Uncle Balt has a stern straight look but no eyes. It is also—I mean my shallow memory—unfamiliar with the thickness of his hair or how, if at all, it was "styled." (How distant that fashionable word is from any history of his life.) What else? His shoes were high and black and laced by means of cleats. You might think you were tying up a ship. White cotton socks oozed out of his shoetops like soda foam. You might think, in such a sandy soil, the past would be easy to dig up. Well, Uncle Balt was a loud tall bitterly beknuckled farming man whose head struck with force when he spat. I distinctly see his spittle darkening the dust in long loose streaks like glacial lakes on maps. Then there was that little bob like a bob of a duck which may have meant "yup." The longjohns he wore were always only somewhat soiled. And now he's gone. I'm half, and the past half of me remembers him. His hands were huge and emerged from the ends of his arms broad as brooms. He wore no rings, no watch, and so no chain, no fob, no jewelry or charms, unless you counted his moustache, which he did say once was made of nose hair and ear wax. One of the cats had had kittens and Uncle Balt said he was taking them to a neighboring farm where they could lead a fine and useful barnyard life. My mother put her hand on my head/neck/back—tip, tip, tap—lightly like a benediction, sanding my skin with glass. She had come down the stairs as if balancing her body on the end of its nose, and I had scooted from beneath the table, reddening my knees on the rough nap of the rug, to cling to her legs for dear life—hers or mine, I'm not sure. It was like clutching a curtain. In the rug were woven ancient vases done in ivory. Ten is a lowered eye, base age.

Shortly Uncle Balt was yelling: EVER HEAR OF WORK, YOUNGSTER? He spelled it. W O R K, A STRANGER. WANT TO GET ACQUAINTED WITH IT? LOSE OUT ON ALL THE LADYDAHIN AND THE LOCAL TOAST SOAK THOUGH, IF YOU DO.

I wanted to lose out. I wanted to lift myself from my red knees and float from that place like the wind itself had—disappear as thin air. I agreed by jumping up and down—how like a puppy—and so the following morning I had to lower my face and put my tongue down in that poison that was killing my mother, tasting it, making the expected face, amusing those men, the sun not yet up in the bar. Then we rode out on ruts to where the tractor and combine had been left like pieces of junk. The water in the water jars was warm; the sandwiches were gray and dry; the morning sun had stopped to talk with the wimmin and seemed never to reach noon; the smell of wheat was everywhere in the warm wind; and Uncle Balt went comfortably on through the day behind the roar of the machines.

Gin probably made my mother's head hum too. Certainly the world loosened its grip, fluttered a bit. I know that much now. But at ten the glass was like dry particles of some former creature sifting down my back, the rug rougher than a towel, her legs like an arm sleeping under a pillow, those urns the pale shape of the visible world.

And when I felt all there was was the blood bunched up and beating in my belly, wasn't I right?

I do keep wondering whether it was the same for my mother as for Uncle Balt—that withdrawal—and whether mine is like either of theirs. I am more than distant from those days. I am distance itself. The advantage of gin is that it looks like water. I stand alone on an empty page like a period put down in a snowfall. They coat Christmas tree ornaments with glitter like that which fell upon my mother. Well, where is the love that does not make more trouble, Rilke once wrote to a friend; and I am reminded of the unfriendly gift at Easter of a rabbit I couldn't care for or bear to destroy, and how it left its droppings nervously along the baseboards and behind chairs; because I understand Rilke: love is an act of acquisition—a takeover bid—and Uncle Balt didn't wish to be acquired—not by his sister or relations, not by kittens crawling over my legs and lap, not by social duties, not by his fields or any element of nature. In a trap, he was ready to chew off a limb. I wonder whether my mother saved what little life she had by driving herself through a fog of drink toward that eventual rebirth in oblivion, or whether it was life itself, her own soft soul, passive as a pudding, she wished release from. The latter is the usual hypothesis. It is the hypothesis of society. I quote a poet against it, but I should not put a poet between us. Or tendentious philosophical concepts. Or schemes out of history. My mother, father, Uncle Balt: first I must understand them, before I can understand them; and the difficulty is that I only want to understand myself, which is what I do when I interpose the poet like a napkin between you— that is, them—their lives—you, yes—and my mind's mouth.

But Uncle Balt got his wish. He lived his death in solitude, without having to suffer the mercies of the church, or the solicitude of the moist eye, the spooks who gather about your bed to tell jokes as long as their faces: soon you will have no desires they can deny; soon the servant in you will have carried out their last request; there will be one less to pain or complain of—how it saddens them;

and even my father thought he felt bad when my mother died, in her asylum, in solitude too, her blood leaking back into her body through her throat.

But Uncle Balt got his wish. I have a picture of him there on that lonely farm, the sky like soil, dirty with one disaster after another, yelling at the elements, maybe; for by now the world must have become a woman for him, nibbling away at his life, bossing his mouth, wearing the paint from his house, thinning his skin, darkening everything by degrees with dust—boy am I in for it— and the hail like bullets falling into those applauding bodies, crops grazed to the ground, a stubble of life the wind will shave.

Surely he must have realized in those final years that his wish had been granted ironically, as so many are in fairy tales, for now he was alone with the grandparents of us everywhere; because when the early myths described creation didn't they suggest a mating of the earth and sky? and what better image of that copulation is there than the funnel of wood and straw and dust the tornado's excited suction shapes: a column according to its outer edges, the classic figure of the phallus; then vaginal on its inner rims, in its windings, hollows, shell-like lips?

Kids from the Conservation Corp, I gather, discovered him. He fell climbing over a fence, they said. The wind blew a bed of dust around him. He'd snapped a leg and consequently fainted. That is their conjecture. Who knows how strong he was by then; how well he'd slept or eaten; or even if he had been faithful to the fields in his former fashion, without the need to rush away from granny's house—as it then had become—in anxiety, disgust, or anger? Disgust. Maybe that's why he ate with a napkin like a loincloth covering his mouth. Slowly silted up the way sand buries a beach, he'd been in his grave near a month when the boys dug him up. He hadn't ripened much. He and his world were eternal as Egypt. Until they found him, I'm willing to bet, his hair had blown lazily about like those heads of oat and wheat he'd picked to check the progress of the crop.

Even then, though, with Uncle Balt's body returning to the dust in the most appropriate Biblical way, wasn't that enormous voice of his perhaps composing a final cry of help at having fallen? wasn't it still far away inside him like something planted—a seed of sound— and might it not break out one day when an innocent spade turns a clod like a cork? to pop forth at the end of that word he was completing?

GARET!

Well, there I go.

I had put the kittens in the center of a spread of papers, but the papers had been scarcely peed on when Uncle Balt carried the kittens away. He was swift, almost deft, about it. I was farmed out with cousins who were quite congenial. That summer didn't end so badly, and my mother came around . . . part way.

At ten, what can one be expected to see, or seize upon, or comprehend? And at my present age and anger, what can I unreservedly remember or deservedly forgive? At ten, though I might have found him odd, I bet a buck I thought that Uncle Knuckle was a lot of fun.

THE REEDBEDS OF THE HACKENSACK

by AMY CLAMPITT

from THE KENYON REVIEW

nominated by Seamus Heaney, William Pitt Root, Grace Schulman and Philip Schultz

Scummed maunderings that nothing loves but reeds,
Phragmites, neighbors of the greeny asphodel
that thrive among the windings of the Hackensack,
collaborating to subvert the altogether ugly
if too down-to-earth to be quite fraudulent:
what's landfill but the backside of civility?

Dreckpot, the Styx and Malebolge of civility,
brushed by the fingering plumes of beds of reeds:
Manhattan's moat of stinks, the rancid asphodel
aspiring from the gradually choking Hackensack,
ring-ditch inferior to the vulgar, the snugly ugly,
knows-no-better, fake but not quite fraudulent:

what's scandal but the candor of the fraudulent?
Miming the burnish of a manicured civility,
the fluent purplings of uncultivated reeds,
ex post cliché survivors like the asphodel,
drink as they did the Mincius, the Hackensack
in absent-minded benediction on the merely ugly.

Is there a poetry of the incorrigibly ugly,
free of all furbishings that mark it fraudulent?
When toxins of an up-against-the-wall civility
have leached away the last patina of these reeds,
and promised landfill, with its lethal asphodel
of fumes, blooms the slow dying of the Hackensack,

shall I compare thee, Mincius, to the Hackensack?
Now Italy knows how to make its rivers ugly,
must, ergo, all such linkages be fraudulent,
gilding the laureate hearse of a defunct civility?
Smooth-sliding Mincius, crowned with vocal reeds,
coevals of that greeny local weed the asphodel,

that actual, unlettered entity the asphodel,
may I, among the channels of the Hackensack—
those Edens-in-the-works of the irrevocably ugly,
where any mourning would of course be fraudulent—
invoke the scrannel ruth of a forsooth civility,
the rathe, the deathbed generations of these reeds?

DREAM VISION

by RAYMOND OLIVER

from THREEPENNY REVIEW

nominated by Thom Gunn and Gary Soto

If I could open only one of those days—
December 6, 1160, Oxford?—
Locked in the Mind where all our story stays,
What would I find? A high medieval quaintness?
Tall men at altars, mantled, stony-faced,
As in Autun's façade? Or men with eyes
Like goggles, limbs at funny angles, braced
To hurl their wavy spears, as at Bayeaux,
In linen? Parchment peasants from the books,
In skirts and puttees, tending tiny sheep,
Gesturing statically with bishop's-crooks?

I see a snow-filled wood, not, as in Frost,
Lovely, but rough, indifferent, like Montana,
Part of the total frozen forest crossed
Only by fragile trails from far-off hamlets
To towns like Oxford there: no dreaming spires
But tufts of cottage smoke in the early distance.
And here a clearing, where the morning fires
Reek of mere wood for heat, not roasting boar.
And from a thatched and earthy A-frame shack
A man comes forth, just for a moment pausing,
Smiling; in words like Dutch he hollers back
To make a woman laugh. I recognize him.

THE DESIRE AND PURSUIT OF THE PART

by HENRI COULETTE

from THE IOWA REVIEW

nominated by Michael S. Harper

I.

Do you feel yourself somehow one
With the mute and russet leaf
And the smoke thereof? Do you?

Back off, then, back off.
Everything here is all but nothing,
And nothing here belongs to you:

Not the rain-gray eye rolling,
Nor the lewd lip canted
(No, none, November),

Not the old men blowing in their hands,
Their feet shuffling,
The axe in the stump,

Nor this one, nor that one,
For the only one is the one before two,
Though the wind says O, says one, says ever.

II.

We motored for some nine hours through the countryside,
Having at least four flats in that time, perhaps five.
The radiator boiled over again and again.

We saw no one on the way. No one at all.
That didn't seem strange in the beginning;
A custom of the country, we thought, to stay hidden.

That was, of course, to ignore our experience
In the capital, where we had been beseiged
By peddlers with every sort of gee-gaw.

Our eyes, though, were fixed, I would hazard,
Too intently upon the subtle shift and shade
Of leaf out of which at any moment, so it seemed,

Butterflies and scorpions might flutter and shudder.
We had read about these matters and others of such like
In Professor Baldassaro Bandini's definitive text.

The road was hardly a road at all. We leaned forward,
Peering through our isinglass goggles, willing
The road to be there, imagining that it was.

Our tempers became short: expletives, interrupted sentences.
Tom's knuckles were white on the steering wheel;
Ned's nails picked at the leather of the map case.

The maps that case contained are of no use to us now
Stalled here in this small clearing up to our hub-caps
In the mud—they stir on the ground like old newspapers.

Tom has wandered off. Ned has gone to look for him.
Is there something going on between them? Something
Unvoiced or never voiced in my presence?

The sky is metallic, shimmering, copper in color.
Water drips from the great fronds. The brass headlamps
Have turned green, and the flying ants are eating the tires.

III.

The whole is not
Implicit in the part.

The part is simply
A part, *a* division,

As in the parting
Of waves, the parting of hair.

Afraid of the crab
In my gut, and the claw there,

Afraid of the spider
In my head, and the web spun,

Afraid, afraid . . .
I get up, cold on the cold

Linoleum,
And make coffee. Jerome

—O glove of light!—
Camels his back, purring.

Miss Coots, the color
Of bone, the color of vein,

Stoops, stiff-kneed,
To her November garden.

It is enough,
Enough for the time being.

AGE

fiction by JANET DESAULNIERS

from PLOUGHSHARES

nominated by Gordon Lish

LAST NIGHT I was seduced. "Lord," you must think, "this I've heard before." But then I could be wrong. I constantly overestimate my powers of intuition. Some days I walk to my store, my small shoebox of a bookshop, and feel the women near the bus stop stare at my balding head, my cracked shoes wound with electrical tape. I turn to face them and say, "It's not so bad." They look confused and I wonder: Were they really looking at me. Were they interested at all, or were they looking past me, to a store window, perhaps at a new pocketbook or spring coat. What do you think? I think you may not be interested in the seduction of a sixty-three year old man, that you may view the seduction of a man past his prime, past ambition, past desire's tap on the shoulder, as a shade perverse, slightly off the scheme of things.

You may be nowhere near sixty-three. Perhaps you are young—your body and mind firm and uncreased. Perhaps you think of seduction in terms of young men and women who move in and out of doorways as if always following some distant strain of music. If so, some day I think you'll find, as I did, those people have only a small role in the final order of things. Not that I don't appreciate them. Not that I don't see their long legs, their faces turned up and open—almost pious in their ease. I see, God, I see. But they are a diversion—bestseller fiction before bedtime. At sixty-three, you will be able to think of at least five things more important. I can: good wine, quiet sleep, easy digestion, less pain, something *new*.

Or perhaps you are older than sixty-three. Perhaps you think of seduction as that one bright glint in a shadowy past—the red scooter when you were nine, or the face of your wife the first morning she touched your arm as you rose from bed, the first time

404

she took *you*—the trembling in your hands and knees. I take your hand in mine. To you, I offer comfort. To you, I say it can happen again.

I wonder if you believe me. I am balding, overweight, and alone. My body hangs from my shoulders like a coat that has lost its shape, its definition. From around my bald spot, my hair grows wild and unstyled. Often I don't comb it. I think, Why should I. I am poor—too poor for cars and clothes and casual drinks. My drinks, when I can afford them, are serious, meaningful. I wash my gray undershirts and socks in the bathtub and hang them to dry over my furniture. I read. That's all. I sit in my tiny, failing bookshop. I hear it sigh, give up and fail all around me, and I read. Otherwise, I do nothing. C.S. Lewis understood the dangers of nothing. He wrote: "Nothing is very strong: strong enough to steal away a man's best years not in sweet sin but in a dreary flickering of the mind over it knows not what and knows not why." C.S. Lewis is right more often than I am. Still, nothing is what I do most days. Like my shop, I gave up. I gave in. I sit quietly inside myself like a motionless pond. But this is important. This is what I'm trying to say: I am all these things, but last night I danced.

I suppose I should tell about the woman. I am impatient with the way this is going. The woman is not the most important thing. There are the places, the days, even the people who remind me of her—all scattered about in a shambles of significance. The woman is at the center, but alone, isolated, she'll look small, maybe ridiculous. Finally, though, she saved me—a save as clean and final and close to the heart of matters as any surgeon's stitch.

Lily is twenty-four. Perhaps I've been too abrupt. I can imagine the young people nodding and the old folks shaking their heads. But Lily is twenty-four, and though I'm hesitant to mention this now, she is also lovely though she's too thin like all the rest of the young ones. Women have lost respect for hips and breasts these days. I'm sure I'll suffer for saying that, but I don't understand. I have always envied women, praised them. Women are balanced, fluid, as if always something about them is in motion. Men are hard, clumsy, unyielding. Women can take men inside them. They can feel men grow inside them and feel themselves grow around the men.

A poet wrote those last two lines—a young poet with small

chapped hands who rented the room above my bookshop for two years and left his poems as a final payment of sorts. The sound of his typewriter came down to me through the vent over my cash register in fits and starts, like an animal fretting over a wound. He wrote only about women. Afternoons, when the lunch hour browsers abandoned me and the sun came through the front window to draw harsh edges around the clutter and the quiet, I imagined him up there, barechested in the heat, crossing his ankles and rocking in his chair, transfixed by the implications of his own words. He knew women though. In his poems, he knew them as I think they might choose to be known—tender and complex, opening slowly, over time, the way a small bud unfolds and unfolds until finally, it overwhelms. That young poet knew women's power; he held it in his mind, examined it. The sad part, the tragic part, is that all this was only on paper. Standing next to a real woman, he unraveled. I wanted to reach out and quiet his shoulders. He blinked, stammered, and the fear moved up in lines around his eyes. But on paper he found solace. There he could study women closely, impose an order upon them he could believe in, and though none of that order was real, none of it workable, its beauty was relentless and blinding. Finally, even I believed. It was a quiet, personal deception—one that caused my first disagreement with Plato, who argued that poets and painters should be denied a place in the City of the Good. I would save that young poet a place if it were my city. But I digress. The poet and what his poems did are a seduction of another kind.

Lily. Lily is a woman—a young one, thin and long-legged, with great eyes and a full but serious mouth. Her hair is long and auburn. She thinks she might cut it when she turns twenty-five. I hope she doesn't; you would, too, if you saw it. Its shine is like a mahogany cabinet. Everything about Lily wants to believe it's tough, unaffected—sensible sandals, no jewelry, never a pocketbook or a hat or a handkerchief, not even an umbrella on drizzly days. She says things like, "Hey. Howya doin'."—but softly, hesitating, as though the gangly familiarity is a ruse she hasn't fully accepted, and in her face there is something distant, quizzical, even sweet. When she stands among the stacks in my shop, I sometimes think if I reached out to touch her, she'd suddenly be gone. Her mouth is always open just a bit, and her eyes are always wide, as if she is standing just outside herself, viewing herself and her small life as a very interested, perhaps awestruck, spectator. She likes books (how else would we have met), mainly fiction, mainly contemporary, and works evenings as a waitress on the Square.

The Square brought Lily and me together. We both hate it—though she works in it and my bookshop leans against it like a poorly dressed cousin. I don't know quite how to describe the Square with fairness. It is a thorn in my side, a raucous painful reminder of the way things are, but it is important—the backdrop against which I've lived out my silly life. When I bought my bookshop in 1950, before the collapse of city neighborhoods, the buildings on the Square housed an upholstery shop, a bakery, a beauty salon, a tobacconist, a market, a movie house and a drugstore that doubled as neighborhood meeting place for the idle and garrulous. Now those same buildings accommodate clothing stores for the very young and very chic and countless bars and restaurants all bursting with overgrown ferns, brass fixtures and tinted glass. Lily works in a restaurant called the Soup Kitchen decorated in (it embarrasses me to say this) a Depression motif with blown up photographs of bread lines and Apple Annies and cold, hungry looking children. A bowl of split pea soup costs $3.95 there.

Sometimes I think I should have left the Square when I had the chance. During the Sixties, a group of young people pooled their tuition money and bought a few of the storefronts that had been abandoned in the rush to the suburbs. They worked hard—refinishing the doors and wood all around the windows, planting small gardens of herbs and flowers in the sooty dirt of the back alley. Sometimes, at dusk, when the cars and buses moved away from the city, when it seemed everyone was leaving, I would sit and have tea with the women who ran the sandwich shop. I liked those people. They were, for a time, fully young and fully earnest. One of them, a carpenter, helped me build new shelves for the north wall. Each morning, he'd arrive with his tools under one arm and his baby daughter under the other. Her name was Star, and she was a fat, good baby; her father used to say she was a baby of character. Mornings she'd sleep through the noise in a crate I'd used to store old magazines, and afternoons she'd sit up eating bananas and watching the door. It thrilled her to hear the bell over the door ring. Even then, my customers were few and far between, but Star was patient, and when one finally did come in, she'd laugh at him and laugh at us and then raise her banana in a kind of cheery salute. By the end of the first day of work, Star and her father and I were friends. When we finished the shelves, I gave them twenty dollars and they gave me a beret. I wore it every day. I let my hair grow. It had just reached the middle of my back when a developer decided he liked the site and offered to buy all of us out. I tried to convince the others to stay, but they had plans—a commune in Vermont, farmland in Arkansas. The carpenter asked me to join him, but I couldn't. This was the only place I knew. All right, I'll say it, I was afraid. I kissed Star goodbye and stayed. For months, I watched the renovation, and sometimes, even with a customer in the shop, I wept at my window.

Now I sit with a picture window view of the way things are. Lily agrees that people have changed less than I thought. I have changed more. The old drugstore came down last week. Late-night bar trade requires more parking than you can believe.

I did not mean to strike so bleak a note. As I tell women I imagine to be watching me in the street: It's not so bad. Lily. Lily waits tables in a tight jersey floor-length dress. It is a silly dress—meant to be sexy and demure at the same time. Lily knows this, but she wears the dress constantly, marketing and running errands in it before and after work. When I mention it, she holds the dress away from her hips as if it were diseased. "I sold out," she says. "Why should I try to hide it." Lily means she makes more money waiting tables four nights a week than I have made in any one week of my thirty-one years of bookselling.

Lily always seems to be caught up in some emotion. This is the part about her that angers me, frustrates me, and yes, even summons up desire. Some of you may think desire after sixty must be something like an echo trapped in a deep cave, but I tell you, if it is an echo at all, it is one that knows no logic, one that has lost its trajectory, its mathematical predictability. I hear it reverberate crazily, bouncing out of nowhere off the wall over my shoulder as I walk home at night, throwing itself up in front of me, randomly, in the shape of a simple dress in the window of Three Sisters or in the color of ripe oranges. Lily knows a similar kind of desire, but one less random, more pervasive. Always Lily seems to be longing for something—better cheekbones, a new job, wisdom, spontaneity.

In someone so young, such silliness is both maddening and charming. A young face touched with longing lights up; so does an old face, I suppose, but you must admit a lost look in young eyes is more appropriate, somehow prettier.

The problem is Lily tries to think about these emotions. Like the poet, she tries to order them, give one precedence over another. She is ill at ease with her longings. When she comes to me to talk about them, to think them out, I watch her grow heavy and careful right in front of me. I watch her pull her arms in, close secret doors, grow old. It angers me. She thinks about her longings so much that finally, before she has decided what to do about them, they pass. I can't help it—when this happens, I have to give her advice. I lean back in my chair until it squeaks, I put one hand on each knee, and then I tell her what to do. She never does it, but I think she believes I never notice that. I used to justify all this by telling myself she was saving all my advice, hoarding it in expectation of the one time she would really need it, and now I know she was.

A few weeks ago, Lily came into my shop with a decision that had to be made. Lily lightens my shop the way Star and her bananas used to. Without them, the shop is simply dark and quiet, and the only way I know to characterize it is to say that I lost control of the clutter years ago. The aisles are narrowing, and some have simply disappeared. I haven't been able to get through to the shelving against the back wall for at least two years. I've forgotten what's back there. But the shop just seems to recede and make room when Lily comes in. She sidles through the stacks and crawls over boxes and stands on crates, all the while crooking her neck so she can read titles. Every so often she'll call out an author she doesn't recognize and ask if she should read him. I pretend to think a moment but always say yes, and then she stands there, holding the book in her hand as if she's weighing it, before she puts it back and says, "I'll remember that."

The day of her decision she leaned against my counter and poked through a box of paperbacks I'd bought from a college kid that day. She said, "I waited on the director of that new dance company tonight. He said I should join. He said they have classes for beginners." I said, "Dance, Lily, you should," and thought of her in tights and leotard. I didn't tell her I thought that. Lily always catches me when I say things women don't like to hear anymore. I know she wouldn't like what I said about hips and breasts.

"I don't know though." She walked to the window and stared out into the street. "It's too late for me to be good. I'm already too old, and I never dance—not even socially. That sounds foolish, doesn't it. Social dancing. Maybe it's all foolish. Frivolous."

I had to interrupt her here. I mean, I thought of Martha Graham and Isadora Duncan.

"Lily, dance is movement," I said. "Movement is life. Everyone should move. Lord, Lily, Aquinas even defines God as the prime mover."

She turned from the window and looked at me.

"He does?"

"Yes."

"I don't know though—if I could do it."

"And you're not too old."

"Maybe. Not really, I guess. I don't know."

She walked around the shop, trailing her hand along the shelves and sometimes stopping to pat the spines of a row of books as if they were all lovely children. Lily punctuates all our conversation with wandering. Often she disappears behind the shelves for long periods. I can't see her. I can only hear her voice. That day she went behind the religion shelf. I think she was looking for Aquinas. Her voice floated out to me.

"But I was going to take that course in literature you told me about. I mean, I don't know a thing about books. I probably haven't read one-fifth of all the great ones."

"Maybe not even one-twentieth."

"See."

I think she was back in the corner when she said that. I began to get angry. I wanted her out in the open. I liked her to look at me when I gave her advice. I raised my voice and my chin, as if searching for her in a crowd.

"Then do it," I said. "Study literature. Go to the university and read the other four-fifths of all great books in the world."

"Maybe I will." She raised her voice to match mine. "I just might."

"Do it," I said and stopped looking for her. "Go."

She was silent for a time, long enough to have read a few pages.

The store was quiet without her voice, quiet the way it is in the afternoon—an oppressive quiet that seems to move in like heat and hover in the six inches of space between my tallest shelves and the ceiling. The quiet made me think of the poet and miss him. I even missed Lily. I knew she wasn't reading. I knew she was back behind a shelf imaging herself as someone else, as someone who had read all five-fifths of the great books in the world, perhaps as someone who said things like, "God is the prime mover."

"Lily."

"What."

"Why don't you just do both?"

"Oh—money."

"Money? You make lots of money. Enough for you and two more like you."

"I'm saving it."

I craned my neck and saw her peeking inside an old armoire I use to store books I want to read before I die.

"What are you saving for? What could you need?"

"I don't know. Something might come up."

"Lily, nothing is ever going to come up. Nothing ever comes up. You know what you should do with that money? I'm serious now. Are you listening?"

"Yes."

"Buy a little red sportscar, Lily. A convertible. Then find a young good man. Lord, buy one of those, too. You can buy anything these days. Then drive around, Lily. Drive around fast until you feel like dancing. Then do that. Dance. That's what you should do, Lily. That's what you should do with your money."

She poked her head from behind a shelf directly in front of me. She surprised me. I could never keep track of her when she was in the shop.

"Are you making fun of me?"

I didn't answer because I wasn't sure. I looked down into a box of books I'd traded for that week—criticism from the twenties. They'd never sell. Lily was out from behind the shelf and in front of me before I could look up.

"What would you do?" she said. Her voice trembled a little. "Would you drive around town, whistle at people and let your hair blow behind you in some silly damn car?"

"Lily, I'd do some silly damn thing."

I was tired of both of us when I said that, and I know I shouldn't have said it. Lily and I had a pact of sorts. You don't accuse someone of doing nothing when you have a pact. So I can't blame Lily for whispering, "You would not. You would not," and walking out the door. I do wish I could blame someone for the way the door closed behind her—quietly, slowly, like the end of some sad story. Even with the melodrama, it frightened me.

For ten days, she was gone; it rained for seven of them. People walked by under newspapers, plastic head scarfs and low, heavy clouds. I missed her. Lord, I read with one eye always on the door. Late last night after closing, she came back. I was reading behind the counter, and though I knew from the knock who it was, I walked to the door slowly. I composed my face. She stood there in her silly dress, swaying. She was out of breath and looked cold. Her face and dress seemed drawn, pulled tight against her, as if she had been running from something that stood right outside the door.

"Are you all right?" I said.

"I've been drinking. I'm cold."

She came into the shop, and I moved behind my counter to my chair, settling in like a judge.

"So what's the problem?" I said.

She looked at me hard until I felt a touch of foolishness at the way I sat, the way I crossed my arms on my chest. Then she said, "I think we should take your advice tonight."

"What advice?"

"I think we should go dancing."

How can I say what I felt when she said that. I was sixty-three years old, and hadn't danced, hadn't thought of it, in over thirty years. I leaned back in my chair, and for once, the squeak startled me. I was cold, and tense, as though some intruder were standing over me, armed with a weapon against which I had no choice. But I could feel the chair against my back. I was in my own shop. I told myself I was safe.

"No, Lily," I said, smiling and shaking my head. "I don't think we should."

"I do. Really."

She was still swaying, but her eyes were firm. I said, "Lily, sit down," but she didn't sit down. She put her hands on the counter

and leaned over until her face was just inches from mine. For a
moment, I thought she might kiss me. I was confused. I wanted
her to. Instead, she looked into my eyes—a long unflinching look,
a look that made me wonder what she saw there.

"I don't want to sit down," she said. "I think we should go
dancing. Tonight. I think you should lock up this store and walk
down the street with me. And I think we should go into that bar
under the blinking purple sign. We should dance."

She took my hand. Maybe that's why I followed her out the
door, or maybe I thought I could bolt down an alley, outrun her, or
maybe she just overwhelmed me, her face that close to mine. We
walked slowly down the street in a fine rain. Lily was looking
straight ahead, as if expecting to meet someone, and she looked
different than she had in the shop, moments before. She looked
frightened and young. I put my mouth next to her ear and said
quietly, "Come on, Lily. I'll walk you home." She raised her head,
and her face was like a child's face.

"When we go in, we'll walk straight to the dance floor, okay? We
won't stop or look around. We'll just walk straight up there. And
I'd like you to hold my hands when we dance."

What could I say? Lord, she was standing in the rain and
shivering. So we went into the bar under the blinking purple sign.
I felt the stares, but I looked only at Lily's dress, drenched and
dragging behind her like a tiny wake. We walked straight to the
dance floor. I took her cold hands and looked at her face. She
looked shy. The music was very loud. People all around us were
dancing. They looked like they were born to dance, bred to dance.
I thought of running again, and then I thought of standing very still
in hope that I might disappear the way a telephone pole or a street
sign can disappear in a landscape that is otherwise alive and in
motion. But Lily said, "We have to move." So we moved, clumsily,
drawing close for protection. I looked at my feet, concentrating
only on moving them back and forth with Lily's, trying to remember anything about dancing. Gradually, the back and forth shuffling became comfortable, or at least automatic. The crowd moved
in so close they didn't matter. I looked up to see Lily watching me,
her mouth open, in surprise, as if the moon had just sat down next
to her.

"We're dancing," she said.

Inside, I felt a delicate tug, the way healing aches when a scar forms, when the body makes peace with its wounds, and then I remembered something. I remembered it the way the blind must remember color or the way the dead must remember life—a memory rising strangely, all at once, like something buoyant moving up through water and exploding onto the surface. I raised my arm and, with it, Lily's hand, and I said to her, "Spin." She looked at me for a moment, and then she smiled and did it. She spun. At that moment, our lives cracked open and held out a small, very important opportunity. In the end, I did not seduce her and she did not seduce me, but something that lived in the very center of her and even of me, that breathed and moved, seduced us both.

🔥 🔥 🔥

BEING AND JUDAISM*

by OSCAR MANDEL

from THE GEORGIA REVIEW

nominated by THE GEORGIA REVIEW, *Herb Leibowitz, and Joyce Carol Oates*

AFTER WALLACE STEVENS:
"The imperfect is our paradise."

I too, undoubtedly, I too
I should have ventured to conceive
this world as turquoise, aware
but softly of the streak which marred
its blue primordial. Not marred,
not so (I too, I should have said):
that darker but still blue distress
enriched the stone's peculiar price,
for blue naively blue, the lake
untampered by its island,
glib blue would make orfèvres yawn,
I too, aware, I should have said.

But could this be? I came too late.
And yet I tried. My fingers held
that delicately irritated stone,
exquisite with sin, until
the symbol failed. "Am I," a Jewess
twelve years old inquired softly
of her elders and her betters,
"the discord that beguiles the song?"

*From a work in progress entitled "The Book of Elaborations," each chapter of which opens with a poem taken from the author's *Collected Lyrics and Epigrams* (Los Angeles: Whitmarsh, 1981).

She was the flimsiest among the dead
and stinking innocently in the ditch.
   A man had pushed that rod of his
between his legs between her legs.
Her skin slumped through her bones. She lay
in her own liquid filth licking
a piece of wood for succulence.
One morning she forgot her mother.
The winter froze two fingers off.
But milk and schoolsong recollections
kept her tough: she trusted God.
At last her turn she reached the ditch,
she knelt, was shot, fell blood to blood,
another elbow slapped across her neck.

I trembled safe across an ocean.
Behind the barbed roses of Connecticut
El Sereno boomed his "all is well."
I could not find, oh Stevens, syntax
for this child, no jewel adequate,
no shape of nature that would tally
or be wholesome (since through rock
and thorn and tiger, symbol-making man
can anodyne his grief). And ever
untranscended, pain stands by,
there is no exile into peace:
still on my lips that excrement
successors will digest to art
but I must suffer brute and fat,
clotting paradise out of my voice.

I accept the man who says, "I will not write of concentration camps; I will write only of lapis lazuli"; but I cannot accept the man who writes acceptingly of concentration camps. I hope I have done Wallace Stevens an injustice in my poem. Most of the time (if I read him right) he has nothing whatsoever to say about evil. This Yankee child of Théophile Gautier is a master of the sheerest sensory revels. America does not have a greater poet. He went wrong only in thinking of himself as a thinker—and here he reminds me, in his own way, of Robert Browning. Both are veritable Casaubons of Intellectual Poetry: the Victorian indefatigable in his wearisome Proof for the Existence of God, the New Englander dreary with his Function of the Imagination. Was it the Puritan in him that whispered, "It is not enough to sing

> The skreak and skritter of evening gone
> And grackles gone and sorrows of the sun;

a man without Concepts is a sinner"? So Stevens made a Concept, and the Concept made Stevens a bore. Once in a while, naturally, another little concept would sneak into a poem, and this is where I think, rightly or wrongly, that I have caught him delivering himself of a thought about human evil; and I do not like what I see.

In my own literary presumptions, I have more readily grappled with concepts of ultimate horror than with the concrete contemporary horrors themselves. I do not grasp these hard in my palm because they scorch me. Before turning extermination camps into poems or stories I would have to live with them and live in them long and deep, and this is something I could do only if I possessed a secret fund of indifference—"the imperfect is our paradise"—or, on the far other side, a Messianic conviction that Art is the necessary and the only redeemer of mankind. Since I do not possess either the fund or the conviction, I have by and large kept hands off, lest they blister without doing anyone any good. There are griefs too terrible for art.

Besides, I would feel ashamed. Shall I make an *objet d'art* out of Auschwitz? Shall I turn a connoisseur's appreciative eye on the corpses of my beautiful cousins, Stella shot while trying to escape from the death-train, Dita gassed to death with her mother—on them and all the others whose pitiful shapes you see in the photographs shuffling to their death in baggy clothes—on that Anne Frank whom I half-meant my poem to evoke—and cry, "Ah, here is something for my palette"—and weigh my words and my rhythms, and the breaks at the end of my lines, to find the most *satisfying* way of conveying the horror to you—and become, if I succeed, a famous writer?

You see what perplexes those of us who believe that, even though an artist may wear the garments of a prophet, missionary, philosopher, or legislator, a close look inevitably reveals, under a hem or inside a collar, a scrap of Harlequin's dubious patches. What? On Strindberg? On Kafka? On Beckett? Yes, on the gloomiest of them all.

I am no better as a reader or spectator, for I impenitently make a large swerve around "lacerating" works of art—motion pictures, plays, novels, perhaps even paintings. I do not want lacerations from Harlequin. Reality lacerates me quite enough, and I don't go begging the artist for more. I am speaking now of these "uncompromising" artifacts which only minimally perform the aesthetic operation Yeats mentions in his poem concerning shabby terrorists:

> All changed, changed utterly:
> A terrible beauty is born.

If I do approach *terrible* art, I do it on condition that the terror has been so far compromised by aesthetic constraints that I am comforted even while I am clawed. But this comfort—the comfort of all that is poetic about poetry—is a betrayal of reality. All tragic or terrible art that succeeds as art must in part enact this betrayal, since, willy-nilly, the success of a work of art turns upon the satisfaction, the pleasure it has given. Many Harlequins and most observers of Harlequins (I mean critics and aestheticians) ignore or oppose this decree of Fate, but the world itself speaks the last word, and removes *unpleasing* works of art from the roll. A mystifying dilemma results. You cannot give pleasure in a work of art whose subject is torture without betraying the truth of torture. And you cannot give torture truly without betraying art.

There is, however, no uniformity imposed on what is intolerable and for whom. I, for instance, happen to find several etchings from Goya's *Disasters of War* too horrible and need to avert my eyes. Picasso's *Guernica*, on the other hand, strikes me as very endurably grim. Stripped of its title, it might easily suggest a lunatic's nightmare and lead one's mind toward a Freudian couch rather than a mass grave. These are examples for me; you will have your own. I can endure ample infiltrations of pain into my pleasure before giving up; but in the end, at the extremity, I do give up. I do not read realistic novels concerning gas chambers, and I do not watch movies about concentration camps. As for arguing that doing so might make me a wiser or better man, might you not speculate instead that spectacles of brutality are insidiously brutalizing, even when moralized? If I had a child, I would rather have him hide in my lapels from a scene of brutality in a motion picture than nag me for a dollar to see it again.

To the extent that I myself have dealt with truths which lacerate me, I have clearly betrayed reality in the service of art. Consider lines like

> Behind the barbed roses of Connecticut
> El Sereno boomed his "all is well."

"Barbed roses"—set against the implicit barbed wire of the death camps—is a case of the purest and rankest aestheticism, designed (success or failure is another question) to delight the mind through intellectual and affective density. But observe, besides, that El Sereno is not only an allusion to that blithe mentality of Stevens which is in part the poem's concern, but also the Spanish word for a watchman. Here then is an exotic touch in Stevens' own manner, and here is the poet-watchman over mankind giving us reassurances. A "deeper" reading will bring out that your Sereno in Madrid is in fact far from reliable. Most ingenious. In the meantime the victim is rotting away in her ditch. I call this a moral scandal.

Both the pain and the moral scandal diminish as the event recedes and becomes history. Successors, says the poem, digest it to art. For the secret of tragic historical art is that the past hurts less than the present. Lucretian indifference works for distance in time even more efficiently than it does for distance in space. This is, in a way, a melancholy thought. Why should I not weep for the victims of Attila with the same brute-fresh tears I shed for Hitler's dead? On the other hand, it is a kindness of Nature to make us cruel; otherwise we would drown in tears, we could not suffer the accumulation of injustice and bloodshed over the ages. Think of those odious Aztecs at their mass murders for the sake of an imbecilic religion. Quaint images for a lovely poem, or a visit to a museum.

II.

It is easy to suppose that the nausea which overcomes me when I imagine the unfathomable scurrilities perpetrated by the Germans owes much to my "being" a Jew myself—and one who came near to taking up a small place in the ditch. But the massacres commanded by Stalin, or by Idi Amin, sicken me equally. Do you suppose I could write a novel, poem, or play imitating, in the manner of Zola, certain scenes we heard of in Uganda, where prison inmates were compelled to kill their fellows by hammering out their brains?

But I want to pause in front of this much-pondered business of "being" a Jew, and to explain the quotation marks I have been using. "To be" in all its permutations is a mischief-maker if ever words made mischief in the world. Surely permanence and impermanence are opposites, and surely opposites deserve different words, and yet we will blandly say, "He *is* angry" and "He *is* bald," as if no difference existed. The Spanish language is not so guilty as ours in this respect, for it offers its *es* and its *está* as approximate responses to this difference. We simply blunder along. Granted that it is useless to keep chiding language for its notorious deficiencies and delinquencies: language seems to have done its duty whenever it has almost done it. We must take up the cudgels, however, when its laziness becomes outrageous and dangerous; and outrage and danger are ever on duty when the issue is Judaism. What do we really mean when we say, "He *is* a Jew"? As soon as we put ourselves on the alert, we discover that some are interested in giving this *being* its meaning of permanence, and others its meaning of impermanence.

Thus in the first year of Israel's independence, the Knesset defined the Jew as follows: "Everyone who considers himself a Jew is a Jew." This was clearly the impermanent view of *to be*. One might be an X on Tuesday, a Jew on Wednesday, and an X again on Thursday. I do not know in what respect this definition bothered the Parliament, because it could have given trouble for opposite reasons: allowing anyone who wanted in to come in, and allowing anyone who wanted out to depart. One can see that either of these alternatives might have displeased. Whatever the reason, the Knesset redefined the Jew in 1978 as follows: "Only a person born of a Jewish mother or who has been converted in conformity with orthodox prescriptions is a Jew." Now both meanings of *to be* were allowed: the permanent one of birth (with the extra caution of specifying the mother), and the impermanent one of conversion and adherence to a creed. This politic duplicity apparently allowed a Roman Catholic to come in if he wanted to, but prevented the son of a Jewish mother to depart if such was his wish. By implication, impermanence was conveniently attached to every other religion, and permanence, conveniently, only to Judaism.

In Communist countries (instructive digression) something like the same magic is performed, whenever convenient, on being or not being a bourgeois. Is a pretext required for getting rid of an enemy? The fact that his father and mother belonged to the middle-class will be dragged into the light, and it will be suggested that the condition of gentility passes ineradicably from parents to children. For one's friends, however, this is not true. Friends can forswear and drop this bad being at will, and slip victoriously out of a tuxedo origin into a present set of overalls.

Of course, Communists do not make of gentility a racial taint, and nothing is said of genes or blood. Not only would such a notion be tough to apply in homogeneous societies, but Marxist doctrine, as we know, is ferociously environmentalist. Therefore, when Communists wish to defame and demolish, they find that gentility is an infection one inevitably catches from one's parents and passes on to one's own children. This witty line of thought serves both doctrine and expediency. Environment, not heredity, is responsible; and this environment creates a being that is permanent or impermanent as the political situation requires.

By this detour we return better equipped to cope with the Jewish question. Not so long ago, race would have been given as the ground of a permanent being for Jews. To race/blood/genes would have been ascribed ineluctable physical characteristics (for example, a crooked nose), or unavoidable psychological traits (a pretty one like loving one's family, or a nasty one like stinginess). This racial doctrine is by no means dead, but professors no longer write treatises to expound it; it has been relegated to the crumbling slums of philosophy. Nowadays, instead, Jewish being—like bourgeois being in the Soviet Union or China—acquires its permanence mostly by inevitable infection. As you were born and raised among admitted and practicing Jews, you necessarily caught Jewishness for life. Your loyalties may be repressed into your subconscious, and your habits may wear a specious veneer, but inspection quickly detects your ineradicable being. Do you love your mother? Obviously a Jewish trait. Are you keen on education? How Jewish! Do you give to charity? Jewish to the core.

This discovery of the body under the blanket is regularly made *ex post facto*. That is to say, the sleuth already knows that the body is there when he shrewdly lifts the blanket. Dropping the metaphor: first the observer learns that his victim did indeed have a Jewish father and mother, or had been exposed to Jewish habits and doctrines, or had himself professed Judaism at one time or another; and next he astutely finds Judaic traits in his man. I recently read a learned essay on Marcel Proust in which his *verve* was authoritatively traced to the Jewish half of his 5.6 liters of blood. In *The Hudson Review* a friendly critic spoke of the "negative undertones of Jewish self-appraisal" in my verse. If I had signed myself O'Toole, he would have called my negative undertones typically Irish. A few years ago a scholar ferreting among the archives discovered that the great Fernando Rojas had been a *converso*. Presently a swarm of shrewd critics from the best American universities revealed that *La Celestina* could have been written by none but a Jew, an observation no one had thought of launching during the four centuries preceding the happy find in the archives. Is this any better, I ask, than the practice of biographers who speak of the "stubborn nose" in their subject's picture in the frontispiece after they have ascertained that he refused to pay his taxes for forty years?

These notions of Jewish permanence are thriving today largely because the Jews themselves cannot bear to see the roster of their tribe depleted. Christians who drop their religion never to give it another thought (or Bolsheviks who convert to capitalism) undoubtedly retain some little flavors of their past, but no one dreams of taunting them for this, assuring them that they cannot cease to *be* what they once *were*, or denying them the possibility of being what they now claim to be. And it is singularly terrifying that Nazi and Jewish fanaticism joined hands across the mass grave to agree that Judaism in ineradicable.

For myself, it now goes without much further saying that I can conceive of "being" a Jew only as a set of loyalties: loyalties to others with whom we exchange these loyalties, loyalties to certain beliefs concerning God and man, loyalties to a history, loyalties to a number of precise customs and rituals. As soon as such loyalties are dropped, a secondary or intermediate state is usually reached. The person no longer *is* a Jew (or a Rosicrucian, or a Socialist, or a Cambodian), but obviously remembers the time when he was, and when he lived with his parents who were Jewish; and he usually retains some minor tastes or habits that are best called subintellectual. This stage allows for ample variations, even when we assume that the "world" does not oppose his change. How old was the man when he converted? How difficult for him was his conversion? How distant were his old creed and habits from the new ones? How well was he really equipped, psychologically and intellectually, for his new self? But this variety must not disguise the central feasibility of conversion. This is clinched a generation or two generations later, when dissolution is completed, if indeed the first of the line had not completed it himself. All of this, incidentally, was granted by some if not all of the fathers of Zionism, for they were convinced that the Jews who refused to settle in the new promised land—Palestine or Uganda—would cease to be Jews and merge into Christian Europe.

III.

Against those of us who perpetuate this civilized Zionist view of free choice, the implacables, after advancing their axiom of permanent being, bring to bear a psychological weapon of which they are astonishingly fond. We who favor dissolution, they cry, are eaten up by "self-hatred." This "argument" is thought to have a devastating effect on its target. Perhaps, for all I know, it has in fact stopped short several would-be defectors and returned them shamefaced to their kin. A less impressionable subject—someone, perhaps, more responsive to ethics than to the pop psychology of the "well-adjusted personality"—might remind the implacables that the best theologians, Jewish and Christian alike, have always recommended hating in oneself that which deserves to be hated: where else does salvation lie? So that, if it is true that we hate ourselves, we can retort with some satisfaction that we have found out our sins and meekly hope to mend them. In reality, of course, this "self-hatred" is a desperate invention. The feeling is not hatred at all but aversion; and it is not aversion for ourselves, but aversion for those who would enforce upon us a being contrary to our will and our convictions. So much for "self-hatred," where little said is more than enough.

The implacables have but a single argument that deserves serious rebuttal. Even if one admits that being a Jew is as mutable "in theory" as being middle-class or being a Socialist (for we do not say to a man, "Once a Socialist always a Socialist")—even if one yields this point, it still takes two (they say) to play the game. Cringe as much as you like (they say); join a Presbyterian congregation; change your name; get a nose-job; tell lies to your children; drop your old friends. But the past is always tensed like an animal ready to spring. Sooner or later one Gestapo or another will sniff you out. You will be not only a toady, but a failed toady at that. In a word, the *others* will not let you.

Recent history, imprinted with the unforgettable mark of the Nazi, makes this a poignant argument, and one must plunge through a dreadful night of emotions to recover one's reason and to grasp once again that the early Zionists were right: Jews can disappear, Jews have disappeared en masse, the *others* have in fact absorbed them. That opposition of the others is anything but a fixture of history. It was, on the contrary, an aberration of history, made possible by a new vision of the permanence of Jewish being. I am referring to the racist theories developed in the nineteenth century, prior to which the offensive characteristics of Jews had usually been imputed to alterable causes. Now, as if to prove that science too can go mad, the cause was inscribed in the "blood," in ancient and irremediable racial defects which intermarriage would only pass into the blood of Christians. The consequence was clear. If the offensive Jew is doomed to be forever offensive, even when he scrubs himself in the baptismal font, then naturally the doors of the clean must be forever barred against him. The clean may watch with amusement or disgust his abject attempts to alter his being, but when they are tired of watching, they should kick him—or gas him. Thus, in effect, spoke the science of race in its "purest" tones. Let us forget for the moment that compromises could be tendered: the candidate for absorption might be instructed, for instance, that if he married a Christian, and if his descendants did so unwaveringly as well, the scum might at last be washed out of the blood.

We can disregard compromises of this sort because the normal spectacle of history is in any event quite the opposite; it is a spectacle of Christians begging, cajoling, bribing, or compelling Jews to convert, like those of Apulia (among many others) towards the end of the thirteenth century. This was the period when the Augustinian dispensation—which tolerated the Jews, though for reasons one may refuse to admire—was giving way to the missionary craze of the Franciscans and Dominicans, guided by a bull from the quill of Pope Nicholas III:

> Summon them [i.e., the Jews] to sermons in the places where they live, in large and small groups, repeatedly, as many times as you may think beneficial. Inform them of evangelical doctrines with salutary warnings and discreet reasoning, so that after the clouds of darkness have gone, they may shine in the light of Christ's countenance, having been reborn at the baptismal font.

Nothing about "once a Jew always a Jew." The range of actions spread in reality from "discreet reasoning" to solid brutality, but the goal was the baptismal font, not the gas chamber. Three centuries later Shylock, cursing all the way, is baptized. His daughter marries a Christian. Everybody takes it for granted that her children will "dissolve." For, the historic aberration of racism notwithstanding, it has always seemed evident that Jews can and do vanish into Christendom.

If this normal course is sometimes forgotten, and if we can so easily choose to forget that the *others* have absorbed masses of Jews in the past, the reason is that no one writes to celebrate the apostate adventure, while libraries do not suffice to hold the rhapsodies to and histories of Jewish solidarity, fortitude, resistance, and spiritual victory. There are words of pity for those who were forced to convert, but no words of relief—because the tragic story was over for them and their descendants—and least of all words of admiration for those who had the strength of mind to cut of their own volition the "rope of sand" which tugs so insistently at the common mind.

Quietly or not so quietly, I repeat, flocks of Jews have disappeared a hundred times since the fall of Jerusalem. Nearly everyone you meet in Spain, for instance, is the descendant of one or more Jews who were baptized (usually under duress) in the fourteenth and fifteenth centuries, led a precarious existence as "new Christians," were about to dissolve into the population in the late sixteenth century when a massive influx of Portuguese *conversos* retarded the natural process, and completed their dissolution in the eighteenth century. Completed it so well that the term "new Christian" came to be applied to the gypsies! Again, almost no one has written the history of this benign solution: hints must be extracted from all but inaccessible works of erudition, or casual asides by historians preoccupied with the more glamorous chronicles of bloody persecution and resistance.

Needless to say, Hitler would not have remembered the Jews if they had converted en masse two thousand years ago. But they would have escaped his notice too if they had allowed themselves to be absorbed, instead of merely unshackled, in the age of Napoleon and Nicholas I. The Nürnberg Laws, whose odious definitions still held when the Final Solution was being carried out, preserved anyone who could produce at least two untainted grandparents. Even the more dubious *Mischlinge* (mixed breeds)—those who were labeled as "first degree"—could hope to survive the ultimate massacre. A strange and awesome spectacle, this compromise with perpetual being, with ineffaceable racial dirt, at the very headquarters of fanaticism.

Now if we ask why, in the nineteenth century and in a Western Europe ever more alive to rational and scientific thought, a considerable segment of the Christian and indeed post-Christian world was switching, so to speak, from obliging to forbidding the Jews to convert, we must dare—all fury notwithstanding—to place much of the blame on the Jews themselves. For the masses of Jews who accepted emancipation but refused absorption played a dangerous game throughout the nineteenth century. Moving from the ghetto to the city, the orthodox traditionalists kept up a way of life singularly calculated to arouse the fury of the mob, or to make them attractive targets for persecutions inspired by the authorities when they needed a faction to persecute. Intensely tribal themselves, these Jews might have considered that others were as tribally minded as they, and that an extravagantly conspicuous minority—conspicuous above all in the trivia of manners, dress, and language which act, alas, as bright signals to other tribes—a minority that competed not only on the economic plane, but also for the sublime distinction of being God's best-loved people—and to top it all, a minority which their powerful hosts and neighbors still looked upon as deicides—taking all this together, they might have considered that their position was *biologically* untenable. The Jews, at once helpless and high in relief, were banking on preternatural virtue in the dominant pack. The right to live at peace which they claimed was a platonic right: a right that lives in the

Cloud-Cuckoo-Land; it was not a right on which a prudent family could sensibly raise its children.

But we must blame the so-called emancipated Jews even more. They were about to replay a half-forgotten Alexandrian tragedy. While the orthodox Jewish community of that city remained content with its status as resident alien without special privileges, a highly Hellenized minority attempted to enjoy the best of two worlds by keeping the faith of their fathers but demanding Greek citizenship. This aroused an extremist opposition and provoked the brutal pogrom of the year 38. Now once again this very particular sort of provocation was enacted. The liberated Jews of the nineteenth century shaved their beards, dressed in the best fashion, learned to speak irreproachable French and German, became physicians and professors, went to hear Rossini—but remained Jews. They too wanted to dine at two tables. And insofar as these Jews competed far more grandly than the orthodox for positions of wealth and power, their situation became even more "difficult and fraught with danger," as Theodore Mommsen wisely warned. They were displaying a perilous optimism with regard to the human species. I suppose that the Age of Enlightenment had misled them. A cheerful trust in mankind blinded them. They could not imagine the rabble-bullies of the twentieth century who would supplant the polite kings and emperors of the nineteenth.

"Blame" is too harsh a word, perhaps. For indeed who could foresee the S.S.? One might reasonably predict a century of legal impediments, discrimination in business and the professions, trivial daily insults, social snubs, the occasional Dreyfus Affair, and sporadic violence incited by the lunatic fringe. I myself would undoubtedly have changed my name and done my best to liquidate an archaic "being," impatient with the tergiversations of my halfway brethren. But who could have foreseen the triumph of the lunatic fringe, and who could have foretold that the optimists were going to drag into the Holocaust those whose wiser course (had all adopted it) would have prevented the slaughter? I blame, then, only in a manner of speaking.

It may be that in the Soviet Union today there are men and women like myself, living in something like a nineteenth-century condition of discrimination and odium without actual massacre, who curse that same shilly-shallying. Let us not forget that when the Bolsheviks triumphed, the Jews *demanded* the separate Soviet nationality which is now *imposed* on them. Once more they were proving the justice of the old accusation that they constituted a state within a state. And once more a foolish optimism with respect to human enlightenment was drawing them into a trap. Surely the Proletarian Revolution would bring about the brotherhood which the Age of Reason, and then the French Revolution, and then Napoleon had somehow failed to beget, and the Jews might remain Jews and yet be equal, equal and loved, amidst their hosts. Instead, the ancient story repeated itself. The State wanted to absorb the Jews and liquidate Judaism; the majority of the Jews offered a "splendid" and "heroic" resistance in favor of their fossil; and the regime countered with the ancient, all too natural, all too animal and human hatred.

But I am not done with the implacables who claim that the others will not let you. Their challenge must be taken up on moral as well as on practical grounds. Must I continue to look upon myself as a Jew solely because that is how the world looks at me? Let me pretend to accept the premise that the door is locked against me, in order to ask whether this is a sufficient reason for giving up the house. Socrates took himself to *be* a pious man. The majority decreed that he *was* an atheist. Should Socrates have renounced his own vision of himself?

Surely we ought to take our stand with Socrates. I am, in and for myself, what I choose to be and not to be. I choose not to be a Jew. Others insist that I am. To show how serious they are, they throw me into a concentration camp. I am still not a Jew. They laugh in my face, and for the proof that has no reply, they shoot me.

Is this an argument?

They call me dog, therefore I bark!

As others see me. As I see myself. I take it that in primitive societies this *Zwiespalt*, this split in two, hardly ever exists. There, boys and girls receive their feeling-of-themselves from their tribe, and when they are grown up they take their turn administering this feeling to the next generation. The possibility of a split between "as others see me" and "as I see myself" must have arisen as soon as the individual was placed in significant, prolonged, and (on the whole) peaceful contact with members of other groups, so that startling new ways of doing and thinking (or simply new trades and professions) offered themselves to his inspection. The possibility of eccentricity, of rebellion, of heresy was born. Perhaps such events took place now and then in the open field and in the forests; but this rubbing together of different ways is clearly a specialty of city life. And even there, it took centuries to develop. It took man centuries to comprehend this idea of freedom.

Such an idea has nothing to do with "free will." Man is not able to invent himself any more than a chemical element is able to choose a reaction. My freedom to be what I choose instead of complying with the dictates of my own or some hostile tribe is nothing but a condition of exposure to a multiplicity of causes instead of a few or only one. It is like a vessel emerging from a quiet channel into a turbulent, toss-vessel sea.

On this sea, prudential advice has its place. Job's friends deserve a hearing. "Why not admit to Yahweh that you are a sinner? Everybody knows you are. Only *you* keep denying it!" Perhaps Socrates should have fallen on his knees and confessed himself an atheist and a perverter of young men. Sometimes it is not "smart" to define oneself against the police's grain. Besides, some choices of oneself are truly mad, and they are mad even if we grant the chooser every moral right to consider himself whatever he desires: thus the loony who calls himself Napoleon, or a Socrates who would claim that he *is* handsome. But other choices—like Job's or Don Quixote's—are less mad than they seem, or mad only for a season. I, for one, have listened attentively to the voice of wise counsel. I postulate that my choice of being is not mad. (If it is, I cannot know it, being mad.) If I am told that my choice is imprudent, or foolish, or useless (that is to say, incapable of imposing itself on society), either I disagree or else I bravely, yes heroically, assert it in your teeth, obstreperous to the end.

IV.

I was but a child when I turned my back on the culture and religion of my parents—long before I could formulate a single thought on the subject. My father took me to the synagogue on the High Holidays. He himself remained all his life deeply Jewish in all his feelings, loyalties, acquaintances, and views, and gave perfunctory but soul-satisfying obedience to ritual. To me, that ritual seemed odious, and downright freakish, from the beginning. I sat deep in the pew-chair, playing with the tassels of my father's prayer shawl—I liked the silky ripple over and under my fingers—

or whispered and giggled with the boy who was sitting behind me.
In front of the tabernacle, weird bearded personages babbled and
dipped their torsos as if possessed. My father showed me the
prayer book and made me read the unintelligible words along with
him, who understood them no better, but who felt the profound
union and unction of faithfulness. The French translation on the
facing pages edified me little more. The remoteness was absolute;
in a word, I was bored.

If only (I hear you say) the mother and father had taken pains to
make Judaism intelligible, interesting, and lovable instead of
offering him their half-baked cake, their neither hot nor cold, their
both here and there. Who can tell? Would Judaism have won the
tug-of-war against Hugo and Verlaine, against the Antwerp of
streetcars, bicycle rides, cinemas, and voluminous steamers
docked at the quays?

Or else, would a reformed service, stripped of medieval para-
phernalia, have won over the boy? It would at least have offered a
simulacrum of continuity with the "real world." But here I am
peremptory. If the gods have given me indeed the blessing of a
clear mind, I know that the man would have quit reformed religion
even more lightly than orthodoxy. Reformed Judaism is as vacuous
as streamlined Roman Catholicism. When our venerable religions,
which were flesh of the flesh of mankind once upon a time,
perpetuate inviolate their doctrines and their ceremonies, they are
so pitifully archaic that one can sympathize with inventions to
bring them up-to-date. But these reforms are like updating a fish
by urging him to breathe good fresh air. Modernized religions
cannot make their divine right stick: they wilt; they become
insipidly sociological, anemic branches of a Consumers' League. It
is another dilemma without an issue.

My father had taken steps, at any rate, to make his charming
little son understand prayers better than he. Once a week a
Hebrew tutor appeared in our house—an advantage which my
poor father, who had gone to work in a Viennese sausage factory at
the age of fourteen, had not enjoyed. But never did teacher
contend with a more mulish pupil. Years went by and I continued
to oppose an inexorable stupidity to the alien language. At thirteen, I (I?) stood chanting in the center of the synagogue, declaring
myself, in words I did not understand, and declared by the
congregation, a grown-up male Jew. This solemn commitment

exhausted all concerned, I think, for soon afterward my parents rid me of the Hebrew teacher and substituted an English master. They may have felt that *their* reputation, at any rate, had been secured by the irreproachable *bar mitzvah*. Be that as it may, suddenly the light filled my brain. The distinction between "I have" and "I am," and the conjugations of these two appealing verbs were mastered at once: and I would have conquered the English language in a year if the war had not broken out and interrupted my lessons just as "to run" was opening to me.

In the meantime I was keeping a small pad arranged in alphabetical order where I entered newly-learned French words with their definitions. This miniature thesaurus meant so much to me that I hastily slipped it into a pocket on the day of our flight from Belgium and kept it with me during the entire exodus. Changing my ambition from French to English proved to be as easy as it is for a rider to leap from one horse to another when keen on his mission: mine had been, from my very boyhood, to add a posy to the grand Florilegium of the Western World.

The only object of veneration that I kept on my shelves was a chunk from the hill in the Ardennes where good King Albert the First had fallen to his death. The authorities had allowed a pious souvenir stand to be built at the foot of the fatal hill. There citizens could buy the commemorative stones, each adorned with a tiny photograph of the king and a couple of flags. How my tears had fallen on the day of his plunge! And how they fell, shortly after, when the young Queen Astrid was killed in a car accident! I purchased sentimental albums concerning my sovereigns, and made my devout, silent oblations, not to the Maccabees, but to the Saxe-Coburg.

Some of my Jewish school friends came from homes similar to mine. Others were being brought up within a more earnest orthodoxy. But I do not recall that such matters were ever discussed among us. My evolution in this respect was proceeding alone, unabetted, unopposed, underground. For all I know, I was the only child of that generation to have so decidedly slipped the leash. Again it was alone, without co-plotters, that I "played hooky" so persistently from the Jewish scouts among whom my mother had enrolled me that I was brought to trial before the club's leading spirits and quite rightfully expelled. Why then was I irrevocably refusing my "Jewish heritage"? Revulsion against my family—the customary revenge of the child against his parents? Not so. I was the darling of the family, coddled and cuddling, and no one was ever less a rebel against my gentlest of parents than I. But I was a timid and cowardly child. The force operating on my unconscious mind must have been, banally enough, a desire to elude derision and blows and to draw on the strength of the dominant group by becoming one of its members. For although the Jewish minority of Antwerp was substantial, strong, and an excellent mother hen to the young, it was distinctively, even ostentatiously, a minority. Many Jews walked about in their caftans, silk hats, long beards, and curly sideburns. Certain teachers did not disguise their anti-Semitism. The Jewish minority very visibly attended the French rather than the Flemish classes in the schools of this most Flemish of cities. Many spoke with "queer" accents (my father's made my face burn red with shame). Yes, we stood out, and I did not want to stand out except to immense advantage. I did not want to be the member of a bizarre minority. If any jeering was to be done, I wanted to be the one to do it.

As it turned out, the tribe I finally joined was not precisely that of the dominant majority, but the band of intellectuals who constitute a sort of congregation within it. Of course it is perfectly possible to be an intellectual *and* a Jew, or an intellectual *and* a Roman Catholic, but it is also possible to be an intellectual *tout court*, and that evidently was enough for me. There was, fortunately, no tincture of madness in this particular "decision" of mine. The *others* did not slam their door in my face. Nor did my progenitors object. And so I quietly learned the signs, the language, the things one says, and even more important the things one takes for granted and leaves unsaid; took the decent course of initiation at the universities; learned to bleed when a beautiful monument is razed, to marvel when a scientist pokes his imagination into a Black Hole, to commune with a Japanese who loves Bach—and to write essays on Judaism or Marivaux.

The essential point, however, is not that I joined this particular band, but that the easily frightened child of a vulnerable group (one which he disliked on other grounds too, as I will presently show), sent out his "feelers"—long before he could engender a theoretical discourse about his motions—towards another group that promised, among other satisfactions, an approved-of haven.

It takes little wit to guess that these "confessions" seem unlovely to you. They seem not so to me, who look upon mankind as an intensely social species (both for good and for ill) where aberrations—what we call nonconformity—may be sometimes heroic, and sometimes necessary for progress, but must also be perilous. When I see the little monkey I was, seeking a place within the pack rather than outside it, I inquire, first, whether he was leaving virtue for vice or intelligence for stupidity; and second, whether, from within the pack, it was his intention to turn, like certain Inquisitors, into a scourge for those who were choosing to cling to the outside they loved. The answer being comforting to both questions, I can look back at the toddler with unclouded equanimity.

But let me take you down a yet darker corridor. Sometime ago, coming upon that well-known passage in *Mein Kampf* where Hitler describes the shock he received when he saw, wandering the streets of Vienna, his first East European Jew, another blow struck me by rebound: I recognized my own revulsion in his. Horrible kinship! My first impulse was to repudiate my own feelings and thoughts: change thy life!—*du musst dein Leben ändern*; the second, to conceal their existence. These then, I said, are the sensations which—carried to their pathological conclusion—led to Auschwitz. But eventually I won my way to a saner view. Were I a saint, I would still share feelings and ideas with any thug. And would Hitler snatch from his bed of dust a subtler victory than the annihilation of the Jews—namely, the extinction of reasonable discourse? Have we not seen scores of thousands discover their Jewish *being* for the sorry reason, flattering to that hooligan, that Hitler persecuted the Jews? For it has almost come to pass—because of Hitler—that we dare not criticize Judaism for a missing button, lest we be thought ready to hang every Jew for it.

Hitler's revulsion—and I shudder as I say it—was in itself normal. I repeat: every species abhors aberrations. Woe to those who deviate, who are too weak to enforce their deviation, but who ostentatiously display it: ghastly trinity of invitations to the Furies. The strange, the outlandish East Europeans Hitler saw were taunting the bull. The rest we know—from the shifty figure of this solitary vagrant, at once genius and dunce, in love with hatred, able and bold to act instead of dream, to the unimaginable luck in the historical combinations that gave him the power and the time to conduct his hatreds to their pathological conclusions.

A fraction of this, the sane fraction, was staged in the little boy's mind. Once a week it was beggars' day in the Jewish world of Antwerp. My mother prepared a cup full of coins and placed it in the vestibule. Every few minutes the doorbell rang. Mother, the maid, or I opened the door, and after the bearded personage had delivered himself of a minimal formality of wailing, we gave him his due. It was a wonderfully organized business of misery. Everyone seemed to regard it as a routine, much like the phases of the moon. For me, in that stage of my life (which could only become thought many years later), the sheer ugliness of these scenes associated itself with every other ugliness: the synagogue and its rituals, the Pelikaanstraat in which the diamond business was transacted in a whirl of high gestures, vociferations, and frantic tuggings at lapels, my Hebrew lessons, the dreary black prayer books, and the Passover ceremony over which my dear father presided in our house, leaving me mostly with an impression of inedible food and bedraggled cheer. Can you conceive, my unfriendly reader, the astronomical distance between all this and Verlaine?

Looking back, I see that this aesthetic revulsion played as important a part in my refusal of Judaism as the urge to dwell unobtrusive and safe amidst a dominant or accepted group. If Judaism had appeared to me robed in beauty, who knows? This satisfaction might have superseded the timid boy's fear of humiliation and persecution. But everything, save the love I bore my parents, worked to thrust me away from my ancestral clan.

Of course, aesthetic receptivity was a thing even less known to myself than my anxiety to conform. God knows I was not born with a "passion for beauty," nor even bred to it. At best I was born with a capacity for acquiring it. But my tastes formed slowly. In my family the tone was one of unaffected simplicity. No one talked about Culture. A few books were read, without any clear notion of Literature. For visual gratification, my parents had their glossy furniture (style Art Deco of the 1930's), a landscape or still-life on the walls, and a few trinkets on the mantelpiece, preferably of a sentimental or innocently lascivious character. My sister and I were never taken to museums, palaces, or (need I say it?) churches. Recreation consisted in long middle-class walks, good hotels, a month at the beach, and many hours on the terraces of cafés. Although the drive to Knokke on the North Sea took us past cities like Ghent and Brugge, it never occurred to anyone to pause for a look at their riches. Now and then my parents went to the opera, and once—once only—I was taken to a matinee in a theater. A celebrated Dutch actor was performing in *The Miser*, and to this day I see him placing two pinches of snuff into his nostrils, sniffing zestfully away, and then prudently picking the snuff out of his nostrils to replace it in his snuffbox. It would please me to report, in the manner of inspired biographers, that "the enchantment of this first encounter with the theater had, unknown to the lad himself, marked him for life: he *would* be a playwright." The truth, however, is that I heartily enjoyed myself, and went home. I do not recollect begging my parents to let me see more plays, or pining away in silence because all I got was Laurel and Hardy at the movies. In short, no one was training me to be an intellectual or an aesthete. On the other hand, my gentle parents were not stopping me. Instead of theaters and museums, I had love—not the worst of foundations, even for an intellectual.

It is clear to me that a subtler infiltration was affecting the growing boy. I owe much, I think, to the city of Antwerp itself: its old district with its mysterious intimations, the fresh rain rubbing its parks till all the leaves shone, its harmonious avenues valanced with chestnut trees, and the cathedral bells in the distance . . . all this mingling delicately with books, with poems. Such influences are as hard to capture in words as the quality of a perfume; and if we name them, how do we know why they take hold in one person and not in another? Why was I the only boy in a large group of friends to drift into another world? Or were there others I know nothing of?

V.

By now you know where I stand. The point at which all my speculations about Judaism end is that the Jews should have converted the day after Constantine changed religion and—adopting a new home, a new nest, a new cozy family—melted into the great world. An interesting chapter in man's history would have closed without harm to anyone, like a drained lake whose waters have gone elsewhere. That which Jews had contributed to mankind: several volumes of great poetry, a monotheism which (I don't know why) most people take as an important advance over polytheism, and ethical conceptions as respectable as those of the Greeks; that, I say, which the Jews as Jews had contributed to mankind *had* been contributed, and over the ruins of the Temple the Spirit of History was whispering the hint: Enough, and beware.

Because this is a psychologizing age, you may wave off this argument of mine on the ground that I myself, poor fool, have thoroughly exposed its dubious origins in my "personal emotional history." But I advise you to drop this weapon. For if it is true that a personal psychological thrust can vitiate an argument, it is equally true that another such thrust can open a man's eyes to realities concealed from his fellows. Who shall decide whether a particular psychological "bias" is benign or malign to a theoretical body of opinions? "You are misled because you were beaten as a child." "No, because I was beaten as a child I see the truth." Nothing comes, you see, of tracing an opinion back to a psychological source.

You must attack me otherwise.

"What harm were we doing by keeping the faith? What justice is there in your advising us to convert? All we asked for is a shop or a farm, the right to work hard for a living, our dear Book, and the hope for a return to the Holy Land. What people more innocent? More undemanding? More modest? More unobtrusive?"

Granted, granted, and granted. You did no harm. You were modest. You worked hard. Justice is on your side. Reason is on your side. They should have left you alone. God knows they should have left you alone. So should a tornado leave a house alone. So should a bull leave a man alone.

But I am not hardhearted enough to take my stand on Justice and Reason. I take my stand on mountains of corpses and floods of blood. Oh sons and daughters of Moses, you *did* keep the faith, and today you are stronger than you have been in twenty-five centuries: rejoice! But not I. I stagger through the corpses, I choke in the blood. Monstrous price to pay for the privilege of staying in the nest where you feel at home. Or are you telling me that your traditions—your dogma—your rites—your moral life—are so astoundingly superior to anything else the world can offer that a thousand massacres should be endured for their sakes?

For this is the lamentable theme they play over and over again, as if to shield themselves from the monstrosity of the sacrifices they chose to incur, and made others incur: the magnificent contribution of Judaism to civilization. We now leave behind us the controversies I have already touched upon. We assume for argument's sake that the Jews *could* have vanished as Jews. But now we ask whether, in consideration of that magnificent contribution, we should not rejoice that they held firm, come hunger, humiliation, or death.

Consider briefly, to begin with, what one might call intramural contributions: Judaism speaking to Judaism, and little said about affecting the rest of mankind. For instance, addressing himself to the "literary creativity" of the leaders of Russian Jewry as late as 1938 and 1939, the historian S. W. Baron exclaims with naïve admiration: "I was amazed to note that in less than two years, East European Jews published more volumes of responsa, halakhic and aggadic commentaries, homilies, kabbalistic (and hasidic) works than in any two decades of the seventeenth century, the heyday of rabbinic learning." This species of learning continues to thrive. I saw it also as a child shimmering in the pale faces of young men studying in one *Yeshiva* or another. Hurrying along the streets, all seemed to be thinly pregnant with yet another aggadic commentary, and impatient for delivery.

I do believe that many of those (and perhaps all who perpetuate this particular order of contribution) would willingly if tearfully pay the tragic price: accept the hecatombs, that is, in order to keep the faith burning in this manner. But the millions of Jews who live outside the inner circle—inner and, let there be no mistake, authentic as no other—need to summon, with somewhat paradoxical pride, the men and women who poured their works of mind and hand into the stream of occidental culture, enriching it and altering its course beyond calculation.

Everyone will admit, I think, that the outpouring that predates the Great Emancipation is really a trickle. Intellectual activity in those many centuries was of the intramural kind already mentioned. Of international figures like Maimonides and Spinoza we have not enough to help the implacables' argument. Nor will anyone claim that the loss of Jewish art (products made by or for Jews) would have dealt civilization an irreparable blow. Jewish art was borrowed. The best synagogues were built on general European models, and the aesthetics of wedding rings, embroidered shawls, silver vessels, book-binding, and so forth, afford us nothing vitally or remarkably original. For the rest, we neither expect nor obtain a Jewish Titian or Bach. The talent, heaven knows, was not wanting; but Jews had survival to think of, not partitas. Indeed, their really influential inventions occurred in the fields of finance and marketing, activities close to the problem of survival. And in the sciences, *everything* was to come.

The argument becomes genuinely weighty only when we contemplate the astonishing flood of products of the Jewish mind and hand without which world history since the age of Napoleon is hardly thinkable. The contention is that if the Jews had converted along with Constantine there would have been no Einstein (and a thousand others) and no Kafka (and a thousand others). Let us for the moment pour into the same vessel contributions that manifest a special Jewish cast (like a painting by Chagall or a novel by Saul Bellow); works with no discernible Jewish character (like those of Modigliani and Soutine or the discovery that matter and energy are interchangeable); and works like Kafka's, into which one may or may not read Jewish features. Let us call a contribution Jewish if it has been made by a son or daughter of Jews *and* sent (so to speak) *extra muros*. There is obviously such abundance and such importance here that a man would be neither a fool nor a brute for declaring that the contributions are sufficient compensation for twenty centuries of oppression and massacre.

I promptly concede at this point that a kind of semi-oppression—something less harsh than dismal pauperization, and obviously something much less harsh than massacre—stimulates the mind as it struggles for ways of overcoming or compensating. In other words, I accept as true the commonplace notion that suffering sharpened Jewish intellects and intensified Jewish energies. If this stimulation occurred during certain periods preceding the Emancipation, it did not, as we have seen, lead to many "extramural" contributions. Only after the opening of the doors (partial and reluctant, or full and loving) could it and did it help to produce the works we are considering. I concede, therefore, that without Judaism (that is to say, if all the Jewish achievers had been born of families Christianized since Constantine, or indeed since Philip II), a distinct loss of intensity would have resulted in our world, bringing about in turn a distinct diminution in the number and power of achievers. Since the specific disabilities imposed on Jews as Jews constitute only one composite cause for major creativity, no one will claim that the Einsteins and Kafkas would have disappeared outright. But neither can anyone affirm that they would all have surged forward as before.

But if oppression is good for the soul (alas), so is opportunity. Directly we think of all the achievers produced by the pressures of Judaism and anti-Judaism, we must enter into our account book veritable armies of potential achievers since our "year zero" whose field of thought and creation was pathetically shrunk in the ghetto or the squalid village:

> But Knowledge to their eyes her ample page
> Rich with the spoils of time did ne'er unroll;
> Chill Penury repressed their noble rage,
> And froze the genial current of the soul.

Instead of one Spinoza, the world might have celebrated twenty; the sciences might have reached in the year 1700 the point at which they stood in 1800 or 1900; and a second Raphael might have lived and painted. This is enough for my argument; but even after the Emancipation, opportunity might have done as much good as oppression did. In short, for every Einstein produced by Judaism, I see another aborted by Judaism, and I make bold to wish that generations of pale youths had turned away from aggadic commentaries to the curricula of Oxford, Paris, or Bologna.

These calculations, distasteful in any case, lead to a blank. The only assertion the implacables can retrieve with certainty is that the especial subject matter (or coloring, or character) of products which are, to begin with, capable of being Jewish would have been lost. I doubt that any anxiety is in order concerning the sciences in which verification is practiced. Even Einstein's discoveries would have been discovered sooner or later without him—if need be by a band of lesser men doing the work of the single genius. But what would have taken the place of works of art in which the Jewish character is at least detectable and at most overwhelming? By our very hypothesis we must grant that, after replacing every Chagall and Kafka with a neo-Chagall and a neo-Kafka (or two other artists who took advantage of opportunities while the first ones sank into a lethargy of unruffled Christianity), the Jewish images and the Jewish "something" would have vanished.

To this, then, comes the loss we can be sure of, and this, in sum, is the "magnificent contribution" that would have disappeared from the world after Titus if the Jews had consented to join with Saul of Tarsus. Science and technology would have advanced undisturbed at worst. A certain number of men and women, lacking the irritant of anti-Semitism, would have lounged instead of achieving. Others, given opportunities denied them as Jews, would have substituted for them. But certain Jewish motifs, inflections, images would have been irretrievably lost to the world.

And now, make your choice. Will you preserve mankind from this loss by perpetuating Judaism and pogroms, or will you accept the loss and cancel the bloody persecutions, the forced migrations, the ceaseless exactions and degradations, and finally the colossal massacre perpetrated by the Germans? If I abolish the gas chambers, will you not let me baptize the Jews of the Roman empire? I wish that I could ask this question of the victims themselves, "stinking innocently in the ditch"; but the dead are famous for their silence. Instead, I will take you, the living, farther with me. Let the Jewish contribution be as magnificent as you choose it to be. *Now* are you willing to pay the ghastly price? Not I. You have been calling me coldhearted while reading these pages—I know you, my sweet reader—but who is coldhearted now? It was not from a cold heart that I cried, two thousand years ago, "Give it up! It isn't worth the blood that has flowed, and the blood that will flow."

Besides, the world is made neither of nor for major achievers and magnificent contributions. Plain families count too. And what does a plain family require? Health, a house, food, schools, work, security, a God to worship. Can these not be found outside Judaism? Are you abjectly "pre-programmed" animals, that you had rather die than change from one custom to another?

Or were you waiting for the world to become more intelligent, more rational, less tribe-minded than you were yourselves? I have said so before: you may as well wait for Cloud-Cuckoo-Land. No one knows better than a faithful Jew what tribal cohesion is. Who is more inclusive and exclusive than the Jew himself? Who is better situated to understand man's distrust of outsiders—that hatred of the "uncircumcised" which leads so easily to pathological conclusions? The Jews can understand that tribalism is natural, is precious, and is terrible. Yet they cry to the heavens because the Christians cannot rid themselves of it.

Let me assure you that if Judaism had been the powerful tribe, I would have cried my cry to the Christians: "Give it up; it is not worth the blood!" and urged them to file into the synagogue.

Today, of course, the Jews *are* the powerful tribe in Israel; they are, at last, a majority; and if the nation succeeds in imposing itself and, secure from Arab attack, perpetuates the luxurious burden of oppressing *its* minority, I hope that the local Arabs will cheerfully get themselves absorbed by their tormentors, Near Eastern like themselves: another very feasible change of being! My own view about this new nation can be guessed. Whether its repossession of Palestine is just, or constitutes an imperialist Gibraltar-like enclave—either way, for me, the price paid for it was intolerably, monstrously high, so high (I speak of twenty centuries of oppression and massacre) as to become a macabre absurdity. The price having been paid, however, and the nation being established—by means of the violence that customarily begets nations—reasonable men and women everywhere are bound to hope that diplomacy will finesse a permanent accommodation, based, one supposes, on the vast unpopulated spaces over which the Arabs dispose. If peace does settle in, a notion like mine—that the Jews would have been better off melting into the crowd than reconfirming their destiny in Palestine—becomes academic. On the other hand, it will be anything but academic if the state of Israel succumbs at last to Arab conquest—an event that will not occur without another impressive slaughter.

And outside Israel? Has Hitler's efficient work sobered the nations? May we suppose that, aside from vestigial hot spots of Jew-baiting, the Cossacks and the S.S. will ride no more? Many anxious Jews are heard to say that the bloodletting is far from over. Any time, anyplace, a storm of violence can fall upon the Jews again, while (short of another "final solution") the old hatred will continue to trigger the old persecutions and the old degradations. If these anxious persons are right, more of my sort should leave their other occupations and plead for the dissolution of Judaism, recapitulating my argument thus: No, the "being" of Judaism is not a permanent being; Yes, Jews can relinquish Judaism and dissolve into the circumambient culture, some in a single generation, others in two or three; and No, not religion, nor ethical singularity, nor customs, nor contributions to the general culture warrant the suffering brought about by the passion to preserve them.

Curiously, though, my own vaticinations are less grim. I think it not impossible that outside of Israel other hostilities, other problems, and other struggles will by and large deflect the attention of Cossacks and S.S. men to come. As a result of this general sense of the future, I have responded but sluggishly to my own doctrines. Coming to maturity in the United States just at the time Hitler was expiring (we hope) in his bunker, I have allowed my favorable habitat to lull me. I have not changed my name. I tell you freely who I am and whence I come. Those who smile at me, and shake their heads, and put into their voice a particular tone of confident world-wisdom to tell me, "You *are* a Jew whether you like it or not; once a Jew always a Jew," are welcome to their wisdom. And if, perchance, we have lived to witness the last hecatomb, my adjuration ends: let Judaism flourish.

VI.

It can flourish, I daresay, without one man's admiration. I am fond of local color and quaint old religions, but not all folkways appeal to me to the same degree. Neither Moslem nor Jewish traditions, for example, make a snug fit into my spirit. The former I know mostly by hearsay; but my distaste for the thousand prescriptions and prohibitions among which orthodox Jews live to this day derives from something approaching intimacy. Concerning these *do's* and *don'ts*, Mr. Poliakov, the historian of anti-Semitism, reproduces an admirable passage from Rousseau: "To keep his people from melting among alien nations, Moses gave them manners and customs that could not be allied to those of other nations; he overloaded them with rituals and special ceremonies; he cramped them in a thousand ways to keep them unremittingly on their toes and make them forever strangers among other men; and all the ties of brotherhood that he placed among the members of his republic were so many barriers that kept them separate from their neighbors and prevented a mingling between them." An all but Darwinian explanation! And one is free to admire these strategies of survival or to deplore them. Admire them, since they enabled the group to survive through thick and thin; deplore them, since they led the group *into* thick and thin. Picture a species of animals, tightly organized and behaving according to deeply ingrained rules. The world changes all around this species but the species itself "declines" to change. As a result, its members are decimated time and time again by a number of newer predatory groups. But a few members always remain alive. They continue unchanged, almost impervious to mutation, and they multiply again, until enough of them appear for a new carnage. Is this admirable? If you wish. But since you have advised me that changing my being is impossible, I shall advise you in turn that keeping it was absurd.

For the rest, these manners and customs dumbfound me. Perhaps the Moslems are worse, but they are known to be living in an earlier stage of history, though in the very shadow of their oil wells. And besides, they live in their lands largely by themselves. Instead, a Jew who will not flip a light on the Sabbath in Manhattan, London, or Sydney is a figure almost farcical. I know a young man—a brilliant physician and musical genius—who refuses to open his refrigerator on the day of rest because the open door throws a switch that lights a bulb. At table a few weeks ago a Jewish guest spoke of a professor at Brandeis University who solves the problem of lighting his house on Saturdays by pressing the switches with his elbow, apparently with the blessing of an influential rabbi. My friend and colleague K. C. assures me that this story must be a joke. But who has not heard of a hundred similar banalities and absurdities that would shame a Papuan? K. C. herself is learned, wise, urbane, but cannot dine at my house because my dishes are polluted. Another colleague of mine is a Russian woman who fled to Israel with her eleven-year-old boy. The boy died and was refused burial because he was uncircumcised. The mother had to allow the little corpse to be put to the knife before she could get it interred. In short, as many follies, pitiful in the context of Western civilization, cover the "ethical beauty" of Judaism as quills on a porcupine's hide. Or do they cease to be follies on account of their "survival value" to the group?

The same question can be asked of a famous Jewish trait, the love of learning. We have all been treated to emotional descriptions of centers of learning in Babylon, study houses in every Polish village, the veneration bestowed on learned boys and men (women were devoted to imbecility), and so on. But it is clear that the learning of rabbis and other masters constituted a powerful means of socio-political control. The supposedly *spiritual* leaders combined in a single person the monarch, legislature, tribunal, propaganda ministry, and police force. This meant that rabbis had to provide themselves with something more than a few metaphysical doctrines concerning God, salvation, angels, etc. They must find a rationale for controlling daily actions in perpetual danger of gravitating towards the norms of the surrounding Christian communities. This they accomplished by giving religious significance to the most minute particulars of life. One could not rinse a cup without divine prescription; and divine prescription was interpreted and enforced by the rabbis. No wonder study houses were the first houses built in every new community! They were the Jewish universities—but also the disguised chancelleries and police stations. Now we also see why so little interest was shown in the afterlife. Cohesion here below was what mattered; and for cohesion a regulation on hair-clipping was more important than dreams of the empyrean.

It is also with a sort of stupefaction that I see the boy I was at thirteen, when my father took it into his head to make a mature Jew out of me. I had just completed the ceremony of the *bar mitzvah;* now, if ever, was the moment to make the boy wrap himself every morning in phylacteries. I have forgotten the precise character and importance of this daily ritual, but I recollect a row of voluble prayers, certain ribbons I placed about my arm and head, and a couple of sinister little black boxes, which I suppose contained some incantations. I contemplate myself at a distance of almost forty years and shake my head. They speak about Africans leaping across twenty centuries in a single generation as they cross from animism to heavy industry. Why cite Africa? I see the tiny lad in the Avenue de Belgique: outside his window the automobiles and streetcars are rolling by. A short walk away is the electric railway. Then the movie houses. The twenty-four story "skyscraper," Antwerp's pride. Two tunnels just finished under the broad river. And myself muttering incantations to Yahweh. It was too wretchedly droll to last. My father struggled from a weak position, for he was not phylacterizing himself. After two or three weeks, he gave up, and the family returned to normal.

But the true *rite de passage* happened later. By then I was fifteen and living in New York. When the Day of Atonement came around, I was naturally expected to fast for twenty-four hours along with the rest of the Jewish world. At noon, after an hour of forced prayers in a shabby neighborhood synagogue, I slipped out to a nearby "luncheonette," sat down on one of its stools, and bought a solid meal. As I masticated, I searched myself for the fatal *ayenbite of Inwit*, that is to say, the bitter sting of remorse. I would not have been absolutely surprised if a thunderbolt had fallen on the luncheonette. But ah, what bliss, my conscience was clear. Not a spiculum of reproach stuck in it. On the contrary, I fell into the marvelous elation of a youth who has passed the test of manhood and established his right to self-determination. In that same year I announced to my father that I would not enter a synagogue again.

Somewhere in Germany, Hitler's despised dust is aging in some tub or pot. I too, had I not trembled safe across an ocean, would have disappeared from earth long, long ago. But in those death-camp days, if they had forced me to the ditch under a gun, I would have been executed by gangsters for a creed, and in the name of a tribe, that I had renounced two thousand years before, and for an identity foisted on me by the Nazis and the Jews alike in horrid collusion against my selfhood. Like that wretch in Plutarch and Shakespeare who—when the assassins were looking for Cinna the politician—cried out in vain, "I am Cinna the poet, I am Cinna the poet!", I would have tumbled into an inglorious, mistaken death.

THAT BRIGHT GREY EYE

by HILDA MORLEY

from IRONWOOD

nominated by Stanley Kunitz

The grey sky, lighter & darker
greys,
    lights between & delicate
    lavenders also
blue-greys in smaller strokes,
                    & swashes
of mauve-grey on the Hudson—
                    openings
of light to the blue oblong
off-center
        where the door to the warehouse
shows—
        the larger smearings darkening
                    deep
into blues
        So alight that sky,
        late August,
early evening,
            I had to
gasp at it,
        stand there hardly moving

to breathe it,   using
whatever my body gave me,
                                    at
that moment   attending to it,
thinking:
              Turner   he should have
seen it,
              he would have given it
back to us,
                  not let it die away
                                      And that other
evening, walking down Bank Street from marketing,
the sky fiery over the river,
                                    luminous but
hot in its flowering also,
                              rich in color
as Venice seen by Guardi—more aflame even,
the sky moving in a pulse,
                              its fire breathing in
a pulse verging on danger—mane of a lioness
affronted.
                  That brilliance—the eye of the lion
filled to the lids with
flame
              And his eyes, Turner's, that bright grey eye
at seventy-six,
                  "brilliant as
the eye of a child"
                        who grew his thumbnail
in the shape of an eagle's claw,
                                    the better
to use it in painting
                        In Kirby Lonsdale, Yorkshire,
where Turner first drew mountain-landscapes,
              I found Blake's *Marriage*
of Heaven and Hell—sold for two guineas, 1821
& Turner aged 46 that year
                              & there I read:
"And when thou seest
an Eagle, thou seest a portion of genius.

                                        Lift up
thy head," says Blake.
                              These afternoons now,
                              late in September, '76,
the sky, the river are lit up
at the end of Bank Street, at Bethune.
                                        The pavement
trembles with light pouring
upon it.
                    We are held in it.
We smile.
              I hold my breath to see if
the cashier in the supermarket
will be gentle with the old lady who cannot
read the price-tag on
a loaf of bread.
                         Then I breathe freely,
for yes, she is helpful, yes, she is
kind.
              Outside on
the pavement, the light pouring itself away
is the light in the eagle's
eye   or the eye of a child
                         (I saw it in a man's eye once:
                         but he's dead now more than
                         four years)
Drawing heat out of
surfaces,
              the light is
without calculation,
                         is a munificence now,
is justified.

GREAT-AUNT FRANCESCA

by JOE-ANNE MCLAUGHLIN

from PLOUGHSHARES

nominated by Hayden Carruth

"Girl, it's taken everything in me
just to keep myself breathing."

Half then all our chickens
picked off by coyotes, the pig gut
he salted with strychnine,
meant for coyotes, eaten by his own
dogs, the burial of the dogs
useless against the coyotes,
the reburials, the coyote hunters
shooting our goats, his stallion
breaking its leg, startled
by something that looked like
a coyote, the shooting of the stallion
the burning of its carcass
and in the rain, burning, burning,
for days, him taking to mint gin,
turning on me with his shot gun,
that night giving me a hand gun,
locking himself in the storm cellar;
I tell you I ran, ran outrunning
the coyotes, ran and told no one.
Please, please don't ask me anything.

INDIAN BOARDING SCHOOL: THE RUNAWAYS

by LOUISE ERDRICH

from FRONTIERS: A JOURNAL OF WOMEN STUDIES

nominated by FRONTIERS: A JOURNAL OF WOMEN STUDIES

Home's the place we head for in our sleep.
Boxcars stumbling north in dreams
don't wait for us. We catch them on the run.
The rails, old lacerations that we love
shoot parallel across the face and break
just under Turtle Mountains. Riding scars
you can't get lost. Home is the place they cross.

The lame guard strikes a match and makes the dark
less tolerant. We watch through cracks in boards
as the land starts rolling, rolling till it hurts
to be here, cold in regulation clothes.
We know the sheriff's waiting at mid-run
to take us back. His car is dumb and warm.
The highway doesn't rock, it only hums
like a wing of long insults. The worn down welts
of ancient punishments lead back and forth.

All runaways wear dresses, long green ones,
the color you would think shame was. We scrub
the sidewalks down because it's shameful work.
Our brushes cut the stone in watered arcs
and in the soak frail outlines shiver clear
a moment, things us kids pressed on the dark
face before it hardened, pale, remembering
delicate old injuries, the spines of names and leaves.

THE EIGHT STAGES OF TRANSLATION

by ROBERT BLY

from THE KENYON REVIEW

nominated by THE KENYON REVIEW, *Naomi Clark, David Ignatow, and Joyce Carol Oates*

IN THIS ESSAY I will not deal with the theory of translation but I will try to answer the question: What is it like to translate a poem? We'll look mainly at the difficulties. The difficulties are all one difficulty, something immense, knotted, exasperating, fond of disguises, resistant, confusing, all of a piece. One translates a poem in fits and starts, getting a half line here, weeks later the other half, but one senses a process. I'm going to simplify the process into eight stages. I mean by that the stages one goes through from the first meeting with a poem to its recreation, when one says goodbye to it. As I've mentioned above, the stages will often collapse into each other, or a single line will suddenly go through all eight stages in a flash, while the other lines lie about looking even more resistant than before. What I will do then is to pretend that all goes in order; but this is an ancient ploy. When one makes a map, one pretends the earth can be laid out flat. But a map helps us to visualize the territory.

I decided not to choose a poem I had already translated, which I would write about from hindsight, but instead I chose virtually at random a sonnet from Rilke's first series of the *Sonnets to Orpheus*, a poem I did not know well. In preparation for this essay, I took the poem to a seminar in German translation and we all worked through the sonnet. The sonnet is this one:

XXI

Frühling ist wiedergekommen. Die Erde
ist wie ein Kind, das Gedichte weiss;
viele, o viele . . . Für die Beschwerde
langen Lernens bekommt sie den Preis.

Streng war ihr Lehrer. Wir mochten das Weisse
an dem Barte des alten Manns.
Nun, wie das Grüne, das Blaue heisse,
dürfen wir fragen: sie kanns, sie kanns!

Erde, die frei hat, du glückliche, spiele
nun mit den Kindern. Wir wollen dich fangen,
fröhliche Erde. Dem Frohsten gelingts.

O, was der Lehrer sie lehrte das Viele,
und was gedruckt steht in Wurzeln und langen
schwierigen Stämmen: sie singts, sie singts!

1

During the first stage we set down a literal version, we don't
worry about nuances—English phrases that are flat, prosaic,
dumpy are fine. We only want the thrust.

Spring has returned again. The earth
is like a child that knows poems;
many, oh many. For the burdens
of her long study, she receives the prize.

Her teacher was hard. We liked the white
in the old man's beard.
Now, how the green [things] and the blue are called,
we dare to ask: she knows it, she knows it!

Earth, on vacation, you lucky one, play
with the children now. We'd like to catch you,
happy earth. Success goes to the happiest.

Oh what the teacher taught her, so many things,
and what is imprinted [or pressed] into roots and the long
difficult stems: She sings it, she sings it!

That is the literal. We notice immediately a problem with the gender of the child. Because Rilke is speaking of earth and a child at once, he is committed, *die Erde* being feminine, to a feminine pronoun, and we'll have to live with that, though we see the child could just as well be male. Earth is "it" in English, so we are already in trouble, and we'll have to face this issue sooner or later.

As we read the literal, our first reaction is: What happened to the poem? Where did it go? So we read the original again and it's still marvelous; so evidently something has been left out—probably the meaning. Before we go farther with a translation then, we have to deal with the issue: What does the poem mean?

2

To find that is what I call the second stage. Some translators just print the literal version; they turn away from this stage. If we enter it, we will need everything we have learned in literature courses, or from our own writing, and all the German we can scrape up in order to penetrate the "problems." Often friends are helpful at this stage, to bring up quirky details that we haven't noticed. Here, for example: Why is this child brought in? And if the earth has to be compared to a child, why a child *"das Gedichte weiss"*? It calls up a typical European schoolroom scene, memorization of poetry; the student who memorizes best, sometimes a girl, wins a prize that the principal perhaps awards her in public at Student's Day. The scene contains the strenuousness and tension of European grade school education. What does that have to do with the spontaneity of spring? That's the first problem.

If we read over our own literal versions, the poem appears to be a sort of depressing testimony to the way school experiences persist in the European adult. It says the earth memorizes poems, gets a prize, and is good at identifying flowers. Then a game at recess appears involving a game of tag, and the poem closes with the child or the earth singing something, no doubt in a school recital. That is what the literal says. If we read over the German, we realize something else or something more is being said, but what?

We go back to the first question. What does grade school education have to do with the spontaneity of spring? In line with that, we ask: Who is this teacher with a white beard or with white in the beard? The white has to be snow, and he winter. Apparently earth knows her own trees and flowers from some memorization work done in winter, the same time school is in session. That's odd. In this stage, it's important to follow every eccentric branch out to its farthest twig—if one doesn't, one pulls the poem back to the mediocre middle, where we all live, reasonably.

The third stanza continues to compare or associate earth and schoolwork. Earth is described now as "*frei*," which in the context means "out of school." During this stage a native born speaker is most helpful—the ambiguous meanings that surround "*weiss*" in line two, "*frei*" in line nine, and "*gedruckt*" in line thirteen, a dictionary will not settle. A native born speaker can shorten the floundering time. Spring apparently resembles the recess time, or perhaps the "play day" some schools have in May. After that we are called immediately back to the teacher. It has been mentioned how strict he is, and now, how many things he teaches. As Americans we tend to get uneasy when our convictions that earth-life and poetry are spontaneous become challenged. The whole mood of American assumptions, of which Whitman is a part, leads us to associate growth—of which the growth from winter to spring is exemplary—with spontaneity, perhaps the spontaneous writing of poetry. But Rilke does not agree with this; he connects growth in this poem—earth growth at least—with discipline, difficulty, routine memorization. This discipline he embodies in the major metaphor: the discipline of learning poems by heart. There is something un-American here, whether by American we mean Whitmanic gladness or the easy stages the "human potential" movement believes in. We don't find our hopeful prejudices supported by Rilke.

A German-born speaker will tell us that "*weiss*" in the second line does not only mean "know" but "memorize," and the context tells us the second meaning is the one used here. "*Beschwerde*" which is related to "burden," "heaviness," "pain," and "difficulty" emphasizes the painful labor involved in growth, as does "*langen*" ("long") before "study," also the word "*streng*" applied to the teacher, and particularly the adjective "*schwierigen*" in the last line, surprisingly given to tree trunks or plant stems. A native speaker will tell us this is not a usual adjective for these nouns at all; so we guess by that that Rilke is laying special emphasis on the difficulty. Whatever the earth achieves therefore she does not achieve through spontaneity. When a poet from another culture contradicts our assumptions, we tend to fudge his point; therefore to struggle with each eccentricity we see is extremely important. Americans are merely twentieth-century readers. Rilke obviously is aware what we, as twentieth-century readers, think, and he violates our expectations consciously. What can it mean that the earth has a teacher? This detail connects to the idea of the evolution of the earth which Rudolf Steiner and others in Germany have written of. If earth has a teacher, it means earth learns gradually as a child does: the whole thing implies the earth has consciousness; one cannot learn and change without consciousness. We feel ourselves drawn here into areas we do not feel confident in, even to ideas we cannot accept. If we cannot accept them, we will resist them as a translator and do a poor job translating the poem. During this stage, then, we test how far we are willing to go. It's clear that the poet is ahead of us, otherwise the poem would not be worth translating; it would have nothing "to say." So we need to estimate how much resistance we have, or we need to sense inside whether we believe, say, in growth by disciplined labor, though it contradicts most cultural assumptions, and whether we believe the earth has a teacher. If we don't, we should let the poem alone and not translate it; we'll only ruin it if we go ahead.

Let's continue with this pursuit of problematic detail. A small problem arises with the ball game. The earth is *"frohliche,"* which Cassell's lists as "joyous, joyful, gay, blithesome, jovial, merry, frolicsome, gladsome." We gather the earth is not repressed, not hard-nosed, not "puritan," to use a cultural term. When Rilke suggests who will win in this game of tag with earth, we would expect it to be "the speediest child" or "the most competitive child." But it isn't so. He uses the same root *"froh,"* and the most joyful child wins, and so "catches" the earth. Here again I feel him violating our expectations, perhaps Christian expectations this time, as opposed to pagan. The Greeks, not much given to sin and savior, always taught that the most joyful child, the most joyful sculptor, the most joyful runner would win. Who gains earth? If the translator believes it is the most repentant, the most sorrowful, the most obedient, he or she should not translate this poem— something will go wrong.

The final problem we notice centers around the curious word

"*gedruckt*" in line thirteen, which is placed next to "roots" or "trunks." "*Gedruckt*" means impressed, pressed on, laid on, stamped, imprinted. It implies a mechanical process. This word belongs to the world of factory presses, work, levers, human forces multiplied, offices, copiers, printing presses, drill presses. What is it doing here? In what sense can a root be "pressed" or "imprinted"? We have to answer it; if we don't, the poem will not be clear. There is enough ambiguity given by the forced movement to another language without additional uncertainty caused by a pious trust in ambiguity which amounts to a refusal to think the question through or risk an answer. What will we do with "*gedruckt*"? We might guess that the imprinting is genetic, as when biologists talk of an animal being "sexually imprinted" at a certain age. But if we accept that, we can't relate it to the singing or the difficulty. Is it possible some words are actually imprinted on the roots? No. Did earth's teacher *impress* this on the plants? I don't think so. Is this some sort of raised lettering, a reference to bark? I don't think so. It is pressed, not raised. How did a sheet-metal press get into this line? We could rephrase the question: How did a printing press get into this line? We see instantly its link with schoolwork because "printed" is exactly how the schoolchild finds the poem which she memorizes. It has been *printed*. After some debate, I adopted this solution, which may of course be wrong, but it allows me to put the details together into a meaningful whole for the first time.

Earth's teacher knows what discipline is, and so earth does. Plants cannot blossom all by themselves. They need earth before they flower. So earth is related to flowers as a human being is to a poem. A poem cannot blossom without a human being; that suggests we should not let a poem lie on the page but should learn it by heart. So out of discipline this enormous blossoming comes and that blossoming from labor lies beneath the excitement that shows itself in the exclamations ending the second and fourth stanzas. It is wonderful to know something, but that is not enough; it also has to be sung, that is, carried by the human body into sound and music, delivered to others, so to speak. Just knowing a poem is not enough. This is quite a different meaning than we arrived at by reading the literal version.

In a good poem, which violates certain secret assumptions, this second stage may take several hours. I spent a long time on this stage alone, some of it arguing over the text with other students and translators. When working with a poem as complicated as this one, the translator can easily get pulled off into a bypath for half an hour; but none of the time is wasted. The more one talks, the more clear Rilke's beliefs become, and so his meaning. He is certain of it, and so the German has a lovely enthusiasm, expressed in lifting, joyful rhythms. If that store of feeling is beyond the translator, he or she should leave the poem be. At the end of this stage, the translator should ask himself whether the feelings as well as the concepts are within his world. If they are not, he should stop. I've had to abandon a number of poems at this point. I remember a Vallejo translation for example; in it I felt Vallejo's feelings toward his own images enter the violet, or grief, range of the spectrum, where I could not follow him. At the age I was, the violet range was not accessible to me, and these feelings can't be faked. In the second stage, we decide whether to turn back or go on.

3

If we decide to go on, we return to our literal version and see where it lost the meanings just found. We redo the literal and try to get it into English this time. We think of the genius of the English language, what its nature is. I'll call that the third stage.

During this stage, we use all we know about the structure of the English language. During the composition of the literal version we followed the word order of the original German, and by doing that found ourselves drawn into the whirlpool of the delayed verb. German gains energy at times by delaying the verb, and even the main noun, so it appears late in the sentence. English gains energy the opposite way, by embarking the main noun immediately and the verb soon after. Most sentences in English that begin with prepositions, with "into" or "upon the" or "for the" tend to be weak in practice; this is not a doctrine but something we observe in reading or writing English. We have to face the issue of the delayed verb immediately, with the third sentence:

Für die Beschwerde
langen Lernens bekommt sie den Preis.

If we say:

For the burden
of her long study, the prize comes to her.

we can feel how dead and flat the lines are. Making the last phrase "she receives the prize" helps, but the lines still feel supine. If we take the main noun and main verb and move them to the front, we can say:

> She receives the prize
> for her long and strenuous study.

It sounds more like English now, and "strenuous" has added considerable energy to the line.

The delayed verb appears again in the green and blue passage of the second stanza. The line: "Now, how the green and blue are called" is not English at all; it belongs to "translatorese," a language never spoken but a language translators know and laugh about. Anything we try will be an improvement:

> So for blue things and green things, we dare
> to ask their names, and she knows them!

That's not marvelous, but it is English and some of the passive, dead mood has disappeared. We feel more confident; we are back in our own language. Leaving the word order of the original poem behind is often painful; beginning translators especially resist it. They feel disloyal if they move the verb, but each language evolves in a different way and we cannot cancel a thousand years of language evolution by our will. Moreover, if we are disloyal to German, we are at the same moment loyal to English. The word order of Spanish is closer to that of English, and this stage is usually less painful when translating from Spanish. So then, after redoing later lines, thinking solely in this stage of the sentence and clause structures natural to English, we would arrive at a new draft. We ignore the sentence structure of the German original, and try to move all sentences bodily into the genius of English. Along the way, we rephrase all other lines as well, so as to avoid being caught in the first phrases that have come to mind. The new version might look something like this:

> Spring has returned once more. The earth
> is like a child who has memorized her poems,
> many, many poems. She receives the prize
> for her long and strenuous learning.

Her teacher was strict. We were fond of the whiteness
in the old man's beard.
As for blue things and green things, we dare
to ask their names, and she knows them!

Earth, now out of class, lucky being, play
now with the children. We want to catch you,
happy earth. Only the happiest succeeds.

How many things the teacher taught her,
and what has been pressed into the roots
and long wiry trunks: she sings it, she sings it!

4

We translated the poem into English in the third stage. In the
fourth stage we translate the poem into American . . . that is, if we
speak the American language. In England, we would translate it
into spoken English. It's the spoken quality that this stage aims at.
The idea that a great poem should be translated freshly every
twenty years is rooted in an awareness of how fast the spoken
language changes. We need the energy of spoken language as we
try to keep a translation alive, just as we need the energy of
written.

Rilke's poems, like those of every great poet, mingle spoken
language and written in the most delicate way; the poem balances
informal tones and formal. But his poetry is never without the
electrifying power that spoken rhythms bring. Rilke's group of ten
"Voices" ("Die Stimmen"), in which a blind man speaks, a suicide
speaks, and a drunkard speaks, carry astonishing and cunning
rhythms, picked up by his ear with its immense feeling for the
rhythms of intimate confession, the accents of desperate conversation, and the dying fall of street language. The aim is not street
language, not slang as such nor the speech rhythms of half-
educated people, but rather the desperate living tone or fragrance
that tells you a person now alive could have said the phrase. Robert
Frost believed in such rhythms and wrote of them brilliantly; he
called the fragrance "sentence sound." Perhaps one in one hundred
sentences we hear or read has "sentence sound." Frost gives a few
examples: "The thing for me to do is to get right out of here" or
"Never you say a thing like that to a *man*"—in this decade it would
be, "You can't say that to a *man*." Another example might be:

"John, you come on right down here and do your work." We might end a poem: "And a lot of the changes in my life go back to that decision," and that line would be English but it would lack sentence sound. The phrasing with sentence sound would be: "And that has made all the difference." As Frost correctly says, it isn't the rational mind that understands these distinctions but the ear and the ear's memory.

So during the fourth stage we begin to need the ear. As we read it over, the opening phrase, "Spring has returned again," which seemed adequate for both first- and third-stage drafts, doesn't sound so good anymore. Suppose we met a friend one day as we left our house. Could we imagine him or her saying, "Spring has returned again"? I don't think so. It doesn't sound right. We may not be able to move this phrase from written English to spoken American, but we can try.

What do we remember people saying to us? I remember: "It's spring!", "Spring is back," "Spring is here again," "It's spring again," "Spring has come again" (not likely, that one). How about "Spring is here, baby"? or "My God, it's spring!" The German definitely has the idea of a cyclical return in it, but we're not sure how important that detail is. For the moment we'll try "It's spring again."

"Viele, o viele," partly because of the "ee" sounds, does not sound bookish in German, but "many, oh many" does sound bookish in American. Suppose a friend comes from the grocery store and says he has bought some potatoes. You want to know how much, and he says, "Many, oh many." It doesn't sound right. His answer would be humorous, but the German here is not. What might he say? How many potatoes? "Lots of potatoes!", "Tons of potatoes!", "Potatoes and potatoes!", "So many potatoes you wouldn't believe it!", "Scads of potatoes!", "Oodles of potatoes!", "Sacks and sacks!", "More than enough!", "A lot of them!", "A ton, a roomful!", "A lot, a lot . . .!" The American language is so astoundingly abundant now in possibilities, that one always ends up with more phrases than one can use, but there's great fun in that too. For the moment we'll choose: "A lot, a lot. . . ."

"She receives the prize for her long and strenuous learning" doesn't sound as if it were spoken language any more. Rarely in speech these days do we let a sentence go so long without a pause. "Receives" doesn't sound right either. We'll try "gets."

> And she gets the prize,
> gets it after study, hard work.

My ear feels better now; it remembers sentences like this, spoken hundreds of times. The sequence is two three-beat phrases, followed by one two-beat phrase, "hard work." That sequence is characteristic in spoken American English.

The next two lines sound all right, but the naming passage I don't like any more. We'll move the "daring to ask" concept to the front of the sentences:

> We feel able to ask what the names of green
> and blue things are, and she knows all of them!

Or

> We feel able, looking at green shades and blue, to ask
> what their names are, and she knows them!

Or

> Asking what this is, so green, and that, so blue,
> seems all right. And she knows the names!

Or

> Asking about the blue, and about the green
> seems right to do, and she knows. She knows!

I'm sure it's clear to the reader now the sort of work one does during this step, and I won't go over the rest of the poem in detail.

Asking the ear about each phrase, asking it, "Have you ever heard this phrase spoken?" is the labor of this draft. The ear will reply with six or seven new phrases, and these act to shake up the translation once more and keep it from solidifying. The language becomes livelier, fresher, lighter. Many translators stop before this stage; some of them have an exalted idea of the poet and think Rilke uses written German; others associate literature with a written language, with written English—many academic translators have this habit—and it never occurs to them to move to the spoken. Nineteenth-century translators in general rarely took this step; it was Whitman, Pound, and William Carlos Williams who sharpened everyone's sense for spoken English and spoken American. The marvelous translation that is now being done in the United States, work that has been going on for thirty years or more, is partly a gift of these three men and their faith that poetry can be composed in spoken rhythms.

The new draft then might look something like this:

> It's spring! The earth
> is like a child who's learned poems by heart,
> a lot, a lot! And she gets the prize,
> gets it after study, hard work.
>
> Her teacher was strict. We were fond of the white
> we saw in the old man's beard.
> Asking about the green—how about that blue—
> seems all right, and she knows all the names!
>
> Earth, now out of school, born lucky, play
> now with the children. We want to play catch,
> glad earth. The most glad catches you.
>
> The teacher managed to teach her so much.
> Astonishing! And what the roots and the long
> strenuous stalks hold in printed form, she sings!

5

We haven't thought about tone yet. Does this last draft have the tone of the German? In what I'll call the fifth stage we need the ear again—not the ear turned outward toward human speech but the ear turned inward toward the complicated feelings the poem is carrying. Each poem has a mood. Harry Martinson remarked that to him a poem *is* a mood. A poem did not come to him out of an idea, but a poem marked a moment when he was able to catch a mood.

To succeed in this stage I think it is important that the translator should have written poetry himself. I mean that he or she needs the experience of writing from mood in order to judge accurately what the mood of a stranger's poem is. We need accurate judgment on mood now because in finding spoken phrases to replace the written we may have thrown the tone off. We may have the wrong "tone of voice" in the new phrases. The spoken language has dozens of tones available; sometimes in American, hundreds. The reason that "Spring is here, baby" doesn't sound right for the opening sentence is not because it isn't *spoken*—it carries a wonderful fragrance of the spoken—but rather because the mood of the original poem is quite different. Many translators stop before this stage; they translate a poem into spoken American and then quit. Pope put Homer into eighteenth-century spoken English and ignored the problem of mood. When in America we force Catullus into hip language it means we have stopped before struggling with this problem. Catullus likes mischievous words and obscene phrases, but he will lay them in among measured Latin rhythms. Overall Catullus's mood is a tender, complicated grief that resembles the mood of Celtic art.

The younger we are, the easier it is to make mistakes in tone. During my late twenties, I translated over sixty poems of Rilke's. A few years ago when I went back to look at them, I had to throw away virtually every line I had done because I had confused Rilke's mood with certain violent moods I had at the time. I had made almost every line more extroverted than it was. I may still be doing that.

Rilke is especially difficult in the matter of mood because German in one of its levels is high-flown. All language has two levels at least: an upper and a lower. We recognize the "upper" in Shakespeare's sonnets: language high-flown, ethical, elaborated, capable of concept, witty, dignified, noble in tone.

We might speculate that in the American language now only the "lower" level is alive. It flows along on earth; it is a physical language that everyone contributes to, warm, intense, with short words, well connected to the senses, musical, capable of feeling. This sensual language is the only one we have; William Carlos Williams used this language by principle when he wrote, and Brecht used the lower level by choice in his German poems. In America the "noble" stream dried out around 1900, against the will of Henry James, and since that time, as Williams declared, the writer has had no choice.

What we have to do then in Rilke is use our one level to carry his two. The problems of tone are tremendous. Pablo Neruda's *Odas Elementales* go into American so much more easily because by 1956, when he wrote them, Neruda too was using only the sensual language. But Rilke in 1920 found both the "upper" and "lower" languages alive, and the presence of both in his work is a part of his greatness. Rilke not only invited in the "noble language" with its immense garden of associations, but he carried it brilliantly. Rilke's richness became especially noticeable during World War II when the Nazis were destroying the resonance of the German language by inserting brutal bureaucratic jargon. A German professor sympathetic with the Resistance told me that in his city the word "Rilke" was a secret password for their Resistance and became so precisely because of Rilke's rich language.

We notice that this problem of "noble language" causes a lot of trouble to translators in their effort to translate Rilke into English. Rilke translations have frequently been nobly dead. The translator, in the effort to rise to the upper or resonating level he senses in Rilke, abandons our living language and resorts to old cloudlike phrases that are now only scenery. He tries, from the best intentions, to retrieve and revive dusty clauses and high-flown diction and stuff them into the poem, with the result that the living language dies, both languages die, and Rilke seems ridiculous. J B Leishman, speaking of a palace in one Rilke translation, says:

> And, dazzlingly from all points manifest
> (like pale sky with diffused illumination),
> by weight of fading portraiture possessed
> as by some deep interior contemplation,
> the palace, in unfestal resignation,
> stands taciturn and patient as a guest.

It is hard to recognize these lines as Rilke's. The vividness is gone and the senses have evaporated. Mr Leishman is not inaccurate, but the translation fails in tone, and that comes from pretending that the aristocratic stream of language is still alive in English. We have to use the feeling stream only; it is grievous, but we have no choice. As I mentioned, Rilke used both languages, but interestingly the simple or feeling language grows stronger as he grows older. Each poem he wrote in the ten years before his death moves toward its own tone fragrance, in contrast to the poems from *A Book for the Hours of Prayer* in which a whole group of poems carry a single tone, often high-flown.

To return to our sonnet, if we read the sonnet that comes just before it in the *Sonnets to Orpheus* and the sonnet just after, we notice great distinctions in mood. The sonnets on each side plunge into memory; number 22 for example sinks into a sort of deep Gothic memory, with slow heartbeats. The sonnet we have, by contrast, is light-hearted, gay, and enthusiastic—the exclamation marks alone indicate that—but the light-heartedness is one that comes after long brooding or long thoughtfulness. The point is not only that "It's spring" but that "It's spring *again*." So the simple statement "It's spring!" doesn't seem quite right now, in mood. Moreover, the stopped sounds in "a lot A lot!" create a pugnacious mood, even though enthusiastic, that "viele, o viele" doesn't have. Moreover we notice that changing the word order of the sentence about receiving the prize has changed the mood of the stanza. In German the prize represents the close of a learning process; but we, by moving the prize to the middle, interrupted the process. The prize interferes with the grief of learning, so to speak. So we'll have to change that.

> It's spring once more. The earth
> is like a child who's learned poems by heart,
> many of them . . . and after hard work
> and long study, she gets the prize.

That's better. Studying the next stanza, I have become uneasy with the tone of "how about that blue." Perhaps we should aim for a softer tone.

> Her teacher was strict. We were fond of the white
> we saw in the old man's beard.
> And we can ask the blue flower's name
> and that green bush—she knows all the names!

I'm a little dissatisfied also with "glad" earth or "happy" earth. Both are too light. Something is wrong with their mood. Neither "glad" nor "happy" carries the dark side, as one feels *"fröhliche Erde"* does. The adjective *"fröhliche"* may be related to the word *Freya*, the ancient Germanic Great Mother. Her joy has a lot of darkness in it. Perhaps Freya's darkness is connected to the luck she brings.

> Earth, now out of school, lucky inside, play
> now with the children, we want to touch you,
> deeply glad earth. The deepest catches you.

"Deeply glad" may be wrong but we'll try it; and I feel better about the mood of that stanza now; it has a little more darkness in it.

But I don't feel the next line is right—there is a lovely enthusiasm in the German "O, was der Lehrer sie lehrte, das Viele," that I don't feel that in the line:

> The teacher managed to teach her so much

The tone is wrong. We feel some praise for the teacher in the German line: "O, was der Lehrer sie lehrte, das Viele." We could try: "The teacher she had, he taught her so well."

We could try leaving out "he":

> The teacher she had taught her so well!
> So much!

The problem is that we're getting caught in the human part of the poem now. Rilke's German, because "Erde" is feminine, is able to hold our attention evenly divided between what the *earth* learns, and what the *school girl* learns: we see with two eyes at once. But because "Erde" is "it" in English, we've lost one eye. We're forgetting the earth. By repeating "she" we're losing some of the deep earth mood, and veering too far toward the more human mood we feel in the girl student. For the sake of tone, we may have to replace that "she" with "earth."

> The teacher earth had taught her so well!
> So much! And what nature printed in roots
> and knotty, slender trunks, she manages to sing!

Summing up, then, in this stage we move to modify errors that may have come in with the emphasis on the spoken. Most of all we open ourselves for the first time to the mood of the poem; we try to be precise about what its mood *is*, distinguishing it from the mood of nearby poems. We try to capture the poem's balance between high and low, dark and light, seriousness and light-heartedness.

6

In the next stage, which I call here the sixth, we pay attention to sound. The question of tone has led to this. If we wonder whether the poem's tone is enthusiastic or melancholic, there is only one thing to do: memorize the poem in its original German and say it to yourself, to friends, to the air. No one can translate well from a poem he or she hasn't learned by heart; only by reciting it can we feel what sort of oceanic rhythm it has, which is a very different thing from analyzing the meter.

When we recite Rilke's German, free from the page, we notice immediately that there is a powerful beat on the opening syllable of the first, third, and fourth lines. This is a rhythm characteristic of pagan poetry; almost all Greek poems begin with this resolute firm stroke on the first syllable, and much of *Beowulf*. Christian poetry gradually evolved toward iambic rhythm, in which the first syllable is somewhat ingratiating, softer, more modest, and prepares the way for the heavier second stroke. Throwing the energy toward the start of the line hints again at the poem's nature, which is more pagan than Christian. A number of phrases: "viele o viele," "Streng war ihr Lehrer," "dürfen wir fragen," "Erde, die frei hat," "fröhliche Erde" start the line with a stroke, a confident assertion, causing a rocking motion.

What's wrong with "a lot! a lot!" as an opening to line three is that it doesn't have this initial stroke. "Many, o many" is better, but the crest doesn't rise high enough. "Viele, o viele" resembles a high rising wave, and the sound "ee" in "viele" helps it to rise. "Ee" is high. The "an" in "many" does not carry the line far enough up.

In our last draft the opening lines read:

> It's spring once more. The earth
> is like a child who's learned poems by heart,
> many of them . . .

We can only get a higher wave in line two by going to an open vowel. We'll try this:

> so many poems . . .

The opening phrase:

> Frühling ist wiedergekommen

also has a rocking motion, and our versions of that sentence so far, though spoken and all right in tone, feel a bit flat: "It's spring," or "It's spring once more." I'd favor trying to pick up some sort of rocking motion.

> Spring is here, has come! The earth
> is like a child who's learned poems by heart,
> so many poems . . .

We're getting there.

We can distinguish in a poem between two sound energies, one in the muscle system and one in the ear. That is very roughly stated. The rocking motion we have spoken of is a body motion, which Donald Hall calls "goat foot" because of its association with Greek drum and dancing. Similarly, in a recent essay Robert Hass struggles to separate certain rhythms felt in the muscle system from meter. "I have already remarked that meter is not the basis of rhythmic form." The body motion alerts the mind and builds tension which is later released. Most nineteenth-century translators, ignoring the distinction, imagined that by following the meter of the original poem precisely they would arrive at the rhythm. But it didn't happen. The translator's job is to feel the body rhythm of the line, but that may or may not lead to the meter. The rocking motions, or body motion, is primary, not meter. Using Donald Hall's metaphor, we can speculate that we can understand the meter in a poem without necessarily experiencing the goat's foot. A flat line, in metered or free verse, may have human feet but not goat's feet.

I've mentioned a second quality of sound—sound calling to sound, which is related to internal rhyme. I don't feel right in talking about that one yet because I'm just learning it myself. But if the reader will memorize the Rilke poem in German and say it over many times, he will understand sound calling to sound without my help.

Keeping these two aspects of sound in mind, and saying the German over many times, I decide to make the following changes in the first stanza:

> Spring is here, has come! The earth
> resembles a child who has learned her poems.
> So many poems! Her study long,
> strenuous, earns it . . . the prize comes to her.

In the next stanza I decide, for the sake of internal rhyme, to change "strict" to "stern." The rhythmical wave in German rises at the left wall with "Nun, wie das Grüne," so we have to do some work with the English rhythm at that point. "And we ask the blue flower's name" is too flat. There's no heavy stroke at the start.

> What names to give to green patches, and blue
> occurs to us, we ask! Earth knows it by heart!

The change helps.

Let's go on to the third stanza. I see that by altering the ninth line I can shift the rhythm over to the left. We had:

> Earth, now out of school, lucky inside, play
> now with the children. We want to touch you,
> deeply glad earth. The deepest catches you.

We'll try:

> Earth, free from school now, joyful, come,
> play with the children. We want to touch you,
> deeply glad earth. The deepest catches you.

Now the "deeply glad" earth passage bothers me. None of the phrases we've tried please me. "Happy earth," "glad earth" . . . "deeply glad earth." The last seems closest. So separating "fröhliche" into an adverb and an adjective may be a solution. Rilke uses two words from the same root, "froh," and we should follow him if we can. "Happy" and "happiest," "glad" and "gladdest" do that, but they are too light. Listening to the German sound, we notice that Rilke uses here the open "oh" sound for the first time in the poem. "Wir wollen dich fangen . . . Dem frohsten gelingts." It's possible that the "aeh" sounds we have been using in "happy" or "glad" are wrong for his mood. I decide to try this:

> Earth, free from school now, joyful, come
> play with the children. We want to catch you,
> wholly glad earth. The most whole gets you.

One can never be sure, when helped by sound to a solution, if the solution is reasonable, justifiable, within Rilke's area of meaning.

After brooding about it, I decide the emphasis on "whole" as opposed to "happy," "glad," or "perfect" is all right. Some associations that cluster around "froh" are carried in our culture by "whole." We notice for example the becoming whole, whole earth, whole-wheat bread, resonate with certain associations around the earth mother. I have to trust my sense of it. I may be wrong, but the line now seems to me more in focus than it was.

The German of the next line has a strong opening beat with "O was der Lehrer. . . ." If I want something like that I'll have to abandon my old line, even though I like it:

> The teacher earth had taught her so well

I'll try "Earth's teacher," and rephrase also the final two lines of the poem:

> Earth's teacher taught her things, so many!
> And the sounds that lie printed inside roots
> and long entangled stalks: she carries and sings them!

I'll set down here, then, a draft worked out after brooding over Rilke's rhythm, which has a strong rocking motion, and the dominant vowel sounds of the poem, and internal and external rhymes.

> Spring is here, has come! The earth
> resembles a child who has learned her poems.
> So many poems! Her study long,
> strenuous, earns it. . . . The prize comes to her.
>
> Her teacher was stern. We loved the white
> that showed in the old man's beard.
> What names to give to the green patch and the blue
> comes to us, and we ask: earth knows it by heart!
>
> Earth, free from school now, joyful, come
> play with the children. We want to catch you,
> wholly glad earth. The most whole gets you.
>
> Earth's teacher taught her things, so many!
> And the sounds that lie printed inside roots
> and long entangled stalks: she carries and sings them!

7

We are nearly finished now. During what I will call the seventh stage we ask someone born into the language to go over our version. Perhaps we go back to the native speaker who helped us in the first draft; if we did not get such help then, we do now; we ask him or her to find errors that have crept in.

For beginning translators, this stage is very painful. As beginners, we tend to give ourselves permission to veer away from the poem's images, pulled away in fact by our private mental horses, and dismay sets in when we realize that some of our best solutions are simply wrong. Hardie St Martin has always performed this reining-in function when I, or James Wright with me, translated from Spanish. Once I remember he found in a single Jimenez poem that I had already worked over for months, and that contained only twenty lines to start with, twenty-two errors that could not be allowed to stand. The error sometimes was in tone, sometimes in image, or slant of image, or I had picked up a South American coloring the word had rather than its Castilian coloring, or I had gotten the rhythm or vowels wrong. None of us can learn a foreign language well enough to pick all these things up.

During this new stage we also have a second chance to ask about the implications of certain words that have begun to bother us. I want to check out my sense of "fröhliche" and "Frohsten" and talk some more about "gedruckt." I didn't notice "schwierigen" so much at first, but now I see it as an unsolved or entangled knot of associations, and I want to know what its German root is. Almost all words that seem abstract now once, as Owen Barfield makes so clear in his book on the history of words, carried a physical motion at the start, perhaps pulling or cutting or lifting. Sometimes knowing the German root helps to choose an English word. If one has a German friend nearby then the labor of this stage can be done gradually, as the problems come up, and that is probably best. But if not, we should take on this stage by will, and consider it as important as any of the earlier stages. We have been slowly possessing the poem and making it ours—we have to do that to bring it alive—but it is possible that we have kidnapped it instead.

8

Our last stage is making the final draft. We read back over all our earlier drafts—perhaps a half line was said better in one of them.

We have to make our final adjustments now. I decide to change the blue and green clause once more, but I won't make many substantive changes. As a result of the conversation around "schwierigen" I've decided to use "involved," and I notice that the n's are coming along well in the final stanza, and "involved" will help that. During this stage we allow ourselves, at last, the pleasure of examining other people's translations of the poem. That is fun we can't deny ourselves after all the work, and we can sympathize with each translator. We don't expect much from J B Leishman, and he doesn't give much.

> Spring has come again. Earth's a-bubble
> with all those poems she knows by heart—
> oh, so many. With prize for the trouble
> of such long learning, her holidays start.

One can see he has had trouble with his rhymes. I believe in working as much as possible with internal rhymes, but I think it's best not to insist on reproducing end rhymes. Nineteenth-century translators often felt obsessive about end-rhyming, and usually did it in exactly the same pattern as in the original poem. Leishman's version shows a common outcome: the translator has to add images that destroy the poem's integrity. There is no mention of earth bubbling in Rilke's poem, and the "start of the holidays" interferes with the learning process he is evoking. Leishman's third stanza reads:

> Eager to catch you, Earth, happy creature,
> play with the children now outpouring!
> Conqueringly foremost the happiest springs.

Leishman is helpful, in a way, because reading his translations one grows determined to retranslate.

Al Poulin, who published *Duino Elegies and the Sonnets to Orpheus* in 1977, is a much better translator. We could look at his first two stanzas:

> Spring has returned again. The earth
> is like a child who's memorized
> poems; many, so many . . . It was worth
> the long painful lesson: she wins the prize.

> Her teacher was strict. We liked the white
> in the old man's whiskers.
> Now when we ask what green or blue is, right
> away she knows, she has the answer!

This is not so bad; good work on the spoken. But rhyming caused trouble again. He wanted to rhyme "earth," and ended up with "worth." Rilke doesn't say whether the prize was worth all the effort or not. Possibly a half-rhyme with "answer" pulled him into "whiskers," which loses some dignity and some feeling of the snow. In general, though he is translating with considerable accuracy, we feel that he stopped his labors after the spoken stage. He does not work on sound. His lines are not joyful in sound. In fact, the *s* sounds dominate: "lesson," "memorized," "prize," "strict," "whiskers," "ask," "answer." The *z* and *s* sounds produce a kind of hissing that encourages anxiety.

His third stanza goes:

> Earth, lucky earth on vacation,
> play with the children now. We long
> to catch you, happy earth. The happiest will win.

He uses "happy" and "happiest" so the "oh" sound doesn't have a chance to enter. Of course one might say that if a translator is doing all the sonnets, he has no time to pay so much attention to one. We understand that, but it is perhaps better to do one carefully than to do the whole fifty-five.

The French translation by J F Angelloz, which he did with Rilke's knowledge, is accurate and clear. We notice that in the third stanza he uses the word "compliqués" to translate "schwierigen":

> O, ce que le maître lui enseigna, l'innombrable,
> et ce qui est imprimé dans les racines et les longs
> troncs compliqués: elle le chante, elle le chante!

To my surprise, I found a commentary on this poem by Angelloz at the back, which I hadn't known of before. Now that we have gone over the poem so carefully, Angelloz' commentary is extremely interesting, and I'll translate it here, roughly, from the French.

Here spring blazes up and fills the poem. Holthusen says that the true season of the *Sonnets to Orpheus* is summer, the season of fullness and possession. But that is a misconception. Rilke had a predilection for transitional times and, especially during the final years of his life, for that transitional time the Germans call, so happily, "Vorfrühling." He saw such transitional times as the creative periods. It was, in fact, at the start of February 1922 that he completed the *Elegies* and the *Sonnets;* it was on the 9th that he wrote "Children's Spring Song" (Frühlings-Kinder-Lied) which he sent to Madama Oukama-Knoop to replace the sonnet beginning "O das Neue, Freunde, ist nicht dies" (published in *Späte Gedichte*, p 97), and to serve as a counterpart to the horse poem (Letter to Madame Oukama-Knoop, February 9, 1922). And, finally, it was at a similar time of the year, in 1913, that Rilke experienced, at Ronda in southern Spain, the incident that inspired this sonnet.

In a convent church he heard a mass accompanied by music, as by bouquets of joyful sound; it was a remarkable music, with a dance rhythm; to it children were singing an unknown text to the sound of a triangle and a tambourine. Rilke considered this sonnet as an interpretation ("Auslegung") of that mass, and he found in it "the mood of spring at its most luminous." He starts, in essence, with a cry of joy that greets the return of spring. Moreover the earth is compared to a child, who knows numerous poems; she receives the prize for assiduous work. But it is wrong to talk of a comparison; in fact, there is an identification going on of the springtime earth, the children singers, and the Orphic poet himself, who, in the second stanza, uses "we." There is a parallel identification of winter, an old man with a white beard, a singing master, whom Rilke does not mention again, and Orpheus, who teaches the art of distinguishing the main springtime colors (green, blue), as he also teaches all creatures to listen. And now, the earth freed from winter, the children, who have learned their poems by heart, and the poet himself, who takes part in the awakening of nature, play tag with the earth, source

of all joys; the victory goes to the most joyful of them.
The sonnet closes in a magnificent harmony: the universal impulse of Dionysius expresses itself in singing; and
all of it—we can think also of the early sonnets—all of it
is Orpheus singing.

I am encouraged by this story. And our interpretation of the poem
is supported by his comments, and what I called "pagan" he calls
"Dionysian." It is possible that the mysterious teacher of the earth
is Orpheus.

Well, then, after studying once more all our earlier drafts, and
making our final sound and rhythm adjustments, and after taking
in what we can from other people's translations and commentaries,
we are ready to set down the final draft. We know that we haven't
captured the original: the best translation resembles a Persian rug
seen from the back—the pattern is apparent, but not much more.
The final version, then, so far, is this:

> Spring is here, has come! The earth
> is like a child who has learned her poems—
> so many poems! . . . Her study, long,
> strenuous, earns it . . . the prize comes to her.
>
> Her teacher was stern. We loved the white
> showing in the beard of the old man.
> What is blue and what is green have distinct names—
> What are they? Earth knows all that by heart!
>
> Earth, free now of school, lucky one, come,
> play with the children. We want to tag you,
> wholly glad earth. The most whole catches you.
>
> Earth's teacher, how much he taught her!
> So much! And what lies printed inside roots,
> inside long, involved stalks: earth carries that and sings it!

𝄾 𝄾 𝄾

THE WOMAN WHO LIVES IN THE BOTANICAL GARDENS

by ALEXIS DE VEAUX

from OPEN PLACES

nominated by Colleen McElroy

is a man. who. sleeping on a hill
and a bench among the Chinese
maple trees lives there. sleeping in her petticoats
of ackee leaf
and banana leaf though neither grows
in this city: O see: how
tall she is the tallest lean: O see:
the delicate spread of her branch
a thickly muscled arm. how it sways there (quiet)
how it dreams
of plantain and rice and the Black Star Line:
O Jah
and the hairless face/the primitive hollow of
cheeks taut: with re
bellion. black with the dust of upturned earth and
the plantings of
memory.
O Jah see
O Jah
see: the barest of black/like an island
and the hair the long: dangling
mats of hair under arm pits; the perfumed hair
laden with anarchy:
hands from the pit of the arm dangling over the bench.

THE WOMAN WHO LIVES IN THE BOTANICAL GARDENS
wears underneath her
banana ackee leaf petticoat the pants of 3
generations: her grand
father's her father's: her own.
THE WOMAN WHO NEVER COMES OUTSIDE
the gates never comes outside the rags
around her pine bark hair;
the reams of rage: O see, O Jah:

THE WOMAN WHO LIVES IN THE BOTANICAL GARDENS/
THE WOMAN WHO LIVES
IN THE BOTANICAL GARDENS: is named South Africa.
See there how she
holds the m-16: how she holds the Gardens hostage.
and the bullets
in her earlobes: bullets at her breasts:
the red green and gold
rage. And the necklace of fallopian tube
and the egg of children
and the bits of blood of hair
in the tumours of the homeland: O
Jah: O Jah: see her how she: stalks the gates.
O Jah/THE WOMAN WHO
THE WOMAN WHO LIVES:
on the squirrels and stray cats of the Garden
LIVES. like a guard dog. gums bared.
teeth pointed: she snap at
the gate:

THERE WILL BE NO   VISITORS
AT THE GARDEN TODAY
OR TOMORROW NEITHER
IN FACT
DON'T COME NO CLOSER:
I REALLY DO MEAN TO SHOOT UP THE MUSEUM
I REALLY DO MEAN TO SHOOT UP THE PARKWAY
I REALLY DO MEAN TO SHOOT UP THE HELICOPTER
SO: DON'T COME NO CLOSER

WHO IS ME??
THIS IS SOUTH AFRICA SPEAKING
BLACK SOUTH AFRICA
AND I AM TAKING OVAH THIS SHIT
I AM TAKING OVAH.

SAPPHICS AGAINST ANGER

by TIMOTHY STEELE

from THE THREEPENNY REVIEW

nominated by Thom Gunn

Angered, may I be near a glass of water;
May my first impulse be to think of Silence,
Its deities (who are they? do in fact they
       Exist? etc.).

May I recall what Aristotle says of
The subject: to give vent to rage is not to
Release it but to be increasingly prone
       To its incursions.

May I imagine being in the *Inferno,*
Hearing it asked: "Vergilio mio, who's
That sulking with Achilles there?" and hearing
       Vergil say: "Dante,

That fellow, at the slightest provocation,
Slammed phone receivers down, and waved his arms like
A madman. What Attila did to Europe,
       What Genghis Khan did

To Asia, that poor dope did to his marriage."
May I, that is, put learning to good purpose,
Mindful that melancholy is a sin, though
       Stylish at present.

Better than rage is the post-dinner quiet,
The sink's warm turbulence, the streaming platters,
The suds rehearsing down the drain in spirals
       In the last rinsing.

For what is, after all, the good life save that
Conducted thoughtfully, and what is passion
If not the holiest of powers, sustaining
       Only if mastered.

TUTKA BAY, ALASKA

by ANITA WILKINS

from THE TREES ALONG THIS ROAD (Blackwells Press)

nominated by Naomi Clark

Wet wordy morning.
Nothing more cranky than
that raven, black burry voice
from the spruce trees.

Flaps down for a clam
on the tide bed.
Flaps back.
In the trees
huddling and cracking.

A black helicopter thuds overhead,
cranky. Looking out for itself.

Up here, they say Raven began the world.

for my father

CONTRIBUTORS' NOTES

DIANE ACKERMAN is the author of three poetry collections and a prose memoir.

JOHN ALLMAN is the author of *Walking Four Ways in The Wind* (Princeton) and two other collections. His work has appeared in *The American Poetry Review, Chowder Review, Memphis State Review* and elsewhere.

JILLIAN BECKER was born in Johannesburg in 1932. She is the author of three novels set in South Africa plus a study of German terrorism in the 1970's, *Hitler's Children*.

CLARK BLAISE is the recipient of a 1983 Guggenheim award. His next novel is *Lusts*.

ROBERT BLY's many books include a translation of Rilke's poems—*The Selected Poems of Ranier Maria Rilke* (Harper and Row). His essay in this volume has just been published by Rowan Tree Press in book form with poems translated by Mr. Bly.

PHILIP BOOTH is the author of six books, most recently *Before Sleep*. He teaches at Syracuse University.

WAYNE C. BOOTH is George M. Tullman Distinguished Professor of English at The University of Chicago. He is President of The Modern Language Association and the author of several books.

RAYMOND CARVER's next collection of short stories has just been published by Knopf. His stories have appeared in *Pushcart Prize* editions I and VI.

AMY CLAMPITT is the author of *Kingfisher* (Knopf, 1983). She received a Guggenheim Fellowship last year.

ANDREI CODRESCU's most recent publication is *Selected Poems*. A new novel is just out from City Lights—*In American Shoes*.

HENRI COULETTE lives in South Pasadena, California. His work has appeared in *The New Yorker, Poetry, The Hudson Review* and elsewhere.

JOHN DANIEL's chapbook, *Common Ground*, is due this summer from Clearwater Press. He will be the Jones Lecturer in poetry at Stanford University for 1983-84.

JEAN DAVIDSON graduated from the Center for Writers at the University of Southern Mississippi. Her work has appeared in *Mississippi Review* and *Sojourner*.

JANET DESAULNIERS is at work on a first novel and lives in Evanston, Illinois.

ALEXIS DE VEAUX is the author of a novel, an award winning children's book and, most recently, of a biography—*Don't Explain: A Song of Billie Holiday.*

WILLIAM DICKEY is the author of five poetry collections—most recently *The Sacrifice Consenting* (Pterodactyl Press). He was awarded The Juniper Prize and an award from The American Institute and Academy of Arts and Letters.

PATRICIA DOBLER's poems have appeared in *Ohio Review, Poetry Now, The Bellingham Review, Tendril* and elsewhere. She is the author of the chapbook, *Forget Your Life.*

ALAN DUGAN's *New and Collected Poems (1961-1983)* will soon be published by Ecco Press. He has won both The Pulitzer Prize and The National Book Award for poetry.

LOUISE ERDRICH is a Turtle Mountain Chippewa who grew up in Wahpeton, North Dakota and attended Dartmouth College. She has taught school, worked road construction and edited a newspaper for the Boston Indian Council.

JANE FLANDERS won the Juniper Prize in 1982 for her book of poems, *The Students of Snow*. She is poet in residence at Clark University.

TESS GALLAGHER's *Willingly* has just been published by Graywolf Press. Her poems have been featured in *Pushcart Prize* editions I and IV.

WILLIAM GASS' story is taken from his novel-in-progress, *The Tunnel.* He is the author of *Omensetters Luck, In the Heart of the Heart of The Country, On Being Blue,* and a number of other books.

ELLEN GILCHRIST is the author of a book of short stories, *In The Land of Dreamy Dreams* (University of Arkansas Press) and a novel, *Annunciations* (Little, Brown). Her short story "Rich" was featured in *Pushcart Prize IV.*

JORIE GRAHAM's poems have appeared in *Ironwood, The Paris Review, American Poetry Review, Antaeus* and elsewhere.

JAMES BAKER HALL's first book of poems, *Her Name,* was published by Pentagram Press in 1982. His second novel, *Music For A Broken Piano,* has just been published. He teaches at the University of Kentucky.

ANDREW HUDGINS, a Wallace Stegner Award winner, has a first book of poems ready for publication. His work has appeared in *The Hudson Review, The Georgia Review, The Southern Review* and elsewhere.

RICHARD HUGO's many publications include nine volumes of poetry, a collection of lectures and essays and two mystery novels. His collected poems will soon be issued. His many awards include the Theodore Roethke Memorial Poetry Prize, a Rockefeller Fellowship, and a Guggenheim Fellowship. He was director of the creative writing program at the University of Montana and editor of the Yale Younger Poets series at the time of his death in October, 1982.

RICHARD HOWARD's eighth poetry collection is soon to be published by Atheneum.

WILLIS JOHNSON lives in Gardiner, Maine and has written several stories about the people of "Prayer for The Dying."

JANE KENYON's first book of poems, *From Room To Room*, was published by Alice James Books. She is at work on a second collection plus a translation of the poems of Anna Akhmatova.

LINCOLN KIRSTEIN is president of the School of American ballet and he is the co-director of The New York City Ballet. He has written extensively on the ballet.

MAXINE KUMIN won the Pulitzer Prize for her poetry in 1973. She was appointed Poetry Consultant to the Library of Congress in 1981.

THOMAS LeCLAIR was a Fulbright lecturer in Greece. His reviews of contemporary fiction have appeared in *The New Republic, The Washington Post, The New York Times Book Review,* and elsewhere.

LI-YOUNG LEE lives in Chicago. This is his second published poem.

GORDON LISH is an editor at Knopf and author of the novel, *Dear Mr. Capote*.

OSCAR MANDEL is the author of seventeen books, the latest of which is *Collected Lyrics and Epigrams*.

BOBBIE ANN MASON's prize-winning short story collection, *Shiloh And Other Stories*, was recently published by Harper and Row.

ROBERT McBREARTY is 28 years old, a graduate of the Iowa Writers Workshop and lives in Santa Fe, New Mexico.

THOMAS McGRATH is the author of several poetry collections, as well as a novel and filmscripts. He has held fellowships from The National Endowment for the Arts, The Guggenheim Foundation, the Bush Foundation and the Amy Lowell Travelling Fellowship.

HEATHER McHUGH's poetry has appeared in *Antaeus, Atlantic* and *Pushcart Prize V.* She lives in Binghampton, New York.

JOE-ANNE McLAUGHLIN has published in *New Letters* and elsewhere. She won the Academy of American Poets award in 1978.

HILDA MORLEY's most recent collection of poetry was *What Are Winds & What Are Waters* (Matrix Press, 1982). She lives in New York City.

JOYCE CAROL OATES' most recent book is *The Profane Art* (essays and criticism). Her next novel is *Mysteries of Winterthurn*.

MARY OLIVER's most recent book of poems is *Twelve Moons*. Her next collection is titled *American Primitive*.

RAYMOND OLIVER teaches at the University of California at Berkeley and has published a book of poetry, *Entries,* with David Godine Co.

CYNTHIA OZICK is the author of the novel, *Trust,* and several short story collections. Her work has appeared in *Pushcart Prize* editions I, V and VII.

Contributors' Notes

STANLEY PLUMLY is the author of the poetry collection, *Out of the Body Travel* (Ecco Press) and other work. He lives in Iowa.

W. D. SNODGRASS teaches in the English Department at the University of Delaware and is the author of several volumes of poems.

ANN STANFORD is the author of six books of poetry, the last being *In Mediterranean Air* (Viking). She is working on a new book of poems titled *Dreaming the Garden*.

TIMOTHY STEELE is the author of two poetry collections: *Uncertainties and Rest* and *The Prudent Heart*.

GERALD STERN was co-poetry editor for *Pushcart Prize VII*. He is the author of *Lucky Life* and a recipient of the Lamont Award.

ELLEN BRYANT VOIGT has published two volumes of poetry: *Claiming Kin* (Wesleyan) and *The Forces of Plenty* (Norton). She lives in Cabot, Vermont.

SUSAN WELCH is at work on a first novel. This is her first published story.

KATE WHEELER is at work on her first novel. She lives in Provincetown, Massachusetts.

RICHARD WILBUR is writer in residence at Smith College. He has recently published a book of poems, *The Mind-Reader,* a collection of prose pieces and several translations. He received the PEN Translation Award in June, 1983.

ANITA WILKINS is the author of two poetry collections, both from Blackwells Press.

🔥 🔥 🔥

OUTSTANDING WRITERS

(The editors also wish to mention the following important works published by small presses last year. Listing is alphabetical by author's last name.)

FICTION

Living Alone in Iota — Lee K. Abbott (Fiction International)
Canned Fish — Rosaire Appel (Mississippi Review)
Harold Munger's Story — Nicholson Baker (Story Quarterly)
The Naked Lady — Madison Smartt Bell (Crescent Review)
Johnnieruth — Becky Birtha (Iowa Review)
The Dignity of Life — Carol Bly (Ploughshares)
from Points In Time — Paul Bowles (Missouri Review)
Greasy Lake — T. Coraghessan Boyle (Paris Review)
Lily — T. Alan Broughton (Ploughshares)
Critics — Frederick Busch (Conjunctions)
The Mexican Donkey — Alvaro Cardona-Hine (Bilingual Review)
The First Wife — Andrea Carlisle (Northwest Review)
Where Saturn Keeps the Years — R.V. Cassill (Hermes House)
from Dictee — Theresa Hak Kung Cha (Tanam Press)
Enough — Fred Chappell (Xavier Review)
The Furlough — Fred Chappell (Writers Forum)
Oliver and August — Carolyn Chute (Shenandoah)
Omar Wicks and The Hippie Massacre — Carolyn Chute (Agni Review)
The African Dodger — Merritt Clifton (Samisdat)
Early Murphy: Eight Sketches — Mark Costello (Missouri Review)
A Conventional Life — Dennis Covington (Greensboro Review)
Souvenir Mercy — Richard Currey (North American Review)
Apples and Pears — Guy Davenport (Conjunctions)

Cutaneous Horn — Millicent G. Dillon (Threepenny Review)

Sambo, or: The Last of the Gibson Girls — Rita Dove (StoryQuarterly)

The Spray Paint King — Rita Dove (Gargoyle)

In Darkness — Pam Durban (Crazyhorse)

This Heat — Pam Durban (Georgia Review)

The Grand Tour — Joan Eades (Bloodroot)

The Ugly Beetle — Philip A. Eprile (StoryQuarterly)

The Dachau Driver — Pamela Erbe (Antioch Review)

"I'm Waiting For The Man In The Moon" — Pamela Erbe (Columbia)

The Red Convertible — Louise Erdrich (Mississippi Valley Review)

Jolson Sings Again — David Evanier (Pequod)

A Summer At Estabrook — William Ferguson (Paris Review)

On the Heights of Machu Picchu — H.E. Francis (Greensboro Review)

selections from Desire — Thaisa Frank (Kelsey St. Press)

The Junkman Sings in Spring — Emanuel Fried (Textile Bridge Press)

Midnight — Abby Frucht (Ontario Review)

Meeting In The Tiring Room — George Garrett (Chelsea)

Wolf-Money Daughter-Dream — Reginald Gibbons (Agni Review)

The Decline and Fall of A Reasonable Woman — Joan Givner (Ascent)

The Bobby Pin — Jaimy Gordon (Gargoyle)

Had I a Hundred Mouths — William Goyen (Triquarterly)

Comfort Stations — John Griesemer (West Branch)

Property — Carla Harryman (Tuumba Press)

The Man Who Cultivated Fire — Gerald Haslam (Maelstrom Review)

As Luck Would Have It — Patricia Henley (Northwest Review)

The Mojado Who Offered Up His Tapeworms to the Public Weal — El Huitlacoche (BiLingual Review)

Motion Of The Heart — Josephine Jacobsen (New Letters)

Protection — Josephine Jacobsen (Epoch)

Holograms, Unlimited — Bev Jafek (Mississippi Review)

Ode To Heroine Of The Future — Tama Janowitz (Mississippi Review)

China — Charles Johnson (MSS)

The Seige — Gayle Jones (Callaloo)
Separate Person — Bill Kinnard (Quilt)
A Life Story — Kenneth Lash (North American Review)
Museum of Love — Ralph Lombreglia (Iowa Review)
Highlights — Michael Martone (Indiana Review)
Underground — Bobbie Ann Mason (Virginia Quarterly Review)
The Two of Them Together — Jack Matthews (Black Warrior Review)
Chicago Jubilee Rag — John McCluskey (Seattle Review)
Asbestos — Lew McCreary (North American Review)
The People-Oriented Bomb of Late America — Joseph McElroy (Grand Street)
The Old Left — Daniel Menaker (Grand Street)
Comic Valentine — Don Meredith (Texas Review)
The Tail of His Luck — Greg Michalson (CutBank)
Office Story — Robert Minkoff (Epoch)
This Light Is For Those At Sea — Kent Nelson (Southern Review)
Hints and Glimpses — Kathryn Nesmith (West Branch)
The Golden Years — Jay Neugeboren (New England Review)
When The Lord Calls — Gloria Norris (Sewanee Review)
The Mirror — Joyce Carol Oates (South Carolina Review)
The Missionary Has Some Thoughts — John O'Brien (Northwest Review)
This Is The World — W.S. Penn (Antaeus)
Fallick: A Frieze — Robert Phillips (New England Review)
Mr. Mintser — Robert Pinsky (Kenyon Review)
The Guests — Nancy Potter (Liberal and Fine Arts Review)
Companions — Melissa Brown Pritchard (Webster Review)
Minnie the Moocher's Hair — Jack Pulaski (Ploughshares)
When I Was a Prince — Jack Pulaski (Ohio Review)
The Amazing Frog Boy — George Rabasa (StoryQuarterly)
Waldorf Salad — Kurt Rheinheimer (Piedmont Literary Review)
Watertower — David R. Schanker (Triquarterly)
The Passover War — L.J. Schneiderman (Kansas Quarterly)
and excerpt from Upstart Crow — Philip Schultz (Kenyon Review)
Stolen Kiss — Robert Shacochis (Paris Review)
The Tuning Fork — Layle Silbert (Salmagundi)
Her Victory. Part One, Making The Break — Alan Sillitoe (Descant)
The Queen — R.D. Skillings (Triquarterly)

How It Had To Be — Jewell Smith (Kenyon Review)
Decoys — Kenneth R. Smith (Triquarterly)
Nijinsky — Maura Stanton (Michigan Quarterly Review)
Tunnel and Walls and Other Ways of Getting There — Sharon Sheehe Stark (StoryQuarterly)
Deep Thought — T. K. Stein (Writ)
from Isaac Looking for Paradise — Steve Stern (Memphis State Review)
The Big Trees of Westchester — Alma Stone (Shenandoah)
The Route As Briefed — James Tate (Antaeus)
Preservation, 1934 — Robert Taylor, Jr. (Quarterly West)
Blue Porcelain Trumpet — Maria Thomas (StoryQuarterly)
Snowbound — Norma Tomlinson (Carolina Quarterly)
The Blue Dress — William Trevor (Antaeus)
Home Economics — Gordon Weaver (Western Humanities Review)
The Dogs In Renoir's Garden — Gloria Whelan (Virginia Quarterly)
Blood Telling — Gayle Whittier (Ploughshares)
When It's Time To Go — John Wideman (Callaloo)
Land Fishers — Robley Wilson Jr. (Antaeus)
The Quick and the Dead — Z. Vance Wilson (Missouri Review)

NONFICTION

Why There Are No Southern Writers — Daphne Athas (Southern Review)
Evelyn Scott: The Woman In The Foreground — Peggy Bach (Southern Review)
The Hours Musicians Keep — Marvin Bell (Antaeus)
Playing And The Two Traditions — Thomas Beresford (Southern Review)
Three Prose Pieces — Stephen Berg (Triquarterly)
from The Pact — Thorkild Bjornvig (Translation)
The Remission of Play — Herbert Blau (Performing Arts Journal)
The Viennese Connection — Leon Botstein (Partisan Review)
Changing Art: A Chronicle Centered on John Cage — Kathan Brown (Triquarterly)
Steaks — Frederick Busch (Iowa Review)

Enclosures: Barbara Pym — Hortense Calisher (New Criterion)

Who I Am — Hayden Carruth (Sulphur)

Fires — Raymond Carver (Antaeus)

Art and Redemption: On Money As Metaphor — Kelly Cherry (Book Forum)

Some Audibility Gaps — Donald Davie (Sewanee Review)

Consummations Devoutly To Be Wished — Helene J.F. De Aguilar (Parnassus)

The Last Year — Paula Deitz (Ontario Review)

Wish I Had Pie — Annie Dillard (Black Warrior Review)

And The Look of The Bay Mare Shames Silliness Out of Me — Wayne Dodd (Ohio Review)

The Politics of Modern Criticism — Denis Donoghue (Bennington Review)

Yeats and Byzantium — William Empson (Grand Street)

In Defense of The Iowa Writers' Workshop — David Fenza (Poet and Critic)

Against Literature As An Institution — Leslie Fiedler (New Boston Review)

Writing — Northrop Frye (Anansi)

Representation and The War For Reality — William Gass (Salmagundi)

The Soul Inside The Sentence — William Gass (Salmagundi)

Hilda In Egypt — Albert Gelpi (Southern Review)

My Face — Gail Godwin (Antaeus)

The Critic As Co-Creator — David J. Gordon (Sewanee Review)

Other Days — John Haines (Graywolf Press)

On Certain Slants of Light Slipping, "Zippy Zappy," From Williams — David Hamilton (Missouri Review)

James Wright, The Good Poet — William Harmon (Sewanee Review)

Iran Face to Face — Curtis Harnack (Aperture)

Talking With Dogs, Chimps and Others — Vicki Hearne (Raritan)

Poetry Without Credentials — Michael Heller (Ohio Review)

The Madonna of Red Hook — David Hellerstein (North American Review)

They That Mourn — Richard Hoffman (Hudson Review)

Human Bone Meal — Ian Jackson (Pacific Horticulture)

Against A Field Sinister — Edith A. Jenkins (Massachusetts Review)

On The Photography of Peter Hujar — Stephen Koch (Ontario Review)
Faces of Writing — Berel Lang (Michigan Quarterly)
The Audible Silence — Lewis Lapham (Yale Literary Magazine)
Reading Foucault (Punishment, Labor Resistance) — Frank Lentricchia (Raritan Review)
Auschwitz-Birkenau — Arnost Lustig (Yale Review)
Double Visions: Olympic Games and American Culture — John MacAloon (Kenyon)
Who's Diphilus — Oscar Mandel (American Scholar)
Nuclear Theater — Bonnie Marranca (Performing Arts Journal)
Voluntary Exile In Italy — Eugenio Montale (Antaeus)
Pictures of My Father — John O'Brien (Hudson Review)
Plotless Prose — Bob Perelman (Poetics Journal)
Inviting The Muse — Marge Piercy (Negative Capability)
Literature, Technology, People — Richard Poirier (Daedalus)
The Right To Read — Igor Pomeranzev (Partisan Review)
Wintering In Southern Chile — Caroline Richards (Minnesota Review)
On Being Against Pornography — Joanna Russ (13th Moon)
The Unfinished House: Notes on Poetry and Memory — Vern Rutsala (American Poetry Review)
Travelling Theory — Edward Said (Raritan)
Noble Numbers: Two In One — Reg Saner (Ohio Review)
Planes Under the Eiffel Tower — Perdita Schaffner (Grand Street)
Oceans of Emotion: The Narcissus Syndrome — John Seelye (Virginia Quarterly)
On An Exact Art (Again) — George Steiner (Kenyon Review)
Clio In China — Fritz Stern (Partisan Review)
Hamlet's Modernity — Isadore Traschen (Southern Review)
The Poetry of Janet Lewis — Helen P. Trimpi (Southern Review)
Roget's Thesaurus and Other Abuses of Style — E.P. Whipple (Clamshell Press)

POETRY

Porch — Betty Adcock (Plainsong)
American Landscape With Clouds and A Zoo — Jon Anderson (Antaeus)

Reading Our Times — Philip Appleman (The Literary Review)

After Yeats — Jane Augustine (Woman Poet — The East)

Late Summer — Marianne Boruch (American Poetry Review)

Like Noah's Dove — Christopher Buckley (New England Review)

The Old Soul-Suck Life — Charles Bukowski (Another Chicago Magazine)

At Grandfather's Place of Work — Christopher Bursk (Quarterly Review of Literature)

Failure Intrinsic — Hayden Carruth (Kayak)

A Hanging: Zomba Central Prison — Frank Mkalawile Chipasula (Contact III)

Chlly Bees Blues — Brenda Connor-Bey (New Rain II)

Down On The Farm — Timothy Dekin (Elpenor Books)

The Olympian — James Dickey (Pressworks)

Settling — W.S. Di Piero (Sewanee Review)

The Station — W.S. Di Piero (Elpenor Books)

Atocha Choo-Choo — Tom Disch (Paris Review)

China Nights — Michael Dobberstein (Quarterly West)

Receiving The Stigmata — Rita Dove (Georgia Review)

Writing With Light — Douglas Dunn (London Magazine)

You Tell Me — Lynn Emanuel (Georgia Review)

Atlantis — John Engman (Sonora Review)

Ira Hayes — Mick Fedullo (Telescope)

Audubon At Oakley — John Finlay (Southern Review)

Message — Carolyn Forché (Iowa Review)

The Fear of Vacuum Cleaners — Linda N. Foster (Laurel Review)

In The Garden of My Lady — Gene Fowler (Second Coming Press)

Bravura — Robert Francis (Field)

Anthropology — James Galvin (Field)

Yonder — Amy Gerstler (Little Caesar)

Daily Horoscope — Dana Gioia (Hudson Review)

Tapestry — Jorie Graham (American Poetry Review)

To A Friend Killed In The Fighting — Matthew Graham (Antioch Review)

Woolgathering — Emily Grosholz (Cumberland Poetry Review)

The Inside-Outside Game — Thom Gunn (Massachusetts Review)

Untitled — R.S. Gwynn (Vision)

Lunch At Bruno's — Mark Halliday (Ploughshares)

The Painter and The Word — Karsten Harries (Bennington Review)

What's Women's Liberation Done To Help Men? He Said — Jana Harris (Lips)

Preparing The Way — Jaenine Hathaway (Beloit Poetry Review)

Payments — Diana O Hehir (Poetry Northwest)

Ophelia — Brenda Hillman (Threepenny Review)

Hidden Rhymes — John Hollander (Antaeus)

Interferon — Miroslave Holub (Field)

Pishkun Reservoir — Richard Hugo (Corona)

The House Among Pines — Cynthia Huntington (Nimrod)

Word Songs — Colette Inez (Images)

Death and Resurrection — Louis Jenkins (Milkweed Chronicle)

Underwater Music — Diane Keating (Exile)

The Imagined Garden — Nicholas Kilmer (Kenyon Review)

Summers of Vietnam — Mary Kinzie (Southern Review)

Lament — Lauie Lamon (Cutbank)

Sexuality Is Foreign Words — Marianne Larsen (Translation)

Till Morning — Leticia (Poetry Project at Tucson Public Library)

The Man Who Lost His Name — Philip Levine (New England Review)

The Tilemaker's Hill Fresco — Laurence Lieberman (American Poetry Review)

Learning To Live — Ligi (Greenfield Review)

After He Called Her A Witch — Susan Ludvigson (Poetry)

Above Challes-les-Eaux — Peter Makuck (BOA Editions)

Relations — MeKeel McBride (Tendril)

Beach Plums — Molly McQuade (Tendril)

Domino — James Merrill (Paris Review)

Something Old and Dark and Strong — James Masao Mitsui (Raccoon)

A Beautiful Death — Andrew Motion (London Magazine)

The Steel — Les A. Murray (Persea)

After Driving Home Through The Valley — Abby Niebauer (Sequoia)

Stanzas — Richard Pevear (Pequod)

Linnet and Leaf — Wyatt Prunty (Sewanee Review)

Lake Crescent — Wendy Ranan (Tendril)

The Rumor — Liam Rector (American Poetry Review)

The Grown Up — Rainer Maria Rilke (American Poetry Review)

Seniors — Alberto Rios (Ohio Review)

Love Song — Pattiann Rogers (Poetry Northwest)

The Man In The Yellow Gloves — David St. John (Antaeus)

The Beginning of Autumn — Sherod Santos (Ploughshares)

Part of That Particular Circus — Glenda Schrock (Threepenny Review)

Division — Grace Schulman (Grand Street)

The Ill — Hugh Seidman (Poetry)

About Atlanta — Ntozake Shange (Book People)

Cautious — Jane Shore (Tufts Review)

Albany — Ron Silliman (Ironwood)

My Weariness of Epic Proportions — Charles Simic (Partisan Review)

In A Time of Peace — Louis Simpson (Hudson Review)

Accepting A Call — William Stafford (Carolina Quarterly)

A Ceremony: Doing The Needful — William Stafford (Field)

Getting Scared — William Stafford (Hudson Review)

Alba — Rusty Standridge (Threepenny Review)

Father Guzman — Gerald Stern (Paris Review)

Turn Your Eyes Away — Ruth Stone (Ploughshares)

Autumn. Grace. The Signatures — Joseph Stroud (BOA Editions)

The Room Above The White Rose — Joseph Stroud (Ironwood)

November — Lucien Stryk (Poetry)

Blue Ridge — Ellen Bryant Voigt (Antaeus)

Feeding — David Wagoner (Iowa Review)

I'd Trade These Words — James L. White (Graywolf Press)

The Ride — Richard Wilbur (Ploughshares)

Going — Miller Williams (Georgia Review)

Lonesome Pine Special — Charles Wright (Field)

After The Shark — William Yarrow (Central Park)

OUTSTANDING SMALL PRESSES

(These presses made or received nominations for this edition of *The Pushcart Prize*. See the *International Directory of Little Magazines* and *Small Presses*, Dustbooks, Box 1056, Paradise, CA 95969, for subscription rates, manuscript requirements and a complete international listing of small presses.)

Abraxas, 2518 Gregory St., Madison, WI 53711
The Agni Review, P.O. Box 229, Cambridge, MA 02138
Ahsahta Press, Boise State University, Boise, ID 83725
The Alchemist, Box 123, LaSalle, Quebec, Canada H8R3T7
Alice James Books, 138 Mt. Auburn St., Cambridge, MA 02138
The Alternative Press, 3090 Copeland Rd., Grindstone City, MI 48467
Alyson Publications, Inc., P.O. Box 2783, Boston, MA 02208
Amanda Blue, P.O. Box 174, Tiffin, OH 44883
American Poetry Review, 1616 Walnut St., Philadelphia, PA 19103
American Scholar, 1811 Q St. NW, Washington, DC 20009
American Studies Press, Inc., 13511 Palmwood Lane, Tampa, FL 33624
Anansi, 35 Britain St., Toronto, Canada M5A1R7
Andrew Mountain Press, P.O. Box 14353, Hartford, CT 06114
Anglican Theological Review, 600 Haven St., Evanston, IL 60201
Another Chicago Magazine, 1152 S. East Ave., Oak Park. IL 60304
Ansuda Publications, P.O. Box 158, Harris, IA 51345
Antaeus, 18 W. 30th St., New York, NY 10001
Antigonish Review, St. Francis Xavier University, Antigonish, Nova Scotia, B2G1C0
Antioch Review, P.O. Box 148, Yellow Springs, OH 45387
Anvil, P.O. Box 402, Winona, MN 55987

The Apalachee Quarterly, P.O. Box 20106, Tallahassee, FL 32304
Appalachian Consortium Press, 202 Appalachian St., Boone, NC 28607
Applezaba Press, P.O. Box 4134, Long Beach, CA 90804
Arizona Quarterly, University of Arizona, Tucson, AZ 85721
Artifact, 919 Orchard Court, Flint, MI 48503
Ascent, University of Illinois, Urbana, IL 61801
Ashod Press, P.O. Box 1147, Madison Square Sta., New York, NY 10159
Asphodel, 613 Howard Ave., Pitman, NJ 08071
Athena Press, 602 S. 4th St., Grand Forks, ND 58201
Aztlan, c/o UCLA Chicano Studies Research Center Publications, 405 Hilgard Ave., Los Angeles, CA 90024

Back From The Dead Productions, 381 Berry St., (2B), Brooklyn, NY 11211
Back Row Press, 1803 Venus Ave., St. Paul, MN 55112
Backstreet Editions, Box 555, Port Jefferson, NY 11777
Barra Head, P.O. Box 7186, Austin, TX 78712
Barton Press, P.O. Box 243, Station "P", Toronto, Ontario, Canada M5S2S8
The Bellevue Press, 60 Schubert St., Binghamton, NY 13905
Bellingham Review, 412 N. State St., Bellingham, WA 98225
Beloit Poetry Journal, P.O. Box 2, Beloit, WI 53511
Bennington Review, Bennington College, Bennington, VT 05201
Berkeley Art Center, 1275 Walnut St., Berkeley, CA 94709
Beyond Baroque Foundation, 681 Venice Blvd., POB 806, Venice, CA 90291
The Bieler Press, P.O. Box 3856, St. Paul, MN 55165
The Bilingual Review, Eastern Michigan University, Ypsilanti, MI 48197
The Biting Edge Press, 410 Central Ave., #6, Sandusky, OH 44876
BkMk Press, University of Missouri, Kansas City, MO 64110
Black American Literature Forum, Indiana State University, Terre Haute, IN 47809
Black Buzzard Press, 5620 S. 7th Place, Arlington, VA 22204
Black Market Press, 1516 Beverly Rd., Brooklyn, NY 11226
Black Warrior Review, P.O. Box 2936, University, AL 35486

Black Willow, 3214 Sunset Ave., Norristown, PA 19403

Blind Beggar Press, P.O. Box 437, Williamsbridge Sta., Bronx, NY 10467

Bloodroot, P.O. Box 891, Grand Forks, ND 58201

Blue Cloud Quarterly, Blue Cloud Abbey, Marvin, SD 57251

Blue Star Press, 163 Joralemon St., Suite 1144, Brooklyn, NY 11201

Blue Unicorn, 22 Avon Rd., Kensington, CA 94707

Blueline, Blue Mountain Lake, NY 12812

BOA Editions, 92 Park Ave., Brockport, NY 14420

Book Emporium, 768 Main St., Willimantic, CT 06226

Book Forum, Hudson River Press, Rhinecliff, NY 12754

Borf Books, Brownsville, KY 42210

Boss, Box 370, Madison Square Sta., New York, NY 10159

Boston Review, 1013 Mt. Auburn St., Cambridge, MA 02138

Bravo, 1081 Trafalgar St., Teaneck, NJ 07666

Broken Streets, 57 Morningside Dr., E., Bristol, CT 06010

Burning Deck, 71 Elmgrove Ave., Providence, RI 02906

Byline, 5805 N. Grand Blvd., Oklahoma City, OK 73118

CSP World News, P.O. Box 2608, Station D., Ottawa, Ontario, Canada K1P5W7

CSS Publications, P.O. Box 23, Iowa Falls, IA 50126

Cache Review, 131 Fishback, Fort Collins, CO 80521

Cache Valley Newsletter Publishing Co., Rt. 3, Box 273, Preston, ID 83263

Cadmus Editions, P.O. Box 687, Tiburon-Belvedere, CA 94920

Callaloo, University of Kentucky, Lexington, KY 40506

Calli's Tales, Box 1224, Palmetto, FL 33561

Calyx, P.O. Box B, Corvallis, OR 97330

Canadian Fiction Magazine, P.O. Box 946, Station F, Toronto, Ontario, Canada M4Y2N9

Canadian Literature, University of British Columbia, Vancouver, B.C., Canada V6T1W5

Capra Press, P.O. Box 2068, Santa Barbara, CA 93120

Carolina Quarterly, University of North Carolina, Chapel Hill, NC 27514

Carolina Wren Press, 300 Barclay Rd., Chapel Hill, NC 27514

Cat's Eye, 1005 Clearview Dr., Nashville, TN 37205

Cedar Rock, 1121 Madeline, New Branfels, TX 78130

The Centennial Review, Michigan State University, East Lansing, MI 48824

Central Park, Box 1446, New York, NY 10023

Chantry Press, P.O. Box 144, Midland Park, NJ 07432

The Chariton Review, Northeast Missouri State University, Kirksville, MO 63501

Charnel House, P.O. Box 281, Stn. S, Toronto, Ontario, Canada M5M4L7

Chelsea, Box 5880, Grand Central Sta., New York, NY 10163

Chestnut Hill Press, 5320 Groveland Rd., Geneseo, NY 14454

Chiaroscuro, 108 N. Plain St., Ithaca, NY 14850

Chicago Review, University of Chicago, Chicago, IL 60637

Cincinnati Poetry Review, University of Cincinnati, Cincinnati, OH 45221

The Clamshell Press, 160 California Ave., Santa Rosa, CA 95405

Clearwater Journal, 1115 V Ave., LaGrande, OR 97850

Cleveland State University Poetry Center, Euclid at E. 24th St., Cleveland, OH 44115

Colorado-North Review, University of No. Colorado, Greeley, CO 80639

Colorado State Review, Colorado State University, Ft. Collins, CO 80523

Columbia, Columbia University, New York, NY 10027

Concerning Poetry, Western Washington University, Bellingham, WA 98225

Confrontation, Long Island University, Brooklyn, NY 11201

Conjunctions, 33 W. 9th St., New York, NY 10011

The Connecticut Poetry Review, P.O. Box 3783, New Haven, CT 06525

Contact III, P.O. Box 451, Bowling Green Sta., New York, NY 10004

Copper Canyon Press, P.O. Box 271, Port Townsend, WA 98368

Corona Publishers, P.O. Box 58, Sta H, Montreal, Quebec, Canada H3G2K5

Cottonwood Review, Box J, Kansas Union, Lawrence, KS 66045

Cougar Books, P.O. Box 22246, Sacramento, CA 95822

Crawl Out Your Window, 4641 Park Blvd., San Diego, CA 92116

Crazyhorse, University of Arkansas, Little Rock, AR 72204

Creative Arts Book Co., 833 Bancroft Way, Berkeley, CA 94710

Cross Country Press, P.O. Box 146, Sta. A, Flushing, NY 11358

Cross Currents, Mercy College, Dobbs Ferry, NY 10522

Crosscurrents, 2200 Glastonbury Rd., Westlake Village, CA 91361

Crossing Press, Trumansburg, NY 14886

Croton Review, P.O. Box 277, Croton-On-Hudson, NY 10520

Crown Point Press, 1555 San Pablo Ave., Oakland, CA 94612

Cumberland Poetry Review, P.O. Box 120128, Acklen Sta., Nashville, TN 37212

Curbstone, 321 Jackson St., Willimantic, CT 06226

Curbstone Publishing Co., Box 1613, New York, NY 10116

Cutbank, University of Montana, Missoula, MT 59801

The Cypress Review, P.O. Box 673, Half Moon Bay, CA 94019

Daedalus, 136 Irving St., Cambridge, MA 02138

D.J.A.'s Writing Circle, P.O. Box 7042, Jacksonville, NC 28540

December Press, 6232 N. Hoyne, Chicago, IL 60659

Denver Quarterly, University of Denver, Denver, CO 80208

Descant, P.O. Box 314, Sta. P, Toronto, Ontario, Canada M5S2S8

The Devil's Millhopper, University of South Carolina, Columbia, SC 29208

Diana's Bimonthly Press, 71 Elmgrove Ave., Providence, RI 02906

Dimension, Box 7939, Austin, TX 78712

Divisions, P.O. Box 18647, Cleveland Heights, OH 44118

Dixie Flyer, P.O. Box 40074, Memphis, TN 38104

The Dog Ear Press, Hull's Cove, ME 04644

Domestic Crude, University of Houston, Houston, TX 77004

Downtown Poets Co-op, GPO Box 1720, Brooklyn, NY 11202

Dragon Gate, 508 Lincoln St., Port Townsend, WA 98368

Dreadnaught Publishers, 24 Sussex Ave., Toronto, Canada

Drenan Press, 23301 Clarendon St., Woodland Hills, CA 91367

Dryad Press, 15 Sherman Ave., Tacoma Park, MD 20916

Duck Down, P.O. Box 1047, Fallon, NV 89406

Duende Press, Box 571, Placitas, NM 87043

Earth-Song Press, 202 Harnell Pl., Sacramento, CA 95825

Earthwise, P.O. Box 680-536, Miami, FL 33168

Elephant Books, Box 999, Dublin, PA 18917

Eleuthera Press, Winnetka, IL 60093

Elpenor Books, Box 3152, Merchandise Mart Plaza, Chicago, IL 60654

Embers, 117 Northwood Dr., Guilford, CT 06437

En Passant/Poetry, 4612 Sylvanus Dr., Wilmington, DE 19803

Epoch, Cornell University, Ithaca, NY 14853

Erespin Press, 115 W. Koenig Lane, 208, Austin, TX 78751

Exile, Box 546, Downsview, Ontario, Canada

Expedition Press, Box 1198, Kalamazoo, MI 49005

Explorations Press, P.O. Box 907, Greenfield, MA 01302

Eye Prayers Press, P.O. Box 16616, San Diego, CA 92116

Fallen Angel Press, 1981 W. McNichols, #C-1, Highland Park, MI 48203

Fedora Magazine, P.O. Box 577, Siletz, OR 97380

Fels and Firn Press, 944 Sir Francis Drake Blvd., Apt. 7, Kentfield, CA 94904

Feminist Studies, University of Maryland, College Park, MD 20742

Fiction Collective, Brooklyn College, Brooklyn, NY 11210

Fiction International, St. Lawrence University, Canton, NY 13617

Field, Rice Hall, Oberlin College, Oberlin, OH 44074

The Figures, 2016 Cedar St., Berkeley, CA 94709

Floating Island Publications, P.O. Box 516, Point Reyes Station, CA 94956

Flower Mound Writing Co., Box 22984, TWU Sta., Denton, TX 76204

Footwork, Passiac County Community College, Paterson, NJ 07509

Fourth Dimension, Box 129, Richford, VT 05476

Front Street Publishers, 22 Sheldon Dr., Poughkeepsie, NY 12603

Frontiers, University of Boulder, Boulder, CO 80309

The G. W. Review, George Washington University, Washington, DC 20052

Galileo Press, P.O. Box 16129, Baltimore, MD 21218

Gargoyle Magazine, P.O. Box 57206, Washington, DC 20037

Gearhead Press, 835 Ninth, N.W., Grand Rapids, MI 49504

The Georgia Review, University of Georgia, Athens, GA 30602

Gourmet Guides, 1767 Stockton St., San Francisco, CA 94133

Grand Street, 50 Riverside Dr., New York, NY 10024

Grass-Hopper Press, 4030 Connecticut St., St. Louis, MO 63116

Gravesend Press, 4392 Bussey Rd., Syracuse, NY 13215

Graywolf Press, P.O. Box 142, Port Townsend, WA 98368

Great River Review, P.O. Box 14805, Minneapolis, MN 55414

Green Horse Press, 471 Carr Ave., Aromas, CA 95004

Greenfield Review Press, RD#1, Box 80, Greenfield Center, NY 12833

Greenhouse Review Press, 3965 Bonny Doon Rd., Santa Cruz, CA 95060

Greenwich-Meridian, 516 Ave. K, S, Saskatoon, Saskatchewan, Canada S7M2E2

Grey Whale Press, 4820 SE Boise, Portland, OR 97206

Guthrie Publishing Co., Box 1, Guthrie, MN 56451

Gypsy Press, P.O. Box 589, New Castle, DE 19720

Hard Press, 340 E. 11th St., New York, NY 10003

Hartmus Press, 23 Lomita Dr., Mill Valley, CA 94941

Helicon Nine, P.O. Box 22412, Kansas City, MO 64113

Hemlocks and Balsams, Lees-McRae College, Banner Elk, NC 28604

Hermes House Press, 851½ S. Illinois, Springfield, IL 62704

Heyeck Press, 25 Patrol Ct., Woodside, CA 94062

High Rock Review, P.O. Box 614, Saratoga Springs, NY 12866

The Hoboken Terminal, 831 Clinton St., 6, Hoboken, NJ 07030

Holmgangers Press, Star Route, Shelter Cove, Whitehorn, CA 95489

Home Planet News, P.O. Box 415, Stuyvesant Sta., New York, NY 10009

Hope Tracks, 109 S. Walnut, Hope, AR 71801

Horse and Bird Press, P.O. Box 67089, Los Angeles, CA 90067

House of Keys, P.O. Box 8940, Cincinnati, OH 45208

The Hudson Review, 684 Park Ave., New York, NY 10021

Image Magazine, P.O. Box 28048, St. Louis, MO 63119

Images, Wright State University, Dayton, OH 45435

Inky Trails, P.O. Box 345, Middleton, ID 83644

Inlet, Virginia Wesleyan College, Norfolk, VA 23502

Inspirational Review Press, Box 110, Yachats, OR 97498

Instead of a Magazine, 768 Main St., Willimantic, CT 06226

Interstate, P.O. Box 7068, University Sta., Austin, TX 78712

Invisible City, P.O. Box 2853, San Francisco, CA 94126

The Iowa Review, University of Iowa, Iowa City, IA 52242

Iowa Woman, P.O. Box 680, Iowa City, IA 52244
I. Reed Books, 2140 Shattuck Ave., Berkeley, CA 94704
Ironwood, P.O. Box 40907, Tucson, AZ 85717
Island Press, Star Route 1, Box 38, Covelo, CA 95248
Ithaca House, 108 N. Plain St., Ithaca, NY 14850

JLAG Review, Box 459, Dept. M, East Douglas, MA 01516
Jam Today, P.O. Box 249, Northfield, VT 05663
The Jargon Society, Inc., 751 Roslyn Rd., Winston-Salem, NC 27104
Journal of Canadian Studies, Trent University, Peterborough, Ontario, Canada K9J7B8
Jump River Press, Inc., 810 Vernon Ave., #4, Madison, WI 53714
Jungle Garden Press, 47 Oak Rd., Fairfax, CA 94930

Kalliope, Fla. Jr. College, Kent Campus, Jacksonville, FL 32205
Kansas Quarterly, Kansas State University, Manhattan, KS 66506
Kayak, 325 Ocean View, Santa Cruz, CA 95062
Kelsey St. Press, P.O. Box 9235, Berkeley, CA 94709
The Kenyon Review, Kenyon College, Gambier, OH 43022
The Kindred Spirit, 408 Maple, Great Bend, KS 67530

La Reina Press, P.O. Box 8182, Cincinnati, OH 45208
Labyris, 223 E. Hillsdale, Lansing, MI 48933
Lake Street Review, Box 7188, Powderhorn Sta., Minneapolis, MN 55407
Laurel Review, West Virginia Wesleyan College, Buckhannon, W. VA 26201
L'Epervier Press, 762 Hayes, #15, Seattle, WA 98109
Limited Editions Press, 8412 Wilbur Ave., Northridge, CA 91324
Linden Press, 3601 Greenway, Baltimore, MD 21218
Lintel, Box 34, St. George, Staten Island, NY 10301
LIPS, P.O. Box 1345, Montclair, NJ 07042
Literary Magazine Review, Kansas State University, Manhattan, KS 66506
The Literary Review, Fairleigh-Dickinson University, Madison, NJ 07940
Little Balkans Press, Inc., 601 Grandview Heights Terrace, Pittsburg, KS 66762
Little Caesar, 3373 Overland Ave. #2, Los Angeles, CA 90034

Little River Press, 10 Lowell Ave., Westfield, MA 01085

Live Writers!, P.O. Box 8182, Cincinnati, OH 45208

Lodestar, P.O. Box 18086, Atlanta, GA 30316

Log Cabin Publishers, P.O. Box 1536, Allentown, PA 18105

Logbridge-Rhodes, Inc., P.O. Box 3254, Durango, CO 81301

Look Quick, P.O. Box 222, Pueblo, CO 81002

Lotus Press, P.O. Box 21607, Detroit, MI 48221

Low-Tech Press, 30-73 47th St., Long Island City, NY 11103

Lowlands Review, 6048 Perrier, New Orleans, LA 70118

Lowry Publishing, 5047 Wigton, Houston, TX 77096

Luna Bisonti Prods., 137 Leland Ave., Columbus, OH 43214

The Lunchroom Press, P.O. Box 36027, Grosse Pointe Farms, MI 48236

MSS Magazine, SUNY, Binghamton, NY 13901

Maelstrom Press, 34 Winter St., Portland, ME 04102

The Manhattan Review, 304 Third Ave., 4A, New York, NY 10010

Marsh Point Press, Peters St., Orono, ME 04473

The Massachusetts Review, University of Massachusetts, Amherst, MA 01003

Matrix, Box 510, Lennoxville, Quebec, Canada J1M1Z6

Memphis State Review, Memphis State University, Memphis, TN 38152

Menomonie Review, University of Wisconsin, Menomonie, WI 54751

Merging Media, 59 Sandra Circle, Westfield, NJ 07090

Mho and Mho Works, Box 33135, San Diego, CA 92103

Micah Publications, 255 Humphrey St., Marblehead, MA 01945

Michigan Quarterly Review, University of Michigan, Ann Arbor, MI 48109

Mid-American Review, Bowling Green State University, Bowling Green, OH 43403

The Midwest Quarterly, Pittsburg State University, Pittsburg, KS 66762

Milkweed Chronicle, Box 24303, Minneapolis, MN 55424

The Minnesota Review, Oregon State University, Corvallis, OR 97331

Mississippi Mud, 3125, SE Van Water St., Portland, OR 97222

Mississippi Review, University of Southern Mississippi, Southern Sta., Hattiesburg, MS 39406

Mississippi Valley Review, Western Illinois University, Macomb, IL, 61455

Missouri Review, University of Missouri, Columbia, MO 65211

Montana Review, 2220 Quail, Missoula, MT 59802

Moody Street Irregulars, P.O. Box 157, Clarence Center, NY 14032

Moonfire Press, 3061 N. Newhall St., Milwaukee, WI 53211

Mothering Publications, Inc., P.O. Box 2208, Albuquerque, NM 87103

Mutante Publik Ink, P.O. Box 39188, Friendship Sta., Washington, DC 20016

NKQ, P.O. Box 26, Kent State University, Kent, OH 44240

NRG Magazine, 6735 SE 78th, Portland, OR 97206

Naiad Press, P.O. Box 10543, Tallahassee, FL 32302

Naked Man, 1718 Vermont, Apt. A, Lawrence, KS 66044

Nantucket Review, P.O. Box 1234, Nantucket, MA 02554

Naturegraph Publishers, Inc., P.O. Box 1075, Happy Camp, CA 96039

Negative Capability, 6116 Timberly Rd., N, Mobile, AL 36609

New Blood Magazine, 1310 College Ave., Suite 1195, Boulder, CO 80302

New Boston Review, 10-B Mt. Auburn St., Cambridge, MA 02138

New College Magazine, 5700 North Trail, Sarasota, FL 33580

New Directions, 80 Eighth Ave., New York, NY 10011

New England Press, Box 1903, Tudor City, 45, New York, NY 10017

New England Review, Box 170, Hanover, NH 03755

New Leaves Review, 41-50 48th St., Sunnyside, NY 11104

New Letters, University of Missouri, Kansas City, MO 64110

New Orleans Review, Loyola University, New Orleans, LA 70118

New Renaissance, 9 Heath Rd., Arlington, MA 02174

New Rivers Press, 1602 Selby Ave., St. Paul, MN 55104

New Seed Press, Box 9844, Berkeley, CA 94709

New Society Publishers, 4722 Baltimore Ave., Philadelphia, PA 19143

New Southern Literary Messenger, 302 S. Laurel St., Richmond, VA 23220

New York State Waterways Project, 799 Greenwich St., New York, NY 10014

Newsart, c/o The Smith, 5 Beekman St., New York, NY 10038

Newsletter Inago, 1616 E. Bantam Rd., #37, Tucson, AZ 85706

Night Horn Books, 495 Ellis St., Box 1156, San Francisco, CA 94102

Nimrod, 2210 S. Main, Tulsa, OK 74114

North American Review, University of Northern Iowa, Cedar Falls, IA 50614

North Atlantic Books, 635 Amador St., Richmond, CA 94805

North Country ANVIL, P.O. Box 148, Yellow Springs, OH 45387

Northwest Review, University of Oregon, Eugene, OR 97403

Nova Scarcity Publishers, Box 1404, Wolfville, Nova Scotia BOP-IXO

O.ARS, Box 179, Cambridge, MA 02238

Oboe, 495 Ellis St., Box 1156, San Francisco, CA 94102

The Ohio Review, Ohio University, Athens, OH 45701

The Ontario Review Press, 9 Honey Brook Dr., Princeton, NJ 08540

Open Hand Publ., Inc., 1904 3rd Ave., #5, Seattle, WA 98101

Open Places, Box 2085, Stephens College, Columbia, MO 65215

Operative Magazine, P.O. Box 785, Willoughby, OH 44094

Osiris, Box 297, Deerfield, MA 01342

Owl and Butterfly Press, 16 Pennsylvania Ave., Los Gatos, CA 95030

Owl Creek Press, 2220 Quail, Missoula, MT 59802

The Pace Gallery, 32 E. 57th St., New York, NY 10022

Pacific Arts and Letters, P.O. Box 99394, San Francisco, CA 94109

Pacific Horticulture, 1914 Napa Ave., Berkeley, CA 94707

Pale Fire Review, 162 Academy Ave., Providence, RI 02908

Pangloss Papers, Box 18917, Los Angeles, CA 90018

Paris Review, 541 E. 72nd St., New York, NY 10021

Parnassus: Poetry in Review, 205 W. 89th St., New York, NY 10024

Partisan Review, 121 Bay State Rd., Boston, MA 02215

Pass Press, 170 Second Ave., #2-A, New York, NY 10003

Passages North, Fine Arts Center, 7th St. & 1st Ave., S., Escanaba, MI 49829

The Pawn Review, 2903 Windsor Rd., Austin, TX 78703

Paycock Press, P.O. Box 57206, Washington, DC 20037

Pebbles and Stone, 6858 Burnside Dr., San Jose, CA 95120

Pembroke Magazine, Box 60, PSU, Pembroke, NC 28372

Penelope Press, P.O. Box 31882, Seattle, WA 98103

Pequod, 536 Hill St., San Francisco, CA 94114

Performing Arts Journal, 325 Spring St., Rm. 318, New York, NY 10013

Perivale Press, 13830 Erwin St., Van Nuys, CA 91401

Persea, 225 Lafayette St., New York, NY 10012

Persephone Press, P.O. Box 7222, Watertown, MA 02172

Michael Joseph Phillips Editions, 430 E. Wylie, Bloomington, IN 47401

Piedmont Literary Review, Box 3656, Danville, VA 24543

Pig Iron Press, P.O. Box 237, Youngstown, OH 44501

Pinchpenny, 4851 Q St., Sacramento, CA 95819

Ploughshares, P.O. Box 529, Cambridge, MA 02139

POEM, c/o R. L. Welker, University of Alabama, Huntsville, AL 35899

Poet and Critic, Iowa State University, 203 Ross Hall, Ames, IA 50011

Poet Lore, 4000 Albemarle St., NW, Washington, DC 20016

Poetics Journal, 2639 Russell St., Berkeley, CA 94705

Poetry, 601 S. Morgan St., P.O. Box 4348, Chicago, IL 60680

Poetry/LA, P.O. Box 84271, Los Angeles, CA 90073

Poetry Northwest, University of Washington, Seattle, WA 98105

Poetry Now, 3118 K St., Eureka, CA 95501

Poetry Project at Tucson Public Library, Box 27470, Tucson, AZ 85726

Poetry Society of America, 15 Gramercy Park, New York, NY 10003

Poor Souls/Scaramouche Books, P.O. Box 236, Millbrae, CA 94030

Porch, 5310 E. Taylor, Phoenix, AZ 85008

Poultry, Box 727, Truro, MA 02666

Practices of the Wind, P.O. Box 214, Kalamazoo, MI 49005

Prairie Schooner, University of Nebraska, Lincoln, NE 68588

Praxis, P.O. Box 1280, Santa Monica, CA 90406

Press of Appletree Valley, Box 608, 138 S. 3rd St., Lewisburg, PA 17837

Press Porcépic, 235 Market Sq., 560 Johnson St., Victoria, BC, Canada V8W3C6

Primary Press, Box 105, Parker Ford, PA 19457

Prism International, University of British Columbia, Vancouver, BC, Canada V6T1W5

The Private Press of Emily Woodward, 217 Ross Ave., San Anselmo, CA 94960

Proof Rock, P.O. Box 607, Halifax, VA 24558

Ptolemy/Browns Mills Review, Box 908, Browns Mills, NJ 08015

Puckerbrush Press, 76 Main St., Orono, ME 04473

Puerto Del Sol, New Mexico State University, Las Cruces, NM 88003

Pulpsmith, 5 Beekman St., New York, NY 10038

Quaecumque Journal, Northwestern University, Evanston, IL 60201

Quarterly Review of Literature, 26 Haslet Ave., Princeton, NJ 08540

Quarterly West, University of Utah, Salt Lake City, UT 84112

Quilt, 2140 Shattuck Ave., Berkeley, CA 94704

RFD, Rte. 1, Box 127E, Bakersville, NC 28705

Raccoon, 323 Hodges St., Memphis, TN 38111

Raritan: A Quarterly Review, Rutgers University, New Brunswick, NJ 08903

Raw Dog Press, 129 Worthington Ave., Doylestown, PA 18901

Real Fiction, 10008 Masonic Ave., San Francisco, CA 94117

The Reaper, Indiana State University, Evansville, IN 47712

Red Cedar Review, Michigan State University, East Lansing, MI 48823

Red Herring Press, 1209 W. Oregon, Urbana, IL 61801

Red Hill Press, P.O. Box 2853, San Francisco, CA 94126

Red Key Press, P.O. Box 551, Port St. Joe, FL 32456

The Red Ozier Press, P.O. Box 101, Old Chelsea Sta., New York, NY 10113

Reflect, 3306 Argonne Ave., Norfolk, VA 23509

The Re-Geniusing Project, 1432 Spruce St., Berkeley, CA 94709

Revista Chicano-Riqueña, University of Houston, Houston, TX 77004

Rhiannon Press, 1105 Bradley Ave., Eau Claire, WI 54701

River Styx, 7420 Cornell, St. Louis, MO 63130

Rocin Press, 30 Central Park South, New York, NY 10019

Room of One's Own, P.O. Box 46160, Sta. G., Vancouver, BC, Canada V6R4G5

The Roving Press, Box 2870-MCCA, Estes Park, CO 80517

S & S Press, P.O. Box 5931, Austin, TX 78763

Sachem Press, Old Chatham, NY 12136

St. Andrews Review, Laurinburg, NC 28352

St. Luke's Press Fine Arts Productions, P.O. Box 1378, South Bend, IN 46624

Salmagundi, Skidmore College, Saratoga Springs, NY 12866

Salome: A Literary Dance Magazine, 5548 N. Sawyer Ave., Chicago, IL 60625

Samisdat, Box 129, Richford, VT 05476

Sands, 17302 Club Hill Dr., Dallas, TX 75248

Santa Fe: Poetry and the Arts, 115 Delgado St., Santa Fe, NM 87501

Search, 59 Sandra Circle, Westfield, NJ 07090

Seattle Review, University of Washington, Seattle, WA 98195

Second Coming Press, P.O. Box 31249, San Francisco, CA 94131

Seems, Lakeland College, Box 359, Sheboygan, WI 53081

Sequoia, Storke Publications Building, Stanford, CA 94305

Serrell & Simons, Box 64, Winnebago, WI 54985

Seven Buffaloes Press, Box 249, Big Timber, MT 59011

The Sewanee Review, University of the South, Sewanee, TN 37375

SEZ, P.O. Box 8803, Minneapolis, MN 55408

Shameless Hussy Press, Box 3092, Berkeley, CA 94703

Shankpainter, Box 565, Provincetown, MA 02657

Shaw, Li Kung, P.O. Box 16427, San Francisco, CA 94116

Shenandoah, Box 722, Lexington, VA 24450

Silver Apples Press, P.O. Box 292, Hainesport, NJ 08036

Silverfish Review, P.O. Box 3541, Eugene, OR 97403

Sing Heavenly Muse, P.O. Box 14059, Minneapolis, MN 55414

Singular Speech Press, 507 Dowd Ave., Canton, CT 06019

Sinister Wisdom, P.O. Box 669, Amherst, MA 01004

Skywriting/Blue Mt. Press, 511 Campbell St., Kalamazoo, MI 49007

Slough Press, Box 1385, Austin, TX 78767

The Small Pond Magazine, P.O. Box 664, Stratford, CT 06497

The Smith, 5 Beekman St., New York, NY 10038

Smoke Signals, 1516 Beverly Rd., Brooklyn, NY 11226

Snail's Pace, 12041 Jetty Circle, RM 4, Garden Grove, CA 92640

Snapdragon, Library, University of Idaho, Moscow, ID 83843

Solus Impress, Porthill, ID 83853

Sonora Review, University of Arizona, Tucson, AZ 85721

Soundings East, Salem State College, Salem, MA 01970

The South Carolina Review, Clemson University, Clemson, SC 29631

Southern Exposure, P.O. Box 531, Durham, NC 27702

Southern Humanities Review, Auburn University, Auburn, AL 36849

Southern Poetry Review, University of North Carolina, UNCC Sta., Charlotte, NC 28223

The Southern Review, Drawer D. University Sta., Baton Rouge, LA 70893

Southwest Review, Southern Methodist University, Dallas, TX 75275

Sou'wester Magazine, Southern Illinois University, Edwardsville, IL 62026

Spindrift Press, P.O. Box 3252, Catonsville, MD 21228

Spirit that Moves Us, 1718 Vermont, Apt. A, Lawrence, KS 66044

Spoon River Poetry Press, P.O. Box 1443, Peoria, IL 61655

Star Line, P.O. Box 491, Nantucket Island, MA 02554

Starlight Press, Box 3102, Long Island City, NY 11103

State Street Press, 67 State St., Pittsford, NY 14534

Station Hill Press, Station Hill Rd., Barrytown, NY 12507

Still News Publ. Co., P.O. Box 353, Port Ludlow, WA 98365

Stone Country, P.O. Box 132, Menemsha, MA 02552

Story Press, P.O. Box 10040, Chicago, IL 60610

Story Quarterly, 820 Ridge Rd., Highland Park, IL 60035

Street Press, Box 555, Port Jefferson, NY 11777

Stronghold Press: Plains Poetry Journal, Box 2337, Bismarck, ND 58502

Studia Hispanica Editors, P.O. Box 7304, UT Sta., Austin, TX 78712

Sulphur, 852 S. Bedford, Los Angeles, CA 96035

Sulphur River, P.O. Box 3044, E. Texas Sta., Commerce, TX 75428

The Sun, 412 W. Rosemary St., Chapel Hill, NC 27514

Sun Dog, Florida State University, Tallahassee, FL 32306

Sun and Moon Press, 4330 Hartwick Rd., College Park, MD 20740

The Sunstone Press, P.O. Box 2321, 239 Johnson St., Santa Fe, NM 87501

Syzygy, Box 18, Rush, NY 14543

Tamarisk, 319 S. Juniper St., Philadelphia, PA 19107

Tanam Press, 40 White St., New York, NY 10013

Tar River Poetry, East Carolina University, Greenville, NC 27834

Telescope, P.O. Box 16129, Baltimore, MD 21218

Tempest, P.O. Box 680-536, Miami, FL 33168

Tendril, Box 512, Green Harbor, MA 02041

Tetrahedron, Inc., P.O. Box 402, Rockport, MA 01966

Texas Review, Sam Houston State University, Huntsville, TX 77341

Textile Bridge Press, P.O. Box 157, Clarence Center, NY 14032

Theater, 222 York St., New Haven, CT 06520

Third Eye, 189 Kelvin Dr., Tonawanda, NY 14223

13th Moon, Drawer F, Inwood Sta., New York, NY 10034

Three Tree Press, P.O. Box 10044, Lansing, MI 48901

Threepenny Review, P.O. Box 9131, Berkeley, CA 94709

Threshold Books, RD 3, Box 208, Putney, VT 05346

Threshold of Fantasy, P.O. Box 70868, Sunnyvale, CA 94086

Thunder's Mouth Press, 242 W. 104th St., #5RW, New York, NY 10025

Timberline Press, Box 327, Fulton, MO 65251

Timely Books, P.O. Box 267, New Milford, CT 06776

Tinkers Dam Press, 1703 E. Michigan Ave., Jackson, MI 49202

Tompson & Rutter, P.O. Box 297, Grantham, NH 03753

The Toothpaste Press, P.O. Box 546, West Branch, IA 52358

Translation, Columbia University, New York, NY 10027

Tri-Quarterly, Northwestern University, Evanston, IL 60201

Truly Fine Press, P.O. Box 891, Bemidji, MN 56601

Turkey Press, 6746 Sueno Rd., Isla Vista, CA 93117

Turnstone Press, 201-99 King St., Winnipeg, Manitoba R3B1H7

Tuumba Press, 2639 Russell St., Berkeley, CA 94705

Uncle Magazine, P.O. Box 1075, CSS, Springfield, MO 65803

Underground Rag Magazine, 931 3rd Ave., SE, Rochester, MN 55901

The Unhinged Voice Press, P.O. Box 4388, Portsmouth, NH 03801

Unicorn Press, Inc., P.O. Box 3307, Greensboro, NC 27402

United Artists, 172 E. Fourth St., (9B), New York, NY 10009

U.S. Catholic, 221 W. Madison St., Chicago, IL 60606

University of Illinois Press, Box 5081, Sta A, Champaign, IL 61820

University of Windsor Review, University of Windsor, Windsor, Ontario, Canada N9B3P4

Unspeakable Visions of the Individual, P.O. Box 439, California, PA 15419

Uranus, 1537 Washburn, Beloit, WI 53511

Uzzano Press, 511 Sunset Dr., Menomonie, WI 54751

Vagabond Press, 1610 N. Water St., Ellensburg, WA 98926

Valhalla, 59 Sandra Circle, Westfield, NJ 07090

Vanishing Cab, 1152 Jackson, #8, San Francisco, CA 94133

Velocities, 1509 LeRoy Ave., Berkeley, CA 94708

The Virginia Quarterly, One West Range, Charlottesville, VA 22903

The Washington Expatriates Press, Box 8862, Washington, DC 20003

Washington Review, Box 50132, Washington, DC 20004

Washington Square Writes, 50 W. 4th St., Rm 331, New York, NY 10003

Webster Review, Webster College, Webster Groves, MO 63119

Wedge, 141 Perry St., New York, NY 10014

Welter, University of Baltimore, Charles at Mt. Royal, Baltimore, MD 21201

West Branch, Bucknell University, Lewisburg, PA 17837

Western Humanities Review, University of Utah, Salt Lake City, UT 84112

Western Sun Publications, P.O. Box 1470, 290 S. First Ave., Yuma, AZ 85364

Westgate House, 1716 Ocean Ave., Suite 75, San Francisco, CA 94112

White Cross Press, Rt. L, Box 592, Granger, TX 76530

Willow Avenue Review, Rte. 2, Box 33, Janesville, MN 56048

Willow Springs Magazine, P.O. Box 1063, Eastern Washington University, Cheney, WA 99004

Wim Publications, Box 367, College Corner, OH 45003

Win Magazine, 326 Livingston St., Brooklyn, NY 11217

Wind/Literary Journal, RFD #1, Box 809K, Pikeville, KY 41501

The Windless Orchard, Indiana University, Fort Wayne, IN 46805

Wingbow Press, 2940 Seventh St., Berkeley, CA 94710

Winter Soldier Archive, 2000 Center St., Box 1251, Berkeley, CA 94704

The Wisconsin Review, University of Wisconsin, Oshkosh, WI 54901

Wistaria Press, 4373 N.E. Wistaria Dr., Portland, OR 97213

Word Loom, Box 43, 242 Montrose, Winnipeg, Canada R3M3M7

Wormwood Review Press, P.O. Box 8840, Stockton, CA 95208

WOT, 657 Ardmore Dr., RR2, Sidney, British Columbia, Canada V8L3S1

WRIT, Two Sussex Ave., Toronto, Canada M5S1J5

Writers Forum, University of Colorado, Colorado Springs, CO 80933

Xanadu, Box 773, Huntington, NY 11743

The Yale Literary Magazine, Yale University, New Haven, CT 06520

The Yale Review, P.O. Box 1902A, Yale Sta., New Haven, CT 06520

Yellow Silk, P.O. Box 6374, Albany, CA 94706

Yellow Umbrella Press, 501 Main St. Chatham, MA 02633

Ziesing Brothers, 768 Main St., Willimantic, CT 06226

INDEX

The following is a listing in alphabetical order by author's name of works reprinted in the first eight *Pushcart Prize* editions.